Table of Contents

G000114026

Part I: A+ Core Hardware

Drew Bird and Mike Harwood
Expert certification book authors,
instructors, and networking specialists

Microsoft

Faster Smarter

A+
Certification

**Take charge of the A+ exams—
faster, smarter, better!**

PUBLISHED BY
Microsoft Press
A Division of Microsoft Corporation
One Microsoft Way
Redmond, Washington 98052-6399

Library of Congress Cataloging-in-Publication Data
Bird, Drew
    Faster Smarter A+ Certification / Drew Bird, Mike Harwood.
       p. cm.
    Includes index.
    ISBN 0-7356-1915-8
    1. Electronic data processing personnel--Certification.   2. Computer technicians--Certification--Study guides.   I. Harwood, Mike. II. Title.

  QA76.3.B514   2003
  621.39--dc21   2003041348

Printed and bound in the United States of America.

1 2 3 4 5 6 7 8 9   QWE   8 7 6 5 4 3

Distributed in Canada by H.B. Fenn and Company Ltd.

A CIP catalogue record for this book is available from the British Library.

Microsoft Press books are available through booksellers and distributors worldwide. For further information about international editions, contact your local Microsoft Corporation office or contact Microsoft Press International directly at fax (425) 936-7329. Visit our Web site at www.microsoft.com/mspress. Send comments to *tkinput@microsoft.com*.

Acquisitions Editor: Hilary Long
Project Editor: Sandra Haynes
Technical Editor: Christopher J. Pierce
Series Editor: Kristen Weatherby

Body Part No. X09-35336

Part II: A+ Operating Systems

"Writing is a solitary occupation. Family, friends, and society are the natural enemies of the writer. He must be alone, uninterrupted, and slightly savage if he is to sustain and complete an undertaking."

Jessamyn West

This book is dedicated to a less savage lifestyle.

Many Thanks To...

The creation of a book is not a simple process. The commonly held perception of the author huddled over a keyboard in the wee hours of the morning is only half the story. There are also many other people—also huddled over a keyboard in the wee hours—who make a book like this possible. Without their commitment to the project and the continous tweaking and tuning, the book you hold in your hands right now would remain a figment of our imagination, and a pretty disorganized one at that. It is with this in mind that we would like to thank the following people for their invaluable help with this project:

Our project editor at Press, Sandra Haynes; Curtis Phillips, project manager; and Andrea Fox, copyeditor, for making things make sense and keeping the project on track. There can be little doubt that your help has made this a better book. Sincere thanks also to Chistopher Pierce for his diligent technical editing. Books like this one stand or fall on their technical accuracy, and Chris's watchful eye has been invaluable in making sure that the material contained herein is as accurate as possible. We would also like to thank the backroom staff of Kerri DeVault and Joel Panchot, for all their help. When our job is done, theirs has just begun, and it's nice to know our work is in safe hands. Thanks also go to Len Newton for his help with the pictures in this book, to Melissa Craft for letting us borrow from her *Faster Smarter Network+ Certification* introduction, and to Kristen Weatherby for tying up some of the loose ends and bringing the project to fruition.

Finally we would like to thank Hilary Long, program manager at Microsoft Press, for her continuing faith in our abilities and her unwavering support of this project.

The contents of this training material were created for the CompTIA *A+ Certification* exams covering CompTIA certification exam objectives that were current as of *May, 2003*.

How to Become CompTIA Certified:

This training material can help you prepare for and pass a related CompTIA certification exam or exams. In order to achieve CompTIA certification, you must register for and pass a CompTIA certification exam or exams.

In order to become CompTIA certified, you must:

1 Select a certification exam provider. For more information please visit *http://www.comptia.org/certification/general_information/ test_locations.asp*

2 Register for and schedule a time to take the CompTIA certification exam(s) at a convenient location.

3 Read and sign the Candidate Agreement, which will be presented at the time of the exam(s). The text of the Candidate Agreement can be found at *http://www.comptia.org/certification/general_information/ candidate_agreement.asp*

4 Take and pass the CompTIA certification exam(s).

For more information about CompTIA's certifications, such as their industry acceptance, benefits, or program news, please visit *http://www.comptia.org/certification/default.asp*

CompTIA is a non-profit information technology (IT) trade association. CompTIA's certifications are designed by subject matter experts from across the IT industry. Each CompTIA certification is vendor-neutral, covers multiple technologies, and requires demonstration of skills and knowledge widely sought after by the IT industry.

To contact CompTIA with any questions or comments:

Please call + 1 630 268 1818

questions@comptia.org

Introduction

Getting started is an apt description for not only the beginning of this book, but also for your work toward achieving A+ certification. CompTIA's A+ is one of the most popular and well recognized certifications that PC technicians worldwide select to advance their technical expertise and launch their careers in the Information Technology (IT) industry. Opportunities for PC technicians can be found in almost every business sector and in almost every town and city in the world. The A+ certification is internationally recognized as the entry-level PC technician certification, and one that has become almost essential for anyone wishing to embark on a career in IT.

This book is intended to start you on the path to A+ certification. What's interesting about CompTIA's A+ certification is that it teaches basic concepts and principles that are not tied to any particular vendor's products. This means that the information you learn while studying for the A+ exams can be applied to almost any environment, regardless of what PC systems they use.

To gain A+ certification you must pass two exams, one based around PC hardware and another that tests your knowledge of popular PC operating systems. This book provides the information you need to study for both of these exams and is organized in such a way that you can clearly see what information refers to what exam.

The exams can be taken at the same time or separately. By passing both exams and becoming A+ certified, you will have proven that you have the requisite knowledge to configure, maintain, and troubleshoot PC systems and their associated software. You will also have proven that you are committed to furthering and proving your knowledge in your chosen field. This alone is the mark of a true IT professional.

This book is organized to help you study for the two A+ examinations that you will have to pass before you can become A+ certified. The majority of the material offers detailed information about the hardware devices, software configurations, and troubleshooting issues you will face as a PC technician.

About CompTIA

CompTIA stands for the Computing Technology Industry Association, which was formed in 1982. The association works with systems integrators and value-added resellers. For more than two decades, CompTIA has helped computing professionals achieve certifications that validate their knowledge and has also helped them launch their careers and earn higher wages.

In providing a vendor-neutral information technology certification series, CompTIA offers many certifications. Just a few are listed below. More are being added as CompTIA grows with the technology industry.

- A+
- Network+
- I-Net+
- CDIA+
- Server+
- E-Biz+
- IT Project+
- Jobs+
- Certified Technical Trainer+
- Linux+
- Security+
- Home Technology Integrator+

This extensive array of certifications enables a computing professional to pursue several different skill sets of information technology. Holding such certifications is undeniable proof that you possess the qualifications, the knowledge, and the skills that are necessary to be successful in the industry.

CompTIA is an association dedicated to advancing the growth of the IT industry. With its history, global reach, and extensive membership (over 13,000 strong), CompTIA has an impact on all areas of the IT industry. It looks closely at industry standards; develops expertise among professionals in the industry; provides business solutions; and offers training, certifications, workforce development, public policy, and technology innovations.

One of the advantages of CompTIA's interest in public policy is its strong influence. When the public becomes more concerned with privacy, antitrust, security, and other technology issues, CompTIA's recommendations carry weight.

CompTIA's certifications are highly regarded throughout the industry, as evidenced by Microsoft's adoption of the A+/Network+ combination or A+/Server+ combination of certifications as acceptable replacements for an elective for the MCSA certification. These certifications encompass the theory of networking protocols through the skills of building and maintaining a server-based computing network and more.

Who Should Read This Book

Two types of people should read this book: those who seek A+ certification and those who are working with PC technology and require reference materials.

The goal of the book is, of course, to help the reader learn the technologies and principles as laid out in CompTIA's A+ objectives. You aren't expected to have a complete understanding of PC technologies before you begin using this book, although any additional knowledge and experience you can gain will obviously help.

About A+ Certification

The A+ certification measures your knowledge of PC hardware, operating systems, basic networking, and troubleshooting. It is geared toward PC technicians who have a basic but thorough understanding of these topics, but who may or may not be working as PC technicians.

One of the advantages of the A+ certification is that it can get you started on the path toward your Microsoft Certified Systems Administrator (MCSA) certification. Microsoft currently accepts a combination of either the A+ and Server+ exams or the A+ and Network+ exams toward the MCSA elective.

To achieve the MCSA, you must first pass at least one Microsoft Certified Professional (MCP) exam and obtain your MCP identification number. Then you should begin taking the A+ and Network+ (or Server+) certification exams and register with your MCP number so that CompTIA will forward your certification information to Microsoft. At that point, you can complete the remaining exams for the MCSA certification, which you can see more about at http://www.microsoft.com/traincert/mcp/mcsa/Default.asp.

There are more benefits to achieving certifications than simply adding letters and, in this case, a plus sign, to your name as it appears on your business card. The certification stands for the body of knowledge you have studied, an achievement that few others can claim, and a particular level of professional competence. Employers and recruiters seek out individuals with CompTIA certifications. With the proliferation of outsourcing in the IT industry, you should know that outsource clients show quite a bit more confidence in certified outsource staff members, and often require that all staff be certified. It's obvious that this certification provides an incredible advantage.

Exam Overview

In creating the A+ certification testing program, CompTIA offers the IT industry a vendor-neutral method of measuring the knowledge of PC technicians. Because the test is vendor-independent, it is useful for people working in any environment. The objectives for each of the exams in the A+ certifications are divided into domains. These domains are weighted to match the job tasks that networking technicians and engineers spend time on during their average workdays.

Knowing the material for the exam is probably the most critical part. However, when you're familiar with the way the test works, you'll find this vital to achieving a passing score. The questions in the chapters that follow will drill you on your knowledge of the technologies, mirroring the types of information you'll face on the real exam.

A+ Exam Objectives

The following is a list of the objectives for both of the A+ exams. You can view these objectives online at *http://www.comptia.org/certification/A/objectives.asp.*

Core Hardware Exam

Domain 1.0 Installation, Configuration, and Upgrading

1.1 Identify the names, purpose, and characteristics, of system modules. Recognize these modules by sight or definition.

- Motherboard
- Firmware
- Power supply
- Processor /CPU
- Memory
- Storage devices
- Display devices
- Adapter cards
- Ports
- Cases
- Riser cards

1.2 Identify basic procedures for adding and removing field-replaceable modules for desktop systems. Given a replacement scenario, choose the appropriate sequences.

- Motherboard
- Storage device
  - FDD
  - HDD
  - CD/CDRW
  - DVD/DVDRW
  - Tape drive
  - Removable storage
- Power supply
  - AC adapter
  - AT/ATX
- Cooling systems
  - Fans
  - Heat sinks
  - Liquid cooling
- Processor /CPU
- Memory
- Display device
- Input devices
  - Keyboard
  - Mouse/pointer devices
  - Touch screen
- Adapters
  - Network Interface Card (NIC)
  - Sound card
  - Video card
  - Modem
  - SCSI

- IEEE 1394/Firewire
- USB
- Wireless

1.3 Identify basic procedures for adding and removing field-replaceable modules for portable systems. Given a replacement scenario, choose the appropriate sequences.

- Storage devices
  - FDD
  - HDD
  - CD/CDRW
  - DVD/DVDRW
  - Removable storage
- Power sources
  - AC adapter
  - DC adapter
  - Battery
- Memory
- Input devices
  - Keyboard
  - Mouse/pointer devices
  - Touch screen
- PCMCIA/Mini PCI Adapters
  - Network Interface Card (NIC)
  - Modem
  - SCSI
  - IEEE 1394/Firewire
  - USB
  - Storage (memory and hard drive)
- Docking station/port replicators
- LCD panel

- Wireless

    - Adapter/controller

    - Antennae

1.4 Identify typical IRQs, DMAs, and I/O addresses, and procedures for altering these settings when installing and configuring devices. Choose the appropriate installation or configuration steps in a given scenario.

- Legacy devices (e.g., ISA sound card)

- Specialized devices (e.g., CAD/CAM)

- Internal modems

- Floppy drive controllers

- Hard drive controllers

- Multimedia devices

- NICs

- I/O ports

    - Serial

    - Parallel

    - USB ports

    - IEEE 1394/Firewire

    - Infrared

1.5 Identify the names, purposes, and performance characteristics, of standardized/common peripheral ports, associated cabling, and their connectors. Recognize ports, cabling, and connectors, by sight.

- Port types

    - Serial

    - Parallel

    - USB ports

    - IEEE 1394/Firewire

    - Infrared

- Cable types

    - Serial (Straight through vs. null modem)

    - Parallel

    - USB

■ Connector types

- Serial: DB-9, DB-25, RJ-11, RJ-45
- Parallel DB-25, Centronics (mini, 36)
- PS2/MINI-DIN
- USB
- IEEE 1394

1.6 Identify proper procedures for installing and configuring common IDE devices. Choose the appropriate installation or configuration sequences in given scenarios. Recognize the associated cables.

■ IDE Interface Types

- EIDE
- ATA/ATAPI
- Serial ATA
- PIO

■ RAID (0, 1, and 5)

■ Master/Slave/cable select

■ Devices per channel

■ Primary/Secondary

■ Cable orientation/requirements

1.7 Identify proper procedures for installing and configuring common SCSI devices. Choose the appropriate installation or configuration sequences in given scenarios. Recognize the associated cables.

■ SCSI Interface Types

- Narrow
- Fast
- Wide
- Ultra-wide
- LVD
- HVD

■ Internal vs. external

■ SCSI IDs

   ● Jumper block/DIP switch settings (binary equivalents)

   ● Resolving ID conflicts

■ RAID (0, 1, and 5)

■ Cabling

   ● Length

   ● Type

   ● Termination requirements (active, passive, auto)

1.8 Identify proper procedures for installing and configuring common peripheral devices. Choose the appropriate installation or configuration sequences in given scenarios.

■ Modems and transceivers (dial-up, cable, DSL, ISDN)

■ External storage

■ Digital cameras

■ PDAs

■ Wireless access points

■ Infrared devices

■ Printers

■ UPS (Uninterruptible Power Supply) and suppressors

■ Monitors

1.9 Identify procedures to optimize PC operations in specific situations. Predict the effects of specific procedures under given scenarios.

■ Cooling systems

   ● Liquid

   ● Air

   ● Heat sink

   ● Thermal compound

■ Disk subsystem enhancements

   ● Hard drives

   ● Controller cards (e.g., RAID, ATA-100, etc.)

   ● Cables

- ▥   NICs
- ▥   Specialized video cards
- ▥   Memory
- ▥   Additional processors

1.10 Determine the issues that must be considered when upgrading a PC. In a given scenario, determine when and how to upgrade system components.

- ▥   Issues may include:
  - ●   Drivers for legacy devices
  - ●   Bus types and characteristics
  - ●   Cache in relationship to motherboards
  - ●   Memory capacity and characteristics
  - ●   Processor speed and compatibility
  - ●   Hard drive capacity and characteristics
  - ●   System/firmware limitations
  - ●   Power supply output capacity
- ▥   Components may include the following:
  - ●   Motherboards
  - ●   Memory
  - ●   Hard drives
  - ●   CPU
  - ●   BIOS
  - ●   Adapter cards
  - ●   Laptop power sources: Lithium ion, NiMH, Fuel cell
  - ●   PCMCIA Type I, II, III cards

Domain 2.0 Diagnosing and Troubleshooting

2.1 Recognize common problems associated with each module and their symptoms, and identify steps to isolate and troubleshoot the problems. Given a problem situation, interpret the symptoms and infer the most likely cause.

- ▥   I/O ports and cables
  - ●   Serial
  - ●   Parallel

- USB ports
- IEEE 1394/Firewire
- Infrared
- SCSI
- Motherboards
  - CMOS/ BIOS settings
  - POST audible/visual error codes
- Peripherals
- Computer case
  - Power supply
  - Slot covers
  - Front cover alignment
- Storage devices and cables
  - FDD
  - HDD
  - CD/CDRW
  - DVD/DVDRW
  - Tape drive
  - Removable storage
- Cooling systems
  - Fans
  - Heat sinks
  - Liquid cooling
  - Temperature sensors
- Processor /CPU
- Memory
- Display device
- Input devices
  - Keyboard
  - Mouse/pointer devices
  - Touch screen

- Adapters
  - Network Interface Card (NIC)
  - Sound card
  - Video card
  - Modem
  - SCSI
  - IEEE 1394/Firewire
  - USB
- Portable Systems
  - PCMCIA
  - Batteries
  - Docking Stations/Port Replicators
  - Portable unique storage

2.2 Identify basic troubleshooting procedures and tools, and how to elicit problem symptoms from customers. Justify asking particular questions in a given scenario.

- Troubleshooting/isolation/problem determination procedures
- Determining whether a hardware or software problem
- Gathering information from user
  - Customer Environment
  - Symptoms/Error Codes
  - Situation when the problem occurred

Domain 3.0 PC Preventive Maintenance, Safety, and Environmental Issues

3.1 Identify the various types of preventive maintenance measures, products, and procedures and when and how to use them.

- Liquid cleaning compounds
- Types of materials to clean contacts and connections
- Non-static vacuums (chassis, power supplies, fans)
- Cleaning monitors
- Cleaning removable media devices

- Ventilation, dust, and moisture control on the PC hardware interior
- Hard disk maintenance (defragging, scan disk, CHKDSK)
- Verifying UPS (Uninterruptible Power Supply) and suppressors

3.2 Identify various safety measures and procedures, and when/how to use them.

- ESD (Electrostatic Discharge) precautions and procedures
  - What ESD can do, how it may be apparent, or hidden
  - Common ESD protection devices
  - Situations that could present a danger or hazard
- Potential hazards and proper safety procedures relating to
  - High-voltage equipment
  - Power supply
  - CRTs

3.3 Identify environmental protection measures and procedures, and when/how to use them.

- Special disposal procedures that comply with environmental guidelines
  - Batteries
  - CRTs
  - Chemical solvents and cans
  - MSDS (Material Safety Data Sheet)

Domain 4.0 Motherboard/Processors/Memory

4.1 Distinguish between the popular CPU chips in terms of their basic characteristics.

- Popular CPU chips (Pentium class compatible)
- Voltage
- Speeds (actual vs. advertised)
- Cache level I, II, III
- Sockets/slots
- VRM(s)

4.2 Identify the types of RAM (Random Access Memory), form factors, and operational characteristics. Determine banking and speed requirements under given scenarios.

- Types
    - EDO RAM (Extended Data Output RAM)
    - DRAM (Dynamic Random Access Memory)
    - SRAM (Static RAM)
    - VRAM (Video RAM)
    - SDRAM (Synchronous Dynamic RAM)
    - DDR (Double Data Rate)
    - RAMBUS
- Form factors (including pin count)
    - SIMM (Single In-line Memory Module)
    - DIMM (Dual In-line Memory Module)
    - SoDIMM (Small outline DIMM)
    - MicroDIMM
    - RIMM (Rambus Inline Memory Module)
- Operational characteristics
    - Memory chips (8-bit, 16-bit, and 32-bit)
    - Parity chips versus non-parity chips
    - ECC vs. non-ECC
    - Single-sided vs. double sided

4.3 Identify the most popular types of motherboards, their components, and their architecture (bus structures).

- Types of motherboards
    - AT motherboards
    - ATX motherboards
- Communication ports
    - Serial
    - USB
    - Parallel

- IEEE 1394/Firewire
- Infrared
- Memory
  - SIMM
  - DIMM
  - RIMM
  - SoDIMM
  - MicroDIMM
- Processor sockets
  - Slot 1
  - Slot 2
  - Slot A
  - Socket A
  - Socket 7
  - Socket 8
  - Socket 423
  - Socket 478
  - Socket 370
- External cache memory (Level 2)
- Bus Architecture
- ISA
- PCI
  - PCI 32-bit
  - PCI 64-bit
- AGP
  - 2X
  - 4X
  - 8X (Pro)
- USB (Universal Serial Bus)
- AMR (audio modem riser) slots
- CNR (communication network riser) slots

- Basic compatibility guidelines
- IDE (ATA, ATAPI, ULTRA-DMA, EIDE)
- SCSI (Narrow, Wide, Fast, Ultra, HVD, LVD (Low Voltage Differential)
- Chipsets

4.4 Identify the purpose of CMOS (Complementary Metal-Oxide Semiconductor) memory, what it contains, and how and when to change its parameters. Given a scenario involving CMOS, choose the appropriate course of action.

- CMOS Settings
  - Default settings
  - CPU settings
  - Printer parallel port—Uni., bi-directional, disable/enable, ECP, EPP
  - COM/serial port—memory address, interrupt request, disable
  - Floppy drive—enable/disable drive or boot, speed, density
  - Hard drive—size and drive type
  - Memory—speed, parity, non-parity
  - Boot sequence
  - Date/Time
  - Passwords
  - Plug & Play BIOS
  - Disabling on-board devices
  - Disabling virus protection
  - Power management
  - Infrared

Domain 5.0 Printers

5.1 Identify printer technologies, interfaces, and options/upgrades.

- Technologies include:
  - Laser
  - Ink Dispersion
  - Dot Matrix
  - Solid ink

- Thermal
- Dye sublimation

■ Interfaces include:

- Parallel
- Network
- SCSI
- USB
- Infrared
- Serial
- IEEE 1394/Firewire
- Wireless

■ Options/Upgrades include:

- Memory
- Hard drives
- NICs
- Trays and feeders
- Finishers (e.g., stapling, etc.)
- Scanners/fax/copier

5.2 Recognize common printer problems and techniques used to resolve them.

■ Printer drivers

■ Firmware updates

■ Paper feed and output

■ Calibrations

■ Printing test pages

■ Errors (printed or displayed)

■ Memory

■ Configuration

■ Network connections

■ Connections

■ Paper jam

▦ Print quality

▦ Safety precautions

▦ Preventive maintenance

▦ Consumables

▦ Environment

Domain 6.0 Basic Networking

6.1 Identify the common types of network cables, their characteristics and connectors.

▦ Cable types include:

  ● Coaxial: RG6, RG8

  ● RG58

  ● RG59

  ● Plenum/PVC

  ● UTP: CAT3, CAT5/e, CAT6

  ● STP

  ● Fiber: Single-mode, Multi-mode

▦ Connector types include:

  ● BNC

  ● RJ-45

  ● AUI

  ● ST/SC

  ● IDC/UDC

6.2 Identify basic networking concepts including how a network works.

▦ Installing and configuring network cards

▦ Addressing

▦ Bandwidth

▦ Status indicators

▦ Protocols

  ● TCP/IP

  ● IPX/SPX (NWLINK)

- AppleTalk
- NETBEUI/NETBIOS
- Full-duplex, half-duplex
- Cabling—Twisted Pair, Coaxial, Fiber Optic, RS-232
- Networking models
  - Peer-to-peer
  - Client/server
- Infrared
- Wireless

6.3 Identify common technologies available for establishing Internet connectivity and their characteristics.

- Technologies include:
  - LAN
  - DSL
  - Cable
  - ISDN
  - Dial-up
  - Satellite
  - Wireless
- Characteristics include:
  - Definition
  - Speed
  - Connections

Operating System Technologies Exam

Domain 1.0 Operating System Fundamentals

1.1 Identify the major desktop components and interfaces, and their functions. Differentiate the characteristics of Windows 9x/Me, Windows NT 4.0 Workstation, Windows 2000 Professional, and Windows XP.

- Contrasts between Windows 9x/Me, Windows NT 4.0 Workstation, Windows 2000 Professional, and Windows XP

■ Major Operating System components

- Registry
- Virtual Memory
- File System

■ Major Operating System Interfaces

- Windows Explorer
- My Computer
- Control Panel
- Computer Management Console
- Accessories/System Tools
- Command line
- Network Neighborhood/My Network Places
- Task Bar/systray
- Start Menu
- Device Manager

1.2 Identify the names, locations, purposes, and contents of major system files.

■ Windows 9x–specific files

- IO.SYS
- MSDOS.SYS
- AUTOEXEC.BAT
- COMMAND.COM
- CONFIG.SYS
- HIMEM.SYS
- EMM386.exe
- WIN.COM
- SYSTEM.INI
- WIN.INI
- SYSTEM.DAT
- USER.DAT

■   Windows NT–based specific files

- BOOT.INI
- NTLDR
- NTDETECT.COM
- NTBOOTDD.SYS
- NTUSER.DAT
- Registry data files

1.3 Demonstrate the ability to use command-line functions and utilities to manage the operating system, including the proper syntax and switches.

■   Command/CMD

■   DIR

■   ATTRIB

■   VER

■   MEM

■   SCANDISK

■   DEFRAG

■   EDIT

■   XCOPY

■   COPY

■   FORMAT

■   FDISK

■   SETVER

■   SCANREG

■   MD/CD/RD

■   Delete/Rename

■   DELTREE

■   TYPE

■   ECHO

■   SET

■   PING

1.4 Identify basic concepts and procedures for creating, viewing, and managing disks, directories, and files. This includes procedures for changing file attributes and the ramifications of those changes (for example, security issues).

- Disk Partitions
  - Active Partition
  - Primary Partition
  - Extended Partition
  - Logical Partition
- Files Systems
  - FAT16
  - FAT32
  - NTFS4
  - NTFS5.x
- Directory Structures (root directory, subdirectories, etc.)
  - Create folders
  - Navigate the directory structure
  - Maximum depth
- Files
  - Creating files
  - File naming conventions (Most common extensions, 8.3, maximum length)
  - File attributes - Read Only, Hidden, System, and Archive attributes
  - File Compression
  - File Encryption
  - File Permissions
  - File types (text vs. binary file)

1.5 Identify the major operating system utilities, their purpose, location, and available switches.

- Disk Management Tools
  - DEFRAG.EXE
  - FDISK.EXE

- Backup/Restore Utility (MSbackup, NTBackup, etc.)
- ScanDisk
- CHKDSK
- Disk Cleanup
- Format

■ System Management Tools

- Device Manager
- System Manager
- Computer Manager
- MSCONFIG.EXE
- REGEDIT.EXE (View information/Backup registry)
- REGEDT32.EXE
- SYSEDIT.EXE
- SCANREG
- COMMAND/CMD
- Event Viewer
- Task Manager

■ File Management Tools

- ATTRIB.EXE
- EXTRACT.EXE
- Edit.com
- Windows Explorer

Domain 2.0 Installation, Configuration, and Upgrading

2.1 Identify the procedures for installing Windows 9x/Me, Windows NT 4.0 Workstation, Windows 2000 Professional, and Windows XP, and bringing the operating system to a basic operational level.

■ Verify hardware compatibility and minimum requirements

■ Determine OS installation options

- Installation type (typical, custom, other)
- Network configuration
- File system type
- Dual Boot Support

- Disk preparation order (conceptual disk preparation)
    - Start the installation
    - Partition
    - Format drive
- Run appropriate setup utility
    - Setup
    - Winnt
- Installation methods
    - Bootable CD
    - Boot floppy
    - Network installation
    - Drive Imaging
- Device Driver Configuration
    - Load default drivers
    - Find updated drivers
- Restore user data files (if applicable)
- Identify common symptoms and problems

2.2 Identify steps to perform an operating system upgrade from Windows 9x/ME, Windows NT 4.0 Workstation, Windows 2000 Professional, and Windows XP. Given an upgrade scenario, choose the appropriate next steps.

- Upgrade paths available
- Determine correct upgrade startup utility (e.g., WINNT32 vs. WINNT)
- Verify hardware compatibility and minimum requirements
- Verify application compatibility
- Apply OS service packs, patches, and updates
- Install additional Windows components

2.3 Identify the basic system boot sequences and boot methods, including the steps to create an emergency boot disk with utilities installed for Windows 9x/Me, Windows NT 4.0 Workstation, Windows 2000 Professional, and Windows XP.

- Boot Sequence
    - Files required to boot
    - Boot steps (9x, NT-based)

- Alternative Boot Methods
  - Using a Startup disk
  - Safe/VGA-only mode
  - Last Known Good configuration
  - Command Prompt mode
  - Booting to a system restore point
  - Recovery Console
  - Boot.ini switches
  - Dual Boot
- Creating Emergency Disks with OS Utilities
- Creating emergency repair disk (ERD)

2.4 Identify procedures for installing/adding a device, including loading, adding, and configuring device drivers, and required software.

- Device Driver Installation
  - Plug and Play (PNP) and non-PNP devices
  - Install and configure device drivers
  - Install different device drivers
  - Manually install a device driver
  - Search the Internet for updated device drivers
  - Using unsigned drivers (driver signing)
- Install Additional Windows components
- Determine if permissions are adequate for performing the task

2.5 Identify procedures necessary to optimize the operating system and major operating system subsystems.

- Virtual Memory Management
- Disk Defragmentation
- Files and Buffers
- Caches
- Temporary file management

Domain 3.0 Diagnosing and Troubleshooting

3.1 Recognize and interpret the meaning of common error codes and startup messages from the boot sequence, and identify steps to correct the problems.

- Common Error Messages and Codes
  - Boot failure and errors: Invalid boot disk, Inaccessible boot device, Missing NTLDR, Bad or missing Command interpreter
  - Startup messages: Error in CONFIG.SYS line XX, Himem.sys not loaded, Missing or corrupt Himem.sys, Device/Service has failed to start
  - A device referenced in SYSTEM.INI, WIN.INI, Registry is not found
  - Event Viewer – Event log is full
  - Failure to start GUI
  - Windows Protection Error
  - User-modified settings cause improper operation at startup
  - Registry corruption
- Using the correct Utilities
  - Dr. Watson
  - Boot Disk
  - Event Viewer

3.2 Recognize when to use common diagnostic utilities and tools. Given a diagnostic scenario involving one of these utilities or tools, select the appropriate steps needed to resolve the problem.

- Startup disks
  - Required files for a boot disk
  - Boot disk with CD-ROM support
- Startup modes
  - Safe mode
  - Safe mode with command prompt
  - Safe mode with networking
  - Step-by-Step/Single step mode
  - Automatic skip driver (ASD.exe)

■ Diagnostic tools, utilities, and resources

- User/installation manuals
- Internet/Web resources
- Training materials
- Task Manager
- Dr. Watson
- Boot Disk
- Event Viewer
- Device Manager
- WinMSD
- MSD
- Recovery CD
- CONFIGSAFE

■ Eliciting problem symptoms from customers

■ Having customer reproduce error as part of the diagnostic process

■ Identifying recent changes to the computer environment from the user

3.3 Recognize common operational and usability problems and determine how to resolve them.

■ Troubleshooting Windows-specific printing problems

- Print spool is stalled
- Incorrect/incompatible driver for print
- Incorrect parameter

■ Other Common problems

- General Protection Faults
- Bluescreen error (BSOD)
- Illegal operation
- Invalid working directory
- System lock up
- Option (Sound card, modem, input device) will not function
- Application will not start or load

- Cannot log on to network (option – NIC not functioning)
- Applications don't install
- Network connection

■ Viruses and virus types

- What they are
- TSR (Terminate Stay Resident) programs and virus
- Sources (floppy, e-mails, etc.)
- How to determine presence

Domain 4.0 Networks

4.1 Identify the networking capabilities of Windows. Given configuration parameters, configure the operating system to connect to a network.

■ Configure protocols

- TCP/IP: Gateway, Subnet mask, DNS (and domain suffix), WINS, Static address assignment, Automatic address assignment (APIPA, DHCP)
- IPX/SPX (NWLink)
- AppleTalk
- NetBEUI/NetBIOS

■ Configure Client options

- Microsoft
- Novell

■ Verify the configuration

■ Understand the use of the following tools

- IPCONFIG.EXE
- WINIPCFG.EXE
- PING
- TRACERT.EXE
- NSLOOKUP.EXE

■ Share resources (Understand the capabilities/limitations with each OS version)

■ Setting permissions to shared resources

■ Network type and network card

4.2 Identify the basic Internet protocols and terminologies. Identify procedures for establishing Internet connectivity. In a given scenario, configure the operating system to connect to and use Internet resources.

■ Protocols and terminologies

- ISP
- TCP/IP
- E-mail (POP, SMTP, IMAP)
- HTML
- HTTP
- HTTPS
- SSL
- Telnet
- FTP
- DNS

■ Connectivity technologies

- Dial-up networking
- DSL networking
- ISDN networking
- Cable
- Satellite
- Wireless
- LAN

■ Installing and Configuring browsers

- Enable/disable script support
- Configure Proxy Settings
- Configure security settings

■ Firewall protection under Windows XP

Taking the A+ Exams

Preparing for the actual exam day is stressful. You've likely burned the midnight oil studying for the test, and you've probably worked through numerous installations and configurations in a practice lab. Despite how busy you are, it is highly recommended that you spend at least 15 minutes per day reviewing material or practicing in a lab to keep the subject matter fresh in your mind.

To sign up for either of the A+ exams, you can go through Thomson Prometric by calling (800) 77-MICRO or accessing the Web site at http://www. 2test.com. You'll be required to select an exam location and time. The company has added directions to its Web site so that testing centers are easy to find. The Thomson Prometric associates will be able to give you directions as well. The company accepts both credit cards and prepaid vouchers in addition to checks, as long as your check is received prior to your test date. You can book both of your tests on the same day, one after the other, or you can choose to take the tests on different days. CompTIA used to require that you take both tests within 90 days but they have now abandoned this requirement.

Test Smart   Before taking the test, you can read the chapter summaries and the Quick Reference section at the back of the book for a fast refresher.

On your test day, you should arrive at the testing center at least 15 minutes prior to your scheduled appointment. Bring two forms of identification, at least one of them with a picture and both with signatures. As you might expect, you will not be allowed to bring in any notes, books, or other reference materials. You are also prohibited from bringing pagers, cell phones, laptops, PDAs, or other electronic equipment into the testing room. Testing centers offer the ability to store your personal belongings.

Keep in mind that some people are natural test takers, while others have more difficulty even though they know exactly the same material. Understanding how the exam works in advance might be of some help. The exam is in multiple-choice format and is given on a computer. The testing center will provide you with pencils and scratch paper. You are given the chance to mark questions that you are unsure about so that you can go back and look at them later on. For each question answered correctly, you will receive points. You should answer every question, even if you're not certain about the answer. If a question is not answered, you will receive no points for it. If you guess, you have a 25 percent chance (or better, if you have made an educated guess to eliminate any obviously wrong choices) of receiving points for the answer. As you can see, it's better to guess than to leave a question blank.

Each exam has a time limit, which is usually more than adequate for reading and responding to each question as well as going over your answers at the end. The better you know the material, the faster you will likely finish. One way you can easily avoid wasting time going back to search for questions you later believe you answered wrong is to always answer the question, even if you aren't certain about your answer. This way, if you end up taking too much time, at least you will have answered all the questions by the end of the exam. If you're unsure about a question, check the box labeled "Mark" so that you'll be able to return to it easily.

You may encounter some scenario questions on the test. These can be time consuming, and it's tempting to skip them with the intent to return to them later. If you do decide to skip and return, make sure you guess an answer and mark the question rather than leave it blank. That way, even if you don't get time to go back and re-read the question you will still have provided an answer.

When you come across a question on the test and you're not sure about the answer, use the elimination technique. Starting at the bottom, look at each possible choice and eliminate it or keep it as a potential answer. If you can narrow your choices down to two possibilities and then take a guess, you have a 50 percent chance of being correct.

After you've finished answering every question, do a quick "click-through" to look for questions that ask you to choose more than one answer. Then make sure that you've selected all the possibilities. During this step, you'll probably find at least one question for which you missed one of the multiple answers.

 Test Smart   Use elimination techniques when you're unsure. Don't dwell on any single question. Mark questions that you want to return to. Don't leave questions unanswered. Run through all the questions as a final check before you finish the exam. And don't worry if you feel nervous; everyone feels the same way.

When you finally submit your answers, a score is generated. This is fairly nerve-wracking because the computer will tell you to wait while the score is being printed before revealing whether you passed the test. The testing center will provide you with a hard copy of your score, which is sealed to ensure its validity. Then the testing center will provide your scores to CompTIA, and if they're passing, the relevant certificate will be on its way to your mailbox. If you didn't pass the first time, you are allowed to register to take the test again.

Once you have taken and passed both of the necessary tests, you will become CompTIA A+ certified.

How to Use This Book

This book is intended to be both a study manual and a reference. Because the book covers both of the exams required for A+ certification, it is divided up so that you can find the information related to each of the exams easily. The first part of the book covers the A+ Core Hardware Exam objectives. The second part covers the Operating System Technologies Exam.

Even though the sections are divided in accordance with A+ objectives, some concepts recur throughout the book. The reason for this is simple: each chapter builds on the fundamentals from earlier chapters, and reminders of those fundamentals ensure that you fully learn the more complex concepts. Once you've finished with the A+ exam, this book can help you with your job as a PC technician.

Your Study Plan

Studying for any exam can be grueling. Given that A+ certification is geared toward those starting a career in IT, it's quite likely that you'll be studying for the exam while holding down a full-time job or attending college or university. To make it easier, this book has been organized to both match the A+ objectives, as well as build up from the basics to more intricate concepts.

At the end of each chapter, you will find a chapter summary that briefly covers the chapter's key points. In addition, each chapter contains exam tips throughout and a set of several questions that will help you study.

To use this book in the most efficient manner, go through it three times, but in three different ways:

1 The first time, lightly skim through each chapter, starting from the beginning, and make certain to read the headings and the exam notes, look at the diagrams, and read anything that catches your eye. This will familiarize you with the material and prepare you for the heavy studying you'll do later.

2 The second time, read each chapter in detail. Try to spend at least 15 minutes every day reading, or more if you have time. Even in small amounts, reading daily will keep the concepts fresh in your mind.

3 The third time, answer the questions at the end of each chapter. For any question that you have trouble answering, go back through the chapter and look up the answer.

In addition to studying, develop a way to test various theories and methods in the "real world." This will be the most effective way to practice installation, configuration, and troubleshooting, all of which appear in later chapters. Ideally, you should have a lab available to practice in. Many students gather old equipment and set up practice labs in their homes.

A day or two before your exam, read through the Check Yourself (before you test yourself) section at the end of this book. This process will help you understand all the concepts tested for on the exam as well as concentrate your efforts on any weak areas. By the time you take the exam, you'll know what it will take to pass it.

Support

Every effort has been made to ensure the accuracy of this book. Microsoft Press provides corrections for books at the following address:

http://mspress.microsoft.com/support/

If you have comments, questions, or ideas regarding this book, please send them to Microsoft Press via e-mail at:

mspinput@microsoft.com

or via postal mail at:

Microsoft Press
Attn: Faster Smarter A+ Certification Editor
One Microsoft Way
Redmond, WA 98052-6399

Please note that product support is not offered through the above addresses.

About the CD

The companion CD contains a fully searchable electronic version of this book. It also contains an electronic assessment, which allows you to take timed practice tests that prepares you for the actual A+ Certification exams. Explanations of the answers to each question on the assessments can be found in separate files on the CD.

Follow these instructions to use the companion CD:

1   Insert the companion CD into your CD drive.

2   If a license agreement does not appear automatically, double-click StartCD.exe in the root folder of the CD. Accept the license agreement to display the starting menu screen.

The menu provides you with links to all the resources available on the CD.

System Requirements

To install and run the contents of this CD, your system must meet the following minimum requirements:

- Operating system:

  - Microsoft Windows 95 or Microsoft Windows NT 4 with Service Pack 6a or later

  - Microsoft Windows 98, Microsoft Windows Me or Microsoft Windows 2000

  - Microsoft Windows XP or Microsoft Windows Server 2003

- Pentium class with 166 megahertz (MHz) or higher processor

- Memory required:

  - Microsoft Windows 95: 12 MB RAM

  - Microsoft Windows 98, Me, and NT 4 SP6a: 16 MB RAM

  - Microsoft Windows 2000, Microsoft Windows XP and Microsoft Windows Server 2003: 64 MB RAM

- Microsoft Internet Explorer 5.01 or later. The electronic assessment requires a full installation of Internet Explorer 5.01 or later. If you do not have Internet Explorer 5.01 or later, you can install Internet Explorer 6 from the Companion CD.

- Hard disk space required:

  - To install the eBook: 10 MB

  - To install Internet Explorer 6 SP1 from this CD: 32 MB

  - To install the electronic assessment: 17 MB

- A double-speed CD drive or better

- 800x600 with high color (16-bit) display settings

- Microsoft Mouse or compatible pointing device

Part 1

A+ Core Hardware

The Core Hardware exam is intended to measure the skills necessary to work with both PC hardware and peripheral devices. To be successful in taking the Core Hardware exam, candidates must demonstrate an understanding of installing, configuring, upgrading, and troubleshooting computer systems. To that end, the following six chapters are designed to prepare you to take and pass the A+ Core Hardware exam.

The questions you are going to find on the A+ Core Hardware exam follow exam objectives as developed by CompTIA. These objectives provide you with the only real insight as to the areas that will be tested. These objectives are organized into topic-focused domains. Each chapter in the book corresponds to these CompTIA domains. For example, Chapter 1 deals with Domain 1.0 and the objectives within that domain. This approach makes finding the information on each of the CompTIA objectives as easy as possible, and, in turn, makes reviewing for the exam that much easier.

Chapter 1

Installing, Configuring, and Upgrading Hardware

Although a computer system might seem like a complex thing, from the perspective of a technician it is relatively simple. That is not to say that a computer is not a highly complex piece of technology, just that it is actually composed of a fairly basic set of parts. Once you become familiar with these parts, the computer becomes a lot less threatening.

To lay the foundation of what is to come, we will start this book with a look at some of the more common computer terms, components, and concepts. These are listed in the CompTIA objectives and will provide a framework for working through the rest of the book and give you an understanding when various components are discussed throughout the book. So, without further ado, allow us to introduce you to your computer, or at least some of its core components.

Note   As mentioned in the front of this book, the chapters are organized according to the Comp-TIA A+ domains and test objectives. What this means is that the following chapter covers Domain 1.0 of the A+ Core Hardware exam in its entirety. Domain 1.0, like this chapter, is extensive and 30% of the exam questions will come from this single chapter. In that light, spend a little more time here reviewing tables and keeping a close eye on exam tips and bulleted points.

Identifying System Modules

System Board/Motherboard

The system board, also known as the *motherboard*, but sometimes referred to as the *mainboard*, is the primary circuit board into which all of the other components connect. In essence, the system board is the part that brings all other parts together. Think about it this way: if your computer threw a party, the motherboard would be the host.

In the early days of PCs, the motherboard provided a socket for a CPU, a place for memory, expansion slots for add-on devices, and some other basic system functions, but not much else. Additional functionality, like connectors for hard disk drives, sound cards, mice, and so on, was provided through expansion cards that plugged into the motherboard's expansion slots. Today's motherboards tend to adopt a more integrated approach, often combining hard disk, floppy disk, video, parallel ports, serial ports, modem, network card, USB, mouse, keyboard, joystick, and sound into the motherboard itself. When a motherboard offers this functionality, it is said to do so "on-board," as in on-board video.

Motherboards come in a variety of sizes and shapes known as form factors. The form factor defines such things as how big a case is required to fit it into, and determines everything from the type of memory and processors used to the connectors and location of the expansion slots.

The two most common types of motherboards used today are the older Advanced Technology (AT) motherboards and the AT Extended (ATX) motherboards. For a detailed discussion on motherboards, refer to Chapter 4.

Power Supply

The power supply is the means by which a computer system gets its "juice." A power supply is necessary because computer components actually use a smaller amount of power, and in a different format, than that which flows out of the wall socket. In practical terms, a computer power supply takes the alternating current (AC) voltage supplied through the cable connecting it to the wall, converts it to direct current (DC), and drops the voltage to a fraction of what was supplied.

The conversion and reduction process generates heat, which is why power supplies have fans built into them to aid cooling.

There are two primary types of power supplies: AT power supplies, which have unique connectors to fit on an AT motherboard, and ATX power supplies designed to work with ATX motherboards. If you ever need to replace a power supply, you will need to ensure that you purchase the correct one for the job.

See Also   *For more information on power supplies, refer to Chapter 4.*

Processor/CPU

Processors, or to give them their proper name, central processing units (CPUs), are the brains of the computer system. They are the means by which all processing in the computer occurs.

Processors come in a variety of shapes and sizes, and the type of processor used must be compatible with the motherboard into which it is to be plugged. In other words, all processors are not compatible with all boards.

Processors generate a significant amount of heat—heat that can damage or even destroy a processor if it is not dissipated. For this reason, processors use metal conductors called *heat sinks* to pull the heat away from the processor, as well as fans that typically mount directly on top of the heat sink to move the hot air away from it. Heat sinks are made with fins that serve to increase the surface area of the sink and so improve the efficiency of the heat dissipation. Figure 1-1 shows a CPU with a heat sink and fan.

Figure 1-1 Processors use a heat sink and fan to help dissipate the heat they produce.

See Also   *For more information on processors, refer to Chapter 4.*

Memory

When we talk about memory, we are referring to random access memory (RAM), which is an essential part of every PC system. RAM stores information temporarily so that it can be used and accessed by the components of the system. RAM is a commonly upgraded component and one that PC technicians will be expected to frequently work with.

See Also   *While Domain 1 of the CompTIA objectives lists memory as an objective, Domain 4 covers it in greater detail. Therefore, a more in-depth discussion of memory can be found in Chapter 4.*

Storage Devices

Just like closet space in our homes, the computer system needs storage space, a place to store all of those documents, MP3s, and programs. When we talk about storage devices, we are most often referring to hard disk drives, though in today's multimedia world the category can also be expanded to include CD, CD-R and CD-RW, and DVD drives, floppy disk drives, Zip drives, tape drives, and even USB devices such as memory sticks. All of these devices make it possible to store files for later retrieval.

There are three basic types of storage—magnetic, optical, and silicon. Magnetic storage devices include hard disks, floppy disks, and proprietary formats like tape and Zip disks. Optical storage includes all of the CD- and DVD-based media. Silicon-based storage is a relatively new addition to this category, and includes storage devices like USB memory sticks and memory cards like those used in digital cameras. At the moment, the cost of these is high and the capacities are low, but as with everything else in technology, prices are falling and capacities are going up. Soon they will offer a viable alternative to other removable media.

Monitor/Display Devices

Computer monitors are one of the means by which we interact with the computer system. A computer can function without a monitor, and in fact some systems can be used in this "headless" fashion, but in general every PC has a monitor.

Monitors come in different types. The traditional cathode-ray tube (CRT) monitor is what you are most likely to see in your travels, but there is an increasing trend toward liquid crystal display (LCD) screens, which are also called *flat-panel displays*.

As far as the CompTIA objectives are concerned, there are two types of desktop monitors, Video Graphics Array (VGA) monitors and Super Video Graphics Array (SVGA) monitors. The difference between the two is that the

SVGA monitor is capable of displaying a higher-definition picture. SVGA monitors are more common nowadays, but if you are working with an older computer system, you might find yourself staring at a VGA monitor. A detailed discussion on installing and configuring monitors appears later in this chapter.

Modem

Modulators/demodulators, or modems, are devices that offer translation services. Their job is to translate the digital signals sent from your computer into analog signals that can be transferred over a conventional phone line. At the other end of the line, another modem is required to once again convert the analog signal back into digital format so that the receiving computer can understand it.

Even though other technologies such as cable Internet access, digital subscriber line (DSL), and Integrated Services Digital Network (ISDN) have become more popular in recent years, dial-up communication (the term given to a connection that uses a modem) is still the most popular form of remote access and Internet access in the world. For that reason, you are very likely to find yourself working with modems and, perhaps more importantly, answering modem-related questions on the A+ exam.

Modems come in both internal and external versions. External modems are housed in a box and normally require an external power supply. Connectivity to the PC can be achieved via serial communication or via USB. Internal modems are installed in an expansion slot inside your computer. Of the two types, internal modems are far more common and, unfortunately for us as technicians, often more problematic in terms of configuration and management. Figure 1-2 shows an example of an internal modem.

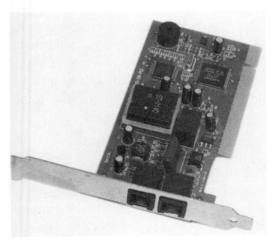

Figure 1-2 Internal modems are more common than external modems, but present more challenges in terms of configuration.

Firmware

Firmware is a program (software) that is stored on a chip (hardware) but is not considered to be software or hardware. In other words, it is between hardware and software—in between soft and hard comes firm. The terms *BIOS* and *firmware* have been used interchangeably and serve to confuse the issue. Firmware simply refers to the programs that are stored in chips and not on hard disks or other such devices.

BIOS/CMOS

In the computer world, it is software that tells the hardware what to do. The first set of instructions given to the computer as it boots up comes from the basic input/output system (BIOS).

The BIOS firmware is stored in the complementary metal-oxide semiconductor (CMOS), a special chip on the motherboard that holds the various BIOS settings. These settings include things like the parameters for the hard disks, the boot order, and the status (either enabled or disabled) of on-board devices. Because the BIOS is firmware, it can be updated, though it requires a special program to achieve this. The process of upgrading the BIOS is referred to as *flashing*. The BIOS can be flashed to provide additional functionality or to correct a problem with the current version of the BIOS. The procedure for upgrading the BIOS is covered later in this chapter.

BIOS settings are configurable through a special program. This program can normally be accessed by pressing a specific key, or combination of keys, on boot-up.

The CMOS is a chip that stores the settings for the BIOS. The CMOS is a type of RAM, which means that if the system is powered down, it will lose its settings. Of course, having to reinstall hardware settings every time the computer is shut down would be very inefficient. Instead, the CMOS RAM is powered by a battery so that its settings will be retained. As with any battery, however, it will at some point lose power and be unable to hold the settings. This situation is seen from time to time when the system boots and the hardware configurations have to be reset every time. Simply replacing the battery corrects this problem.

Ports

One of the terms you are going to hear with great frequency when working with computers is *ports*. The term ports is actually very broad and can refer to many different things. As you will see throughout this book, ports refer to the physical connectors the system uses to communicate with other system devices. Ports of this nature carry names such as COM1 or COM4, and are used by devices like the mouse or modem to communicate with the system. Another port type, LPT ports, can be used by printers to facilitate communication between the printer and the computer.

Field-Replaceable Modules   While working with computers, you are likely going to encounter the term *field-replaceable module (FRM). FRM* refers to any device that can be replaced "in the field." Generally FRMs do not require any special tools, conditions, or skills to be replaced. For instance, you would not show up at a work site and begin to repair a monitor; it is more likely that you would simply replace the monitor. Components that are considered FRMs include mother-boards, power supplies, hard drives, CD-ROM drives, and floppy-disk drives—basically, anything that can be replaced, without the need for specialized tools and equipment, by technical personnel.

The basic idea behind FRMs is to save time and, of course, money. Most organizations would rather not pay the PC technician to spend time trying to repair a device that can be replaced quickly. Time is a critical consideration. Most users are unwilling to wait for you to repair a device and some-times will hardly wait patiently while you replace the component. When replacing FRMs, consider the following:

- ■ **Replace with a Similar Component**   Whenever possible, replace the failed compo-nent with a similar or identical one. For instance, if a network card fails, replacing it with a card that has the same speed and uses the same drivers can save you a lot of addi-tional work.

- ■ **Replace the Correct Component**   Before taking the old component out and replacing it with the new one, follow the troubleshooting steps to ensure that you are replacing the correct component. For instance, before replacing the video card, make sure that the problem is not with the monitor.

- ■ **Ensure Functionality**   After replacing the FRM, test it for functionality. If it's a new com-ponent, care must be taken to ensure that it works with the current hardware configuration.

- ■ **Put the System Back to Normal**   As a matter of courtesy, after replacing a component, return everything back to its original state. If you moved the user's papers, stationery, or other equipment during the process, put it back.

Identifying System Resources

Throughout this book, you are going to see many references to system resources and configuring devices to use them. Essentially, the computer system is a collection of interconnected and interrelated components all needing to communicate with each other. Each computer component needs to be assigned system resources to allow this communication to take place. There are three types of system resources that components use: input/output (I/O) addresses, interrupt requests (IRQs), and direct memory access (DMA) channels.

I/O Addresses

All computers have a number of I/O devices attached to them such as printers, scanners, floppy drives, hard disks, and just about every other component you can think of. Each of these devices requires a unique I/O address. An I/O address is the hexadecimal address of an area of memory that is used by the peripheral device to exchange information with other devices in the system. You can think of it as a kind of mail slot for the device.

Note   I/O addresses are expressed in a numbering system known as *hexadecimal*. The lower case *h* is appended to the number to indicate this. Hexadecimal is a numbering system based on 16 characters—the numbers 0 through 9 and the letters A through F. Although you will not be required to understand the hexadecimal numbering system for the A+ exam, it is a useful thing to understand when working in the real world.

Some core components, such as the hard disk controller or video graphics card, have I/O addresses reserved for them, while other devices such as printers need to have I/O addresses assigned. I/O addresses are assigned to add-on peripheral devices through Plug and Play, or you can manually assign I/O addresses. Plug and Play is far and away the preferred method for resource assignment. You can view I/O address assignments on a Microsoft Windows PC using Windows Device Manager, as shown in Figure 1-3.

See Also   *For more information on using Windows Device Manager, refer to Chapter 7.*

Figure 1-3 You can view the I/O addresses assigned to devices in Windows Device Manager.

Not only does each component require an I/O address, but each component must use a unique I/O address. This means that when a new device such as a network card or modem is installed in the system, it cannot be assigned an I/O address already being used by another device. If two devices are assigned the same I/O address, one or both devices will fail to function. Table 1-1 identifies the default I/O addresses that are assigned to various devices within the system.

 Test Smart Each component attached to the computer requires a unique I/O address to communicate with other devices in the system.

Table 1-1 Standard I/O Address Assignments

I/O Address	Device
1F0–1F8	Hard disk controller
200–207	Game I/O
278–27F	Parallel port (LPT2)
2F8–2FF	Serial port (COM2)
320–32F	Hard drive controller, 8-bit ISA
378–37F	Parallel port (LPT1)
3B0–3BF	Monochrome graphics adapter
3D0–3DF	Color graphics adapter
3F0–3F7	Floppy drive controller
3F8–3FF	Serial port (COM1)

(handwritten margin notes next to table: "1F0–177 → secondary HDC", "1F0–1F7 → primary HDC")

 Test Smart When studying for the A+ exam, ensure that you know the I/O addresses for key system components such as the COM ports, floppy drive, and hard drive.

Standard IRQ Settings

Once a computer component has been assigned an I/O address, it is able to communicate with other devices and the CPU within the system. However, there needs to be some mechanism by which the devices can initiate communication with the CPU; for that the system uses interrupt request (IRQ) lines. IRQ lines are used in the system to notify the CPU that a peripheral device has started or completed a task. When the CPU receives an interrupt request from a peripheral device, the CPU can identify the device by its unique IRQ.

When working with IRQs, there are a few things to keep in mind. Most components need to have a unique IRQ, whether it is located on the motherboard or it is an add-on device. Secondly, devices should not share an IRQ address; if they do, one or both devices will fail to function. There is one caveat here, because Plug and Play has the ability to share IRQs if necessary; just more of that Plug and Play magic. In modern systems, Plug and Play manages the assignment of IRQ addresses, which greatly reduces the chances of assigning the same resources to two devices. As technicians, we do not have the liberty to trust Plug and Play to manage resources because there will be those times when we will need to troubleshoot IRQ assignments. To do this, we need to have a clear idea of which IRQ is used for which device. Table 1-2 shows system IRQs and the components that use them.

Table 1-2   IRQ Assignments

IRQ Address	Device
IRQ 0	System timer
IRQ 1	Keyboard
IRQ 2/9	Open (cascade to IRQ 9)
IRQ 3	Default IRQ for COM2 and COM4
IRQ 4	Default for IRQ 1 and COM3
IRQ 5	LPT2 (often used with audio cards)
IRQ 6	Floppy drive
IRQ 7	LPT1
IRQ 8	Real-time clock
IRQ 9	Redirect to 2
IRQ 10	Open
IRQ 11	Open
IRQ 12	Open (often used with PS/2 mouse)
IRQ 13	Math coprocessor
IRQ14	Primary hard drive controller
IRQ 15	Secondary hard drive controller

 Test Smart   Be sure to study Table 1-2 closely before taking the A+ exam.

Notice in Table 1-2 that IRQ 2 and 9 are connected; there is a good reason for this. Early PCs only had a small number of devices, so the original IRQ controller that supplied eight IRQs was more than sufficient. As PCs developed, more IRQs were needed, which meant that another IRQ controller was needed. The addition of another interrupt controller was made simple by the fact that the second controller was accessed through an interrupt on the first controller. IRQ 2 was set aside for this purpose. In essence, the two interrupt controllers are linked—or, to give it its proper term, *cascaded*—through IRQ 2. This cascading function provides 16 IRQs (0–15) without requiring a fundamental redesign of PC architecture.

DMA Addresses

Direct memory access (DMA) is a method used by peripheral devices to access the system's main memory and store data without having to use the CPU. This frees up the CPU to focus on other tasks. DMA data transfers from peripheral devices are held in a special area of memory known as a *buffer*.

Devices using DMA use channel assignments to bypass the CPU and access the main memory directly. DMA access is not used by every device on the system but might be used by disk drives, tape drives, and even sound cards. Table 1-3 shows the DMA channels and devices that use them.

Table 1-3   Default DMA Channels

DMA Channel	Device
0	DRAM refresh
1	Sound card
2	Floppy disk drive
3	ECP parallel port
4	DMA controller
5	Open (sound card)
6	Open
7	ISA hard disk controller

Like the other resources mentioned in this section, two devices cannot share a DMA channel. Operating systems today assign DMA channels through Plug and Play; however, some legacy devices require that DMA channels be set using jumper settings. You can view DMA channel assignments in Windows using Device Manager. Figure 1-4 shows the DMA channels used.

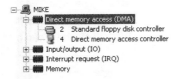

Figure 1-4 You can view the DMA channels in use through Windows Device Manager.

Peripheral Ports, Cabling, and Connectors

Although the multitude of cables running out of our computer system can make an eyesore, for now at least, we need these cables to provide the physical connections between various computer components and allow the transfer of information between devices.

As you probably already know, there are many different types of cables used in the computer world. Cables use copper or fiber optics to transmit data signals. In the context of this CompTIA objective, we are concerned more with copper-based cables than fiber-optic cable, which is almost exclusively associated with computer networking.

Working with Cables

Cables are relatively simple things to work with. In most cases it's just a matter of plugging one end into the computer and the other into the peripheral device. To make things even easier, most cable connectors are either made so that they will only fit into a connector one way, or "keyed" so that it's easy to tell which way the connector should fit. Add to that the fact that many cables look different from other cables, and what you have is a simple way of connecting devices.

Cable Types

Cables often come in two forms, shielded and unshielded. *Shielded* cables have a wire mesh or foil added between the inside wire and the outer sheath designed to protect the cable from outside interference. *Unshielded* cables are cheaper but do not offer a great amount of extra protection against outside interference.

Serial vs. Parallel Communication   Besides being ports, the terms *serial* and *parallel* also refer to a method of communication between devices. *Serial communication* is called such because the data travels across the wire in series—that is, one bit at a time. Think of it as a single checkout in a busy grocery store. This makes serial communication relatively slow, but at the same time, simple. Many devices, such as mice, make use of this simple form of communication. Serial communication is identified as the RS-232 standard. A discussion of the RS-232 standard can be found in Chapter 6.

Parallel communication is faster than serial communication because it transmits data in parallel—that is, 8 bits at a time. It's like having eight cashiers working in that crowded grocery store.

Test Smart   Be sure you know the difference between serial and parallel communication for the A+ exam.

Peripheral Ports

There are a number of different peripheral ports used by the computer system, each of which is used to connect certain types of peripherals. Each port also uses a specific design of connector and a number of pins to make the physical connection. It is likely that you are already familiar with many of these ports and use them daily. Be sure, however, that you know the names associated with each port for the A+ exam.

> **Note**   Objective 1.4 requires that you be able to identify common ports and connectors. In this section, we first look at the purpose of the peripheral ports you will find on a PC. Then, in the next section, we look at the physical connectors used for these ports.

Serial Ports

Serial ports are most commonly used for connections to mice and modems, though they are also used for a multitude of other devices as well. They come in 9-pin and 25-pin versions, and use the DB-9 and DB-25 connectors, respectively. Typically, a PC will have at least one, if not two, serial ports. Serial port 1 (COM1) is typically reserved for the serial mouse, and if you have a modem connected to your system, it will often occupy serial port 2 (COM2). Like most other devices connected to the computer system, the serial ports require both an I/O and IRQ address to function. Table 1-4 shows the resources used by serial ports.

Table 1-4   Default Resources Used by Serial Ports

Port	IRQ	I/O Address
COM1	IRQ 4	3F8h
COM2	IRQ 3	2F8h
COM3	IRQ 4	3E8h
COM4	IRQ 3	2E8h

Test Smart   Before taking the A+ exam, be sure you can identify the resources used by serial ports.

Parallel Ports

Parallel ports are used primarily for connectivity to printers, but they can also be used for connecting to other devices such as scanners and external storage devices. Parallel data transfer is faster than serial, which makes the parallel port more suitable in these instances. Most systems are equipped with only a single parallel port, but it is possible to add more ports if needed. When connecting a printer to the parallel port, we use a DB-25 connector on one end and a 36-pin Centronics connector on the other. Figure 1-5 shows the connectors on a parallel printer cable.

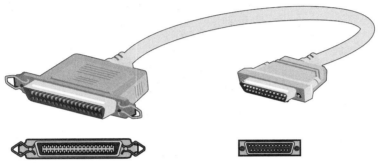

Figure 1-5 A parallel printer cable uses a DB-25 connector to connect to the system and a 36-pin Centronics connector to attach to the printer.

Like any other device, parallel ports require system resources. Table 1-5 shows the default resources used by parallel ports.

Table 1-5   Default Resources Used by Parallel Ports

Port	IRQ	I/O Address
LPT1	IRQ 7	378
LPT2	IRQ 5	278

Joystick Ports

Gaming has always been a popular function for a PC, so much so that all but the earliest PCs (and servers) come with a game or joystick port.

USB Ports

USB is increasingly being seen as the interface of choice for devices like digital cameras, external hard drives, and the like. USB offers many advantages over other interfaces, such as serial, including faster speeds, bidirectional communications, powered connections, and plug-and-play support. PCs and laptops now come with at least two, if not four, and sometimes six, USB ports. For more USB ports, you can add hubs to provide support for a maximum of 127 devices (though this theoretical maximum is not really practical). There are currently two versions of USB available. USB 1.1 has a speed of 12 Mbps, and USB 2.0 has a maximum speed of 480 Mbps. The USB 2.0 standard (also referred to as *Hi-Speed USB*) is designed to be backward compatible from the peripheral end, meaning that you can connect a USB 2.0 device to a USB 1.1 port on the computer, though it will obviously only operate at USB 1.1 speeds.

IEEE 1394

IEEE 1394, or FireWire as it is more commonly known, is a hot-swappable interface used for installing all manner of external devices, from hard disk drives to digital cameras and MP3 players. FireWire has a maximum speed of 400 Mbps and supports up to 63 devices. FireWire's consistently high data rates make it popular in applications such as camcorders, where large volumes of data need to be transferred at high speeds.

Peripheral Connectors

Having looked at the peripheral ports commonly found on a PC, we can now look at the physical connectors used by these ports. The following sections describe some of the more commonly used ones. A picture is worth a thousand words, and in the following sections, we provide a brief description of each port and a picture.

 Test Smart   You will be expected to be able to visually identify the various peripheral ports on the computer.

DB-9

DB-9 connectors are used for serial communication ports. Most PCs will come with at least one DB-9 port, though most come with two. Some PCs will have one DB-9 connector and one DB-25 connector.

DB-15

DB-15 ports are used for joystick, or game port, connectors. Most PCs will come with a single DB-15 connector, though it is possible to add more if you need to connect more devices. Figure 1-6 shows a DB-15 joystick port.

Figure 1-6 Most PCs have a single joystick port but you can add more if needed.

DB-25

Nowadays, the most common application for a DB-25 connector is a parallel port. When used as a parallel port, the DB-25 connector on the back of a PC is a female connector. In the past, DB-25 male connectors for serial ports were also common, but most PCs now use DB-9 connectors for this purpose. DB-25 connectors are also used with some external SCSI implementations. SCSI is discussed later in this chapter. Figure 1-7 shows examples of a DB-9 and a DB-25 connector.

Figure 1-7 DB-9 connectors are used with serial ports, and DB-25 connectors are used with both serial and parallel ports.

RJ Connectors

Registered Jack (RJ) connectors are small plastic connectors used for connecting multiline cables. RJ connectors have a flange that acts as a locking mechanism when it is inserted into its receptacle. There are two RJ connectors commonly associated with PCs—RJ-11 and RJ-45.

RJ-11 The RJ-11 connector is used for telephone cables. In a PC environment, The RJ-11 connector can accommodate up to six wires, but in telephone cable applications only two or four wires are used. Most commonly you will see RJ-11 connectors on phone cables when working with modems.

RJ-45 RJ-45 connectors are used with twisted-pair network cabling. They can accommodate up to eight wires. They are slightly larger in size than RJ-11 connectors, which makes it easy to distinguish between the two. Figure 1-8 shows examples of both RJ-11 and RJ-45 connectors.

Figure 1-8 RJ-11 connectors (left) are used with modems, and RJ-45 connectors (right) are used with twisted-pair network cables.

BNC

British Naval Connectors (BNC connectors) are used in networks that use thin coaxial cabling. BNC connectors have a kind of "twist-and-lock" (or push-and-turn) system that uses locating pins on the receptacle. The connector is aligned with and pushed onto the pins, and then twisted into place. At the end of the twist, the connector locks into small depressions in the twist groove. If you have ever replaced a light bulb that used a bayonet fitting rather than the more common screw fitting, you'll get the idea. You can see an example of a BNC connector in Figure 1-9.

See Also *See Chapter 6 for more information on networks using thin coaxial cabling.*

Figure 1-9 BNC connectors are used with thin coax network cabling.

PS/2 Mini-DIN Connectors

Mini-DIN connectors were first used in PCs by IBM in their PS/2 range of personal computers, which is how they came to be known as PS/2 connectors. DIN connectors get their name from Deutsche Industrie Norme, the German standards organization that created them. Mini-DIN connectors are used for connecting mice and keyboards to PCs. The term *Mini-DIN* is used because the connector is smaller than the standard DIN keyboard connector.

DIN-5 Connectors

DIN-5 is the connector type associated with the old-style AT keyboard connectors. DIN-5 connectors have five pins that are arranged in a crescent shape at the bottom of the connector. A "key" at the top of the connector is provided for correct orientation in the socket. With the advent of the newer-style Mini-DIN (PS/2) keyboard connectors, DIN-5 plugs have all but disappeared from new systems. Figure 1-10 shows examples of DIN-5 and Mini-DIN connectors.

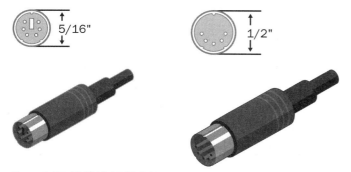

Figure 1-10 PS/2 Mini-DIN (left) and DIN-5 (right) connectors are used to connect keyboards and mice.

USB Connectors

The universal serial bus interface has two types of connectors associated with it. A small, flat-looking connector is defined as the host or hub connector. A smaller, squarer connector is defined as the peripheral connector. Although this is the defined method of dealing with USB connectors, it is not uncommon for peripheral devices to have a host-type connector. In this case, the cable has the same connector on both ends. Figure 1-11 shows an example of a typical USB cable. On the left of the picture is the host connection, and on the right is the peripheral connection.

Type A (host or hub)   Type B (peripheral)

Figure 1-11 USB cables have one end for peripheral devices and one for the host.

Host USB ports are oblong slots with a protrusion in the middle. The protrusion acts as a key, ensuring that the USB plug cannot be inserted incorrectly. Peripheral connectors are shaped so that they can only be inserted one way.

IEEE 1394 (FireWire)

IEEE 1394, or FireWire, ports come in both four- and six-pin versions. In each case, one side of the connector is shaped to ensure that it can only be plugged in correctly. Figure 1-12 shows an example of an IEEE 1394 port and connector.

Figure 1-12 IEEE 1394 ports come in both four- and six-pin versions.

Installing and Configuring ATA/IDE Devices

ATA/IDE is the interface of choice for today's systems. Most of the CD-ROMs and hard drives you install in systems are going to use the IDE interface. If you find yourself working on a server or very high-end workstation, you might run into some SCSI hard disks and peripherals, but expect to spend the majority of your time working with IDE devices. The popularity of IDE is due in part to the fact that the IDE interface provides excellent performance for a reasonable price.

Before we go any further, we should clear up the names surrounding IDE. First off, the terms AT Attachment (ATA) and Integrated Device Electronics (IDE) are one and the same; both define a type of hardware interface that is commonly used to attach devices such as hard drives and CD-ROM drives to a computer system. For the purposes of this book, we will usually refer to the ATA/IDE interface simply as IDE.

The IDE interface can be traced way back to companies such as Compaq and IBM, who, in the early stages of hard disk development, were actively trying to find a way to integrate the hard disk controller right on the hard disk itself. At the time, the reason for attaching the controller card was simply to save a bus slot so it could be used by another expansion device.

As computers advanced and it became clear that all PCs would come with hard drives, companies started to modify and improve the IDE interface. Unfortunately, in these early stages of IDE hard disk development, there were no standards in place for the advancement for the interface, and compatibility issues began to surface. It wasn't until the late eighties that standards were developed for the IDE interface and not until early 1994 that the first formal ATA standard, ATA-1, was approved. Today, we have several IDE standards and those earlier ones are now obsolete. The following is a brief look at the ATA standards and where we are today.

- **ATA-1**   The ATA-1 standard was formalized in an attempt to eliminate compatibility issues that were arising with the ATA interface. This compatibility problem was particularly evident when drives from different hardware manufacturers were linked together as a slave and a master.

- **ATA-2**   The ATA-2 standard, also known as *Fast ATA* (a name that made SCSI supporters smile), offered significant speed improvements over the ATA standard. Another notable addition was the support of logical block addressing (LBA). LBA is simply a means for the computer to recognize hard drives larger than 504 MB. For those of us with partitioned hard disks, this came as a welcome addition. The ATA-2 standard, like its predecessor, has been retired.

Note   Often, the term *EIDE* (Enhanced IDE) is used when discussing the ATA-2 standard. EIDE was developed by Western Digital Corporation and the term is used interchangeably with the term *ATA-2*.

- **ATA-3**   ATA-3 introduced the self-monitoring analysis and reporting technology (SMART), a technology that allowed the device to monitor itself while allowing the operating system to notify the user of potential device failure. ATA-3 also introduced new security features that allowed devices to be password-protected. Surprisingly, the ATA-3 standard did not enhance transfer speeds; therefore, the ATA-3 standard was not well received in the marketplace. ATA-3 had the shelf life of bananas.

- **ATA-33 (ATA/ATAPI-4)**   Things started to get more interesting with the introduction of the ATA-33 standard, which is also referred to as *ATA/ATAPI-4*. This standard, the first of the Ultra-DMA (UDMA) standards, introduced many improvements, bringing us considerably closer to where IDE technology is today. The other major feature of the ATA-33 standard was AT Attachment Packet Interface (ATAPI). ATAPI is an interface extension that accommodates devices such as CD-ROM and tape drives. Finally, the ATA-33 interface introduced a new 80-conductor, 40-pin cable. It was intended to reduce or eliminate interference, but as it turned out, it was not necessary for use with ATA-33.

- **ATA-66 (ATA/ATAPI-5)**   The ATA-66 (ATA/ATAPI-5) standard was published as recently as 2000, and as ATA-33 doubled the speed of ATA-3, ATA-66 doubled that of ATA-33. The ATA-66 standard did require the use of a new 80-conductor, 40-pin cable to connect the hard disk to the system.

- **ATA-100 (ATA/ATAPI-6)**   All of this brings us to where we are today. The latest and greatest standard in the works is the ATA-100, which will be using the latest DMA transfer modes, allowing data transfers at 100 MBps. Once again, the 80-conductor, 40-pin cable is required.

Enhanced IDE

The original IDE standard, ATA-1, had one major drawback, a restrictive size limit. The upper drive capacity for IDE was 540 MB and hard drive capacity soon outgrew this limitation. To get around this restriction, we were forced to partition hard drives into smaller sizes that could be recognized by the system. As a solution, the EIDE technology was developed. EIDE, introduced with the ATA-2 standard, added support for hard drives with capacities up to 8.4 GB. It wasn't very long ago that we marveled at the size of the 8.4-GB hard disks, but anyone who has looked at the specs of a modern computer knows that we have far surpassed the 8.4-GB capacity. To accommodate larger disks, developments known as the INT13 Extensions were added to the ATA-2 standard, allowing for support for much larger hard drives.

IDE Transfer Modes While sitting in math class, did you ever wonder how algebra would apply in the real world? We had the same feeling when learning about IDE transfer modes. Essentially, the ATA/IDE interface uses two communication methods or, as they are known, *transfer modes*. The two modes are the Programmed Input/Output (PIO) and the more recent direct memory access (DMA) mode.

PIO was the original standard and uses the computer's CPU to manage the transfer of data; therefore, the CPU is responsible for executing the instructions that transfer the data to and from a hard drive. Unfortunately, the use of the CPU to manage data transfer to and from the hard drive creates considerable overhead and demands the CPU's attention at all times when accessing the hard drive. There are several PIO modes: three of these were defined by the original ATA standard; the last two were added when the newer ATA-2 standard was approved. PIO modes ranged from 0 to 4, with PIO mode 4 offering data transfers speeds of 16.6 MBps.

In terms of performance, using the CPU to manage the transfer of data to and from the hard disk is unacceptable. A better data transfer method was needed, and in the late 1990s, the DMA transfer method was developed. DMA data transfer does not require CPU resources to transfer data to a hard disk; rather, devices uses the system's memory to transfer data back and forth, allowing the CPU to focus on other tasks.

Like PIO, several distinct DMA modes have been developed for the IDE interface. Today, our newer hard drives use UDMA transfer modes, which make the original PIO transfer speeds look like they are standing still. How does knowing about hard drive transfer modes help in the real world? We'll tell you as soon as we figure out why 2 + x = y.

Connectors, Jumpers, Masters, and Slaves

One of the primary limitations of the IDE interface is the number of devices that can be attached. Modern motherboards include two IDE connectors, known as the *primary* and *secondary controllers*; each of these allows two devices to be attached. That makes a total of four IDE devices that can be attached to a system. Furthermore, IDE devices can only be attached internally; IDE does not support the connection of external devices such as printers, scanners, or external hard disks.

Test Smart   IDE devices allow only four devices to be connected to the system, two on the primary IDE controller and two on the secondary controller.

Four interconnected IDE devices might sound like enough but oftentimes it isn't. Consider that the primary hard disk and the CD-ROM take two of the four, so if you want to add a second hard disk, DVD-ROM drive, and maybe a CD burner, you can run out quickly. Figure 1-13 shows the primary and secondary IDE controllers.

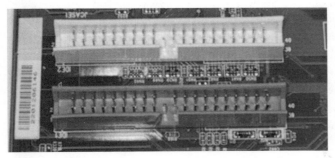

Figure 1-13 Modern motherboards come with two IDE controllers on the board.

To differentiate between devices using the same IDE channel, each device needs to be designated as either a master or a slave. The terms *master* and *slave* can be a bit misleading because the master device does not really have any special capabilities regarding the slave device, and for the most part, they are equals. The only real functional difference between the two drives is that the computer will look first to the master drive and then to the slave drive. In other words, the master gets the PC's attention first. The master drive on the primary IDE channel is given the "C:" designation, and the slave gets the "D:" designation, making the master the one that the system is booted from.

To designate a device (hard disk or CD-ROM drive) on an IDE channel as a master or slave, you use jumpers located on the device. The jumper settings and locations might be slightly different from manufacturer to manufacturer; however, they are all very similar. If the jumper settings are not clearly marked on the device, the specifications of each device are readily available on manufacturer's Web site. Of course, in the absence of solid information, more than one technician has used the trial-and-error method when trying to find the master and slave jumper settings. If the jumpers are set incorrectly (for instance, two masters or two slaves on the same IDE channel) the system might be prevented from booting and the hard drive specifications will not be recognized in the system's BIOS. Figure 1-14 shows the jumper pins and a jumper used to make master/slave settings on an IDE hard disk.

Figure 1-14 The master/slave jumper pins are shown between the IDE connector slot and the power socket.

Hard Drive Addressing and Translation One additional consideration when installing hard drives is that of hard drive addressing and translation. Address translation is a way of getting around the limitations imposed by old BIOSs that can't recognize any more than 540 MB of space on a hard drive. Using address translation, rather than letting the BIOS identify each sector location by its head, cylinder, and sector address, the sector location is accessed using a linear value that is then translated by the hard drive. There are three valid modes when using translation: normal, which means there is no translation, logical block addressing (LBA), and large. Of these, LBA is fastest but it's not supported by certain drives.

In order for translation to work, both the BIOS and the hard drive must support it. Another important consideration is that you must not change the translation status after the drive has data on it. Doing so can cause the data on the drive to become corrupt.

Cable Select

Instead of using jumpers to distinguish between the master and slave device on an IDE channel, the IDE cable itself can do it using the cable select option. Besides the jumper setting for the master and slave on an IDE device, there is one typically listed as c/sel or cs that configures the devices to use the cable select option. When the jumpers are set to cable select, the cable connectors determine master and slave status. The master device will be the one at the end of the IDE cable, and the slave will be the one using the middle IDE cable connector.

> **Note**   When it comes to attaching IDE devices, a data connector for the cable has to be connected to the device, and a power connector coming from the power supply needs to be attached. However, the most common error made when installing IDE devices is to bend the pins when installing the device. It is frustrating to be installing your new hard drive only to bend the pins and wonder if the warranty still covers it.

Installing and Configuring SCSI Devices

The Small Computer System Interface (SCSI) has been with us in one form or another since the late 1970s. Because of its speed and reliability, SCSI is the interface of choice for server systems and high-end workstations. However, due to its relative cost and complexity, it is not commonly used with desktop computer systems.

One of the more obvious advantages SCSI has over IDE is the number of devices that can be connected. While IDE can connect only two devices per channel and only connect those devices internally, SCSI can hold up to 16 on a single cable, using both external and internal devices. Interconnected SCSI devices are referred to as a *SCSI chain* or *bus.*

Unlike IDE hard disks, which have the hard drive controller built onto them, SCSI hard disks require an external controller known as the SCSI host bus adapter (HBA). The host adapter might be an expansion card, but newer systems sometimes have it integrated into the motherboard. The host adapter typically has two connectors (though more are possible), one to attach external SCSI devices and one to connect internal SCSI devices. The SCSI host adapter will require the use of system resources, including an IRQ and I/O address, but each individual device on the SCSI chain will not. Remember that the HBA is considered to be one of the devices in the SCSI chain. For example, if you are using a SCSI chain that supports 16 devices (called *Wide SCSI*), you would actually be able to connect only 15 devices.

SCSI Termination

When installing or working with SCSI devices, one of the things to be mindful of is the termination of the SCSI bus. The SCSI bus is essentially an electrical transmission line with data flowing back and forth through the line. When signals reach the end of the SCSI bus, they must be stopped and not allowed to continue traveling up and down the SCSI bus. The bouncing of signals once they reach the physical ends of the SCSI bus is known as *signal reflection* and causes chaos for newly sent signals. A special terminator is therefore required to absorb the signal as it reaches the end of the SCSI bus.

For signal termination to work, there must be a termination device at both ends of the SCSI bus, and a SCSI bus can have only two terminators on a single bus. The issue of termination with SCSI is very important to understand; when things are not working properly with a SCSI device, termination issues are often the reason. Figure 1-15 shows the proper termination for a SCSI bus.

> **Note**   Many SCSI devices have terminators built into them and are set to "On" by default. These must be disabled if the device is configured to be in the middle of the SCSI bus.

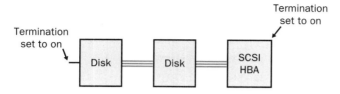

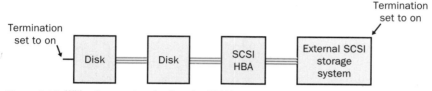

Figure 1-15 Without proper termination, the SCSI bus will not function correctly.

SCSI IDs

In the world of IDE, devices are distinguished by using the master and slave settings; in a SCSI environment, we use SCSI IDs. Each and every device connected to a SCSI chain must have a unique ID. These IDs are typically set using jumpers or switches on the SCSI device. The ID numbers range either from 0 to 7 for some SCSI implementations or from 0 to 15 for others. The priority for SCSI devices is represented by the highest number; 7 has the highest priority for Narrow SCSI, followed by 6, and then 5...well, we think you get it.

 Test Smart   When working with SCSI, the higher the ID number, the higher the priority.

SCSI Cabling and Connectors

In terms of complexity, there is no comparison between IDE devices and SCSI devices—SCSI can be a nightmare. Nowhere is this more evident than in a discussion about SCSI cabling and connectors.

SCSI cables can be either internal or external, unlike IDE cabling, which is restricted to internal cabling. If you haven't already guessed, internal SCSI cables allow devices to be attached within the computer, and external SCSI cabling connects devices outside the computer. These two types of cabling are vastly different in their construction. Because external cabling is outside of the protective computer case, it is at greater risk to interference from electrical devices and the like, and therefore, the cabling has to be made to handle the unique challenges that an external environment presents.

All of the precautions used by external SCSI cables make the manufacturing process complex, so they do not come cheap. Internal SCSI cables do not require the protection that external cabling demands, so they are simpler to construct and more affordable. Internal SCSI uses two different types of cable, a flat cable similar to the one used with IDE devices and a specially designed twist-and-flat cable. The twist in the cable is to increase the resistance to electrical interference. Figure 1-16 shows a standard and twist-and-flat internal SCSI cable.

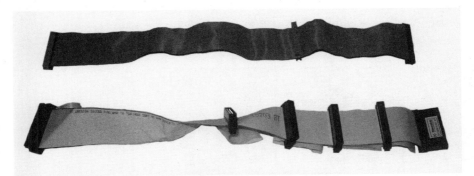

Figure 1-16 SCSI cables come in both standard and twist-and-flat internal cables

SCSI Connectors

Whether they're using an internal or external cable, devices have to be physically attached to the cable. That is where connectors come into play. As with everything else involved with SCSI, there is more than one option, depending on what your needs are. There are several connector alternatives for external and internal connectors.

External SCSI Connectors

The types of external connectors used by SCSI have changed quite a bit over the years. If you were a technician working with SCSI a few years ago, you would most likely have seen the 50-pin D-shell connector and the 50-pin Centronics connector. These connectors were used in the original SCSI standards but are not used today. Figure 1-17 shows the female Centronics and 50-pin SCSI external connectors.

50-pin external SCSI
Centronics connector

50-pin Centronics
female connector

Figure 1-17 Two of the connectors associated with external SCSI are the female Centronics and the 50-pin external SCSI.

Warning   Apple computers and some other peripheral devices use a 25-pin D-shaped SCSI connector that is similar in appearance to a standard PC parallel port. Using the 25-pin SCSI connector in a standard parallel port, however, can damage the port.

More modern SCSI implementations use a new high-density D-shell connector. A narrow 50-pin and a wide 68-pin version of the high-density cable are available and in common use today. In addition to the high-density cables, we have the Very High Density Cable Interconnect (VHDCI) connectors. VHDCI connectors come as a wide 68-pin option only and are sometimes referred to as *micro-Centronics connectors*. Figure 1-18 shows a VHDCI connector.

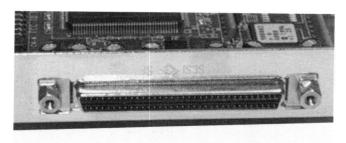

Figure 1-18 Another type of commonly used connector is the VHDCI external SCSI connector.

Internal SCSI Connectors

Internal SCSI connectors are different altogether and are considerably cheaper than their external counterparts. The two most common internal connectors are the regular-density and the high-density connectors.

- **Regular-density connectors**   Regular-density connectors were widely used on older SCSI devices. The regular-density connector resembles the connectors for internal IDE devices except that the SCSI version has 10 extra pins. These 50-pin internal connectors are most often seen with legacy SCSI devices. Technicians working with SCSI today are more likely to encounter high-density connectors.

- **High-density SCSI connectors**   High-density connectors were introduced with the SCSI-2 standard. With high-density connectors, pin spacing was reduced, making the connectors themselves much smaller and easier to work with. High-density connectors can come in a narrow 50-pin unshielded version as well as a 68-pin wide version. Figure 1-19 shows the different internal SCSI connectors.

Standard 50-pin female

High density 68-pin male

Figure 1-19 Internal SCSI connectors come in 50-pin and 68-pin varieties.

SCSI Types and Standards

Over the years, there have been many SCSI standards developed. The problem is, they are confusing and it takes a bit of concentration to get them straight. The general SCSI categories are known as SCSI-1, SCSI-2, and SCSI-3, with SCSI-2 and SCSI-3 having a number of different implementations within them. The A+ exams will certainly not require you to have a detailed knowledge of SCSI standards, but an awareness of them and how many devices they support will be required. Table 1-6 shows the various SCSI standards and the characteristics of each.

Table 1-6 SCSI Standards

Standard	Maximum Transfer Rate	Maximum Number of Devices
SCSI-1	5 MBps	8
Fast SCSI-2	10 MBps	8
Fast/Wide SCSI-2	20 MBps	16
Ultra SCSI	20 MBps	8
Ultra Wide SCSI	40 MBps	16
Ultra2 SCSI	40 MBps	8
Wide Ultra2 SCSI	80 MBps	16
Ultra3 SCSI (Ultra160)	160 MBps	16
Ultra 320	320 MBps	16

[handwritten margin notes:] HVD is earlier implementation of differential voltage.

← LVD Low Voltage Differential 25m cable 12m ultra 16 devices

Note   When looking at the number of devices that a SCSI standard supports, some sources include the host adapter (SCSI interface card) as a device. Therefore, some sources might report the number of SCSI devices supported as 7, while other sources cite it as 8.

Tip   For easy reference, remember that Narrow (non-Wide) SCSI implementations use an 8-bit bus, irrespective of the SCSI version.

Jumper Block Settings

When configuring SCSI controllers and devices, you will commonly need to configure jumpers. The jumpers will often use binary numbering to configure the SCSI ID. If there are three jumpers, the maximum value is 7 (4 + 2 + 1). So, in this scenario, the leftmost jumper pins (when jumpered closed) will be worth 4, the middle will be worth 2, and the rightmost will be worth 1. To get a value of, say, 5, you would configure the jumper block as on, off, on. For 6, you would jumper on, on, off.

On Wide SCSI implementations, there might be four jumpers. With four jumpers the maximum value will be 15 (8 + 4 + 2 + 1). Again, by configuring the jumpers from left to right you can define any value between 1 and 15.

It's a RAID!

Many of us operate our computer systems with a single hard drive, but in many cases, extra, or redundant, hard disks are used for fault tolerance. When used in such a configuration, we are incorporating something called a *redundant array of independent disks* (RAID). The function of RAID is quite simple, to provide a method to safely store and access data in case of hard disk failure. There are several different RAID designs that can be used, known as *RAID levels*. They range from RAID 0 to RAID 5 with a few other odd ones such as RAID 0+1 or RAID 10 thrown in to confuse things. As far as the A+ exam goes, there are only three levels you need to know about, RAID 0, 1, and 5.

In a RAID 0 configuration, data is written across multiple hard disks. For instance, when you save information, some of it is stored on the first hard disk, some on the second, and so on. This process is known as *disk striping*. When data is written to multiple hard disks simultaneously, it allows for faster data throughput, significantly increasing overall performance. RAID 0, sometimes referred to as *disk striping without parity*, is not a fault-tolerant RAID solution. If one hard disk fails, the data stored on all disks is lost and must be reinstalled from backups. Because RAID 0 is not fault tolerant, it is rarely used in real-world applications. RAID 0 requires a minumum of two hard disks.

RAID 1 is an easy and cheap fault-tolerant solution. RAID 1, also known as *mirroring*, writes data twice to separate hard disks, making an exact mirrored copy of the data. In this case, if one of the hard disks were to fail, there would be an exact copy that can be accessed. RAID 1 requires two hard disks.

The final RAID solution mentioned in the CompTIA objectives is RAID 5. RAID 5 is similar to RAID 0 in that it stripes data across several hard disks. Unlike RAID 0, however, RAID 5 requires a minimum of three hard disks with one hard disk being used for parity information. If one of the hard disks were to fail in a RAID 5 configuration, this parity information is used to re-create the data from the damaged hard disk, allowing the data to be recovered.

Test Smart A detailed knowledge of RAID is not required for the A+ exam; however, a basic understanding of the three RAID levels and how many hard disks are required for each is necessary.

Installing and Configuring Peripheral Devices

In today's computing world, we have a multitude of peripheral devices that we need to know how to configure and install on a computer system. Many of the procedures and strategies used to connect and manage these devices are common throughout. This gives us some very general installation guidelines to follow.

Installation Made Easy

It used to be that if you wanted anything done to a computer system, users would pack up their system and head down to the computer store and pay someone to do so. Not so much anymore. Tasks once the domain of the computer "techies" have been made increasingly simple, allowing many home users to perform their own system upgrades and add peripheral devices themselves. Once, when we opened a discussion of configuring peripheral devices, we talked about compatibility, manual resource assignments and the like. Today, however, unless there is a problem, installing all manner of peripheral devices is managed through the Plug and Play magic. Today when we install peripheral devices such as Uninterruptable Power Supplies (UPS), digital cameras, printers, scanners, modems, and virtually any other device, the installation procedures follow some generic and common steps. Most devices would be installed in the following manner:

Read the manual: The documentation that came with the device is the best for discovering those installation guidelines. Depending on the OS used on the system, the installation procedures are likely to vary, the manual will let you know. If the manual is lost, the manufacturer's Web site will likely provide the same information.

Obtain the latest drivers: One of the biggest battles we face in modern installations is having the correct drivers on hand. Windows may have built in drivers for the device which typically work well but if not, you may have to obtain the drivers from the manufacturer's Web site.

Physically connect the peripheral device: With our modern OSs, once the device has been physically connected, it will likely be detected by Plug and Play. If it has, Windows will attempt to install drivers for the device. If it cannot find those drivers, you will be prompted to supply those drivers.

If a device does not work after being connected and doesn't install after these steps, you will switch to troubleshooting mode, discussed in Chapter 2.

Now that we have outlined the general procedures for adding peripheral devices to the PC, we can look at some of the specifics for certain devices.

Monitor/Video Card

Some components are a little more difficult to upgrade than others, and while there is nothing particularly tricky about monitors and video cards, there are a few additional considerations we need to be aware of.

Monitors

Monitors are the means by which we visually interact with the PC. How they display images is an important element in how comfortable we are when using the system and so, to a technician, understanding what defines how an image appears on the screen is important.

Note   Energy Star is an accreditation given by the EPA to devices and appliances that are designed to save energy and so reduce impact on the environment. As monitors use more power than any other PC component, the EPA has been approving conforming monitors for many years. Energy Star-compliant monitors have advanced power-saving features like being able to switch to standby automatically if there is no data signal. Nowadays, it is hard to buy a monitor that is not Energy Star compliant, but you should still make sure that any new monitors you buy carry the Energy Star accreditation.

Refresh Rate   The refresh rate defines how fast the picture on the monitor is redrawn. Most monitors today are capable of refresh rates of 65 Hz and higher, though many people consider 80 Hz as the ideal starting point for configuring the refresh rate. Even if you are able to set the refresh rate of your monitor considerably higher (100 Hz), you should be wary of doing so unless you are completely sure that the monitor can handle it.

Although the general rule of thumb is the higher the refresh rate the better, the best refresh rate for a given situation will depend on the monitor, the video card, and the user. Some users might see a flicker of the screen when the refresh rate is set to a certain number, while other people (including you) might not. Moving the refresh rate up by one setting can eliminate the flicker.

Note   Monitors have a specific range of refresh rates that a given monitor can accommodate, but most also specify a recommended resolution and refresh rate. These are the settings at which the manufacturer believes the monitor will work best, and they should know.

Resolution   Perhaps more than any other characteristic, the resolution defines how the picture appears on the screen. The resolution is defined by the number of pixels from left to right (the horizontal resolution) and from top to bottom (the vertical resolution). The best resolution has as much to do with the preferences of the user as it does with what the monitor and video card are capable of. Some users like low resolution and big chunky icons. Others seem to prefer squinting to see microscopic icons on a monitor that is configured to a resolution somewhere between here and the afterlife. Monitors are capable of a certain resolution, and the actual resolution used by the monitor is dictated by the video card.

Dot Pitch   The dot pitch of a monitor is defined by how far apart the pixels are on the screen. The actual measurement refers to how many 1/100ths of a millimeter dots of the same color are away from each other. The lower the dot pitch value, the better the picture will be. Today's modern monitors have dot pitches around the low .20s, for example .21 to .25. As with most other things, it is possible to get both higher and lower dot pitches. Unlike resolution and refresh rate, the dot pitch is fixed, and not determined by the video card—it is defined by the hardware of the monitor.

Video Cards

There was a time when video cards were simple affairs, their function being to make sure a picture, any picture, appeared on the monitor. Nowadays, things are more complicated as graphical operating systems, applications, and games make the need to have high-quality video on the PC a necessity, not a luxury.

Video Card Resolution   The maximum resolution offered by a video card depends on the color depth (the number of colors being used) and is limited by the amount of memory on the video card. For example, an SVGA resolution of 800×600 using 16 million colors will require 2 MB of video RAM. On modern video cards this consideration is irrelevant because most come with at least 16 MB of RAM, but if you are configuring an older system you will need to know how much RAM is required for a given resolution and color depth combination. You can see a list of the requirements in Table 1-7.

Table 1-7   *Memory Requirements for a Given Resolution and Color Depth*

Video Standard	Color Depth/Resolution	16 (4-bit)	256 (8-bit)	65,000 (16-bit)	16 Million (24-bit)
VGA	640×480	.5	.5	1	2
SVGA	800×600	.5	1	2	2
XGA	1024×768	1	1	2	4
SXGA	1280×1024	1	2	4	4
UXGA	1600×1200	2	2	4	8

Installation Considerations   Video cards are one of those expansion cards that PC technicians will become very familiar with replacing and upgrading. Like any other expansion card, there are a few considerations to keep in mind during the upgrade process.

- **Slot compatibility**   In addition to the standard slot types (PCI, ISA) that are used by video cards, there are also video-specific bus slots such as VL-Bus and AGP. Make sure the video card you intend to install in the system is compatible.

- **Video shadowing**   Video cards have read-only memory (ROM) on them that contains routines for frequently performed functions. *Video shadowing* is the term given to copying the contents of this ROM into RAM, which can yield a small improvement in performance. Be aware, though, that enabling video shadowing can cause stability problems with some systems, so if you enable shadowing and then begin to experience odd and seemingly random system problems, you might want to try turning it off.

- **Drivers**   Whenever you install a new video card, it is very important that you use the correct and most recent drivers for the card. If the wrong drivers are used, you might get a poor display or no display at all. Refer to the manufacturer's Web site for the most recent drivers.

Aside from these considerations, you should find that video cards are relatively straightforward peripherals to install, and hopefully they won't cause you very many problems.

Modem

Unlike most other peripheral devices, modems can be either internal or external. Of the two, external modems are typically easier to install and configure. When connecting an external modem to your computer, the modem plugs into a COM or serial port on the back of your computer. If your modem is plug and play capable, it will be automatically detected and installed. If not, you will need to manually install the modem and device driver into the operating system. The external modem will not need its own resources; rather, it uses the IRQ and I/O address of the port it is plugged into.

To install an internal modem, the case will have to be taken off and the modem installed into one of the system's free expansion slots. The funny thing about internal modems is that even though they are internal, they still require the use of one of the system's COM ports. Though not physically cabled to that port, they will use the resources of that port. Modems can be assigned COM ports provided no other device is using those resources. When it comes to assigning a COM port to your modem, remember that COM1 and COM3 share an IRQ and COM2 and COM4 share an IRQ. This means if another device is using COM3, you cannot use COM1, and the same for COM2 and COM4. Legacy modems used jumpers to determine the IRQ and I/O address that it would use; today, Plug and Play manages modems for us.

Whether the modem is internal or external, there are two RJ-11 sockets built into it. One of the sockets is to used to connect the modem to the telephone jack on the wall. This socket is often labeled as the *Line* socket. This is used to dial a remote location such as an ISP. The other RJ-11 socket, usually labeled *Phone* on the modem, is used to connect a phone so it can be used when the modem is off.

Test Smart   The Line socket on the modem connects the modem to the wall jack, and the Phone socket is used to connect a phone to the modem.

Installing Floppy Drives

The procedures for installing floppy drives are similar to those for installing other devices such as CD-ROMs, hard disks, or tape drives. What we have is a cable that connects the device to the motherboard and a power connector to provide the power to the device. The floppy drive connects the floppy controller using a 34-wire flat ribbon cable and a 34-pin connector. The floppy drive cable is typically gray with one edge marked red or sometimes blue. The color markings identify that end as pin 1 of the cable; pin 1 of the cable has to be aligned with pin 1 of the floppy drive.

When attaching the floppy drive to the motherboard floppy controller, you must also take care to connect it in the correct way. Pin 1 of the cable must attach to pin 1 on the floppy controller. On most motherboards pin 1 is clearly identified, but on some others it can be a bit of a mystery. You don't have to worry much because a cable installed in reverse will not hurt the system—but the floppy drive will not work. You can tell if the cable is in reverse because the floppy drive LED will stay lit. If this is the case, switch the cable around the other way.

Note   On our modern systems, the floppy controller is built directly onto the motherboard in the same way the IDE controllers are. On earlier computers, the floppy drive controller was often attached to an expansion card. In either case, the same installation procedures apply.

Computers can have two floppy drives installed with both attaching to a single cable. The floppy drive that is connected to the end of the 34-pin cable will be given the A: designation; the floppy drive that is attached to the middle cable connector will be designated as the B: drive. The differentiation is made using a twist in the cable between the two connectors. Figure 1-20 shows the floppy cable and the connector on a floppy disk drive.

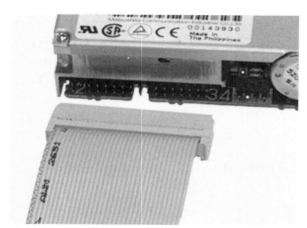

Figure 1-20 When connecting the floppy drive, pin 1 of the cable must be attached to pin 1 of the floppy controller.

USB Peripherals and Hubs

USB has emerged as the number one method of connecting peripheral devices to the computer. The reasons for this are simple: it is very fast, and because of plug and play, easy to install. Add to that the fact that USB devices are hot swappable (that is, they can be plugged in and out of the system without powering off), and one would wonder why we use the old parallel and serial ports.

All manner of devices can be attached to the system using the USB interface. The USB system will provide power to some devices, such as mice and keyboards, but other devices, such as printers, scanners, and external hard disks, will require their own power. Most computers come with one or two USB ports, allowing two USB devices to be attached to the system. Today, however, we often need more than two USB ports; that is where USB hubs comes into play.

As mentioned earlier, USB can support up to 127 devices, but how can this be done with only the few USB ports that come with the computer? USB hubs are external devices that can attach to one of the system's available USB ports. Once attached, you will have access to all of the available ports on the hub. USB hubs typically have four to eight additional ports, and other hubs can be added to each of these to add more devices. Figure 1-21 shows an example of a USB hub.

Figure 1-21 USB hubs are used to increase the system's available USB ports.

One last thing to note about hubs is the power requirement. A USB hub can use power supplied by the USB system or it can have an external power supply. Because of the power demands it puts on the USB system, it is often better to use a USB hub that provides its own power.

Test Smart   When connecting USB peripherals, the maximum cable length between two devices is 5 meters.

IEEE 1284

The IEEE 1284 standard defines parallel communication. Standard printer connections are IEEE 1284, and so when buying cables for printers you might well see IEEE 1284 mentioned.

See Also   *More information on managing and configuring printers can be found in Chapter 5.*

Installing and Configuring Peripheral Devices on Portable Systems

Portable computer systems often bring with them their own set of challenges. We can still add on many of the devices such as modems and floppy drives, except we never open the case to do so. In this section, we look at some methods we use to install devices on a portable computer system.

Docking Stations and Port Replicators

We all need somewhere we can hang our hats, and portable computers are no exception. While portable systems give us mobility, many of us use them as much in the office as we do remotely. In such a circumstance, we can use docking stations and port replicators to give our portable computers a more desktop feel.

Docking stations allow us to easily attach all manner of peripheral devices to portable systems, including monitors, external hard disks, scanners, printers, digital cameras, and just about any other device you can imagine. All we need to do is attach peripheral devices to the docking station unit and leave them connected. When the portable system is attached to the docking station, all those connected devices will be accessible to the portable system just as if you were working with an ordinary desktop system.

> **Note**   Docking stations are designed for use with specific portables only. If you want to use a docking station, you will need to use one designed by the manufacturer to be used with yours.

Port replicators provide similar functionality to that of docking stations but are not as versatile. Port replicators will often provide a base to quickly attach some core peripheral devices such as keyboards, mice, monitors, and printers. Port replicators also provide a simple means to connect such devices simply by attaching the portable system to the port replicator.

PC Cards

In the desktop world, if we want to attach a new network card to the system, we need to remove the case and install the new card. Portable systems do not require us to take anything apart. Adding devices such as modems, network cards, and sometimes even memory is done using PC Cards.

In the early 1990s, the Personal Computer Memory Card International Association (PCMCIA) set out to establish standards by which peripheral devices could be connected to portable computers. The result is the PCMCIA, or as it is more commonly known, the PC Card. PC Cards are about the size of a credit card and provide us with hot swappable devices that can more easily be added to a system than their desktop counterparts.

PC Cards come in three types, appropriately named Type I, Type II, and Type III. The difference between these cards is in their designed function and their thickness. Type I cards are 3.3 mm thick and were originally designed for flash memory. Type II cards, the most common, are 5.0 mm thick and used for devices such as modems, network cards, and other I/O devices. Type III PC Cards are 10.5 mm thick and are used for hard drives.

   Test Smart   Be ready to answer questions on the three types of PC Cards and what they are designed for.

Infrared Devices

Infrared communication provides us with the ability to attach devices such as keyboards and mice to our systems without the need for physical cabling. To accomplish this, infrared devices communicate with the computer using light waves instead of cables. Infrared communications are not lightning fast, providing up to 4-Mbps transfer speeds. They are limited in distance as well; the sending and receiving devices in the infrared communication can be no more than 1 to 3 meters apart.

Infrared communications are known as a point-to-point, line-of-sight technology. This means that the sending infrared device must be facing the receiving infrared device for the communication to happen. If anything blocks the line of sight between the devices, the communication might fail. Modern computers and some printers come with built-in infrared ports; other systems require an external or internal infrared adapter to be installed. Internal adapters install like any other expansion card, and external adapters are connected using the system's serial or USB port.

When connected to the system, infrared devices require system resources like any other component, and Windows versions 9*x* through 2000 offer Plug and Play support for infrared devices, making the assignment of these resources automatic.

See Also   *More information on wireless communication can be found in Chapter 6.*

Note   You might see infrared communication on the A+ exam referred to as *IrDA*.

Increasing Performance   In the computing world, the name of the game is speed, and as such, we are always looking for ways to optimize our systems and increase performance. Of course, when we talk about increasing performance, the most obvious assumption is to upgrade the memory and the CPU, and while these are common upgrades, there are several other components to consider. For instance, if you are on a network, you may want to increase your network card from a 10 Mbps card to a 100 Mbps card. If the network infrastructure supports such an upgrade, the performance is greatly increased. To increase data access times, try to replace your old ATA-33 hard disk with a new ATA-100 hard disk. Further, to increase the performance of those graphic-intensive applications such as games, invest in a specialized video card that may use a faster expansion slot and has plenty of its own onboard memory. The point is, if your system is suffering poor performance in a specific area, try and isolate the component that will target that area. And then just for kicks, upgrade the processor and memory anyway because that's cool to do. Before upgrading any component, however, make sure you follow some basic principles and outlines later in this chapter.

Upgrading: The Neverending Story

One thing that you can be sure of when you are working with computers is that contentment with one's computer is a fleeting thing. One minute it is fast enough, but in the blink of an eye our satisfaction fades and we want a bigger hard disk, more memory, and a faster CPU. As far as computers are concerned, the grass is definitely greener on the other PC. Upgrading has become a fact of life in the computer world, and as a technician you can expect to become very familiar with the process of upgrading all manner of PC components. As such, you can expect a few upgrading questions to appear on the A+ exam.

Upgrading the Processor

It seems like faster processors are introduced on a weekly, if not daily, basis. For most of us who are satisfied with our current processor, the release of a new one goes largely unnoticed. Still, the time will come when either the processor you are using quits or it simply can't provide enough processing power, and you will need to upgrade.

Tip   Before installing a new processor, take the time to review the documentation that came with it. The documentation provides the exact installation instructions and other important installation and handling considerations.

The ability to support a higher level of processor will depend on the physical configuration on the motherboard, the capabilities of the board chip set, and the system BIOS. In some cases, the BIOS might need an update to accommodate the new processor. Often, a new processor was not designed to be used with some boards, and you might find yourself replacing the processor and motherboard at the same time.

See Also   *Refer to Chapter 4 for a discussion on the physical form factors of processors and the motherboards they are designed to work with.*

Steps in a Processor Upgrade

Successful processor upgrades do not happen by accident; rather, they follow some pretty clear guidelines. Removing and upgrading a processor without a good idea of what you are doing can cause undesired results. Following are the steps for upgrading a processor.

See Also   *When handling any hardware, it is important to understand the damage that static electricity can do to your components. The potential damage from static electricity is easily preventable. Refer to Chapter 3 for information on dealing with static electricity.*

■   **System inspection**   Before upgrading the processor, closely examine the inside of the case. It is good to get a look at what you are in for. Does your existing processor fan and heat sink provide adequate cooling for the new processor? Does your motherboard physically support the new processor? Pay close attention to the processor form factors and the socket or slots used on the motherboard because this will determine what kind of processor can be installed in the system. Keep in mind that, even if the physical connection is correct, not all processors will work in all motherboards. Furthermore, refer to the motherboard documentation to determine the processor speeds that the board can support.

■   **Removing the old processor**   The difficulty involved in removing a processor is determined somewhat by the motherboard used and by the type of socket or slot the processor is situated in. If it uses a zero-insertion force (ZIF) socket, the first thing to do is disconnect the heat sink and fan from the processor. Many heat sinks clamp right to the base of the socket, and care should be taken when unlatching the clamps. Once the heat sink is out of the way, ZIF sockets use a release lever to free the processor from the socket. Lift this locking lever, and when the lever is in its full upright position, the processor should slip right out.

Tip   Once the CPU is removed, it is often treated with complete disregard. However, it's a very good idea to gently put it in an antistatic bag. If things go wrong with the new processor, you might need to put the old one back in to keep the computer up and running.

Slot processors are not any more difficult to remove than socket processors, although there are a few other considerations. Slot processors are not clamped down with a locking arm; rather, slots generally use release mechanisms at either end of the processor. Pentium III slot processors, for instance, use retention mechanisms to hold the processor in place and provide very firm seating for the processor. Removing the CPU from the slot requires a little sleight of hand. First, pull one retention mechanism, freeing one side of the processor with one hand, and then swing the other side out with the other hand. The point is, if it is your first time removing a processor from a slot form factor, take the time to figure out how it is best removed.

■ **Installing the new processor**   When you're installing the new processor, there is one simple rule: always follow the documentation provided with the processor. There can be issues even for something as seemingly straightforward as a CPU installation. For instance, if you have just purchased a new Pentium III for your system and you confirm that the motherboard uses Slot 1 with retention mechanisms, that might not be enough. Some of the original Single Edge Contact Cartridge packages used retention mechanisms not recommended with the Pentium III cartridge. In fact, if you were to make the simple mistake of using the wrong retention mechanisms with your new Pentium processor, you might be voiding your warranty.

■ **Setting up the motherboard**   Most modern high-end motherboards will automatically detect the speed of the new processor. There are, however, motherboards that still require jumper settings. When the setting of these jumpers is required, refer to the motherboard manual to find the location of the jumpers on the motherboard, and adjust the jumpers accordingly.

■ **Final check**   Before powering up the system, be sure to check that the processor is securely seated and that the fan and heat sink are properly attached to the processor.

Overclocking   Hang around the IT lunch room long enough, and you are certain to hear someone relating a tale of overclocking and how you can squeeze more performance out of the CPU with a simple jumper setting. These are the folks who are best not to be doing a CPU upgrade. Overclocking the CPU simply refers to setting the CPU to run faster than it was intended to. This has become a fairly common practice for some desktop users, but it is not recommended. Overclocking a CPU decreases the lifespan of the CPU through overwork or overheating, and it is hard to get a warranty on a CPU intentionally set to ignore the manufacturer's recommendations. Quite simply, overclocking and computers just don't mix.

What If It Doesn't Work?

The first thing to remember when trying to isolate a problem with your newly installed processor is not to panic. Of course, these are the same instructions given to you when there is a fire in the building; in reality, we would panic in both situations.

One of the most common errors that occurs after a processor upgrade is that the computer simply won't start. After that feeling in the pit of your stomach goes away, ensure that the processor is properly seated in the slot; if it is, ensure that no pins were bent on the processor during the upgrade. The next place to look is at the jumper settings for that processor; ensure that the multiplier and the clock speed were set correctly. Also look into whether a BIOS upgrade is needed to support the processor. If all seems in order, you might have a faulty processor.

Memory Upgrades

It seems like nowadays, no matter how much memory a computer is using, it always needs more. It wasn't too long ago that members of the IT community experienced RAM envy over a 32-MB module; now we barely raise an eyebrow when we see a system running with 512 MB or even 1 GB.

Somewhere along the way, perhaps because RAM upgrades became fairly cheap and easy to do, people started believing that upgrading RAM was a cure-all for the majority of performance-related system issues. More has become better, but in reality, a RAM upgrade can be a fruitless endeavor if done for the wrong reasons. That said, if nothing else, upgrades can prevent the humiliation of being the only computer owner on the block with only 64 MB of RAM.

When to Upgrade Memory

There are some obvious and not so obvious times when a RAM upgrade is needed. The most common reason today for a RAM upgrade is to accommodate software demands. Today's software packages demand a lot from the RAM, and though they state a minimum RAM requirement, in real-world applications, the listed minimum is often not enough.

Memory—You Can Bank on It

Before you can upgrade your memory, you will need to have a basic understanding of memory banks. Each and every modern motherboard includes one to four RAM slots. Collectively referred to as *memory banks*, these banks match the speed or width of the processor's data bus.

Steps in a RAM Upgrade

Upgrading the system's memory is often the easiest upgrade you can perform, which is probably why many nontechnical people are doing their own memory upgrades these days—bad news for PC repair shops. There are really only a few things to be mindful of when performing a memory upgrade; this section walks you through the general procedures.

See Also *The various types of memory are covered in Domain 4 of the CompTIA objectives. This domain is covered in Chapter 4.*

Note Don't forget the ESD precautions when handling memory.

- **Inspect the system** When upgrading your memory, you will have to crack open the case and check out a few details. First, look at the available sockets to see how many there are, how many are available, and what type they are, whether SIMMs or DIMMs. It would be unwise to start an upgrade and then find out you bought 96 MB of 72-pin SIMMs when you needed a DIMM module. As part of the inspection, it would also be a good idea to check the motherboard manual to see if there are any socket restrictions or memory capacity issues.

  While you have that motherboard manual open, you might want to see what type and speeds of memory the system supports. For example, DIMM memory comes in different speeds: 66 MHz, 100 MHz, and 133 MHz. It might be that the system was designed to function with a particular speed. This is typically only a consideration when working with older computers and newer memory. Some systems will operate with different speed DIMM modules, but others will instantly halt as soon as the system boots. The general rule of thumb when installing memory is to never mix your RAM.

- **Removing old RAM** Removing the existing RAM is a straightforward process. Ensure that the power is turned off, and as an extra precaution, disconnect the power connectors from the motherboard because some motherboards maintain a live circuit even when the system is switched off. It is also a good idea to take the few extra seconds to disconnect any cables that might get in the way. It might take a few seconds to reconnect them later, but it is time well spent because trying to install RAM can be tricky enough without the additional hurdles.

Note One not-so-common consideration is the issue of gold and tin RAM connectors. Memory has been manufactured with both tin and gold connectors; the tin connectors were introduced to reduce the cost of the RAM modules. The only thing to remember with the two is that it is not a good idea to mix them together; meaning, match the tin modules with the tin sockets, and the gold with the gold.

■ **Installing new memory** Installing RAM in a system takes a little concentration and focus. This is not a good time to rush to get the job done. Both SIMMs and DIMMs are keyed, ensuring that the memory is installed in the correct way. With new memory, make sure the module is correctly aligned before applying force. SIMMs and DIMMs do not install the same. SIMMs are inserted on an angle, not straight in. Tilt the RAM slightly; if it's aligned properly, it should slide in with very little effort. Because these modules fit in at an angle, the order in which they are placed into the socket comes into play. When you're inserting SIMMs, the lower banks are filled first to allow for the angle insertions. DIMM modules fit straight into the socket. DIMM installation often takes more force than does installation of their SIMM cousins.

■ **Final check** After the RAM is installed, take a few minutes to make sure that the RAM is seated properly and all of the cables are reconnected. Once done, you are ready to boot up the system.

■ **Testing the new RAM** It doesn't take long to see if the RAM has been installed correctly. If all works as it should, the system will boot up with the new RAM configuration. Often, however, the system will halt and require that you access the BIOS to save the new RAM configuration. To do this, simply enter the BIOS and then exit, saving changes on exit. It is not usually necessary to actually make changes; just go in, save, and get out. Refer to the troubleshooting techniques provided in the next section if the computer does not boot after installation.

DIMM + SIMM = ? One question that seems to arise regularly is whether you can mix older SIMM memory with the newer DIMMs? The answer is—absolutely maybe. It might be that the BIOS does not support this type of configuration, in which case you might have the option of upgrading the BIOS so both types of memory are recognized. If the BIOS cannot be updated, the answer is no. Some motherboards do not support this type of configuration and others claim to, but getting the memory to work together is nearly impossible. The best practice in most cases is to simply use a single type of memory.

Troubleshooting the Memory Installation

Troubleshooting the memory installation is not a difficult process, but there are a few steps to follow, starting with the most obvious possibilities and heading toward the remote ones.

Confirm that the RAM module is properly seated in the socket and that it is in the correct socket. Many RAM failures are due to the seating of the RAM. If necessary, remove the newly inserted RAM and reinstall it.

Remove the new memory and replace it with the old memory to help isolate the problem. If the system boots with the old module installed, try putting the new module in a different socket; this will determine if the problem is with the RAM or perhaps with the socket itself. Also, try the new module with and without the old RAM installed to eliminate any compatibility issues between the types of RAM.

Confirm socket requirements. Some computers can be very specific about where RAM goes in the sockets. Some computers require the largest RAM module to be in the lowest bank, and others require all memory sockets to be filled. Confirm socket considerations with the motherboard manual and manufacturer's Web site.

By now you are wondering if the new RAM you purchased is a dud, and it could well be. Were you using the appropriate ESD-prevention practices? The last step you could take is to try the RAM module in another system to see if it works. If it does not work in another computer, then it is most likely a return. If it does work, then it would seem to be a compatibility issue.

Signs That You Have Gotten into Some Bad RAM

While upgrading RAM is often a simple process, troubleshooting when the upgrade goes wrong is another thing. Having a computer that won't boot is the most obvious sign that there is a problem with the upgrade, but there are a few others to be aware of.

- **General protection faults**   If you notice that the system is being plagued with those annoying general protection faults or fatal exception errors, the problem might be RAM-related. If these errors occur frequently after a RAM upgrade, remove the new RAM module and see if the system continues to get the errors.

- **Error in RAM size**   From time to time, the size of the new RAM is misrepresented in the power-on self test (POST) RAM check. It can be somewhat deflating to have installed 512 MB of new RAM and have only 256 MB show up. Though there are a couple of different factors that can cause this, generally speaking, the most common cause is incompatible RAM. It is possible, however, that misreported RAM can be a result of exceeding the RAM capacity that the board will support.

■ **Computer shows a blank screen upon boot-up** This will happen from time to time with a RAM upgrade, and usually it is the result of a poorly seated RAM module or during the install, another expansion card was dislodged.

■ **Computer freezes** A sign that RAM is failing might be that the operating system freezes up. If this happens after an upgrade, it is likely a result of the memory.

Upgrading Hard Drives

Outside of RAM, perhaps the most common upgrade is that of hard disks. While once we wondered how we would possibly fill that 2-GB hard disk, we are now out of space and wishing for a new 100-GB hard disk. Upgrading hard disks is likely going to be a frequent occurrence in your role as a PC technician. This section looks at the specific steps involved in upgrading an existing hard drive with a new one. One disclaimer, however: the procedures included in this book assume that the data has been adequately backed up and will not cover the process of transferring data from one drive to another.

Note Capacity is not the only reason to upgrade a hard drive. Newer hard drives have the ability to transfer data at increasingly faster speeds. For those systems that need to process data fast, upgrading to the faster hard drives is a common strategy.

Before we dive right into the hard drive upgrade, it might be a good idea to list a few common handling precautions when working with hard drives. Without proper handling, it is possible that you can damage the drive before it even has a chance to power up. Take these precautions:

■ The new drive should remain in its antistatic bag until it is ready to be installed.

■ Handle the drive by the corners or sides, keepings your hands off of the circuitry.

■ Do not apply undue pressure to the top of the hard drive.

■ Make sure all system power is off before installing the new drive.

■ Use the correct screws when mounting the hard drive.

Upgrading SCSI Hard Drives

Installing a new hard drive into an existing SCSI bus is typically a straightforward process, at least as long as you follow some basic guidelines.

▦ **System inspection**   Before doing the SCSI upgrade, it is a good idea
to have an understanding of what is currently in the system and how it
is configured. Document such things as termination location and type,
connector types on the SCSI host adapter, SCSI IDs being used, and
cabling. Some systems have their cabling labeled to make some sense
out of the cabling strategy, but just as many do not. Remember, you
might be installing the SCSI device in a system that already has multiple SCSI hard disks, CD-ROM drives, and tape devices. The sheer mass
of cabling and connectors can get very confusing, so make a lot of
notes.

▦ **Set the jumpers**   The next step in the SCSI installation procedure
involves setting the SCSI hard drive's jumpers. All devices on a SCSI
bus must have a unique ID. These IDs can be 0 through 7 for Narrow
SCSI implementations, and 0 through 15 for Wide SCSI. If you're
upgrading and replacing a hard drive, the ID of the drive being
replaced is typically used. If you are adding a hard drive, you need to
determine which IDs are available for you to use.

▦ **Configure termination**   A SCSI bus has to be terminated at the
physical ends of the bus to prevent signal reflection. When installing a
hard drive, you must ensure that termination is set properly. The SCSI
host adapter will often be used as the terminator for one end of the
bus, leaving the last device on the bus needing termination. If the new
drive you are installing is the last one on the bus, you will have to set
the termination. For termination issues specific to the device you are
installing, refer to the manufacturer's Web site, where such information
is readily available.

▦ **Mounting the drive and attaching the cables**   The physical installation of the drive into the system is not a difficult task, but there are a
few points to keep in mind. Secure the drive in the system with the
screws that came with the hard drive, or use the correct-size screws,
and do not over tighten them. Other than that, mount the drive facing
the right direction, and you should be set.

With both the SCSI host adapter and hard drive installed, the cables can be
connected. If the cables are sufficiently marked, they can be attached quite easily. When attaching the cables, ensure that pin 1 on the cable is aligned with pin
1 on both the hard drive and the SCSI host adapter. Very little force is required
when attaching cables, so if you find yourself pushing hard, you might be bend-
ing a pin.

See Also   *If after installing a new SCSI device things do not work, you will need to troubleshoot. Troubleshooting SCSI devices is covered in CompTIA Domain 2, which is located in Chapter 2.*

Upgrading IDE Hard Drives

So you have deleted all the unnecessary files (and perhaps a few necessary ones) and shifted data from drive to drive, but you are still short of room. Nothing left to do but upgrade your hard drive. When it comes time to upgrade your IDE drive, at least you can take comfort in the fact that it is generally easier than upgrading SCSI drives. Still, an upgrade is an upgrade, and they all bring with them an element of danger. Well, perhaps not danger, but it can still be exciting.

Tip   When you're using IDE drives in a master and slave configuration, it is recommended to use drives from the same manufacturer. Though there are disk standards in place, problems can still arise when connecting two different drives.

- **System inspection**   Before installing that monstrous new IDE drive, take a look inside the computer case. When it comes to IDE drives, there are a few things to be on the lookout for. If you are replacing an existing IDE drive, check its designation (whether it was a master or slave), and configure the new one accordingly. If you're installing a new drive, check the installed IDE devices for their designations. You might have to make an existing IDE drive a slave and make the new one a master. Ensure that the cables have sufficient connectors, and at the correct spacing intervals, to which you can attach the new devices.

- **Set the jumpers**   It is very difficult to set the jumpers after the drive is installed, not only because it is very difficult to determine which pins the jumpers are set on, but also because the jumpers themselves can be well hidden and out of the reach of the technician's fingers. Most jumper settings are listed on the hard drive itself and clearly list the jumper placement for master, slave, and cable select.

- **Mount the drive and attach the cable**   Use the manufacturer's recommended mounting procedures, found in the hard drive documentation. For the most part, mounting simply involves finding an empty slot in the case and securing the drive in place with the appropriate screws or clips. Once mounted, the next step is to attach the IDE cable to the new drive. The trick with attaching the IDE cable is simply to match pin 1 of the cable to pin 1 of the device. The red strip on IDE cables represents pin 1 for the cable. When you're attaching the cables to the hard drive, ensure that they are lined up so no pins are bent in the process. As with any other device, hard drives need power, so connect the power cable to the drive, and you are ready to go.

■ **Final inspection**   Double-check the cabling within the system to make sure nothing has been dislodged. When you're working within the crowded space and with the shorter IDE cabling, it is quite common to accidentally pull the cable from the motherboard IDE controller. Also, check the power connector and cables to other devices, as they can often get dislodged in the upgrade process.

Test Smart   If only a hard drive and a CD-ROM drive are used in the system, it is a best practice to connect each device to a separate IDE channel.

Upgrading the BIOS

When the computer system is first started, it must access the BIOS program. The BIOS program provides the instructions the computer needs in order to boot. Without these instructions, the CPU, for example, has no means or method to talk with the rest of the system, neither hardware nor software.

Because hardware needs to have access to the BIOS instructions every time the computer is started, it makes sense to have these instructions stored permanently on the system itself. Read-only memory (ROM) provides this permanent storage. Once data and BIOS programs have been written to the ROM chip, it cannot be removed. What happens, however, when the system requires an upgrade or modification to the existing BIOS ROM program? That's when electrically erasable programmable read-only memory (EEPROM) comes into play.

Tip   ROM is often referred to as *nonvolatile memory,* meaning that unlike a system's main memory, it does not lose its information when the system is powered down.

EEPROM is a little friendlier than the traditional ROM chips, bridging the gap between the system's main memory and the ROM chip by having characteristics of both. It can receive new information like main memory and can hold this information when the computer is powered down. EEPROM, also referred to as flash RAM, allows the changing of the programs held on the chip. EEPROMs are updated with the use of programs that can be downloaded from the manufacturer in a process called *flashing.* Upgrading a BIOS refers to the process of flashing the EEPROM chip to update its programs.

Flashing can be a dangerous process. If the upgrade flash process is disrupted, for example, by a power outage, or the computer shuts down unexpectedly, the BIOS chip can be damaged and there is really no fix for this. Of equal concern is trying to flash the wrong upgrade to the BIOS chip. While some manufacturers make intelligent programs that can sense a mismatch, others don't. Similar to power disruptions, flashing the wrong upgrade can also permanently damage the BIOS chip.

Portable Systems

As a technician, you can expect to upgrade portable systems as well as desktop systems. In terms of frequency, portable systems are not upgraded as much. This is often due to the cost of the portable components and the many components that are integrated onto the motherboard of a portable system. There are, however, a few components you will be expected to know how to replace and upgrade on a portable system.

Battery

One of the key requirements for portable computers is that they are portable. Portable systems all use batteries to provide their power when not plugged in. These batteries are usually nickel-metal hydride (NiMH) or lithium ion (LiIon) types. Of the two, LiIon batteries provide more and longer power and are therefore used more often on modern portable systems. Older portables use the NiMH batteries.

The batteries in the portable system are recharged whenever the portable is plugged into a wall socket. The life expectancy of a fully charged battery depends on the type of portable and the applications being used. In general, two to four hours is what you can expect before needing a recharge.

Like any other rechargeable battery, the ones in portable systems do not last forever and one day will refuse to provide sufficient battery power. In this case, a new battery will need to be purchased from the manufacturer and placed in the portable system. Accessing the battery on a portable system is straightforward, and replacing the old one with the new takes only a few minutes.

Hard Drive

Like our desktop systems, the hard disk in our portable systems might need to be upgraded at some point. The hard disks used in portable systems are more compact than their desktop counterparts, but in terms of performance and actual hard disk space available, they are similar. To replace the hard disk in a portable system, it is certainly best to follow the instructions laid out by the manufacturer of the portable system. In general, however, all you really need to do is find out if the system's BIOS supports a larger hard disk, how to access the hard disk in the portable system, and then if all checks out, replace the hard disk. Figure 1-22 shows a hard disk used in a portable system as compared to one in a desktop.

Figure 1-22 A hard disk used in a desktop system (left) is much bigger than one used in a portable system (right).

When working with hard disks in portable systems, we are at a disadvantage in that they cannot be easily swapped out to transfer files or troubleshoot. With desktop systems, for example, it is common to slave a hard disk in another desktop system. To get around this, we can use a special adapter cable that allows us to slave a portable hard disk into a regular PC. Doing so can help us isolate whether there is something wrong with the hard disk or with the hard disk controller in the portable system.

Note   Upgrading I/O devices such as network cards and modems is done by swapping out PC Cards. The different PC Cards used in portable systems were covered earlier in this chapter.

Memory

One of the more common upgrades to a portable system is memory. Upgrading the memory in a portable system is similar to the process of upgrading memory in a desktop system; however, you might need to check the reference manual to see where the memory is added. Some portable systems require that the keyboard be lifted out to access the memory slots; on others, you can access the memory slots from underneath the system.

One notable difference from desktop systems when upgrading memory in portable systems is in the memory itself. Portable memory has a different shape than regular DIMM memory. Known as *small outline DIMMs* (SO-DIMMs), it is specifically designed for use in portable systems. Figure 1-23 shows a picture of a SO-DIMM.

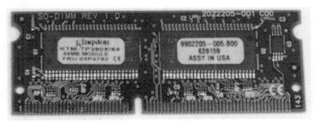

Figure 1-23 SO-DIMMs are used in portable systems.

The Upgrade Review

Before running down to your local computer store and filling your basket with all manner of components, we thought we would mention a few more things to keep in mind before using that bank card.

- **Bus Type**   If you are buying an expansion card, ensure your system has the correct bus slot and that one is available. A new AGP graphics card is great but not so useful if all you have is PCI slots.

- **Power**   Many of the new components we add or upgrade on our systems require more from our power supplies than was intended. As part of the upgrade process you may have to upgrade that power supply to ensure you have enough juice.

- **BIOS**   If you are adding components such as a hard disk, ensure that the BIOS will support the disk. Some of the newer and larger hard disks are not recognized by some of the older BIOSs, and while some of them can be upgraded, others cannot.

- **Memory Compatibility**   Upgrading memory is straightforward as long as you ensure that you purchase the correct memory in terms of speed and physical design. There are several different types of memory available, so before upgrading ensure that you read the manual or refer to the Web site of the manufacturer who made your system to verify that you have the right stuff.

- **Processor**   Not all motherboards can take all processors, so ensure that the processor you plan to upgrade works with the motherboard before purchasing. Further, newer processors require more cooling than older processors, so when upgrading confirm that the cooling method you are using is tested to work with that processor.

Upgrades are a fact of life in the PC world; the trick to avoiding problems with them is to do your homework and verify that the component will work with your system. Once confirmed, there is little left but to install it and sit back and enjoy your upgrade—at least until something better comes along.

If you are installing a legacy device as part of the upgrade process, you will need to ensure that it will function with your system and be sure to get the latest drivers from the manufacturer's Web site.

Key Points

- Firmware is a program that is stored on a chip but is not hardware or software.

- The BIOS provides the first set of instructions to the computer as it boots up.

- The CMOS holds the system's BIOS settings and permanently stores those settings using an on-board battery.

- All devices connected to the system require system resources, including IRQ addresses, I/O addresses, and sometimes DMA addresses.

- System resources need to be unique to the device.

- A field-replaceable module (FRM) refers to any device that can be replaced in the field.

- Most cable connectors are either made so that they will only fit into a connector one way, or "keyed."

- Serial communication is called such because the data travels across the wire in series—1 bit at a time.

- Parallel communications are faster than serial communications because they transmit data in parallel—8 bits at a time.

- A PC will have at least one, if not two, serial port. Serial ports use a DB-9 or DB-25 connector.

- The RJ-11 connector is used for telephone cables; RJ-45 connectors are used with twisted-pair network cabling.

- BNC connectors are used in networks that use thin coaxial cabling.

- PS/2 Mini-DIN connectors are used for connecting mice and keyboards to PCs.

- DIN-5 is the connector type associated with the old-style AT keyboard connectors.

■   IEEE 1394 (FireWire) is an interface used for installing all manner of external devices, from hard disk drives to digital cameras and MP3 players.

■   The ATA standards specify the developments in IDE technology.

■   IDE can have up to four devices attached, two on the primary controller and two on the secondary IDE controller.

■   An IDE bus uses the master and slave settings to differentiate between devices.

■   When installing SCSI devices, each device requires a unique SCSI ID and the SCSI chain must be terminated at both ends.

■   Modems can be internal or external. Both internal and external modems require one of the system's COM ports and the resources assigned to it.

■   When installing peripheral devices, make sure pin 1 of the cable matches pin 1 of the device.

■   If a cable is attached in reverse when connecting a floppy drive, the floppy LED will stay lit.

■   USB hubs are used to add more USB ports to a system.

■   The USB bus supports up to 127 connected devices.

■   Docking stations and port replicators are used to provide a base for laptop systems.

■   PC Cards are used in portable systems to add peripheral devices and sometimes memory.

■   Infrared provides wireless connection between devices and the computer system. Infrared operates at speeds up to 4 Mbps.

■   System performance can be enhanced by upgrading computer components such as the CPU, memory, hard disk, and the BIOS.

Chapter Review Questions

1 What is the standard I/O address assignment for LPT1?

    a) 378-37F

    b) 2F8-2FF

    c) 3F0-3F7

    d) 3F8-3FF

Answer a is correct. The standard base I/O address for LPT1 is 378-37F. Answer b is incorrect. This is the base I/O address for the second serial port on a system. Answer c is incorrect; this is the base I/O address for the floppy drive controller. Answer d is incorrect; this is the base I/O address for the first serial port on the system.

2 What is the default IRQ for COM1?

    a) IRQ 1

    b) IRQ 2

    c) IRQ 3

    d) IRQ 4

Answer d is correct. The default IRQ for COM1 is IRQ 4. Answer a is incorrect. IRQ 1 is the default IRQ for the keyboard. Answer b is incorrect. IRQ 2 is the IRQ for cascading to the IRQ ports 9 and above. Answer c is incorrect. IRQ 3 is the default IRQ for COM2.

3 Which DMA channel is used for the floppy disk drive?

    a) 0

    b) 2

    c) 3

    d) 4.

Answer b is correct. DMA channel 2 is used for the floppy disk drive. Answer a is incorrect. DMA channel 0 is used for the system timer. Answer c is incorrect. DMA channel 3 is used for the ECP parallel port. Answer d is incorrect. DMA channel 4 is used for the DMA controller.

4 How many bits does a parallel interface transmit at one time?

    a) 1

    b) 2

    c) 4

    d) 8

Answer d is correct. A parallel interface transmits data 8 bits, or 1 byte, at a time. All of the other answers are incorrect.

5 What kind of connector would you associate with a joystick port?

a) DB-15

b) DB-9

c) DB-25

d) RJ-11

Answer a is correct. Joystick ports use DB-15 connectors. Answers b and c are incorrect. Both of these connectors are associated with communication ports like serial (DB-9 and DB-25 male) and parallel (DB-25 female). Answer d is incorrect. RJ-11 connectors are associated with telephone connections.

6 What is the maximum number of devices you can have connected to a USB port?

a) 1

b) 6

c) 164

d) 127

Answer d is correct. You can have up to 127 USB devices connected to a single USB port. All of the other answers are incorrect.

7 Which of the following are transfer modes used on ATA drives? (Choose three.)

a) PIO

b) DMA

c) SDMA

d) UDMA

Answers a, b, and d are all correct. PIO, DMA, and UDMA are all valid types of transfer modes associated with IDE drives. Answer c is not a valid type of transfer mode.

8 What kind of cable is required when using a drive with an ATA-66 or higher interface?

a) 40-pin, 40-conductor

b) 80-pin, 80–conductor

c) 80-pin, 40–conductor

d) 40-pin, 80-conductor

Answer d is correct. ATA-66 drives require a 40-pin, 80-conductor cable to operate. Answer a is incorrect. The 40-pin, 40-conductor cable was used with ATA standards before ATA-66. Answers b and c are not valid cable types used with IDE/ATA drives.

9   You are installing an IDE CD-ROM drive into a system with one hard drive already in it. The CD-ROM drive came with its own data cable. In what configuration are you most likely to install the CD-ROM?

   a)   As the master on the primary IDE channel

   b)   As the slave on the primary IDE channel

   c)   As the master on the secondary IDE channel

   d)   As the slave on the secondary IDE channel

Answer c is correct. Where possible, you should distribute devices between IDE channels. Because you have a data cable, the best position for the new CD-ROM drive is as the master on the secondary IDE channel. Answer a is incorrect. The hard drive will almost certainly be the master on the primary IDE channel. Although answers b and c are valid choices, they do not suggest the best placement for the new CD-ROM drive.

10   When using cable select on an IDE bus, on which connector would you put the slave device?

   a)   It doesn't matter

   b)   The one nearest the system board connection

   c)   The one farthest away from the system board connection

   d)   Either, as long as the jumpers on the device are set to either master or slave

Answer b is correct. When using cable select, the device on the middle cable connector (the one nearest the system board connection) is designated as the slave device. Answer a is incorrect. When using cable select, the location of the device on the cable defines its master/slave status. Answer c is incorrect. When using cable select, the device on the end of the cable (farthest from the system board connector) is designated as the master. Answer d is incorrect. When using cable select, the jumpers on the devices must be configured to be cable select, not master or slave.

11   What things must you consider when implementing SCSI? (Choose three.)

   a)   Termination

   b)   Device IDs

   c)   Master/slave configurations

   d)   Compatibility of devices

Answers a, b, and d are correct. When implementing SCSI devices, you must consider termination, device IDs, and device compatibility. Answer c is incorrect. SCSI uses IDs to identify devices on the bus. Master/slave configurations are associated with IDE implementations.

12 What is the maximum data transfer rate of Ultra3 SCSI?

a)   40 MBps

b)   80 MBps

c)   160 MBps

d)   320 MBps

Answer c is correct. Ultra3 SCSI, also known as Ultra160, has a maximum data transfer rate of 160 MBps. Answer a is incorrect. 40 MBps is the maximum data transfer rate of Ultra Wide SCSI and Ultra2 SCSI. Answer b is incorrect. 80 MBps is the maximum data transfer rate of Wide Ultra2 SCSI. Answer d is incorrect. 320 MBps is the maximum data transfer rate of Ultra320 SCSI.

13 Which of the following monitor characteristics is fixed and cannot be changed by the user?

a)   Refresh rate

b)   Resolution

c)   Contrast

d)   Dot pitch

Answer d is correct. The dot pitch of a monitor cannot be changed by the user. All of the other characteristics listed (refresh rate, resolution, contrast) can be changed by the user.

14 How much video memory is needed to display a resolution of 1024x768 at 256 colors?

a)   .5 MB

b)   1 MB

c)   2 MB

d)   4 MB

Answer b is correct. To display an SVGA resolution at 256 colors, you will need 1 MB of video memory. All of the other answers are incorrect.

15 After installing a new, larger hard drive in an older system, the OS is only able to see 540 MB on the drive even though it is a 4-GB drive. Which of the following will you need to do to correct the problem?

a)   Obtain and install a 40-pin, 80-conductor cable.

b)   Reinstall the OS so that it can recognize the larger hard drive.

c)   Upgrade or replace the BIOS on the drive.

d)   Upgrade or replace the BIOS in the system.

Answer d is correct. Older BIOSs only supported drives up to 540 MB. If your system only detects 540 MB of a new drive, you will need to upgrade or replace the BIOS. Answer a is incorrect. The type of cable being used will not have a bearing on how much space can be seen on the drive.

Answer b is incorrect. Reinstalling the OS will make no difference. Answer c is incorrect. The BIOS on the drive, even if it has one, will not determine how much space can be seen on the drive.

16 You arrive on-site to perform a service call. You find that a new IEEE 1284 cable has been sent to the site to help you fix the problem. What kind of problem are you dealing with?

   a)   A printing problem

   b)   A FireWire-related problem

   c)   A SCSI problem

   d)   A network problem

Answer a is correct. IEEE 1284 is the designation given to the parallel communications used. Therefore, it is most likely that you are working on a printing problem. None of the other answers are valid.

17 What is the result of configuring video shadowing?

   a)   Routines defined in the video card ROM are stored in RAM on the system.

   b)   An amount of memory equal to the amount of video RAM is set aside for use by the video card.

   c)   Routines defined in the video RAM are stored in ROM on the system.

   d)   Instructions are processed in system RAM instead of on the video card RAM.

Answer a is correct. When you enable video shadowing, instructions stored in the video ROM are transferred to RAM and executed from there, which can result in a small performance improvement. All of the other answers are incorrect.

18 What is the resolution of Super VGA?

   a)   1280×1024

   b)   1024×768

   c)   800×600

   d)   640×480

Answer c is correct. SVGA is defined as a resolution of 800×600. Answer a is incorrect. A resolution of 1280×1024 is defined as SXGA. Answer b is incorrect. A resolution of 1024×768 is defined as XGA. Answer d is incorrect. 640×480 is defined as VGA.

19 You have a USB hub plugged into a USB port on a system, and three devices plugged into the USB hub. How many IRQs will you need to accommodate these devices?

a) 3

b) 4

c) 1

d) 5

Answer c is correct. The only IRQ required is that used by the USB controller. The devices on the USB chain all share this one IRQ. All of the other answers are incorrect.

20 What is the default base I/O address for the first serial port (COM1)?

a) 378-37F

b) 2F8-2FF

c) 3F0-3F7

d) 3F8-3FF

Answer d is correct. The default base I/O address for the first serial port on a system is 3F8-3FF. Answer a is incorrect. This is the base I/O address for the first parallel port. Answer b is incorrect. This is the base I/O address for the second serial port on the system. Answer c is incorrect. This is the base I/O address for the floppy drive controller.

Chapter 2

When Good Components Go Bad

It has been said that death and taxes are the only guarantees in life. PC technicians can add one more to that list of certainties—troubleshooting. Despite all of our best efforts, things can go wrong with our computers: a mouse quits rolling, a floppy disk drive stops reading, a hard drive stops spinning, or the printer stops, well, printing. These are just a few of the myriad of troubleshooting problems you will be called on to solve in the role of PC technician.

While no book can completely prepare you for what you are going to encounter when actually supporting and troubleshooting PCs, we can give you an idea of which components are more likely to fail and some areas to check when they do.

 Test Smart You will want to pay close attention to the material presented in this chapter. Diagnosing and troubleshooting weighs heavily in the CompTIA objectives; 30 percent of the exam focuses on the material in this chapter.

Identifying and Troubleshooting System Component Errors

When you strip a computer system down to its basic components, there are not really very many components that we have to worry about, at least in terms of troubleshooting. In fact, many system errors can be isolated to one of a very few system components. The real trick when troubleshooting is being able to identify what failure symptoms are associated with what component. For instance, how does a system behave when the memory is failing, or a processor? Over time, you will be able to quickly identify common failure symptoms and easily isolate the component at the root of the problem. Don't expect to develop this level of troubleshooting awareness right away; it takes time working with computers before you will be able to do that.

To give you a few ideas of what you are looking for in terms of component failure, we will take a look at some of the more common system components and the signs and symptoms of failure, and a few ideas on how to correct those problems.

Making It Easy   When a computer or component fails, the mind of a PC technician will often become full of potential problems and complex resolutions. In reality, the solution to most of our computer problems is far from complex. When approaching any system problem, look for the simple things like an unplugged cable or an incorrect user name and password combination. Keep it simple and look for the easiest and most obvious solutions first. For example, if a monitor fails to turn on, check that it is plugged in before replacing the video card. This probably sounds ridiculous, but you might be surprised at how people go out of their way to make things more difficult than they need to be. In the CompTIA exam, be ready for questions that look for the easiest solution first.

I/O Ports and Cables

The ports on the back (and front) of a PC are the source of many troubleshooting tasks, as are the cables that plug into them. Fortunately for the PC technician, the associated troubleshooting steps are relatively straightforward.

Troubleshooting Cables

However it happens, cabling can always seem to find a way of failing. Sometimes the cables get shipped that way, other times they get inadvertently damaged. Troubleshooting cable-related problems is not always easy and is often overlooked. If you suspect a cable-related problem, there are a number of tests you can perform. Most common is to swap out the cable with a known working one to see if the problem is remedied. If you do not have the extra cable with you, the faulty cable can be temporarily swapped out for one that works from another device. When inspecting cables for problems, consider the following:

- **Bent or damaged cables**   Any bends or crimps in the cable could indicate damage to the cable. Better to replace than to wonder.

- **Loose connectors**   Not all cables are equal, and some are simply not as durable as others. Test the ends; if they are loose, they might not be making an adequate connection.

- **Cable length**   There are standards that specify how long certain types of cable can be. These maximum cable lengths are quite adequate for most cable types, but they can be surpassed. To prevent exceeding these limits, be aware of your cable's length requirements.

- **Cable location**   Signal integrity can be compromised depending on where the cable is located. Cables near air conditioners, motors, or any large electrical devices might have interference concerns. This does not, of course, apply to media such as fiber-optic cable.

Note   It is a good idea to have known working spare cables on hand to swap out in a moment's notice when troubleshooting cable-related problems.

Troubleshooting Ports

Troubleshooting ports is a little more involved than troubleshooting cabling because in addition to the physical aspect, there is also a BIOS or software consideration that can affect the configuration.

Serial Ports

Serial ports are one of those PC components likely to cause you few problems. Typically they either work, or they don't, but mostly the former. That said, when serial or COM ports are causing you problems, there are a few more steps in the troubleshooting process than there might be with other port types.

In addition to the normal considerations like interrupt request (IRQ) assignments, it is also possible to configure serial port characteristics from within the operating system. The settings for a serial port can include the number of data bits, the number of stop bits, and the parity settings for the port. The most common setting for these parameters is 8,1,None, as in 8 data bits, 1 stop bit, and no parity. On Windows systems, the configuration for the serial ports is managed through the Ports icon in Control Panel.

Note   When you are having a problem with a device such as a modem or mouse that is connected to the serial port, don't discount the settings for the port as a possible cause.

Parallel Ports

In the real world of PC troubleshooting, you will not find yourself spending a lot of time troubleshooting parallel ports. Of course, now that we've said that, the parallel port in your system (and ours too, most probably) is bound to fail. The parallel port is the 25-pin female DB connector showing on the back of your system. Most often we use the port for printers but it can also be used for many other external devices such as scanners, Zip drives, and even external CD-ROMs.

More Info   For a picture of 25-pin DB connectors, refer to Chapter 1.

When troubleshooting a parallel port connection, there are three key things to keep an eye on: the physical cable, the cable connections, and the settings for the parallel port in the BIOS or operating system.

The best place to start when troubleshooting a parallel port problem is with the physical cabling. This includes verifying that the cable is securely attached to the computer and the connected device, and that the connection points do not have bent pins. An often-used strategy when testing the physical connectivity is to swap out the cable itself with a known working one to quickly eliminate a broken cable as the cause of the malfunction.

Once you are convinced that the cable and the physical connections are not at the root of your problems, you will need to verify that the parallel port itself is recognized by the operating system. One area to check is the system's resources in the BIOS and the operating system. The parallel port typically uses I/O address 378 and IRQ 7 (LPT1). If other components are attempting to use these resources, the parallel port might not work.

Barring any resource conflicts with other devices, the parallel port should be visible and accessible from within the OS. If there is a resource conflict with IRQs or I/O addresses, they will need to be modified before you can access the parallel port. However, parallel port conflicts are rare because they are reserved and, by default, not used by other devices. If there aren't any resource conflicts, verify that the parallel port has not been disabled in the BIOS.

Note   If the parallel port is not motherboard mounted and has stopped working after you have been rummaging around inside the case, double-check that you have not inadvertently unplugged the parallel port cable from the motherboard.

USB Ports

Like many of us, USB devices rely completely on plug and play. The end result of this reliance is that when it comes to USB devices, there is little we need to do to control or configure them. In your travels you are likely going to find that USB is one of those technologies that works most of the time, especially with newer operating systems. However, for those times when you just can't get the USB working, consider the following:

- **Installation**   For the most part, the USB devices will install easily. If they do not, you will need to check in Windows Device Manager to be certain that the USB controllers are functioning correctly. If any of the entries listed under USB Controllers is displayed with an exclamation point in a yellow circle, it is not functioning and those USB devices cannot be used. The problem can often be corrected in the system's BIOS. From within the BIOS, verify that the USB controller is being assigned an IRQ address.

- **Device drivers**   Being Plug and Play, USB will automatically try to install the drivers for your USB device. When the OS cannot find the drivers, you will be prompted to supply the necessary drivers. Ensure that you are using the correct and most recent drivers from the manufacturer's Web site.

- **Firmware**   In normal operation, USB devices are added and removed from the system in seamless operation. Sometimes, though, you will encounter situations where this does not happen. For example, you might find that when a USB device is removed and then re-added, two instances of that device are detected by the system. To get around such peculiarities, you might need to update the firmware for the USB device and, in fact, might even need to update your BIOS firmware in the process.

- **Power**   Some USB devices require external power to operate. An example of such devices are external hard disks. Other devices such as USB memory sticks require very little power and plug directly into the system, drawing the power from the system itself. When troubleshooting, ensure that the devices that require external power are in fact receiving it.

IEEE 1394/FireWire

Troubleshooting considerations with FireWire ports are very similar to those associated with USB in that you need to check provision of power, cabling and physical connections, and software configuration. If you are using a hub, you need to make sure that the hub is powered on.

Infrared

Like most of the other ports discussed here, infrared ports have both a software and hardware configuration. If you are experiencing infrared connectivity problems, you will need to check the port configuration of both the sending and receiving devices.

Some additional considerations with infrared ports are that you must check the connectivity between the two devices. In nearly all cases, a direct line-of-sight path is required between the two devices. Any obstacles between the two points, no matter how small, can affect the performance of the infrared connection. In addition, the two devices must be basically in-line. A generally accepted rule is that the two devices must be within 30° on both a horizontal and vertical axis. Further, you should also consider that the range of infrared in data communication applications is relatively short. If you are having problems, try moving the devices closer together—the closer the better.

SCSI

By SCSI ports, CompTIA is almost certainly referring to the fact that SCSI is a commonly used interface for external devices such as hard disk arrays, tape drives, and even scanners. These external devices connect to the system using external SCSI ports. Some of the types of ports used for this purpose were discussed in Chapter 1.

Using external SCSI devices involves many considerations, not the least of which is that all of the normal SCSI installation issues such as configuration of SCSI IDs, device compatibility, and bus length must be observed, in addition to the following:

- **Port compatibility**   A number of different cables and connectors are used with external SCSI devices. You will need to make sure that you have the correct cable for the application and that it is securely connected.

- **Termination**   External SCSI devices extend the SCSI bus beyond the confines of the system case making it necessary to remove termination from the SCSI host adapter, which will no longer be the end of the SCSI bus.

Because SCSI troubleshooting can be somewhat difficult, in addition to these considerations you should also check other SCSI specifics such as cable length, correct assignment of SCSI IDs, power for external and internal devices, and the configuration of the SCSI host adapter, which is discussed later in this chapter.

Hardware Loopback Plug

Hardware loopback plugs, also known as hardware loopback connectors or loopback adapters, are simple devices designed to redirect outgoing data signals back into the system. The simple effect of this is that the system believes that it is both sending and receiving data. The loopback plug is used in conjunction with diagnostic software that will test the incoming and outgoing signal.

The end result is that the port can be tested to see if it is sending and receiving information correctly. It is a simple and easy way to see if a port is working correctly. Hardware loopback plugs are available for a number of different ports including serial ports, RJ-45 ports, parallel ports, and SCSI ports. Figure 2-1 shows a serial loopback adapter.

Figure 2-1 A hardware loopback plug tests the functioning of a port.

 Test Smart   For the exam, recall that the function of the loopback plug is to test the functioning of a system's ports.

Motherboards

Since the motherboard is the major component in the system, problems with motherboards have a tendency to impact the operation or performance of the system in a significant way. One of the most common sources of problems with motherboards is the BIOS/CMOS.

BIOS/CMOS

Discussed in Chapter 1, the BIOS maintains the system's hardware settings, and the CMOS is a type of memory that holds these settings. The CMOS is nonvolatile memory and retains the BIOS settings using an onboard battery.

One of the more common errors you will hear about regarding the BIOS or CMOS is the loss of system settings or system time. This is almost certainly the result of a dead or dying CMOS battery. When the battery fails, the BIOS settings stored in the CMOS are erased when the system powers down. The fix is simply to replace the CMOS battery.

Test Smart   An indicator that the CMOS battery might be going is the CMOS checksum error. This error is often displayed on boot-up when the CMOS battery begins to fail.

A second problem with the BIOS has to do with installing new hardware on a system with an older BIOS. The BIOS might not be able to accommodate newer hardware and so cannot be used by the system. This is often seen with new hard drives when the entire capacity of a hard drive is not recognized by the BIOS. The only solution in this case is to refer to the manufacturer's Web site and download an update for the BIOS. Updating the BIOS is referred to as flashing the BIOS. There will not always be an update for the BIOS, and it might be that the hardware you are trying to install will not completely work with the current BIOS. Your choice from there is to update the entire system.

Warning   Flashing the BIOS incorrectly might cause irreparable damage to your system. Ensure that you follow the manufacturer's guidelines when flashing the BIOS.

POST Audible/Visual Error Codes

When troubleshooting a system, one of your best friends along the way might prove to be the power-on self test (POST) process. The POST process provides a mechanism to test whether the hardware you installed is actually recognized by the system. In essence, the POST is essentially a self-diagnostic routine that ensures lower-level hardware is present and accounted for. A full POST routine runs every time the system performs a cold boot, which is turning the system off and then right back on again. We have all seen this process when our system powers up and the system's memory is counted and the drives detected. This is all part of the POST magic.

Test Smart   A complete POST check is performed only from a cold boot of the system. A warm boot will run through portions of the POST process, such as the memory check, but not the entire thing.

As we discussed in Chapter 1, anything that is amiss can be reported by the POST with a series of beeps, or information messages. Interpreting beeps can be very difficult as the beep codes are not universal among BIOS manufacturers. To discover the exact beep codes for the BIOS you are using, you might need to refer to the BIOS manufacturer's Web site. To give you some idea of what to expect from the beeps, Table 2-1 provides examples of beep codes for AMI and Phoenix BIOSs and their meanings. Keep in mind, the ones used on your system might vary and you should consult system documentation to ensure that you are "reading" the codes correctly.

 Test Smart   Each and every POST process must verify the processor, video, and memory.

POST Cards   As a PC troubleshooter, it is essential to understand what is going on in the POST process. Sometimes, it is difficult to understand the POST error messages and in many cases a system might lock before giving any error message. In such cases, we have another tool we can use to troubleshoot the POST errors—the POST diagnostic adapter card.

POST diagnostic cards work with any operating system and display detailed information on the POST process. *POST diagnostic cards* are expansion cards that are plugged into the system, and once the system is restarted, error messages are reported via onboard LEDs. POST diagnostic cards are very useful and can isolate a problem easily, and in the process might prevent upgrading or replacing the wrong component.

Table 2-1   Examples of POST Beep Codes for AMI and Phoenix BIOSs

Number of Beeps	Error	Possible Cause
1 short beep	Memory refresh error	Faulty memory or incorrectly installed memory
2	Parity error	Faulty or incorrect memory
3	Base memory error	Faulty or incorrectly installed memory modules
4	Timer not operational	Possible main board failure
5	CPU error	Faulty or incorrectly installed processor
6	Keyboard error	Faulty keyboard or keyboard controller
7	Processor exception interrupt	Possible faulty processor
8	Video card error	Faulty or incorrectly installed video card
9	ROM checksum error	Incorrect version of BIOS ROM
10	CMOS shutdown error	Faulty main board
11	Cache memory error	Faulty or incorrectly installed cache chips
1 long, 3 short beeps	Conventional or extended memory test failure	Faulty or incorrectly installed memory
1 long beep	Successful completion of post	System should boot normally

Numeric Error Codes

In addition to the auditory beep codes, during the boot process we might also see a series of displayed error codes. Of course, we would rather not have these error codes flash on our screens but they can certainly make troubleshooting a bit easier. Numeric error codes work in classes or ranges. For example, motherboard numeric errors range from 100 to 199. Table 2-2 shows the numeric code classes and Table 2-3 shows some specific error codes you won't want to see within those classes.

Table 2-2   Numeric Error Code Classes

Error Code Classes	Description
100–199	Motherboard errors
200–299	Memory or RAM errors
300–399	Keyboard errors
400–499	Monochrome video errors
500–599	Color video errors
600–699	Floppy drive errors
1700	Hard drive errors

Table 2-3   Specific Numeric Error Codes

Error Code	Description
161	Dead CMOS battery
201	Failed or incorrectly installed memory
301	Keyboard not plugged in or is faulty
601	Floppy drive or floppy drive controller has failed
1101	Serial card is faulty
1701	Hard disk drive controller is faulty

The error codes listed in Table 2-3 are not used in modern Pentium-class systems; rather, we use simple text message error codes. Makes you wonder why we didn't do that in the first place. The text messages will tell you straight what the issue is. For instance, you might receive something like "HDD Controller Failure" or "Floppy drive failure." Just how easy can they make it for us technicians?

Peripherals

Any piece of equipment that is connected to a PC could be considered a peripheral. For that reason, including it as a heading in the objectives makes it difficult to determine what CompTIA is referring to in terms of troubleshooting procedures. So, rather than trying to cover troubleshooting steps for a specific peripheral, here are some general points to consider:

■ **Don't forget the system, don't discount the peripheral device**   One of the first things you should determine when trouble-shooting a peripheral device is whether the problem is with the peripheral or whether it is with the system. You need to determine which it is at the first opportunity as it will have a major bearing on your investigations and potential solutions.

■ **RTFM—Read the free manual**   Almost without exception, computer peripherals come with a manual that is laden with all manner of facts. Very often, they also include a troubleshooting guide. Given that, you would think that the manual would be the first stop for someone trou-bleshooting a problem. But it isn't. For some reason, many techs feel that reading the manual is akin to giving up. It isn't, and don't be drawn into ignoring this most useful of resources.

■ **Visit the manufacturer's Web site**   If you are having a problem, chances are that someone has had it before you. In this case, it is likely that the manufacturer has looked at the problem and formulated a solution. In many cases, a trip to the manufacturer's troubleshooting knowledge base will yield the information you need to cure your peripheral problems.

There is more general troubleshooting information later in this chapter.

Computer Case

In the great scheme of computer problems, cases are unlikely to be the cause of very many headaches. Apart from the fact that computer cases are generally sup-plied with power supplies, which we will discuss next, they are basically little more than a metal box.

That said, they do perform a very important function in that they provide the physical means to hold all of the computer components in sufficient prox-imity that they can be connected. The design of the computer case also has a lot to do with the thermal dynamics of the system. The processor fan can pull the excess heat away from the processor but that heat then needs to be dumped out of the box. That is why computer cases have vents and grills on them.

An additional consideration for cases is that they come in many shapes and sizes. Smaller cases that have the space for, say, three or four storage devices might not make the ideal case for a server system. In contrast, a server case with space for 10 or 12 storage devices, additional fans, and a large power supply will be intrusive, from both a space and noise perspective, in a general office setting. When it comes to cases, one size does not fit all.

> **Note** Some higher-end systems have tamper sensors on the case. If the cover is removed while the system is running, the tamper switch senses the removal and immediately cuts the power. Of course you should never remove a cover while the system is running, but the fact that tamper resistant switches exist should discourage you even further.

In terms of straight troubleshooting, the biggest consideration with the computer case is that the covers and any blanking plates are in place. Without them the cooling characteristics of the system can be affected.

Power Supplies

As you will see in Chapter 3, power supplies are one of those components that we do not spend our time fixing; we simply replace them. Power supplies contain capacitors that hold a charge and thus deliver a potentially fatal electric shock. With that in mind, our job is not to repair the power supply but simply to isolate it as the cause of a problem and replace it.

When it comes to power supply failure, the power supply itself might fail, which is easy to determine because the system does not get power and nothing starts. Another common symptom of a failed power supply is a system that periodically turns off. This is often because the power supply is not supplying enough consistent power to the system. The only solution in both instances is to replace the power supply. A little more subtle is the power supply fan. These fans often begin to fail well before the power supply unit itself fails. The result of a faulty fan is a unit that cannot adequately cool itself, and either the power supply will burn out or the system might shut down unexpectedly. Power supply fans typically make a lot of noise when they are beginning to fail, often giving the technician ample time to replace the power supply. Also, some motherboards now come with sensors that can trigger an alarm if the fan stops operating or the processor starts overheating.

 Test Smart A computer system that periodically and spontaneously reboots can mean that the power supply is not providing enough power to the system to keep it going.

> **Warning** If just the fan fails inside the power supply, you might be tempted to simply replace the fan and carry on. This is not recommended because you will need to open the power supply to do so, which as we described earlier can be a hazardous proposition. Even if the fan fails, it is a best practice to replace the entire unit.

Using a Multimeter

A *multimeter* is used for troubleshooting or testing power-related issues in the system. It's used to test four key power areas: AC voltage, DC voltage, continuity, and resistance. The multimeter itself uses two connector probes, one negative and one positive, an analog or digital display, and a switch to select the type of power test you want to perform.

There are many ways of using a multimeter, but one of the most common operations is testing the power output from the power supply, which is a relatively simple process. To test the power output:

1   First, turn the PC off, but leave the power cable connected to the wall outlet.

2   Take one of the power connectors (the ones that power a hard disk, floppy drive, or CD-ROM are the easiest) and insert the black probe of the multimeter into one of the black wires on the power connector.

3   Insert the red multimeter probe into the red wire of the connector. Set the multimeter to 20 volts and turn the PC on. The readout of the multimeter should be around +5V.

4   Turn the PC off and repeat the procedure, this time connecting the red wire of the multimeter to the yellow wire of the power connector.

When you power the PC on, the multimeter should give you a reading of approximately +12V. In each case, some deviation in the voltage is acceptable, but not too much. In the case of the 5V test, the figures should be between +4.8 and +5.2V. In the 12V test, they should be between +11.5 and +12.6V. Any other figure indicates that you are either measuring the power incorrectly, or that the power supply is having a problem.

In the world of PC troubleshooting we typically use the multimeter to measure the voltage, continuity, and resistance (ohms) between two points. Figure 2-2 shows an example of a digital multimeter.

Figure 2-2 A digital multimeter is used to test the power in a system and its components.

Measuring Resistance

When troubleshooting, measuring resistance is one of the elements you are going to become more familiar with. To test the resistance of a device such as a power connector or cable, you must first ensure that there is no power running through it. For instance, if you are testing a power cable, ensure that it is completely unplugged from the system and the wall before starting. If you are testing a component that is inside the case, you must ensure that the power supply is unplugged from the wall socket. Once the power is confirmed to be off, set the multimeter to measure ohms and touch the multimeter probes to the circuit you want to test. The result will be displayed on the multimeter dial or display. To test a cable such as an IDE cable, place one of the probes into pin 1 of the cable and another into pin 1 on the other end. If the cable is working, you should receive a reading indicating that there is continuity. If no reading is present or if a faulty reading is presented, there might be a faulty connection with the probes or a bad cable. We wouldn't suggest throwing out too many "faulty" cables until you really know how the multimeter works.

Measuring Voltage

If you suspect that a power supply or a battery is faulty and want to test your theory, the multimeter is your tool. When measuring voltage with the multimeter, you need to ensure that the positive side of the multimeter connects to the positive side of the target device and the negative to the negative—kind of like connecting the jumper cables to your car battery. Ensure that the multimeter device is set to measure voltage and when the probes are attached, the voltage will be displayed.

> **Warning**   Be sure that you fully understand the procedure for testing power output before starting your diagnosis. Power supplies have potentially dangerous voltages that can at best damage your multimeter and at worst cause fatal injury.

 Test Smart   For the A+ exam, remember that looking for a defective or broken cable is done by setting the multimeter to test ohms, and testing power supplies and batteries is done by testing the voltage.

Slot Covers?

OK, here is a real mind bender. The CompTIA objectives list slot covers in the troubleshooting section, but we are not sure how you would do that! Slot covers are those metal tabs we remove to make room for expansion cards. The simple rule is to use a slot cover when there isn't an expansion card in the slot. This seals the opening, preventing dust from getting inside the system and also allowing better air flow in the case to keep the system cool. For the test, you might need to know why and when we would use slot covers, but it's unlikely that you will be required to troubleshoot a slot cover.

Test Smart   Though they might seem not to have a purpose, slot covers must be in place to prevent dust from entering the case and maintain proper air flow in the case. This serves to prevent overheating.

Front Cover Alignment

Like slot covers, discussing the front cover alignment of a PC might seem like an odd topic in a discussion of troubleshooting, but also like slot covers, it is actually a natural inclusion. Having the front cover of a system incorrectly aligned can affect the cooling characteristics of the case, as well as obstruct access to buttons and, in some extreme cases, even prevent access to CD-ROM drive drawers or floppy disk drives. If a user complains that they are unable to insert a floppy disk into a recessed floppy drive like that found on some computers, you might want to check the front cover alignment.

Storage Devices and Cables

Today's computer systems come at the very least with a floppy drive and a hard drive, a CD-ROM drive, and in many cases a CD-RW and/or DVD-ROM drive. In addition, new storage devices are finding their way into desktop systems including DVD writers, external storage, and USB static memory devices.

Floppy Drive

We no longer rely on floppy disk drives (FDDs) as much as we once did—most of the stuff we need to save exceeds the 1.44-MB capacity of floppy disks. However, almost every computer still has a floppy drive, so it is another device that you, as a PC technician, will be required to support.

Troubleshooting floppy drives is typically not a difficult process. Sometimes a floppy drive will fail completely, but this is not very common. Other times it might work intermittently, reading some floppy disks and not others. In such cases, it is often best to clean the floppy drive heads to see if the problem is resolved. There are two ways to do this. The easy way involves using a floppy disk drive cleaning disk, which can usually be bought from an office supply or computer store. The other way is to remove the case of the floppy drive, and clean the heads with some denatured alcohol and a cotton swab. The bottom line, however, is that floppy drives are so inexpensive (and non-serviceable) that they're not devices we would normally take apart if broken. Instead, we are more likely to replace one at the first sign of a problem.

The following is a list of a few symptoms of a failing floppy drive and possible resolutions.

- **Floppy drive light stays on**   This is a very common problem and easy to resolve. If the drive does not function and the floppy LED stays on, it is often because the floppy drive cable has been attached incorrectly. Refer to Chapter 1 for the proper procedure for installing a floppy drive. As with some of the other errors discussed in this chapter, this is only likely to occur on a drive that has been newly installed.

- **Floppy drive light does not come on**   In contrast to the LED staying on is the problem of the light not coming on at all. This indicates that the drive is not getting power. Check the power connections to the floppy drive.

- **System halts saying a floppy drive cannot be located**   If the system cannot detect the floppy drive during the POST process, the system might stop and indicate that the floppy drive cannot be found. This is because the BIOS has configuration settings for a floppy drive and if the system cannot find the drive, it stops. You can then either change the BIOS settings to remove the floppy drive configuration (if the system doesn't have one) and boot normally, or power down the system and ensure that the floppy drive is correctly installed.

- **Error message when accessing the floppy drive**   If you are working within the operating system and attempt to use the floppy drive, you might get an error indicating that the disk in the drive is not formatted or the device cannot be accessed. If this happens with a single floppy disk, it might simply be a faulty disk and not the floppy drive itself. If the same error message occurs with several disks, it is more likely that your floppy drive has failed. Sometimes cleaning the floppy drive heads will correct the problem or the floppy drive needs to be replaced.

Hard Drives

Of all the components in the computer, hard disk drives (HDDs) can be the most unnerving of them all to troubleshoot. This is not because they are more difficult to troubleshoot than any other component, but with hard drives, the stakes are much higher. Hard drives are the component responsible for maintaining user data, and in most environments, the loss of data is far more costly and more difficult to remedy than any problems with all the other computer components combined.

Given the importance of hard drives and the data they contain, extra caution needs to be taken when troubleshooting them, which will often include making a full backup of the contents of the drive before trying to fix it. Better to be safe than sorry.

There are two types of hard drives you will be working with, SCSI and IDE. In terms of troubleshooting, IDE drives are much easier to work with; troubleshooting SCSI devices can leave even the most seasoned PC troubleshooting veterans scratching their heads.

Troubleshooting IDE Devices   Many of you already have experience working with and troubleshooting IDE devices, whether it was upgrading to a larger hard drive or adding a second one to a system. IDE hard drives are the most common used today and the ones you can be guaranteed at some point to be troubleshooting. When troubleshooting IDE hard drives, there are two areas to keep in mind: external considerations such as cabling, and internal factors, including the overall health of the hard drive and any damaged clusters or sectors. Damaged clusters and sectors are basically areas of the hard disk platters that have been damaged and are no longer suitable for storing data.

In Chapter 1, we reviewed the procedures and methods for installing IDE hard disks, but a quick review is in order before talking about troubleshooting an IDE hard drive installation. If two devices are connected on an IDE chain, one must be set as the master, and the other must be set as the slave. You set the master and slave settings by using jumpers, typically located at the back of a hard drive. If the Cable Select option is being used, set the jumpers accordingly. There can only be one master and one slave on each IDE channel. With that in mind, here are some areas to be aware of when troubleshooting an IDE hard drive.

- Ensure that pin 1 of the cable is aligned correctly to pin 1 of the IDE channel. On most cables pin 1 is denoted by a red strip running down one side of the cable.

- Verify that the master/slave jumpers are correctly set.

- Confirm that the IDE disk is getting power and the power connector is securely attached.

- Check the IDE cable to ensure that it has not become disconnected from the motherboard.

- Sometimes the IDE cable itself might be faulty. To determine if this is the case, swap it out with a known working one.

Note   Believe it or not, you might have everything configured correctly on the IDE chain and it still fails. This is sometimes because some devices and hard disks are not compatible with each other. If you are sure everything is correctly set and things still do not work, the problem might lie with incompatible hardware.

To verify that the hard drive is installed and recognized by the computer system, you can go into the system's BIOS settings and confirm that it detects the hard drive. Modern BIOSs automatically detect the presence of a new hard drive and add the settings for it. Older BIOSs might require that you do this step manually. If the hard disk is detected but is shown as the wrong size, it is often not a problem with the physical installation, but means that the BIOS needs to be updated to accommodate the size of the new hard disk(s).

 Test Smart   If after you install a new and larger hard drive, you find that the BIOS does not recognize the drive's full size, you might need to upgrade the BIOS. If after installing a new and larger drive, the operating system doesn't recognize the full capacity of the larger drive, you might need to update the OS software.

Tracking Down Bad Sectors and Clusters   If you haven't yet encountered a hard disk with bad sectors and clusters, don't worry—you will. Even when an IDE hard disk is physically installed correctly, you are not out of the troubleshooting woods yet. Sometimes damage can occur to the actual hard drive, creating bad sectors on the disk itself, and in turn corrupting the hard disk and the data contained on it. This might happen through everyday wear and tear or it can be a result of the hard disk being dropped, kicked (or drop-kicked), or otherwise abused. Even improperly shutting down the computer system, sustaining power surges or spikes, or being victimized by viruses might cause the problem. The results of such events can range from destroying the entire hard disk to damaging just a few files contained on it. Either way, it's not good.

Many symptoms can indicate that there are problems with your hard disk. Some of these include:

- Missing or corrupt files
- Clunking or grinding noise caused by the read/write heads coming in contact with the platters
- Inability to run or execute a program
- System does not boot and indicates an error such as a missing operating system, or the inability to find Command.com

Such indicators do point to a failing hard disk, but not always. For example, a virus could easily cause any of the problems just listed. So how can you tell the difference? That's where software troubleshooting utilities come in.

Ruling out that hard disk problems are related to virus activity is as easy as installing a virus checker and scanning your computer. If you suspect that there are bad sectors or other such anomalies, operating systems include utilities that give the hard disk a thorough test to see what is actually going on with the hard disk. The utility primarily used with Windows client systems such as Windows 9*x* and Windows Millennium Edition (Windows Me) is ScanDisk. On computers running Windows 2000 and Windows XP, the program is called CHKDSK, commonly referred to as Check Disk. This program can be set to run automatically as part of a regular maintenance of the hard disk, or it can be set to run manually when a problem is suspected. When run, the program can scan your hard disk and identify any bad sectors or clusters on it. This process can take a very long time but be patient, it is worth it.

Does This Look Infected to You?   One of the more difficult tasks when troubleshooting system errors is determining whether the problem is virus, hardware, or software related. Unfortunately, there are no black-and-white guidelines that can easily distinguish between them, but over time it will be easier to identify where the problem lies. One thing that helps in the process is to always ensure that you are using a robust and up-to-date virus solution. To do otherwise will make the troubleshooter's life a whole lot more difficult. Another tactic PC technicians use to help win their battle with viruses is to stay on top of what viruses are out there and what they are designed to do. Armed with this knowledge, it becomes easier to identify the presence of a virus. To learn about virus threats, refer to Web sites from companies such as Symantec (*www.symantec.com*) and McAfee (*www.mcafee.com*). These sites offer detailed information on viruses and the damage each of them can do to a computer system.

> ***See Also***   *More information on these tools can be found in Chapter 9.*

CD/CD-RW Drives

On most of our computer systems, the CD-ROMs get quite the workout. As with many of the other components listed in this section, CD-ROM problems can be a result of actual failure of the device or incorrect installation. Of the two, an incorrect installation is most often the cause.

As with hard disks, CD-ROMs can either be SCSI or IDE; however, the cost of SCSI CD-ROMs makes them less popular than their IDE counterparts. With performance being similar between the two, SCSI CD-ROMs are not often seen. Troubleshooting a SCSI CD-ROM follows the same basic principles as trouble-shooting SCSI hard drives, discussed previously. This includes verifying termina-tion, SCSI IDs, cabling connectors, and cable length. There is also a chance that the SCSI CD-ROM device itself is damaged, although this is not common.

Troubleshooting IDE CD-ROM drives is not complicated. Checking the physical connection follows the same guidelines as verifying the physical con-nectivity with IDE hard drives. This includes checking the master/slave settings and cable connections.

If the CD-ROM drive is physically attached to the system and you are still unable to access it, the drive itself might be damaged. It is often a good trouble-shooting step to swap out the CD-ROM drive with a known working one and see if the problem persists.

If the problem is that the drive gives errors while reading, you can buy spe-cial cleaning CDs, which can be used to clean the lens within the drive. Often, all that is needed to "fix" a CD-ROM drive that is operating erratically is to run it for a couple of minutes with the cleaning CD and all is well.

In most cases, the same steps that are relevant to troubleshooting CD-ROM drives apply to troubleshooting CD-RW drives as well. There are also some other considerations, however. One of the most significant of these might be that with CD-RWs, the correct, device-specific, software drivers are normally required. Whereas most OSs can detect the presence of a CD-ROM drive and often use a generic driver quite satisfactorily, in many cases the OS software will install a CD-RW as a CD-ROM drive and so you will not be able to use it as a writer. So, if you are installing a CD-RW into a system, make sure that you install the correct drivers for the device.

Note   Although many CD-R and CD-RW drives advertise high write speeds, in practical use the actual maximum write speed might be slower. In some cases it might be that the media doesn't like being written at such a high speed. If you are consistently having problems writing a CD, try bringing the write speed setting down a notch or two.

DVD/DVD-RW Drives

Nowadays, it is very common for systems to come with a DVD drive and increasingly DVD-RW units. Because DVD units are almost identical in their physical and logical operation to CD units, troubleshooting these devices fol-lows almost exactly the same processes.

Tape Drives

Generally speaking, tape drives tend to be the domain of server systems rather than desktop PC systems, making the need to troubleshoot them relatively uncommon. The following are some of the things that you should consider when troubleshooting tape drives.

- **Check physical connections**   Tape drives can be either internal or external units. In either case, if you are having problems you should check the data cable and the power connections.

- **Use a cleaning cartridge**   Cleaning the mechanism on a tape drive is considered a routine maintenance task, but if you are having problems reading or writing to a tape it is also the first step in the troubleshooting process. Use the correct cleaning tape for the drive—for the best results periodically use a new cleaning cartridge.

- **Don't discount the cartridge**   As unpalatable as it might be, there are times when there might simply be a problem with the tape that you are trying to read from. In these instances, you can try the tape in another tape drive, but the likelihood is that the data is gone. This is just another good reason why you should always keep more than one copy of critical data.

Removable Storage Devices

Any problems you encounter with removable storage are likely to be with the connection method rather than the devices themselves. For that reason, if you are having problems with a removable storage device, check the physical connection and, if the device has one, the external power source. Outside of that, the general troubleshooting steps for your removable storage device are much the same as those for nonremovable storage. Perhaps the only exception to this advice is that many external storage devices require special software drivers. You should ensure that these drivers are correctly installed and configured.

Cooling Systems

The cooling systems within a PC are vital to its correct operation. Without any one aspect of the cooling, your system might overheat, causing permanent damage to key (and typically expensive) components. For that reason, it is essential that PC technicians understand the cooling components within a system and the functions they perform.

Fans

Fans are quite simply the most important component in keeping your system operating at an acceptable temperature. A system generally has at least two fans, one on the CPU and another in the power supply, but it is becoming increasingly common to have one or even two additional fans in the system case to further aid the cooling.

For a system to be cooled adequately, all of the fans should be connected and operating. If one of the auxiliary fans fails, it might be OK to continue running the system for a short while until it can be replaced, but if the fan in the power supply or on the CPU fails, the system should be powered off immediately and not used again until the fan has been replaced. The heat generated by both a CPU and a power supply can burn that component out very quickly if it is not cooled correctly.

Modern system boards have sensors that can detect when a CPU fan fails, causing an alarm to sound. If your system board has such a feature, you should make sure you understand how it works and that it is enabled.

If you have to replace a fan, make sure that you use the same size fan and that you install it in the correct orientation. It is possible to install a fan so that it is blowing air into the system case rather than sucking it out. As you can imagine, this is not a good thing.

Heat Sinks

Given that a heat sink is an inanimate lump of metal, troubleshooting it is a relatively straightforward process. Provided that the heat sink is squared directly on the chip that it is cooling, and provided that the heat sink has a good contact with the chip, albeit through an adhesive paste, heat sinks should not pose you any problems. Do look out for broken fins, though. These fins serve to increase the surface area of the heat sink and although one or even two being broken off is unlikely to cause a problem, a large number of broken fins can affect the surface area of the heat sink sufficiently to affect its cooling capabilities.

Liquid Cooling

Although fans and heat sinks do a good job of conducting the heat away from a CPU, they still rely on one thing—air—to move the heat around. With CPU speeds increasing, it looks like we are starting to push the limits of what this air-based cooling system has to offer, which means that we will have to look for something stronger.

The answer is liquid cooling. In much the same way that cars use a liquid-filled system with a radiator to pull heat away from the engine, systems for CPUs that use a liquid-filled heat sink and a "radiator" on the rear of the PC are starting to appear in PC systems. At this point the systems are expensive, difficult to install, and still evolving, but over the next couple of years you can expect to see more and more of these liquid cooling systems appearing in high-end server and desktop PCs. One secondary benefit of these systems is reduced noise. Whereas fans, and the airflow they produce, create noise as they run, liquid-based cooling systems use an impeller within the liquid that is almost silent.

One thing to note is, at this point, liquid-based cooling systems are only being considered for CPU cooling. It is likely that other areas of the PC such as the power supply will continue to be cooled by fans for some time to come.

Temperature Sensors

Because of the potentially damaging effects of heat buildup, many mother-boards now include heat sensors that can be configured to trigger alarms or even shut off devices if the temperature within the system case reaches a certain level. If your system board (or any other device installed in your system) comes with these temperature sensors, you should make yourself familiar with how they work, and also with how they are enabled and disabled. Typically, you will leave temperature sensors enabled and set to conservative levels to prevent damage to the system in case of overheating.

Test Smart   Configuration of temperature sensors is typically performed through the motherboard BIOS.

If you receive an alarm from one of the temperature sensors, you should investigate as soon as possible. Typically, if a system has been running for some time without a problem and then the heat sensor alarm goes off, a component like a cooling fan has failed or something is blocking one of the vents on the system case itself. If the alarm goes off on a new or recently upgraded system, it could be that there is simply not enough cooling capacity. In this case, you will need to look at adding additional fans or improving airflow to accommodate the increase in heat production.

Processor/CPU

In the years that we have been involved in repairing and maintaining computer systems, we can count the number of failed processors on a single hand. Most processor failures we have encountered are the result of *overclocking* (configuring the processor to run at a higher speed than it was designed for) or *overheating*, which are for the most part preventable processor disasters. With that in mind, there are two key areas to watch when working with potentially failed processors: installation and overheating.

Note   If you are working with a newly installed processor, you should not discount the possibility
that it might be faulty. Processors are extremely sensitive devices, and it's not unheard of for them
to be faulty upon delivery, or to become faulty during the installation process.

Processor installation was covered in Chapter 1, but as far as troubleshooting is concerned, if the processor was installed incorrectly it might not work at all or work at the wrong speed. Some people overclock their processors to increase processor performance, although this practice is not as prevalent as it once was. While this might work, for a while at least, it also increases the work the processor has to do, forcing it to operate beyond what it was designed to do. Overclocking a processor can destroy it immediately or it can shorten the life of the processor. We don't recommend overclocking the processor.

A second problem associated with processors is overheating. Today's processors operate at very high temperatures and use a heat sink and fan to dissipate the heat. The problem is that processor fans periodically fail, and when they do, the processor cannot keep cool. If a processor were to operate too long without a fan, perhaps even minutes, the processor can overheat and burn out. There is no way to recover a burned-out processor; it is reduced to an item for show and tell.

You do not need to keep taking off the case of a computer to see if a fan is failing. A failing fan typically makes a noise that an astute PC technician will suspect as a potential problem. If you do hear an unusual noise coming from the computer system, pop off the case and see if the fan is still functioning. Processor fans are cheap, and replacing them is a straightforward process. So if you suspect a fan is failing, it might be better to just replace it to be sure.

Test Smart   Nowadays, many processors have fans that are fed with power directly from the
motherboard. This makes it possible to monitor the fan status via software.

Memory

A memory error can be one of the more common errors you are going to encounter as a PC technician. The problem with memory errors is that they are deceptive and might not look like memory-related errors at all. Some symptoms such as beep codes during the POST process can easily indicate a memory problem, but other symptoms such as page faults and system lockups can also indicate a memory error. The problem is these symptoms do not necessarily mean the problem is related to memory, only that it is a suspect.

See Also   *Refer to the section titled "POST Audible/Visual Error Codes" earlier in this chapter for information on POST errors.*

When you do believe that memory is at the root of the problem, there are some specific troubleshooting steps you can perform, including:

- **Verify memory compatibility**   If you have newly installed RAM, confirm with the manufacturer's Web site that it is compatible with your current configuration.

- **Confirm memory configuration**   Depending on the motherboard, it might be necessary to match equal capacity memory modules in available banks. Refer to your documentation or the motherboard manufacturer's Web site to determine what the configuration requirements are. Refer to Chapter 1 for memory installation.

- **Confirm installation**   Sometimes a memory problem is nothing more than poorly seated module. When troubleshooting memory, it's a good idea to carefully remove the RAM and reinsert it. Make sure that it is seated properly in the slot and that it is securely in place.

- **Replace the modules**   It might be necessary to remove and replace the memory modules systematically to help determine the one that is causing the problem. In other words, remove memory modules one at a time (or one bank at a time in older systems) to see if you can identify the defective module. If you have spare, known to be good RAM, this process is slightly easier.

- **Clean contacts and connectors**   If the memory in your system is old or the inside of the case is particularly dirty, the contacts and connectors might need to be cleaned. Refer to Chapter 3 for more information on how you can safely and effectively clean connectors.

Test Smart   If your system is freezing periodically and you suspect memory is the cause, a good strategy is to swap out the RAM and see if the problem is corrected.

As well as these steps, there are software utilities that can be used to test RAM, although this assumes that the system is running in the first place, enabling you to run the program.

Display Device

When it comes to troubleshooting the display, there are two possible scenarios you will encounter: no display and bad display. Of the two, staring at a blank screen seems more dramatic, but it's often easier to isolate and troubleshoot. Bad display can be a bit trickier.

Troubleshooting a Blank Display

Staring at a blank screen can seem like a huge problem but in reality, when you have no on-screen display, the problem is often quite easy to isolate. As we know from Chapter 1, there are two separate components that give us our display, the monitor and the video card. Therefore, when we are troubleshooting a display problem, we have two components to look at...so to speak.

Monitors   Troubleshooting monitors is typically a simple process with most problems being easy to isolate. The first step we would suggest when troubleshooting display problems is to verify that there is a connection between the monitor and the video card. When a connection is made between the monitor and the video card, assuming that the monitor is one of the modern power-saving models and that the PC is turned on, the LED on the front of the monitor will turn a solid green. When a connection is not detected, the LED is often a flashing or solid amber. On older monitors, the LED will most likely be green no matter what the state of the connection.

Note   Don't forget—check the simple things first. If you are troubleshooting a monitor issue, check that the power cable has not become disconnected from the monitor.

If the problem is not the cable, another place to look is the monitor's settings. Monitors typically have a series of buttons on the front, allowing you to change the brightness, contrast, and other settings of the monitor. Oftentimes, the settings might have been changed and are preventing a display. Perhaps the simplest example of this is when the brightness has been turned all the way down. The picture is there—you just can't see it!

 Test Smart   One simple way to isolate the cause of a display problem is to swap out the monitor with a known working one. If your new monitor works, the problem lies with the old monitor and not the video card.

Troubleshooting Poor Display

Far more common than troubleshooting a completely blank screen is troubleshooting poor display. You will often be faced with the problem of a blurry screen, a screen with low resolution, or a screen that flickers constantly. Like troubleshooting a system with no display, the problem with a poor display can be traced to either the monitor or the video card. To troubleshoot poor on-screen display, consider the following:

- Verify that the latest drivers are being used for the video card. This simple procedure can fix a number of display anomalies. To get the latest drivers for the video card, go to the manufacturer's Web site.

- Verify the settings on the monitor. New monitors allow you to make very specific configuration changes, normally through an on-screen menu system. Adjusting these settings will change how the monitor displays information on the screen. You should also check the monitor settings in the OS to ensure that your monitor and video card are configured correctly.

If the on-screen image is fuzzy, this can often be fixed by degaussing the monitor. Over time, the monitor picks up a weak magnetic charge that interferes with the system's display. To remove this charge, you use a degauss button located on the monitor or select the degauss option from the monitor's menu selection screen. Some smaller monitors might not have a degauss function, but larger ones do.

Sometimes, though not often, a bad monitor cable can cause on-screen errors. The symptom of a bad monitor cable is a display with a blue, red, or green tint to it. Wiggling the cable will often return the display to normal but this cable will have to be replaced eventually.

Input Devices

Input devices are where "the rubber hits the road" so to speak in the interaction with the user. As a result, as well as the normal wear and tear considerations, you must also consider the human factor when troubleshooting these generally trouble-free devices.

Keyboard

One of the first things we do when troubleshooting a keyboard problem is to reseat the cable connection at the back. Keyboards are hardy devices and little things such as loose cables are more often the cause of a keyboard failure. If the keyboard is connected correctly and you still can't type, the next thing you might try is to swap the keyboard out with a known working one. This eliminates the actual keyboard as the root of the problem. If the good keyboard still fails, you are looking at a failed keyboard controller. This is not good, as the controller is built right onto the motherboard and generally is not replaceable. If the keyboard controller has failed, instead of replacing the motherboard you can use a keyboard that doesn't use that port. For example, if the faulty keyboard controller is for a PS/2 port, perhaps use a keyboard with a USB connector.

Test Smart   If you are called to fix a keyboard that continually beeps even after the system is restarted, you have a stuck key or there is something pressing down on a key.

Mouse/Pointer Devices

Try using your computer system without the assistance of the mouse and you will discover how awkward life is without it. Fortunately, mice are fairly simple devices and they do not regularly fail. The most common problem with mice is erratic cursor movement on the screen or unresponsive cursor movement. This is often an indicator that the mouse ball and/or the inside of the mouse is dirty and in need of a good cleaning. The rollers on the inside of the mouse might need to be scraped and cleaned.

See Also   For more information on cleaning the mouse, refer to Chapter 3.

Some mouse errors are far more complex than a simple cleaning can fix. Of course a severed mouse cable would qualify as such, but other problems are a little less obvious. If you find that you boot up your system and you are unable to move the cursor around the screen, there are a few things to look for. First and most obvious is to check that the mouse is actually plugged into the computer. If it is, try to reseat the cable connection; sometimes it just comes loose. A second possible problem is a resource conflict. Each device connected to the computer system requires system resources such as an IRQ and I/O address. When two devices use the same resources, there is a conflict preventing one or both devices from functioning. Of course, chances are that a resource conflict will only occur if a new device has been installed or you have reconfigured a device already installed in the system. Much as people would have you believe otherwise, computers do not reconfigure themselves, and resource conflicts on a system where nothing has been changed are extremely rare.

A PS/2 mouse typically uses IRQ 12, so if you power up your system and the mouse isn't working, another device might be trying to use IRQ 12, creating a resource conflict. A serial mouse can also be involved in a resource conflict with other devices such as a modem that use serial port resource assignments. If your serial mouse is connected to COM1 or COM3, it will be using IRQ 4; if it's connected to COM2 or COM4, your mouse will be using IRQ 3. You need to make sure that if devices like internal modems are installed in your system, they are not conflicting with other serial devices.

If the mouse is properly connected and you have confirmed that there is not a resource conflict, the best course of action is to swap the mouse out with a known working one to help isolate the exact cause of the problem.

As well as mice, many people now use other pointing devices with their systems including trackballs and graphics tablets. Trackballs are almost like an inverted mouse, so many of the same troubleshooting steps that apply to mice apply to trackballs. Graphics tablets generally employ a special pointing device or a pen that is used to draw on a flat surface—the "tablet." The most important consideration with a graphics tablet is that the surface of the tablet must be kept very clean. The best way to do this is with a damp cloth.

Touch Screen

There is something really cool about touch screens—you just peck away at the screen with a fingertip and away you go (so much more 21st century than using a keyboard). In fact, touch screens are a relatively mature technology, having been around for well over a decade.

Touch screens are commonly found in point of sale (POS) systems and in other specialized applications such as Internet kiosks and information terminals. They are not often found connected to PCs in normal office environments.

In addition to the standard video cable, which provides the communication of the picture between the system and the screen, touch screens also utilize an additional connection, either through the serial port or via a proprietary interface card, to receive and process the information from the touch screen itself.

Because touch screens are specialized pieces of equipment, actual servicing of the screen itself is best left to those with the relevant experience. As far as basic troubleshooting goes, in addition to checking that the physical connections are secure, you will also need to determine that the software configuration for the screen is correct.

Adapters

The vast array of adapters used in today's PCs makes troubleshooting them a varied and frequent task. In the following sections we explore some of the more common troubleshooting procedures with some of the more common adapters.

Network Interface Card

Network interface cards (NICs) are another one of those components that, if handled and installed correctly, will give you very few hassles along the way. When a network card does fail in a system, the computer will no longer be able to access the network to which it was connected, whether this is the Internet or an internal network.

If you suspect a faulty network card, check the following settings before replacing the card:

- **I/O settings**   If any new hardware has been added, check to see if there is an I/O address conflict. Use the specific hardware reviewing tools to see if this is the case.

- **Network card drivers**   An incorrect driver might make a card work improperly. Even if the driver installed is assigned by the operating system, visit the manufacturer's Web site to get the most recent driver available.

- **IRQ conflicts**   Although nowadays, with plug and play, IRQ conflicts are not as frequent as they were, they are still a concern. Review your operating system logs to ensure that there are no conflicts.

- **Card settings**   Make sure all of the card's network settings are correct. One wrong setting and things could just not work.

- **Network card LED**   Most modern network cards have an LED on them, called the *link light*, which is used to tell if there is an active connection to the network. If you cannot access a network, check to see if the LED is lit. If it is not, there might be a problem with the network card installation or setup.

Note   In some environments, network support technicians have spare network cards available to be swapped into a system at a moment's notice. As much as possible, use duplicate network cards to those already in the machine. This will prevent driver-related problems and decrease potential downtime associated with swapping out a card.

Sound Card

In the old days of computers, fighting with sound cards and audio problems was a common occurrence, leaving many of us to make our own sound effects for those early dungeon games. Today, installing and assigning resources to a sound card is normally no more difficult than physically installing the sound card and turning your computer on. If you are using legacy sound cards, the same cannot be said. Many of these old cards still use jumpers to set their resources. You might need to check with the manufacturer's documentation if you are setting system resources manually using jumper settings.

When troubleshooting sound problems, there are three key areas to focus on: the physical installation, the sound card drivers, and the software setup.

In Chapter 1, we explored the installation of sound cards. If there is no sound coming from the system, the sound card might not be correctly installed. Of course, if your sound card is built into the motherboard, this is not possible. Sound cards are installed into the system in the same way that other expansion cards are, with older sound cards using legacy ISA slots and newer sound cards using the PCI slots. You might need to remove and reseat the card to ensure that the connections are being properly made between the card and the expansion slot. One common error in the physical setup is to connect the sound jack from your speakers to the wrong port, such as the microphone port. It is worth double-checking to ensure that cables are correctly attached.

A second area to look at when there is no sound coming from the computer is the sound card drivers. Even if you are using the drivers that shipped with the audio card, you might need to take a trip to the manufacturer's Web site to get the latest drivers. Only with the latest drivers can you be sure that you have the correct ones.

A final area to check is the software you are using within the operating system. Believe it or not, a large majority of sound-related problems are fixed by simply turning the volume up or on in the operating system. Like we said before, troubleshooting is often about finding the easiest solution.

Video Card

Video cards are one of those components that, once they are installed and working correctly, rarely go bad. If you suspect that the video card has failed, confirm that it has been properly installed and securely attached in the appropriate expansion slot. If it is an old one that has quit working, replace the video card with a known working one. If the new video card works, the old one is simply faulty. The old card is typically thrown out, or returned to the manufacturer if still under warranty.

Modem

Over the years, we have probably fought more with modems than any other computer component. In the days before plug and play, modems were often a nightmare to configure and resource conflicts were a common occurrence. Today, the assignment of resources to modems is handled automatically, at least for newer modems that support plug and play. For all those legacy modems that still use jumpers and are not plug and play, you might need to roll up your sleeves and go a few rounds with your modem.

As with other components, when troubleshooting a modem it is very important to start with the simple fixes. Though not always the solution, these simple fixes can save a lot of your valuable troubleshooting time. The simple fixes as far as modems are concerned include:

■ Verify that the phone jack and power cable (on external modems) are correctly installed.

■ Modems often share a phone line, and if someone else is using the phone you might not be able to dial out.

■ You need a dial tone to use the modem. If you are unable to connect using the modem, ensure that you have a dial tone.

If one of these simple fixes does not get the modem working, you will need to dig a little deeper. The first thing to check is whether the operating system detects the modem you have installed. All major operating systems provide the mechanisms to do this—in Windows you can view installed hardware from within Device Manager. If your modem is detected, it will be listed there. If it is detected but does not function, it might be that you need to update your modem drivers and verify that there are not any resource conflicts. If your modem is not detected by the system, you might need to confirm that it is physically installed correctly. Table 2-4 provides a summary of the areas to check when trouble-shooting a modem.

Table 2-4   Summary of Modem Troubleshooting

Symptom	Possible Solution
The modem stops working.	If the modem stops working, check whether new hardware has been added that might be causing a resource conflict. If new software was added, verify that the modem settings have not changed.
The modem keeps hanging up after making a connection.	Verify that the modem settings are correct. Also, you might need to download and install the latest modem drivers.
The modem is not connecting at correct speed or is operating slowly.	If a modem is connecting more slowly than it should, verify that you have the latest drivers installed. The problem can also be a result of poor phone line quality (often referred to as line noise), which is something you cannot do very much about.
The modem makes a connection but cannot authenticate.	This is often caused by the wrong user name/password combination. Verify that you are inputting the correct settings.
The operating system cannot find the modem on a COM port.	This can often be fixed by moving the modem onto another COM port or checking the configuration of the port to make sure it's correct.
The modem dials but cannot connect.	Ensure that the correct phone number is being dialed.
The modem gives an error that it cannot make a connection to the server.	Verify that the protocol settings are correctly configured to access the server.

As you can see from the preceding table, there are plenty of areas to look at when troubleshooting the modem connection. Once you have fought with one or two of them, it gets easier. But when you are just getting used to troubleshooting modems, don't be afraid to call tech support or your ISP—it can and will save you a huge amount of time.

Modem Commands

When working with and troubleshooting modems, we often use something called the *AT command set*, to help in the process. The AT commands are used from a communications application, such as the HyperTerminal utility in Windows, and talk directly to the modem. The modem in turn responds to the commands, providing us with information we can use in the troubleshooting process. Some of the most commonly used AT commands are included in Table 2-5.

Table 2-5 Commonly Used AT Commands

Command	Result
ATA	Sets the modem to auto answer
ATH	Hangs up an active connection
ATDT *phone number* or ATDP *phone number*	Dials the specified *phone number* using tone (T) or pulse (P) dialing
ATZ	Resets the modem
AT13	Displays the name and model of the modem
ATX	Resets the modem to a predefined state

Test Smart   Before taking the A+ exam, make sure that you know the functions of the commonly used AT commands.

SCSI

Working with SCSI devices can be a frustrating experience, and if things start to go wrong you might find yourself burning the midnight oil as it were. If it's any comfort at all, most SCSI-related difficulties can be isolated to a very few causes. In light of this, perhaps the most important thing to remember when a system that uses SCSI devices starts to go down is not to start pulling things apart too soon. The key is to take a step back, take a breath, and start with the basics.

The following sections describe some of the basic considerations when troubleshooting SCSI hard drives.

> **Note**   As with all troubleshooting procedures, when you're working with SCSI systems, be sure to make only one change at a time. Making multiple changes confuses the issue and prevents you from knowing what the exact remedy to the problem was.

Termination   Many SCSI-related problems can be traced to improper termination issues. Installing SCSI devices and termination was discussed in Chapter 1, but in a nutshell, each of the physical ends of a SCSI bus must be terminated to prevent signal reflection. Improper termination can be tricky to isolate because it might appear to work at first, and because the problems created by improper termination might be intermittent. What you might notice is that data is being lost from time to time, or the system periodically hangs. It might even be that the system will not boot at all, or some of the SCSI devices won't be recognized. To prevent these often hard-to-track-down problems, it's absolutely necessary to ensure proper termination from the start. Remember, a SCSI bus needs termination at both ends of the bus and nowhere else.

> **Note**   When troubleshooting SCSI termination, it might be necessary to connect and test devices one at a time. Finding termination problems on a fully loaded SCSI bus can be difficult to do.

Cable Connections   Given the complexity of connecting SCSI devices, it's often easy to overlook the obvious. But when troubleshooting a SCSI problem, the whole issue could be as simple as whether the SCSI cables are securely attached or connected at all. Before calling your SCSI vendor and complaining of faulty equipment, take a quick look to see if all of the cables are properly attached. It only takes a second and can reduce downtime if it is that simple. Like improper termination, loose cables can cause intermittent problems.

All external SCSI cables come with a means to securely connect them to the system. Whether the mechanisms are the locking clamps of the Centronics connectors or the thumbscrews of the D-shell connectors, they need to be fastened down securely.

Broken Cable   Though this is most often not the case, SCSI cables do fail, and if low-quality SCSI cables were purchased initially, this is even more of a concern. If you suspect a faulty cable, visually inspect the cables to ensure that the pins are not bent and that they make a good connection. It is a good idea to check for strains or cracks on the ends of the cable. Some of the more expensive cables have a strain relief mechanism designed to protect the cable, but this doesn't always provide the necessary protection.

Cable Length   Exceeding the recommended SCSI cable length is not a good idea. If the total length of the SCSI cable exceeds the recommended length, do not be surprised when problems arise. Cable-length specifications for the various SCSI standards were listed in Chapter 1.

SCSI IDs   Conflicts are sure to arise if you try to have two SCSI devices on the same bus trying to use the same ID. Each device on a SCSI bus must have a unique ID. So when troubleshooting your SCSI configuration, ensure that each of the devices has a unique ID assigned to it.

Test Smart   If after installing a new hard drive, whether a SCSI device or IDE, the device does not work, the first area to check is the physical installation. This includes the cabling and hard drive settings.

IEEE 1394/FireWire, USB

IEEE 1394 and USB adapters are used when either the system needs more ports, the system does not have any of its own, or the system ports are no longer functioning. IEEE 1394 and USB adapter cards are typically very basic with little or no configuration options on the hardware level. From a software perspective, the cards will either come with specific drivers or rely on the drivers supplied with the operating system. For this reason, you should check that the correct drivers are either supplied for your OS or that they are downloadable from the Internet.

Within the operating system, the additional IEEE 1394 or USB ports provided by the card will appear as if they are standard system devices.

Portable Systems

Portable systems present their own unique troubleshooting problems because in general they are all proprietary. That is to say that you generally can't just go to your local computer store and buy replacement parts off the shelf. Generally speaking, replacement parts have to be specially ordered, and they are normally only available through an authorized dealer.

PCMCIA

PCMCIA cards are designed to be rugged devices, making them very reliable. Because PCMCIA cards can be plugged and unplugged while the system is powered on, the main problems that you will experience with PCMCIA cards are related to drivers or the detection process by the OS.

The biggest problem with PCMCIA cards is that not all cards are supported by all OSs. You need to be very careful with PCMCIA cards, especially if you are trying to use an older PCMCIA card with an older OS such as Windows 9x. If you are buying a new card and using a current or recent OS, you shouldn't have any problems but it is still worth checking.

Another thing to consider with PCMCIA cards is correct insertion. The card must be fully inserted in order to make the correct contact with the pins within the interface. Remember from Chapter 1 that PCMCIA cards come in a variety of sizes. You must ensure that you are using the correct card for the correct slot.

Batteries

One of the major differences between batteries and other components is that while other parts might continue operating indefinitely, batteries are guaranteed to fail sooner or later. Even though the modern battery technologies used in today's portable systems are designed to withstand irregular charging schedules, eventually their capacity to hold a charge will diminish to the point where they must be replaced.

> **Note**   Although software-configurable power schemes such as those found in Microsoft Windows might increase the usable time available on each charge, they generally don't improve the longevity of the battery.

In nearly all instances, batteries in a laptop must be replaced with a model-specific battery. For this reason, you will often have to order the battery through an authorized reseller. In certain cases you might be able to buy a generic replacement battery but this is becoming less and less common.

Before you replace a battery for a portable system, you should make sure that the battery is indeed the problem. Often your local electronics store will be able to check a battery to see if it is dead. There is nothing worse than spending upward of $100 on a new battery for your laptop only to find that it is the internal charger or some other related component that is the problem, and not the battery at all.

Docking Stations/Port Replicators

Like batteries, docking stations and port replicators are specific to the portable system that they were designed to be used with. Therefore, the first trouble-shooting step for these is to make sure that the correct docking station or port replicator is being used. Once this is determined, you can then move on to more specific considerations.

If you are experiencing a problem with a single function or peripheral, you should concentrate on determining that the correct settings are being used for that device and that any drivers are installed and configured. Because certain operating systems can be used in multiple configurations, often to cater specifically to docked/undocked configurations, you should make sure that the device is enabled in the current profile being used. If you have done all of this and you are still having problems with the device, you might need to turn your attention to the device itself.

If none of the devices or functions provided by the docking station or port replicator are available, you should concentrate on making sure that any external power connections are secure and that the connection between the portable system and the docking station are complete and correct. The interface between the docking station and port replicator may be difficult to see, making it necessary to feel" that the connection has been completed rather than seeing it. If this is the case, try removing the portable system from the docking station and reinserting it.

Finally, always consider that the docking station or port replicator adds an extra layer of complexity to the troubleshooting process. In the past we have encountered devices that simply will not work when connected to a docking station that would work if connected directly to the portable system. For that reason, you should always try a direct connection, thereby eliminating (or implicating) the docking station or port replicator as the source of the problem.

Troubleshooting Procedures and Best Practices

Ask 10 PC technicians about best troubleshooting practices, and you will no doubt get 20 different approaches. Fortunately, despite the range of strategies to PC repair and troubleshooting, there are some common threads. This section will outline the general troubleshooting procedures that you are likely going to follow when presented with a troubleshooting situation. Over time, you will find that it becomes second nature to perform these steps and you'll do so without really thinking about them.

Determine the Severity of the Problem

When repairing PCs, you'll find there are some problems that have a major impact on the user and what they need to do, and some problems that are at best an annoyance. A failed hard drive, for instance, is far more important than a sound card that doesn't work. PC technicians have to be able to tell the difference between the small stuff and the big, and that isn't always easy. When it comes to any PC repair, the first and foremost concern is whether there is any potential for a loss of data. Problems that fall into this category are malfunctioning backup devices, corrupt hard disks, or virus activity. Make no mistake, when it comes to problem severity, those related to losing data will always take precedence.

Note   Network users have a very different priority list. If their e-mail is down or their printer doesn't print, they will be more panicked than you would if your tape backup device has suddenly stopped working. Acknowledge users' frustration, but keep your priorities straight.

Gather Information Necessary to Isolate the Problem

One of the most important steps in troubleshooting a problem is actually finding the problem itself. Admittedly, this sounds like common sense, but the process of gathering information to make an accurate problem diagnosis is often over-looked. The only way to really get the information needed to isolate the prob-lem is to ask the right questions. For instance, if a user is complaining of data loss, appropriate questions can determine who is experiencing data loss, when is it happening, how frequently is it happening, and what exactly is meant by "missing" data. With these answers, it is possible to begin to isolate the cause. It is then possible to determine if the data loss is a result of human error, software error, or hardware error without ever touching a computer. Information gather-ing might seem like a waste of time, but in fact, it can significantly increase your efficiency in isolating the problem and can decrease the amount of time it takes to fix the problem.

Efficient information gathering is also about knowing where to find the information you need. To get the right information, there are three key sources to use: first, the user who reported the problem; second, the system itself; and third, your own senses.

Interviewing Users

PC technicians know that getting accurate information from a user can often be a very difficult endeavor. A nonprinting workstation or the inability to access a certain Web page will often be relayed to the administrator as "the computer is busted." Dig a little deeper into the problem, and you will get slightly more helpful input, including "I was just sitting here and it stopped working," or the ever popular "It was working fine yesterday, but today it doesn't."

Gathering information from users often requires finely tuned communica-tion and interpretive skills, and can resemble a game of charades more than a tech support session. It is important to remember that many users have limited technical knowledge and are quite happy with that. Your job is to glean as much information from them as you can, including the frequency of the problem, the applications being used, whether the problem has occurred in the past, whether they have modified the system in any way, and if there have been any error messages displayed (and if so, which ones).

Interpreting Computer Errors and Generated Logs

Computers and operating systems provide their information in the form of log files, alerts, and messages. Although it's helpful to have events documented, sometimes the logs and error codes can be as difficult to understand as the most confused user. For instance, your system could be experiencing trouble and reports the error code 513xx0067. Sometimes, it would be just as easy to rebuild the system as track down the error. Still, the information is there, and a call to the operating system support line, or a visit to the operating system manufacturer's Web site, with the log information in hand, can probably help you get the answer to your problem.

Using Your Senses

Never underestimate the power of your own senses to determine the cause of a problem. We are not talking about ESP here, but our five senses. If, upon entering a room, you notice that there is smoke coming from the computer, talking to users or checking logs might be an unnecessary step in the troubleshooting process. Visual inspections of equipment are often part of the PC technician's daily routine. Eyes, ears, and nose play an important role in isolating and preemptively troubleshooting a problem.

Tip Although a room full of users and customers can get very noisy, pay attention to the sounds of your equipment. Fans, for instance, will typically give a grating noise before they fail, giving technicians time to preemptively troubleshoot the issue.

Determine the Potential Cause or Causes

After the information is collected, you can begin to determine possible causes. Asking the appropriate questions can narrow the issue down to a few possible options; and after this is done, you can make a list of the potential problems and decide which ones should be tested first. As stated several times, it is a good idea to start with the easiest things first and work from there. For instance, if it is determined that a client computer cannot access the network, check the cabling before changing network settings, and before replacing the network card as well. Before all of those steps, verify that the computer is turned on; take nothing for granted. Often, even in the midst of a seemingly complex problem, the easiest solution is the right one.

Fix the Problem

After all of that, you are now ready to fix the problem. If all goes according to plan, the problem you have isolated is the cause, and its fix will be the remedy.

All too often, however, despite our best efforts, the fix does not work, and you have to start from step 1 and try again.

Note   One of the most important things to remember when troubleshooting is not to go into a panic mode. This can lead to a knee-jerk reaction, and you might find yourself fixing the wrong or a nonexistent problem.

Review and Document

Often neglected as a troubleshooting step, keeping records about the troubleshooting procedures along the way is perhaps one of the most vital aspects of any troubleshooting procedure. When documenting a troubleshooting procedure, be sure to write down each step you took and the result. Remember that it might not be you reading this documentation the next time something goes down, so make sure that the steps you took can be followed by someone else. In fact, assume that you are writing for someone else; this often encourages a little bit better writing.

Key Points

- Loopback plugs test the functioning of a port and work with many different port types.

- A system losing time and hardware settings might need to have the CMOS battery replaced.

- The BIOS might need to be upgraded if it cannot recognize new hardware.

- The POST process tests hardware and reports errors with beep codes, numeric error codes, and text messages.

- The computer case performs an important function in creating appropriate airflow through the computer.

- When a power supply fails, the system might be unable to start or it might spontaneously power down. Power supplies should be replaced and not fixed.

- Multimeters are devices used to verify the power to the system and individual components within the system.

- Slot covers are used to prevent dust from getting into the system and to manage airflow.

■ If a floppy drive LED stays lit or does not come on, verify that the drive has been correctly installed with a power connector and the floppy cable the right way.

■ Before troubleshooting hard drives, it is a best practice to first back up the data.

■ When troubleshooting SCSI devices, verify termination and cabling, and that each device is using a unique ID.

■ When troubleshooting IDE hard disks, ensure that the master/slave settings are correct and that the IDE cable is correctly attached.

■ Many systems now come with DVD or even DVD-RW drives. Troubleshooting procedures for these drives are similar to those of CD-ROM drives.

■ In addition to fans and heat sinks, liquid cooling systems are becoming available for PC systems. Processor failure is often a result of overheating or incorrect installation.

■ Some symptoms of memory failure include system hangs, page faults, and incorrectly identified memory size.

■ Memory failure is often caused by improper installation and handling of RAM chips.

■ When troubleshooting a possible memory error, replace memory with known working RAM to see if the problem is corrected.

■ When troubleshooting poor display quality, verify that the video card is using the latest video card driver.

■ Display errors can be a result of the monitor or video card. Swapping out the monitor with a known working one can help isolate the cause.

■ When a system's mouse fails, verify the cable connection and that there are no resource conflicts.

■ Touch screens have an additional connection that carries the signal for the input back to the computer, normally through the serial port.

■ For nonfunctioning audio, look for resource conflicts, verify the drivers used, and check that the device is properly cabled.

■ When troubleshooting modems, verify cabling and modem drivers, and that there are no resource conflicts.

■ Slow modem speeds might be caused by incorrect drivers, line noise, or incorrect settings.

■   The AT command set is used to test and verify the modem's operation.

■   Batteries in portable systems do not last indefinitely. They must normally be replaced with model-specific units.

■   Many operating systems can accommodate hardware profiles for docked and undocked configurations.

■   Troubleshooting is a systematic process involving several steps, including determining the severity of a problem, gathering information about the problem, identifying potential causes of the problem, fixing the problem, and documenting the problem.

Chapter Review Questions

1   You have been called to troubleshoot a keyboard problem where the system halts during the POST process and indicates that a keyboard is not connected. You verify the connection and then swap out the keyboard for a known working one. The problem still exists. Which of the following is most likely the cause of the problem?

a)   Resource conflict

b)   BIOS needs to be updated

c)   Keyboard cable is faulty

d)   Onboard keyboard controller is faulty

Answer d is correct. If you swap out one keyboard for a known working one and the keyboard is still not detected, this indicates a problem with the keyboard controller. Such errors are rare but are seen occasionally. Answer a is incorrect because a resource conflict would not be evident that early in the boot process and the keyboard has default resources assigned to it. Answer b is incorrect because the current BIOS must be able to detect primary components such as the keyboard. Answer c is wrong because a known working keyboard was used.

2   Which of the following must you confirm when troubleshooting SCSI hard drives? (Choose three.)

a)   Termination

b)   Master/slave setting

c)   SCSI ID on each hard disk

d)   Cable connections

Answers a, c, and d are correct. When troubleshooting SCSI hard disks, you might need to verify that the SCSI bus is properly terminated, that each hard disk has a unique SCSI ID, and that the cables are correctly and securely attached. Answer b is incorrect as master/slave settings are used with IDE hard disks.

3 Your system displays an error code message of 301 when the system is booted. What does the 301 error message relate to?

a) Floppy drive controller

b) Memory

c) Keyboard

d) Hard drive controller

Answer c is correct. If the POST process halts with a 301 error message, it has detected a problem with the keyboard. Most often this means that the keyboard is not properly connected. Answer a is incorrect; the floppy drive controller would give an error message in the 600 range, typically error code 601. Answer b is wrong as memory errors are in the 200 error code range. Answer d is wrong as hard drive error codes are in the 1700 numeric error code range.

4 You have just installed a new serial mouse on your computer but now you find that the system freezes when the modem is used. What is the likely cause of the problem?

a) The system does not support a serial mouse.

b) The serial mouse and modem are using the same IRQ address.

c) The serial mouse and modem are using the same expansion slot.

d) The modem drivers need to be updated.

Answer b is correct. If two components are using the same resources such as an IRQ address, one or both of the components might fail to function. Answer a is not a valid answer. Answer c is incorrect as two devices cannot physically share an expansion slot. Answer d is incorrect. The drivers might need to be updated, but if a device stops working after another is added, the most likely cause is a conflict with the newly installed device.

5 You attempt to retrieve files copied to a floppy disk on another system from your system's floppy drive and an error message is displayed indicating that the floppy disk is not formatted. Which of the following steps are you most likely going to perform?

a) Try a different floppy disk.

b) Replace the floppy drive.

c) Format the floppy disk.

d) Verify that the floppy cable is not inserted backwards.

Answer a is correct. If a floppy drive cannot read a floppy disk, the first thing to try is using a known working floppy disk. This eliminates the disk itself as a cause of the problem. Answer b is incorrect; it might be necessary to replace the floppy drive itself but only after failed floppies have been ruled out as the cause of the error. Answer c is incorrect as formatting the floppy disk would cause you to lose the data on it. Also, as you have just copied data to the disk on another system, you know that the floppy disk is OK and does not need to be formatted. Answer d is incorrect; if the floppy cable is inserted backwards, the LED would stay lit and the drive would be inaccessible.

6 You have installed a new modem but the modem seems slow when used. Which of the following would explain the modem's speed? (Choose two.)

a) The modem is using the wrong or old drivers.

b) There is a resource conflict with the modem and another device.

c) The phone line is already being used.

d) There is noise on the telephone line.

Answers a and d are correct. If the modem is using older or the wrong device drivers, the modem might not function as it should. To verify, check the manufacturer's Web site to ensure that the correct ones are being used. Noise on the telephone line and a weaker signal can also affect the speed at which a modem operates. Answer b is incorrect as a resource conflict would likely cause the modem to fail altogether and not reduce its speed performance. Answer c is incorrect because if the phone line were already being used it would not be possible to dial out with the modem.

7 You enter a room and notice that a computer is making a loud grinding noise. Which of the following two components would you suspect might be failing?

a) Power supply fan

b) CPU fan

c) Memory

d) Monitor

Answers a and b are correct. If you hear a louder than normal grinding noise from a computer system, you will need to check both the power supply and CPU fans. Both will typically make noise when failing. Answers c and d are incorrect as neither of these will make a noise when failing.

8 A user calls you and complains that their computer is running poorly and many applications no longer function correctly. After asking the user, you determine that they have recently installed a program from the Internet. Which of the following are you most likely to suspect as the cause of the problem?

a) Failing hard drive

b) Dead CMOS battery

c) Computer virus

d) Power surge

Answer c is correct. In this scenario, the first area to explore would be to verify that the system does not have a virus. It might be that the program downloaded from the Internet has been infected with a virus and is adversely affecting the entire system. Answer a is incorrect. A failing hard drive could cause the symptoms identified in the question; however, because an application was recently added from the Internet, the first step would be to rule out virus activity. Answer b is incorrect as a dead CMOS battery would not create the problems identified in this question. Answer d is incorrect. Although a power surge could cause errors, it would first be necessary to rule out virus activity.

9 Which of the following AT commands is used to hang up an active connection?

a) ATH

b) ATZ

c) ATB

d) ATV

Answer a is correct. The AT command ATH is used to hang up an active modem connection. Answer b is incorrect as the ATZ command is used to reset the modem. Answers c and d are not valid AT commands.

10 You are troubleshooting a computer that does not display anything on its monitor. You suspect that the monitor might be faulty. Which of the following troubleshooting steps would you first perform?

a) Verify that the operating system recognizes the video card.

b) Swap out the monitor with a known working one.

c) Swap out the video card with a known working one.

d) Verify in the POST process that the monitor is detected.

Answer b is correct. If you suspect that a monitor has failed, the quickest way to determine if this is the case is to swap out the monitor with a known working one. If the new monitor works, the problem was likely the old monitor. Answer a is wrong because it would not even be possible to view the OS if the monitor were faulty. Answer c is incorrect as swapping out the video card would not address a problem of a faulty monitor. Answer d is also wrong because you would not be able to troubleshoot or even see the POST process results if the monitor were faulty.

11 One of the computers you are working on has a failed processor. Which of the following are likely causes? (Choose two.)

a) Overclocking the memory

b) Overclocking the CPU

c) Incorrect BIOS settings

d) Failed processor fan

Answers b and d are correct. If a processor is overclocked or if the CPU fan fails, the processor can burn out and need to be replaced. Answer a is incorrect as it is not possible to overclock the memory. Answer c is incorrect as incorrect BIOS settings will not cause the processor to fail.

12 You are working on a computer system that inexplicably shuts down. Which of the following might explain the problem?

   a)   Failed monitor

   b)   Failed peripheral device

   c)   Incorrect master/slave jumper settings

   d)   Faulty power supply

Answer d is correct. When a power supply is unable to provide consistent power to the system, it might simply turn itself off without apparent cause. The solution is to replace the power supply. Answers a, b, and c are incorrect as none of these answers would cause a system to periodically shut down or reboot.

13 You are troubleshooting a floppy drive and determine that the LED on the drive stays on. What is the cause of the problem?

   a)   Installation of floppy drive

   b)   Faulty floppy drive

   c)   Resource conflict

   d)   This is normal operation for a floppy drive

Answer a is correct. If the LED on a floppy drive stays lit, the most likely cause is that the floppy drive cable has been incorrectly installed. Most often, the cable has been attached to the floppy drive in reverse. Answers b, c, and d would not cause the floppy drive's LED to stay lit.

14 Which of the following components is associated with the 600–699 numeric error code range?

   a)   Hard drives

   b)   Motherboard

   c)   Floppy drives

   d)   Memory

Answer c is correct. Floppy drive errors are associated with the 600-699 error code number range. Answer a is incorrect as color monitors are associated with the 500-599 numeric error code range. Answer b is incorrect; motherboards are associated with the 100-199 range. Answer d is wrong as memory-related errors are reported in the 200-299 error code range.

15 You have just installed a new 15-GB hard drive but it is not recognized by the BIOS. Which of the following troubleshooting steps would you perform? (Choose two.)

   a)   Check the master/slave jumper settings.

   b)   Check the physical cabling.

c) Replace the CMOS battery.

d) Run ScanDisk or Check Disk on the hard disk.

Answers a and b are correct. If you have just installed a new hard disk and it is not recognized by the BIOS, you will need to verify that the hard drive has been correctly installed. This requires that the physical cable connections and the master/slave jumper settings are correct. Answer c is incorrect as a failed CMOS battery would not prevent the BIOS from detecting an installed hard drive. Answer d is incorrect as it would not be possible to access the hard disk to run ScanDisk or Check Disk unless it is recognized by the system.

16 You are interviewing a computer user to help isolate a problem. Which of the following questions are you going to need to ask? (Choose two.)

a) How long have you owned the computer?

b) Where was the computer purchased?

c) What applications were being used when the problem occurred?

d) Have there been any recent changes to the system?

Answers c and d are correct. When trying to isolate a problem, it would be very helpful to know what was being done with the computer when the error occurred and whether there have been any recent changes to the system that might have caused the problems. The other questions listed would not provide any valuable insight into the problem.

17 Recently your computer has periodically been displaying a CMOS checksum error when the system starts. What would explain this error?

a) Faulty memory

b) Invalid CMOS memory

c) Incorrect CMOS version

d) Failing CMOS battery

Answer d is correct. When a CMOS battery begins to fail, a CMOS checksum error message is sometimes displayed during boot-up. All of the others are invalid.

18 Which of the following tools can you use to test a computer's serial port?

a) POST card

b) Loopback plug

c) Serial inspector

d) Serial online cable

Answer b is correct. Loopback plugs are devices that can be easily used to test the functionality of the serial port. All other answers are invalid.

19 Which of the following are reasons to ensure that slot covers are used? (Choose two.)

a)   To prevent UV damage to internal components

b)   Improve airflow within the case

c)   Keep dust out

d)   To reduce susceptibility to eavesdropping

Answers b and c are correct. The systems slot covers are best to keep in place to keep dirt and dust from getting inside the case and to help ensure that there is good airflow and cooling within the case.

20 You suspect that several components are not getting sufficient power. Which of the following tools are used to test the power connectors?

a)   Loopback plug

b)   Multimeter

c)   Anemometer

d)   Diameter

Answer b is correct. A multimeter is used to measure power output and can be used to diagnose correct operation of a power supply. Answer a is incorrect; a loopback plug is used to test operation of data ports and connections. Answer c is incorrect; an anemometer is a device used to measure wind. Answer d is invalid.

Chapter 3

An Ounce of Prevention...

Somebody much wiser than us once said that an ounce of prevention is worth a pound of cure. This is certainly true in the world of computers. Pound of cure aside, PC preventative maintenance is a little like eating healthy—we know it's a good thing but when no one is looking we put away the tofu and bran and find the nearest drive-thru. At the end of the day, seasoned computer technicians are well aware that a few moments spent cleaning, inspecting, and caring for computers can prevent hours spent replacing, troubleshooting, and repairing them. In fact, regular cleaning of our computer and peripherals will prolong the life of both.

Domain 3.0 of the CompTIA A+ objectives focuses on the products and procedures that we, as PC technicians, use as part of our preventative maintenance regimen. In addition, the objectives within this domain include topics on PC safety, including a discussion of the potential hazards when working with computer components such as lasers and high-voltage equipment. Both of these objective areas are addressed in this chapter.

Preventative Maintenance Products

Walk into any grocery store today and you will be able to locate rows of shelf space dedicated to cleaning products and supplies. Some of these cleaning products are abrasive, some smell like lemon, and others claim to soften your hands while you scrub. Of the myriad products out there, which ones do we use to clean our computers? Do we need softer hands?

Some of these cleaners are obviously wrong for our needs. For example, we are unlikely to use silver polish to clean an LCD screen but would we use regular window cleaner? What's the best for getting bacon bits out of the keyboard or greasy fingerprints off a monitor? In this section we answer these questions and identify the products to use for cleaning computer components and even provide a little personal insight gleaned from a few mistakes we've made over the years.

Mean Time Between Failures You might hear someone refer to the fact that preventative maintenance can increase *mean time between failures* (MTBF). This well-used acronym is used to describe the average time a component is expected to work without failing. Finding the actual MTBF for some components such as keyboards and mice is difficult as they typically run for a long time. Other components such as hard disks, which comparatively speaking fail frequently, have published MTBF times so that you can use this information in your purchasing decisions.

Whether preventative maintenance really increases MTBF is a source of some debate. Some would say that preventative maintenance simply allows you to realize a product's full MTBF. Others would say that it extends it. Either way, for a given device there is no way to really know if your preventative maintenance steps make a difference.

Liquid Cleaning Compounds

Most of us are aware that computer systems and associated peripherals are sensitive devices; they do not like a lot of water and most cleaning products available. So what can we use?

Water and a Damp Cloth

In the high-tech world, one of the most often used cleaning supplies is the very nontechnical soapy water and lint-free damp cloth. Considering that the exterior of most computers and peripherals is plastic or metal, a damp cloth and a little soapy water are just great for cleaning these surfaces. There are a few caveats here, however. The cloth must only be damp and not wet. The last thing you want to do is spill drops of water onto the actual components of the system. Before wiping down the outside of components, you need to unplug them. Water and electricity don't mix. Finally, the water and damp cloth solution is for cleaning the exteriors of devices only, not the internal components. There are better "solutions" for those.

Denatured (Isopropyl) Alcohol

For cleaning the inside of some components such as floppy drives, or more specifically floppy drive heads, we can use a little alcohol. The cleaning solution is typically applied with a lint-free swab directly to the heads. When we say lint-free swab, we don't mean a regular cotton swab, as often the cotton itself can jam up the very components we are trying to clean.

Even with denatured alcohol moderation is the key. You will find that when cleaning components, you only need a little alcohol on the swab. One caveat with alcohol is to not clean moving parts within components that use lubricants, such as the gears and drive motors in CD-ROMs, floppy drives, and printers. For many of these, the alcohol will clean off the lubricants that need to be there.

Regular Glass Cleaner

One of the first impulses when cleaning some computer components is to reach for the glass cleaner. In truth, glass cleaner has limited application for cleaning computer equipment. Its use should be restricted to cleaning the display screen of a CRT monitor. Glass cleaner should never be used to clean an LCD screen; it can eat right through it!

Test Smart   Regular glass cleaner should never be used to clean LCD displays.

In terms of liquid cleaners, water, denatured alcohol, and glass cleaner are all you will really need. The trick then is deciding which of these cleaners to use with which component. To give you some idea, we will look at some common computer components and peripherals and what it takes to clean them.

Warning   It is a best practice to make sure the computer component or peripheral device you are cleaning is unplugged before cleaning. This includes everything from mice to monitors and keyboards.

■   **Mouse**   The average mouse is a virtual playground for all manner of germs and bacteria. The outside of the mouse can often be cleaned using a little elbow grease and a damp and soapy cloth. On the inside, some people recommend using an eraser to clean the mouse ball. This is a double-edged sword; it can clean the ball but it has an abrasive effect and can cause small canyons on the surface of the ball and change its shape. As you can imagine, this affects the proper functioning of the mouse. A better solution is to once again use a damp cloth to wipe off the mouse ball. This should be enough to get it clean and smooth off the surface. Do not soak the mouse ball, and make sure it is dry before putting it back in its home. To clean the inside of the mouse, we would not suggest using any liquid cleaners. If the rollers on the inside are dirty, the dirt on them can be gently scraped off. In addition, a can of compressed air can be used to blow out the dust and dirt. Regular maintenance on mice can greatly prolong their life but if you find yourself working in an environment where you are supporting hundreds of computers, this can be a time-consuming task. Given the relatively low cost of mice, in some cases it might be easier just to replace the mouse with a new one if it starts giving you trouble.

■ **Keyboard**   The keyboard probably needs to be cleaned more than any other computer component. Most experts (if there is such a thing as a keyboard cleaning expert) suggest using distilled water to clean the surface areas of the keyboard. Using only distilled water is an important consideration as any soap or iron in the regular water can cause as many problems as it cures. We have seen some people completely soak their keyboards in distilled water and have them function normally afterward. Such an approach might work well on older, $20 keyboards, but the newer, more advanced, and more expensive keyboards require a bit more TLC. The underside of the keys can often be cleaned using just a can of compressed air. You will be surprised by what comes flying out from underneath those keys. The keyboard's surface areas typically require little more than a damp, lint-free cloth using a little distilled water. Some spills such as coffee or other liquids might require that you remove keys to get underneath them to clean. Spills such as cola, which can leave your keys sticky and nonfunctioning, might require that the keyboard be soaked in distilled water, which is OK because at this point you really do not have anything to lose. The best preventative advice we can offer on preventing spills is simply to never drink liquids around the keyboard. One important thing to remember when cleaning a keyboard is to ensure that it is completely dry before reconnecting it to the computer. This can sometimes take more than 48 hours.

 Test Smart   When cleaning keyboards, ensure that they are first disconnected from the computer and completely dry before using them again.

■ **Monitor**   If keyboards are the device we clean the most, monitors have to be a close second. Most often the display screen is simply dusty and all that is needed is to wipe the display with a lint-free cloth. For stains or spills, the best way to go is regular glass cleaner, provided, as we mentioned earlier, that it is not being used on an LCD screen. If you are using a spray cleaner, it's best not to spray the cleaner directly on to the monitor. Instead, first squirt it onto a lint-free cloth and then use that. To make things a little easier, you can also purchase presoaked antistatic cleaners that resemble little towelettes. These do a great job of removing the dust from the display. The outside of the monitor can be cleaned using a damp cloth and the vents can be cleaned using some compressed air. As mentioned earlier, to prevent water from getting inside the vents, do not use a cloth that is too wet. Again, the monitor must be unplugged before any cleaning can take place.

Warning   Do not clean the monitor while it is plugged in! Be sure the monitor is disconnected from the PC and unplugged from the electrical outlet before cleaning.

■   **LCD monitor**   The first rule of thumb is to never allow any moisture to get into your LCD monitor. If you notice moisture on your screen, wipe it off gently with a soft cloth before powering on your monitor. If for some reason moisture has managed to get into the LCD monitor, leave the monitor in a warm area until the water has had a chance to evaporate. As with CRT monitors, LCD screens are often as easy to clean as wiping them with a lint-free cloth. If you do need to rub off a stain or other such blemish, you can use a small amount of distilled water on a lint-free cloth and wipe the stain, but only when the LCD screen is completely off. Do not apply too much pressure to the screen—doing so can damage the interior of the panel.

Test Smart   If you power up an LCD monitor with moisture in it, the electrodes can become corroded, leading to permanent damage.

■   **Floppy drive**   Floppy drives can quickly get full of dust, and over time this will cause them to fail or at the least not function as they should. The trick for floppy drives is a little denatured alcohol on a swab to clean the floppy drive heads. To remove the dust from inside a floppy drive, you might have to use a non-static vacuum (discussed later in this chapter) or a few shots of compressed air. Like some of the other components discussed here, if the floppy drive refuses to work even after a cleaning, it might actually be more economical (though not as environmentally friendly) to replace the floppy drive with a new one.

Cleaning Contacts and Connectors

The computer itself is full of contacts and connectors that must be clean in order to function as they should. If dirt or grime gets on these connectors it can prevent a proper connection between devices, or the dust itself can cause *electrostatic discharge* (ESD). To be clear, the types of connectors and contacts we are talking about are those found on components such as expansion cards and memory modules.

See Also   *There is a more detailed discussion of ESD later in this chapter.*

If you ask around, you are certainly going to receive a number of different ideas for cleaning contacts and connectors. Some of these are valid, some are actually more damaging than leaving the dust on the connectors. The most accepted method of effectively cleaning contacts is to use a lint-free swab to rub a little denatured alcohol on the contact. This will certainly remove any dust and dirt and ensure that clean contact is made. If you are having periodic trouble with an expansion card or memory module, it might be worth your time to clean the contacts and see if the problem is resolved.

One of the more common methods used to clean contacts is to use an ordinary eraser. Erasers have been used to clean contacts as far back as we can remember and actually do a very poor job of it. The problem with erasers is that they often leave more residue than they remove, and the ever popular pink erasers have chemicals in them that can actually harm the contacts. If you are convinced that erasers are the way to go for cleaning contacts, ensure that you use a white eraser as it is less likely to cause damage than a pink one. Personally, we would recommend avoiding erasers and sticking with the denatured alcohol or specialized contact cleaning solutions, which can be purchased from electrical supply stores.

One final technique we should mention is using emery cloth, which is essentially a very fine sandpaper, not unlike the type used to file your fingernails. This can be used effectively to clean contacts and connectors. Care must be taken not to run the cloth over the circuit board itself, as this can damage it. Also, if you are using emery cloth, be sure to do only one or two strokes. Any more might actually start to erode the contacts.

Non-Static Vacuums

As mentioned earlier, dust is an enemy to computer systems. One of the tools you are likely to see used in the war against dust is a *non-static vacuum*. Non-static vacuums are seen in most PC repair shops and are used for sucking the dust out of the computer case, keyboard, power supplies, and even peripheral devices (not to mention the crumbs from lunch!). However, before running to the closet and grabbing the Electrolux, it should be pointed out that non-static vacuums are specifically designed for use with computers. Regular vacuums actually create a storm of static electricity and can damage the components you are trying to clean. Save those for the carpets.

Compressed Air

For those who are not fond of vacuuming, there is another method you can use to remove the dust from inside the computer case and peripherals—compressed air. Compressed air is sold in cans and, as a computer technician, having one or two cans in your toolkit is a definite must. The compressed air is well suited for cleaning fans, power supplies, and those hard-to-reach places. The biggest drawback with compressed air is that the dust is blown everywhere. The best method is to use compressed air on the outside of a device. Some technicians prefer to use their own compressed air by blowing on components. While this is not a terribly bad thing, human breath is moisture laden and so not ideal for this purpose.

Working with Power

Part of the role of the PC technician is to be aware of the environmental factors that might affect the functioning of a computer system. One of the more important environmental factors to be aware of is power. Several power conditions can cause problems. The most common of these include

- **Sag**   A drop in power supply that only lasts a short period, a *sag* is generally the most common type of power anomaly.

- **Brownout**   A *brownout* is a drop in supply voltage that lasts more than a few seconds.

- **Spike**   A *spike* is a sharp and very sudden increase in line voltage that pushes the supply voltage above an acceptable threshold.

- **Surge**   A *surge* is an unacceptably large increase in supply voltage that lasts longer than a spike. This condition is also known as a swell.

- **Noise** *Noise* is interference can cause the supply voltage to be inconsistent.

- **Blackout** A *blackout* is a complete failure in power supply.

Test Smart Before taking the A+ exam, ensure that you are familiar with the power conditions in the preceding list.

Any of the power threats in the previous list can cause a loss of data and even damage the computer equipment. Your role as a PC technician then becomes protecting computer systems from these threats. To do this we commonly use two types of devices, *uninterruptible power supplies* (UPS) and *surge suppressors*.

Warning Power-related problems are the single highest cause of data loss, an estimated 10 to 15 percent higher than computer viruses.

Uninterruptible Power Supplies

Part of the planning for potential power hazards will often include the installation of a UPS system. Our reliance on computer systems has meant that we must protect against all possible interruptions in service, and power is no exception. UPSs provide protection against fluctuations and loss in power, thereby allowing equipment to continue running.

What Is a UPS?

At its most basic, a UPS is simply a box that holds a battery, a built-in charging circuit, and an inverter. Its function is to power the computer in case of a power outage, and to provide sufficient time to allow a computer user to properly shut the system down and prevent data loss. Figure 3-1 shows a UPS in action.

Figure 3-1 A standard UPS system protects your equipment.

Note An *inverter* is a piece of electrical equipment that converts power from one format to another. In the case of UPS systems, the inverter is used to convert the power from the battery, which is DC power, into AC power, which is used by the connected equipment.

When the power supply is good, the battery is charged. When the power fails or does not meet requirements, the battery supplies power to the equipment connected to the UPS.

This description is true of an *offline* UPS, and though the UPS's function of supplying power to the computer might sound simple enough, today's UPS systems are far from simple devices. As well as providing protection from actual power outages, modern UPS systems come equipped with a host of other features as well as a variety of methods of monitoring power activity.

To ensure that connected equipment is not affected by a loss of power, offline UPS systems are designed to make the transfer between standard power and battery power very quickly. The actual interval is usually measured in milliseconds and is known as the transfer time. The power supplies of equipment connected to the UPS are sufficiently insensitive to not notice this very tiny interruption in power and so continue operating uninterrupted.

In contrast to offline UPS systems, today it is far more common to find *online* UPS systems with intelligent management features. Online UPS systems are more suited to use with sensitive equipment as they always supply power to connected equipment through the batteries. This provides two benefits. First, it means that in the case of a power failure, there is no transfer from main power to the UPS battery, eliminating the slim possibility that the connected equipment might not detect the switch or, even less likely, that the UPS might fail to switch over correctly. Second, the constant supply of power from the batteries in online UPS systems makes it is very easy to condition and regulate the power.

Smart or Dumb?   UPS systems are sometimes referred to as being smart or intelligent. That does not mean they are able to balance your checkbook; rather, they have the ability to supply information on their current state and configuration to an outside entity. The correct term is actually "intelligent," as the phrase SmartUPS is a registered trademark of American Power Conversion (APC), which is one of the largest manufacturers of computer UPS systems.

Information supplied by the UPS is passed to a management component, which might be a piece of custom software supplied by the UPS manufacturer, a software component built into a network operating system, or a special network management system. The communication between the UPS and the software can be achieved through a variety of means. Nowadays the most common method is via a special cable that is plugged into the UPS and the serial or USB port of the computer, though other methods such as direct network connection are increasingly becoming more popular.

Note   No one actually refers to UPS systems with no intelligence as dumb, although it would be kind of fun if they did!

Why Use a UPS?

The purpose of a UPS is relatively clear: it conditions and guarantees constant and good-quality power to computer components. This power quality is very important to computers because it addresses three main concerns:

- **Hardware damage**   Fluctuations in power can damage hardware components.

- **Data loss**   As well as damaging the physical hard disk, fluctuations in power can also damage data held on the drive. In addition to damage caused in this way, it is also worth remembering that modern network operating systems make extensive use of caching. Data is held in memory to speed up access, but only while that memory has power to it. Lose the power—lose the data.

- **Availability**   Possibly the most obvious use of a UPS is to guarantee that the system will be available even if there is no utility power.

Test Smart   If a system is not protected from power fluctuations by a device such as a UPS, both data and/or hardware can be damaged.

What Gets Connected?

Before plugging your computer and all peripherals into that UPS, there are a few things to bear in mind. The most important of these is that the UPS is powered by a battery. The more components that rely on the UPS, the shorter the time the battery can keep all of the equipment live. For this reason, you should typically plug only essential components into the UPS, like the CPU itself or those components that maintain the data. Components in general and especially laser printers are not well suited to being attached to the UPS as they draw too much power from the battery in the event of power failure. However, if the need arises, UPS manufacturers can advise on specific solutions that might be able to support this kind of high-draw device.

> **Note**   Some utilities and independent companies offer power-testing facilities for new and existing equipment. If the opportunity presents itself, having power checked in this way before connecting computer equipment to it is a wise move.

UPS Best Practices

UPSs are relatively low maintenance, but a UPS that receives no maintenance is likely to come back and haunt you—at exactly the wrong time. One of the most common assumptions about UPS systems is that the batteries last forever. They don't. If you think about it, it's not unreasonable. Rechargeable batteries in every other place we use them do not last forever, and UPSs are no exception. So, periodically, UPS batteries must be replaced and, although it's not a complicated procedure, special considerations must be used when disposing of used batteries.

In most cases, if you buy replacement UPS batteries from your UPS manufacturer they will accept your old batteries from you for safe disposal. If, for any reason, you can't take advantage of such disposal services, be sure to observe local ordinances and dispose of your used batteries in a safe and responsible manner. Although the actual battery life will normally be between four and six years, this can vary greatly depending on how the UPS is used.

Surge Suppressors

When it comes to power protection, the Cadillac device is certainly the UPS. However, many of us have Cadillac tastes on a Pinto budget and that's where surge suppressors come in. Surge suppressors are designed to help filter out power spikes and surges, and reduce line noise. Surge suppressors are not as versatile as a complete UPS solution; however, they are able to protect against everyday power-related problems. This makes them very useful in protecting nonessential systems from damage so you can reserve the expensive UPSs for protecting servers and the like.

The effectiveness of surge suppressors varies greatly, with the underlying rule being the more you pay, the better protection you have. The cheaper surge suppressors are really nothing more than a regular power bar with limited ability to handle spikes or surges. It really is a matter of getting what you pay for. Figure 3-2 shows an example of a surge suppressor.

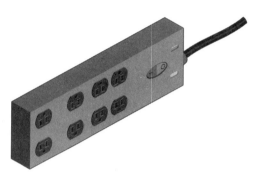

Figure 3-2 A surge suppressor is the minimum level of protection a computer should have against power irregularities.

Note   Surge suppressors are often bought as separate devices, although many UPSs have surge suppressors built in.

Test Smart   One big power spike can wipe out your surge suppressor. In case of an electrical storm, the surge suppressor might not be able to protect the system. Your best option is to unplug the PC and wait for calmer skies.

Storing Components for the Future

When you start to work with computers you will soon find out that you have plenty of spare hardware components lying around. These components often have to be reused and are invaluable for quickly fixing problems. To be effective, however, these components need to be in working order, and proper storage helps to ensure that they work as well as they did when you put them away.

The threats to computer hardware are the same when they are in the computer system as when they are out. These threats include water damage, ESD, and so on. When storing components such as expansion cards, we must also protect against these issues. The best way to store components such as memory, motherboards, or processors is to return them to their original packaging, as when they were shipped from the manufacturer—but how many of us actually have kept the original box and packaging? Not many. In lieu of the original packaging, components should be sealed inside antistatic bags. These bags will prevent the effects of ESD on stored components.

Once inside the ESD bag, it is best to store components in a cool dry place. Too much heat and too much moisture can be a huge problem as you are more likely to get electrostatic buildup in these conditions. If you are storing components such as hard disks or tape cartridges, it's best to keep them well away from magnetic sources and high-voltage devices. Follow these basic guidelines, and those older stored components will be as good as on the day you bought them.

Handling High-Voltage Equipment...or Not

Safety concerns are not always about those things that can happen to the computer; there are also threats to the technician. Most of the components we work with are more afraid of us than we are of them, but there are some key ones that deserve our utmost respect. These include the system's power supply and the CRT (cathode-ray tube) monitor.

Warning   If you ever work with high-voltage equipment, make sure that the device you are working on is unplugged and that you are not wearing antistatic straps. High-voltage equipment doesn't really concern itself with ESD, and the straps could actually attract voltage from high-voltage devices.

Monitors (CRTs)

Whenever a monitor doesn't work as it should, whether it is too blurry or displaying misplaced colorful lines down the center, there is a temptation to take the case off and fiddle around in an attempt to fix it. However, fiddling is never something you want to do inside monitors; there is high enough voltage inside to kill you—even after it has been unplugged!

Monitors use capacitors that retain a charge even after the device is unplugged. If you absolutely must work on a monitor, you will need to discharge it. The techniques for doing this fall outside the scope of the A+ objectives. Also, make sure the monitor is turned off before even attempting to take the cover off. The bottom line is that monitor repair is best left to those who really know what they are doing and are certified to do so.

Power Supplies

Like CRT monitors, power supplies use capacitors that maintain a charge long after they have been unplugged. This makes them as dangerous to work with as CRTs. The problem with power supplies is that they do fail from time to time and the temptation might be to save a few dollars and repair an old one. Don't be fooled; it isn't worth it. Unless you really know what you are doing, there is no need to work on a power supply. Most power supplies ship with large yellow warning stickers on them alerting you to the dangers. They are not there simply for decoration.

All power supplies have an internal fan in them, not unlike the fan used to cool processors. On occasion, this fan fails but the power supply is still OK otherwise. In such a case, many technicians choose to replace the fan and continue with the same power supply. Because the actual power supply case has to be removed to do this, it is recommended that even when a fan fails, the power supply be replaced.

 Test Smart   Even if only the power supply's fan fails, it is recommended that you replace the entire power supply and not the internal fan.

If you do find yourself holding a power supply with the case off, make sure that you do not have any ESD straps on and that the device is unplugged.

Warning   If you do find yourself working with a monitor or power supply, ensure that the power is disconnected and you are not wearing any anti-ESD devices.

Disposing of the Junk

We are constantly upgrading our computer components, from monitors to printers, but how much thought do we give to actually getting rid of that old equipment? Many of us don't really know how and end up storing those old monitors and printers somewhere around the house. There is a better way. In this section, we look at how to get rid of all that old equipment and in an environmentally friendly way, and in the process, you might even free up some shelf space in your house.

Monitors (CRTs)

Since the days of the XT 8088, 286/386, and 486 computers, there have been monitors needing to be thrown out. The problem with monitors is that they contain chemicals such as mercury and lead that can contaminate the soil. This greatly restricts where and how they can be disposed of.

There are a few ways to get rid of those older monitors. Perhaps the best is to check if there is a local organization that might need a donation. Some places will be more than happy to get a slightly used monitor to use, and this is a good way of recycling. Also, many communities have a hazardous waste program that can assist you by either taking your old monitor or giving you the name of someone who will. Unfortunately, it can be a bit of work to safely dispose of that old monitor but it is worth it. Such devices have no place in a landfill, and in many cities it is even illegal to dispose of old computer equipment in this way.

Batteries

Batteries are of course not unique to computer devices, but nonetheless it is important to dispose of them properly. The computer-related batteries we need to get rid of periodically include the UPS battery, laptop batteries, and even the battery on your motherboard. These batteries contain chemicals including mercury, lithium, and nickel-cadmium, all of which can and will contaminate water and soil. For this reason, they should not just be thrown out in a landfill site. To properly dispose of batteries, you need to follow local hazardous waste guidelines and most often take the batteries to a recycling depot. UPS batteries are of a particular concern and must be carefully disposed of as in many cases they are very large—some as large as truck batteries.

Toner Kits/Cartridges

Some companies go through toner kits and cartridges as fast as they go through coffee filters. Even the average home user can go through a few each month. The end result is millions of old toner kits and cartridges that have to be disposed of. Unfortunately, each of these old cartridges still has a little toner left in it that can contaminate soil and water. Moreover, the plastic and metal that they are made of can take thousands of years to decompose. The bottom line is that there is no room for these in a landfill site either.

Today, perhaps more to save money than for environmental concerns, many people are refilling toner and ink cartridges and reusing them. This form of recycling is very effective in terms of reducing the number of toner kits and cartridges being disposed of. However, there is a common complaint when using refilled cartridges. The print quality is often not as clear as with a new one, and refills can be harder on the printer than new cartridges. Still, for many companies and home users, refilling old cartridges is an ideal environmental solution, not to mention an effective way of saving money.

Many local print shops and even the manufacturer will often buy back or at least take used print cartridges and resell them. This is often the easiest method to get rid of them. Another option is to dispose of them according to local hazardous waste guidelines.

Chemical Solvents and Cans

There are not a huge number of chemical solvents and cans used in the computer world, but there are some, such as a used can of compressed air or xylene, which is sometimes used for cleaning rollers on dot matrix printers. When you do come across such chemicals and cans, you will need to dispose of these in a similar fashion as any other hazardous household product. Many local communities sponsor hazardous waste drop-off sites. These are ideal for disposing of old computer chemical solvents.

Material Safety Data Sheet

To help us decide how to dispose of harmful products and components, we have the *material safety data sheet (MSDS)*. An MSDS is a detailed document that contains instructions for handling, transporting, and disposing of particular products. MSDSs are often shipped with a product, such as a monitor, but if not, are generally available from the manufacturer. You can use your favorite Internet search engine to find an online MSDS. Alternatively, you can go to *www.msdssearch.com* to see a few sample MSDSs.

Electrostatic Discharge—Enemy Number 1

One of the acronyms you are likely going to encounter over and over when flipping through books that deal with PC hardware is ESD (electrostatic discharge). ESD is a natural enemy to computer hardware and protecting against the ESD threat is an important consideration for PC technicians.

What Is ESD?

Have you ever moon-walked across a nylon carpet and then opened the door? Of course you have. If the result was a spark between you and the doorknob, congratulations, you have achieved ESD. The spark that bridges the gap between your finger and the doorknob is static electricity, and it can damage almost every component in your PC. Even if you are not given to doing Michael Jackson impressions, just making normal movements or not moving at all can cause a static buildup in your body. The static keeps building until it can discharge itself into something made of metal. Examples include memory chips, hard drives, expansion cards, and just about every other component of a computer system.

Hidden ESD

One of the scariest aspects of ESD is that if a device or component receives an ESD charge, it might not—in fact, most usually will not—stop functioning immediately. Instead, it sits inside your computer, just waiting for the worst time to stop working. This is known as *degradation*, which refers to the fact that the effects of ESD are not felt right away but over time they get worse until the component fails. This delayed reaction to ESD is perhaps why people are not more careful when observing ESD precautions. If the results of ESD were more immediate, or more evident, perhaps everyone would be just a little more careful.

Hidden ESD can really make your life difficult, as a component could fail and troubleshooting could be very difficult. Of course the effects of ESD are not always subtle. Improper handling of a memory chip can immediately prevent the module from functioning, and you are left wondering if that new 256-MB RAM was faulty when you bought it or was handled wrong. When ESD causes the immediate malfunctioning of a component, it is called a *catastrophic* failure. Although the immediate failure of a device seems more dramatic, it is often better than the degradation of a component. In terms of troubleshooting at least, it makes things a bit easier.

Test Smart   Dust and other debris inside your computer case can cause a hidden ESD effect. Over time, the dust can hold a small electric charge and this will eventually begin to degrade the performance of internal components.

ESD Protection Devices

Over the years, there have been a number of methods designed to assist in the struggle against ESD. Different ones are used for different situations, but whenever hardware is handled, one of the following methods and products should be used.

- **ESD wrist strap**   *Antistatic wrist straps* are designed to filter out static charges and safely discharge them. An ESD wrist strap has a strap that fits around your wrist (bet you could have guessed that) and an attached cable. The cable attaches to an earth ground such as the grounding wire of a wall outlet. The cable uses a 1-mega-ohm resistor to negate the effects of ESD.

- **Antistatic mat**   For those that do not want to wear antistatic jewelry, you can use an *antistatic mat*. When you use an antistatic mat, the component you are working on is placed right on top of the mat. The function of the mat is to dissipate the charge of anything that might come into contact with it. Like the ESD wrist straps, ESD mats use a cable to attach to a grounding source. A variation on the antistatic mat is the antistatic floor mat. A technician would be required to stand on a floor mat to prevent ESD.

- **Antistatic spray**   You can also buy an *antistatic spray*; it's kind of like an antistatic deodorant. The function of antistatic spray is to remove the static effect from clothing. Antistatic spray is not as effective as the antistatic mats or wrist straps.

- **Antistatic bag** While most technicians choose not to use *antistatic bags*, they are worth another mention in this section. When working with components, it is best to leave them in their antistatic bags as long as possible. When not working with components, it is always best to leave them in their antistatic bags. Some people choose to take components out of their antistatic bags and place them on the outside of the bag when working on them. However, the outside of the bag offers no ESD protection.

Key Points

- Denatured alcohol is often used to clean floppy drive heads and contacts and connectors.

- Regular glass cleaner can be used to clean the display screen of a regular CRT monitor but never an LCD screen.

- The plastic or metal casing housing computer equipment is best cleaned using a damp cloth and a little soapy water.

- Computer equipment should be completely turned off and unplugged before cleaning. It should not be plugged back in again until it is completely dry.

- The most accepted method of cleaning contacts and connectors is to use a lint-free swab and denatured alcohol.

- Non-static vacuums are specialized vacuums designed for cleaning the inside of computer equipment and peripheral devices.

- Compressed air is often used to blow dust out of the computer case or other hard-to-reach areas—on the computer, that is.

- Computers are susceptible to a variety of power-related problems including sags, spikes, surges, brownouts, noise, and blackouts.

- UPSs use a battery to keep computer equipment functioning in the event of a power failure.

- UPSs can be offline, with no management features, and online, offering a full range of management capabilities.

- Non-mandatory equipment such as monitors and laser printers should not be connected to the UPS.

- Surge suppressors are designed to filter out power spikes and surges.

- Electrical storms can damage a surge suppressor. In the event of an electrical storm, unplug all computer equipment.

- Components should be stored in their original packaging or in anti-static bags.

- High-voltage equipment such as monitors and power supplies use capacitors and should be left to professionals.

- Computer equipment should be disposed of using local hazardous waste guidelines and not in the landfill.

Chapter Review Questions

1 Which of the following are you most likely going to use to clean a mouse ball?

a) Compressed air

b) Damp, soapy cloth

c) Denatured alcohol

d) Eraser

Answer b is correct. The best way to clean a mouse ball is with a little soapy water and a lint-free damp cloth. It is important not to replace the ball until it is completely dry. Answer a is incorrect; compressed air might be able to blow a bit of dust from the surface of the ball but the soapy water can get the surface of the ball cleaner. Answer c is incorrect as the denatured alcohol can harm the mouse ball. Answer d is incorrect as an eraser can change the shape of the mouse ball.

2 You have decided to repair your own monitor. Before starting to work, which of the following must you ensure you do? (Choose two.)

a) Unplug the monitor.

b) Discharge the monitor.

c) Wear an antistatic device such as an ESD wrist strap.

d) Refer to the MSDS.

Answers a and b are correct. Before working on a monitor, you have to make sure that it is unplugged and that you have discharged it. Remember that the CRT monitor uses capacitors that maintain a charge even after the device is unplugged. Answer c is incorrect; you should never wear an antistatic device when working on high-voltage equipment. Answer d is incorrect; the MSDS is a document that provides information on disposing of equipment, not fixing equipment.

3   You hear on the news that there is going to be an electrical storm. What is the best way to protect your computer?

a)   Attach a surge suppressor.

b)   Place the computer on an ESD mat.

c)   Attach a grounding wire between the computer and ground on the wall outlet.

d)   Unplug the computer system.

Answer d is correct. In the case of an electrical storm, it is best to unplug all of the components from the wall socket. This includes all cables, even the modem. Answer a is incorrect as in the event of an electrical storm the surge suppressor might not be able to protect the device and might be damaged in the attempt. Answer b is incorrect, as an antistatic mat will not help electrical surges from a storm. Answer c is incorrect, as attaching grounding wires anywhere would not help in the event of a storm.

4   Which of the following components are you most likely to connect to a UPS system?

a)   Laser printer

b)   Monitor

c)   CPU tower

d)   Bubble jet printer

Answer c is correct. A UPS system is powered by a battery, and the less equipment attached, the less power is drawn from the battery in a power failure. With this in mind, the most critical components to hook up to the UPS are those that maintain the data, such as the CPU tower itself. Answers a, b, and d are incorrect; monitors and printers draw too much power from the UPS and are not mission critical in terms of availability.

5   You have two old monitors stacked up in your garage. What is the proper way to dispose of them? (Choose two.)

a)   Donate them.

b)   Try to repair them and sell them.

c)   Follow the instructions as presented by the manufacturer's MSDS.

d)   Dispose of them in the local landfill.

Answers a and c are correct. A good way of recycling old computer equipment is to donate it to someone else who can use it. Failing that, you should follow the instructions provided in the MSDS to ensure safe disposal. Answer b is not correct. Monitors hold very high charges and should not be repaired unless you have received specialized specific training that allows you to do so safely. Answer d is not correct. Monitors contain numerous chemicals and pollutants that make them unsafe, and often illegal, for disposal in a landfill.

6   Which of the following best describes a sag?

a)   A drop in power supply that only lasts a short period

b)   A sharp and very sudden increase in line voltage that pushes the supply voltage above an acceptable threshold

c)   A drop in supply voltage that lasts more than a few seconds

d)   Complete power failure

Answer a is correct. A sag is a short drop in power that can often cause the computer to reboot. Answer b is incorrect; a spike is a sharp and very sudden increase in line voltage. Answer c is incorrect; this describes a brownout. Answer d is incorrect as it describes a blackout.

7   You need to clean the inside of the computer case. Which of the following are you likely to use?

a)   Non-static vacuum

b)   Compressed air

c)   Denatured alcohol

d)   Breath

Answers a and b are correct. Both non-static vacuums and compressed air are safe and effective ways to clean the insides of a computer system. Answer c is not correct. Denatured alcohol is used for cleaning components such as the read/write heads of floppy drives, not for cleaning the inside of computer systems. Answer d is incorrect. Human breath contains moisture, which does not make it ideal for cleaning inside of computer systems.

8   Which of the following can a UPS *not* provide?

a)   Short-term power to components

b)   Protection against power sags

c)   Long-term power to components

d)   Protection against power spikes

Answer c is correct. A UPS is powered by a battery and therefore cannot supply long-term power to components. The function of the UPS is to provide the time necessary to shut the system down cleanly and potentially save data and hardware. Answers a, b, and d are functions that a UPS can provide.

9   Why would you choose to use a vacuum designed for computers
rather than a regular vacuum?

   a)   Computer vacuums are cheaper.

   b)   Computer vacuums are specifically designed for dust.

   c)   Computer vacuums have less ESD.

   d)   Computer vacuums are smaller.

Answer c is correct. Computer vacuums are specifically designed to clean without producing harmful ESD. Answers a, b, and d are not valid.

10   Which of the following best describes an online UPS?

   a)   Online UPSs last longer than offline UPSs.

   b)   Online UPSs always filter in power to components.

   c)   Online UPSs are cheaper.

   d)   Online UPSs produce less ESD.

Answer b is correct. Online UPS systems always filter a bit of power to components and in case of
power failure, components can automatically shift to battery power. This is not true of offline UPSs.
Answers a, c, and d are invalid and not necessarily true of online UPS systems.

11   Which of the following would be methods used to clean contacts and
connectors?

   a)   Emery cloth

   b)   Eraser

   c)   Denatured alcohol

   d)   Soapy water

Answers a and d are correct. Both an emery cloth and a little denatured alcohol on a lint-free swab
are acceptable methods of cleaning contacts and connectors. Answer b is incorrect because erasers often leave as much residue as they clean off. Answer d is incorrect; water is never good to use
on or near electrical circuitry.

12   Which of the following best describes a power brownout?

   a)   A sharp and very sudden increase in line voltage that pushes the
supply voltage above an acceptable threshold

   b)   An unacceptably large increase in supply voltage that lasts longer
than a spike. This condition is also known as a swell

   c)   A drop in supply voltage that lasts more than a few seconds

   d)   Interference that causes the supply voltage to be inconsistent

Answer c is correct. A brownout is a drop in the voltage supply that lasts more than a few seconds. Brownouts are a common problem in many areas. Answer a is incorrect; this describes a power spike. Answer b is incorrect as this describes a power surge. Answer d is incorrect as this describes power noise.

13 Which of the following would you install to manage power surges?

a) Online UPS

b) Line suppressor

c) UPC system

d) Surge suppressor

Answers a and d are correct. A line conditioner or an online UPS system can be used to filter out power surges. Answers b and c are not valid power devices.

14 Which of the following are not a commonly found antistatic measure?

a) Antistatic mats

b) Antistatic collars

c) Antistatic wrist straps

d) Antistatic floor mats

Answer b is correct. Antistatic collars are not commonly used antistatic measures. Answers a, c, and d—antistatic mats, wrist straps, and floor mats—are all commonly used in the war against ESD.

15 A user calls you to tell you that her PC has "gone quiet," but is still running. Upon investigation, you determine that the fan in the power supply is no longer running. What should you do?

a) Replace the fan.

b) Do nothing—the system will run adequately with just the passive cooling features.

c) Replace the power supply.

d) Reverse the polarity of the fan so that the motor runs in the opposite direction.

Answer c is correct. Even though fans in power supplies can be replaced, the power supply enclosure has components that can give you an electric shock. Therefore, you should not replace the fan unless you have received specialized training that allows you to do so. Answer a is incorrect for the same reason noted in the explanation of answer c. Answer b is incorrect. Power supplies must be cooled to run effectively. Answer d is not valid. Reversing the polarity would cause the fan to spin in the opposite direction, if it were working, which it is not.

Chapter 4

Motherboards, Processors, and Memory

There are so many different computer components and peripherals that, as a PC technician, you may never work with all of them. There are, however, those core components that you will have to work with no matter how hard you try to avoid it. Three of these components are the motherboard, processor, and memory. In this chapter, we take a look at each of these components, including what they are designed to do and how they are configured. There is a lot of ground to cover when discussing these components, so sit back, grab a snack, and let's get started.

Processors

Processors have been described as everything from the heart of the computer to the brains and pretty much every other vital organ in between, excluding possibly the liver and the kidney, which are more likely going to refer to a field replaceable unit. Regardless of the analogy you wish to use to describe the processor, the fact is that without it the computer will not function and without the correct processor, the computer will not function as well as it should. As an A+

technician, you will be expected to know which processors are used in a particular situation and the characteristics of the various processors available today.

Processor Characteristics

When discussing processors, there are many acronyms and terms you will need to have a handle on to make sense out of the discussion. To combat unnecessary confusion and frustration, we thought it a good idea to explain a few of the concepts surrounding processors before jumping right in. You can expect to see these terms in the actual A+ exam.

Processor Packaging

Processors are "packaged" and shipped in a variety of different form factors. This doesn't refer to how the chip is transferred through the mail—instead, it refers to the physical construction of the chip. If you have ever had the opportunity to open up a few computer cases, you have no doubt already noticed this. Of the available form factors, the most commonly used today are the *pin grid array (PGA)* processor packaging and the *Single Edge Contact Cartridge (SECC)*.

   PGA packaging is no doubt the one you are most familiar with and the most widely used. PGA chip packaging can be easily identified, as PGA processors are rectangular with hundreds of tiny metal pins on the bottom. Most PGA processors plug directly into the motherboard using zero-insertion force (ZIF) sockets. ZIF sockets typically have a metal arm on one side used to clamp the processor down in place. PGA processors have to be carefully aligned to fit into the ZIF sockets to prevent bent pins, which could damage the processor. Figure 4-1 shows a variety of PGA processors.

Figure 4-1 PGA processors

   Another type of processor packaging is the SECC or *Single Edge Processor Package (SEPP)*. As the name suggests, the SECC processor package is a cartridge processor and, in appearance, is similar to the game cartridges used with

Nintendo 64, just a little wider and a whole lot more expensive. The processor itself in a SECC package is concealed within a protective plastic cover; all you see are the markings on the outside of the case and the contacts that connect into the motherboard. The difference between the SECC and SEPP packaging is that a SEPP package does not have a protective plastic cover as does the SECC. SEPPs are associated with Intel's Celeron processors and of the two, SECC is now more common.

Introduced with Intel's Pentium II range of processors, the SECC processor does not use pins and ZIF sockets—instead, it is mounted into its own integrated circuit board or "slot" on the motherboard. Cartridges are plugged into the motherboard in a similar fashion as a regular expansion card. Figure 4-2 shows a SECC processor.

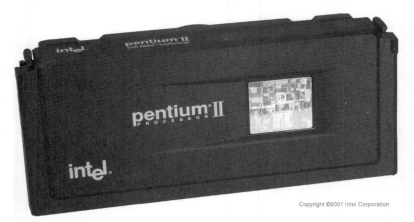

Copyright ©2001 Intel Corporation

Figure 4-2 SECC processor

Processor Sockets and Slots

When it comes time to install a new processor, the issue of sockets and slots will arise. In a perfect world, processors and their motherboard sockets would always be a match; unfortunately, this is not a perfect world. The past few years have seen the introduction of many new processor types and new sockets in which they fit. Before purchasing that new high-speed processor, it is best to see if the motherboard provides the correct socket or slot type.

The physical differences between sockets and slots are quite evident. Sockets, typically referred to as ZIF sockets, are recognized by their numerous holes, which align with the pins on the bottom of a compatible processor. The lever on the side of the socket is then used to secure the processor in place. There are a few variations in socket design, but the look of the socket remains primarily the same. Socket 7, used by the original Pentium-class computers, featured 321 pins;

the Pentium Pro socket uses a 387-pin design. Those hoping to put their new Pentium Pro processor in a socket 7 are going to have some difficulty.

Note   Remember, the Z in ZIF stands for "zero." If you are breaking a sweat installing a ZIF processor, something is not right.

For the most part, Intel has favored the socket and slot form-factor designs. AMD, all the way to the recent AMD K6-III, continues to utilize the original socket 7 form factor. With the introduction of the Athlon processor, however, AMD finally broke free of socket 7 and started using the Socket A design. Figure 4-3 shows a standard socket 7 form factor and compatible processor.

Figure 4-3 Socket 7 form factor and compatible processor

Slot form factors are entirely different from the socket design. Slots are associated with the cartridge type of processor, though many are not restricted to using only cartridges. Sometimes, a slot-to-socket adapter (SSA) is used in place of a cartridge processor and accommodates the socket-type processors.

The original slot connector, appropriately named Slot 1, was first introduced with the Pentium II processor, which was shipped in the SECC processor package.

Note   To confuse things, the Slot 1 receptacle is often referred to as the Single Edge Contact or SEC. So, if at some point you are asked to plug a SECC into a SEC, you heard correctly.

Since the development of the Slot 1 SEC, a new slot has been designed, Slot 2. Slot 2 is used for higher-end Pentium II processors, Pentium III processors, and for Intel's server-class Xeon processors. Intel's new Itanium processors provide a new slot form factor, Slot M. As you read through the descriptions of the various processors, pay close attention to the sockets they use. This material will most certainly appear on the A+ exam. Figure 4-4 shows the Slot 1 connector and compatible processor.

Figure 4-4 Slot 1 form factor and compatible processor

Processor Cache

When you go to buy a computer system, it is not uncommon to hear the salesperson boast that the computer they are trying to sell has a Pentium-class processor with 512 KB of level 2 cache. Such claims are often met with a blank stare and a shrug of the shoulders—by both the person buying the computer and the person selling it. So what exactly is processor caching?

In very simple terms, a cache is used to store recently accessed data in a memory location for quick retrieval. Caching is kind of like the counter space in your kitchen; it is easier and faster to grab a knife off the counter than to keep going to the drawer for it. Of course, the more counter space you have, the more you can keep on the counter. Similarly, it is easier and faster for the processor to grab data from its cache than it is to go get it from RAM or the hard disk. The more caching the processor has, the more it can hold before needing to go elsewhere to get it. So now when someone tells you that a processor has 512 KB of processor cache, you can nod knowingly and tell them that that is indeed a lot of counter space.

As far as processor cache is concerned, there are three kinds, level 1 (L1) or internal cache, level 2 (L2) or external cache, and level 3 (L3) cache. Of the three, L1 is the fastest and is integrated directly into the processors—and has been since the 486 processors. Fast it may be, but the cache size is also small (because it has to fit on the chip). L1 cache is typically 16 KB to 32 KB in size, but many of today's newer processors are tripling this number. This space is often large enough to hold some data but it is primarily used for caching instructions and the like.

In recent processor designs, L2 cache has been integrated into the processor packaging. Previously, it had been built into the motherboard. Today's L2 caches are 512 KB and up, more than enough space to store frequently accessed data and commands.

In the newest generation of PC systems, a new level of cache, level 3, is being used. L3 cache is typically situated between the processor and the system memory and is used as a holding place for frequently accessed data from the main memory. In a sense, L3 cache is taking the place of L2 cache on processor designs that now incorporate L2 cache into the processor or processor packaging. A good example of this architecture is the Intel Itanium processor.

Now that we know a little more about the jargon used when talking about processors, we can take a look at the processors we can expect to encounter both in the real world of PC repair and on the A+ exam.

Processor Types

Given that every computer system has to have a processor, and that there are millions of computers on millions of desks, you may think that dozens of competing manufacturers are out there trying to get a piece of the sizable processor pie. In fact, this is not the case. In the IBM compatible PC market, there are really only two major competing processor companies—Intel Corporation and Advanced Micro Devices (AMD). Of the two, Intel holds the lion's share of the market but increasingly you do not have to look hard to see a system with an AMD logo on the case. Coming in a distant third is a company called Cyrix.

The competition between these two companies has pushed processor development forward at a staggering pace, with both AMD and Intel boasting a large array of available processors. We'll start our specific processor discussion by looking at Intel chips.

Note   As you read this, you may be wondering why some processors such as the early AMD offerings and the Intel 386 and 486 processors are not included. The answer is simple; they are older technologies and not included in the A+ exam. If you want to do a little research on these older processors, refer to AMD's Web site at *www.amd.com* and Intel's Web site at *www.intel.com*.

Intel Processors

Intel has been churning out processors since 1971, which, when you think about the proliferation of computers, is really not that long ago. Although the processors of today bear only a passing resemblance to those of the past, the lessons learned by Intel along the way have made it one of the world's foremost CPU manufacturers.

Intel processors are actually designed for specific purposes. The current range extends from the low-cost Celeron series to the high-performance (and high-price) Itanium series. Expect the lower-end processors to be used for desktop systems while the more pricey processors are aimed at inclusion with server systems.

Pentium Processors   Way back in 1993, many of us were modifying the speeds of our 486 Intel processors, a process known as *overclocking*, trying to squeeze out every last drop of performance, with more than a few processors burning out in the process. To satisfy the increasing need for speed, Intel introduced the Pentium processor, which presented a whole new era for personal computing. The Pentium processor offered buyers a leap forward in terms of processor performance and functionality. The original Pentium chip used a new architecture that provided many enhancements over previous processors. Before it was replaced by the Pentium II, the Pentium processor had been made available in the following speeds: 60, 66, 75, 90, 120, 133, 150, 166, 200, and 233 MHz. The Pentium 60- and 66-MHz versions used a 273-pin PGA, 5 volts DC, and connected to the motherboard using socket 4. The higher-level Pentiums used a 296-pin PGA and connected to the motherboard via socket 7 and 3.3 volts DC. Refer to Figure 4-3 earlier to see an example of a socket 7 ZIF socket and compatible processor.

Note   For those of you who have skipped ahead, processor sockets were discussed earlier in the "Processor Characteristics," page 138.

Multimedia Extensions (MMX) Look back into the history of Intel processors, and you are sure to come across the term MMX, which is the unofficial abbreviation of multimedia extensions. MMX was introduced by Intel as a mechanism for improving the video and audio processing capabilities of its processors. MMX actually consists of 57 processor instructions geared specifically toward the improvement of sound and video processing. Although the first series of MMX-capable Pentium chips was actually named to reflect the added capability, subsequent chips simply included the technology but dropped the moniker. In fact, all Intel processors since the original Pentium MMX have included the MMX functionality.

Pentium Pro

An interesting addition to the Pentium CPU range was the Pentium Pro, which was introduced in 1995. The Pentium Pro was the first processor aimed directly at the PC server market. It was specifically targeted at those organizations that needed, and were prepared to pay for, the extra power and speed offered by a specialized processor.

Note   In terms of performance, there is no doubt that the Pentium Pro offered more than its plain-name brother, with support for 4GB RAM, 256 or 512 KB of L2 cache, and processor speeds from 150 to 200 MHz. The big news was that the L2 cache was physically attached to the CPU by a 64-bit bus, effectively making it two chips in one. This configuration meant that the Pentium Pro chip was quite large and used a special 387-pin socket 8 motherboard connector. The Pentium Pro processor required 3.3 volts. Figure 4-5 shows a Pentium Pro processor and the socket 8 motherboard connector. The Pentium Pro was optimized for 32-bit operating systems such as Windows NT.

Figure 4-5 An Intel Pentium Pro processor and socket 8

Pentium II

Introduced in May 1997, Intel's Pentium II processor offered a new level of power for personal computers. Originally available with speeds of 233, 266, and 300 MHz, Intel also introduced speeds of 333, 350, 400, and 450 MHz before replacing the PII with the PIII. Intel hit on the idea of connecting the processor and the L2 cache directly, but this meant that the Pentium II had to have its own special socket, which led to the introduction of Slot 1. Refer to Figure 4-2 to see an example of a SECC processor. Refer back to Figure 4-4 to see an example of a Slot 1 connector.

Test Smart   For the A+ exam, be prepared to identify a Slot 1 connector on a motherboard.

The Pentium II boasted MMX technology and a 100-MHz front-side bus on the faster models. The addition of 32 KB of L1 cache and 512 KB of L2 cache made the Pentium II a major improvement over the standard Pentium. Pentium II processors require 3.3 volts DC to operate.

> **Note**   If you do any reading about CPUs, you will come across the term *front-side bus (FSB)*. This term refers to the connection between the CPU, the main memory, and the rest of the system board. It is in contrast with the back-side bus, which refers to the connection between the CPU and the L2 cache.

Pentium II Xeon

Although the uptake of the Pentium Pro CPU was somewhat limited, it proved to Intel that there was a valuable market for high-end, high-performance CPUs designed to work in servers. With this is mind, Intel released the Pentium II Xeon chip in July 1998. The PII Xeon uses another proprietary connection method: Slot 2.

The PII Xeon processor package came with a choice of 512, 1,024, or 2,048 KB of L2 cache and a rather large heat sink to take care of the extra heat generated by the new chip. In fact, the heat issue was such a concern with the Xeon processor that a sensor was built into the chip to detect overheating. The original Xeon processor ran at 450 MHz, but faster models were added over time.

Pentium III   One of Intel's best-selling processors of all time is the Pentium III. Currently, Pentium III processors are available at speeds between 450 MHz and 1.4 GHz. PIII processors are available for systems with both a 100-MHz and a 133-MHz system bus. The PIII processor incorporates 32 KB of L1 cache and 512 KB of integrated L2 Advanced Transfer Cache. One of the biggest selling points for the PIII processor, particularly for the home market, is the introduction of new SIMD (single–instruction, multiple-data) technology, which is effectively an extension of the MMX technology discussed earlier.

An interesting aside to the Pentium III story is that it was with this version that Intel began uniquely identifying each chip with an ID number. Privacy groups and watchdogs complained that this was an invasion of people's privacy because it allowed software to use the number to track the computer. Corporate customers liked the idea because it provided a mechanism for tracking their processors, and conversely, thieves didn't like it for the same reason. There are two versions of the PIII chip available, one that uses a Single Edge Cartridge Connector-2 (SECC2) and another that uses a Socket 370 "flip chip" PGA interface. Both require between 1.3 and 2.05 volts DC to operate.

Pentium III Xeon   March 1999 saw the release of the PIII Xeon, which, as with the Xeon processors before it, was designed for use in servers and very high-end workstations, and used the SECC2 connector. The PIII Xeon processor accommodates a 133-MHz system bus and 256 KB of Advanced Transfer Cache. Figure 4-6 shows the Pentium III Xeon processor.

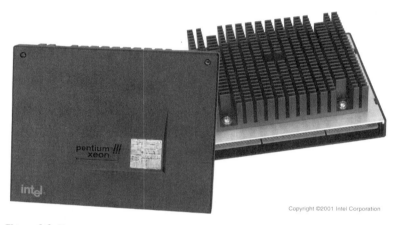

Copyright ©2001 Intel Corporation

Figure 4-6 Xeon processor

Celeron   The Celeron processor is intended mainly for home and value business use. The Celeron has been available in a variety of speeds up to and including the 766-MHz version, which supports a bus speed of 66 MHz, while the 800-MHz- to 1.4-GHz versions support a bus speed of 100 MHz. Today's Celeron processors offer speeds up to 2.2 GHz and bus speeds of 400 MHz.

The original Celeron processor was based on the Pentium II chip, but with the advent of the Pentium III, Intel also, after a period, released the Celeron II, which was effectively a Pentium III with some of the cache disabled. Again, the Celeron II is aimed at the home and value business market. Even though the Celeron II is different from the original Celeron, it's still marketed as simply a Celeron processor.

Celeron processors come in two varieties. One is similar to the Pentium II SECC but without the protective cover. It is referred to as a Single Edge Processor Package (SEPP). Later Celerons came in a standard pin variety and used a Socket 370 receptacle. Figure 4-7 shows the Celeron PGA. In terms of cache, early Celerons had caching disabled, which hurt their marketability. Today, Celerons are available with 16-32 KB of L1 cache and up to 512 KB of L2 cache.

Note Some Celeron processors use a Socket 370 form factor, and one Celeron processor uses the Slot 1 design. An adapter is needed to fit a Socket 370 Celeron into a Slot 1 connector. Just another reason to research the sockets and slots before buying that new processor.

Figure 4-7 Celeron PGA

Pentium 4 The Intel Pentium 4 provides some impressive new features, including a 400- and 533-MHz system bus, enhanced multimedia capabilities through the use of Intel's Streaming SIMD2 Extensions, and a host of other performance-enhancing features. Today, the Pentium 4 line of processors is used in every type of system, including desktops, servers, and laptops.

One interesting aspect of the Pentium 4 is that it was initially designed to work only on systems that use Rambus DRAM (RDRAM—see the section on memory later in this chapter). However, Intel realized that this might be a barrier to the uptake of Pentium 4 processors and has quickly moved to develop a Double Data Rate (DDR)-SDRAM-compliant version of a chip set that supports the Pentium 4 processor. Today's Pentium 4 processors are available in a 478-pin or 423-pin PGA package, require between 1.1 and 1.8 volts DC to operate, and hit speeds up to 3.08 GHz.

Itanium The newest addition to the Intel family is the Itanium chip. The Itanium, which is based on Intel's new Explicitly Parallel Instruction Computing (EPIC) technology, is Intel's first 64-bit processor. The Itanium operates at bus speeds of between 733 and 800 MHz. The Itanium is targeted at the high-end server market and is a potential replacement for the Xeon series of processors. The Itanium will use a new interface system called "Slot M," which incorporates the processor and a power supply unit on one (large) module.

For a brief look at the key features of the various Intel processors, refer to Table 4-1.

Table 4-1   Summary of Intel Processors

Processor	Form Factor	Voltage	Speeds	L1 Cache (KB)	L2 Cache (KB)	Socket
Pentium	273- or 296-pin PGA	3.3 or 5	60–233 MHz	16	256–512 (On motherboard)	Socket 4, 5, or 7
Pentium Pro	387-pin PGA	3.1 or 3.3	150–200 MHz	16	256–1 MB (Integrated cache)	Socket 8
Pentium II	242-pin SEC	3.3	233–333 MHz	32	512 (Integrated cache)	Slot 1
Pentium III	242-pin SECC or 370-pin PGA	1.3–2.05	450 MHz–1.3 GHz and higher	32	256–512 (Integrated cache)	Slot 1 or PGA 370
Celeron	SEPP or 370-pin PGA	1.3–2.05	Up to 2.2 GHz	16–32	0–512	Socket 370, Slot 1
Pentium 4	478-pin or 423-pin PGA	1.1–1.8	1.7–2.8 GHz	8	256–512	PGA 478 or PGA 423
Itanium	Slot M	1.7	733–800 MHz	32	96	Slot M

 Test Smart   When reviewing for the A+ exam, make sure you are familiar with the information provided in Table 4-1. Pay close attention to the sockets or slots used by the various processors.

AMD Chips

It would be unfair to suggest that Intel has always had the PC processor market entirely to itself; in fact, over the past couple of years, AMD has made serious inroads into Intel's market share. Although Intel is hardly looking for handouts, the rise of AMD has certainly caused Intel to focus on the task at hand in a market that at one point it almost completely dominated.

AMD's chips have evolved over the years and are increasingly being used in server environments. In this section, we will focus on AMD's current processor offerings.

3DNow! Just as Intel developed MMX technology to increase the performance of multimedia-intensive applications, AMD developed a system called 3DNow! technology. Like MMX, 3DNow! allows programmers and software developers to take advantage of additional instructions that provide enhanced graphics, video, and sound. Although the standard relies on the fact that software must be specifically written to take advantage of the additional features, developers seem to be recognizing the increasingly large market share that AMD is garnering, and more and more 3DNow!-compliant packages are becoming available.

K6-II Available in a variety of clock speeds up to 550 MHz, the AMD K6-II processor was generally adopted only for home and small-business use. The K6-II provided support for 3DNow! and used a Socket7/Super7 motherboard interface. All K6-II processors use 3.3 volts.

> **Note** We decided to start our discussion of AMD processors with the K6 series, but AMD did produce a series of processors called the K5. You are unlikely to encounter any questions on the A+ exam about the K5, so we omitted it from our discussion.

K6-III Although targeted at power home and business users rather than at server markets, the K6-III processor boasts some impressive statistics. First off, it has a 64-KB L1 cache and a full-speed 256-KB L2 cache. Designed to fit into a Socket7/Super7 motherboard, the K6-III supports a 100-MHz bus speed and comes with 3DNow! support. As with the AMD K6-II, the K6-III is packaged in a 321-pin Ceramic Pin Grid Array (CPGA) arrangement.

Duron

Introduced in 1999, the Duron processor is basically AMD's answer to Intel's Celeron processor, in that it is targeted at the value segment of the market. The Duron processor is currently available in speeds up to 1.3 GHz. The Duron includes a 128-KB L1 cache (considerably more than the Intel Celeron or Pentium III) and a 64-KB L2 cache, which is synchronized to the processor speed. It also supports a 100-MHz system bus. As with other AMD processors, the Duron supports 3DNow! SIMD instruction sets, providing increased capabilities in graphic and audio applications. Although the Duron is not sold or designed for use in server roles, its cost and performance advantages mean that, in some cases at least, it can be used for light server applications.

Athlon In essence, the Athlon is the competitor of the high-end processors from Intel, such as the Xeon and the Pentium 4. Like the Duron, the Athlon utilizes Socket A motherboard connections. The Athlon has 128 KB of L1 cache and 256

KB of L2 cache, all of which runs at full CPU speed. This is a factor that has won over many admirers, especially considering that the Pentium III, which was the Athlon's main competitor, offers just 16 KB of L1 cache. The Athlon was also designed to take advantage of the DDR-SDRAM (see the section on memory later in this chapter), which further improves overall performance.

Currently, the Athlon processor is available in a range of speeds, including 1.0, 1.1, and 1.2 GHz and higher. Although many server purists still insist on Intel processors, AMD is growing ever stronger, building a reputation for providing reliable yet cutting-edge technologies at an affordable price. Figure 4-8 shows an Athlon processor.

Figure 4-8 Athlon processor

AMD Opteron and Athlon XP   AMD, looking to loosen Intel's hold on the high-end processor market, recently released two new processors, the Opteron and Athlon XP.

The more powerful of the two processors is the Opteron, which takes the fight directly to Intel in the high-end server processor range. As with the Intel Itanium, the Opteron is a 64-bit processor with advanced features, such as new registers and the ability to address 4.5 million gigabytes of RAM, as opposed to the 4 gigabytes addressable by 32-bit processor architectures. The Opteron supports speeds of 2 GHz and higher, with a 266-MHz front-side bus.

The Athlon XP, which is less of a force than the Opteron, is aimed at the high-end desktop and entry-level server market. Even so, it still boasts many of the features of its big brother, including 64-bit processing.

Cyrix

Bringing up the rear of processor development are the Cyrix processor offerings. Cyrix, now owned by VIA Technologies, developed the 6x86 series of processors. The 6x86-P Cyrix processors ranged from 120 to 200 MHz, which functioned at roughly the same speeds as the Pentium equivalents. Anyone who had owned or worked with these processors was well aware that they operated at high temperatures and overheating was a problem. A 6x86L version of the processor was developed to operate at lower temperatures. Cyrix still makes a few lower-end CPUs such as the Cyrix M-II, which like the AMD processors, uses a socket 7 form factor. Another Cyrix processor, the VIA C3, uses a Socket 370 ZIF socket.

Keeping It Cool One of the biggest considerations regarding CPUs is heat dissipation. When a CPU is running, it can generate a quite astonishing amount of heat. This heat, if not moved away from the processor, can damage the processor itself or other components within the computer. Although CPU cooling should be considered as part of the overall thermal considerations of a system, CPUs are always cooled directly. The two most common methods of directly cooling CPUs are heat sinks and fans, which nowadays are always used together.

Heat sinks follow a simple rule. The larger the sink, the more heat it can dissipate. For this reason, larger, more powerful CPUs require larger heat sinks. In addition to pure size, almost all heat sinks utilize fins to maximize the surface area through which the heat can be dissipated. The addition of a fan (or two) aids the cooling process by drawing cooler air across the surface of the heat sink.

Because the rate of cooling is vital to the correct performance of the processor, many manufacturers now ship processors with the heat sink and fan already attached. The fan is often easy to remove because they do occasionally fail, but the heat sink is normally attached to the processor by the use of a glue or paste. Running a system without the correct heat sink and fan can lead to component failure in pretty short order. Running with no heat sink or fan at all borders on the insane.

Memory

Like processors, random access memory (RAM) is an essential part of every PC system. RAM stores information temporarily so that it can be used and accessed by the components of the system. It is interesting to note that, while processors have progressed at an incredible pace, the development of faster memory technologies has, until recently, been sedate by comparison.

When working with RAM, there are two distinct types that you will encounter: static RAM (SRAM) and dynamic RAM (DRAM). SRAM, which is much faster but more costly than DRAM, is used for cache memory in systems. DRAM, which has become very affordable in recent years, is now cheap enough to make it possible to use it in large quantities in PC systems.

Static RAM is so named because it holds data in a different way than does dynamic RAM. Static RAM uses capacitors and can hold data indefinitely, whereas DRAM must be continually refreshed to make sure the data is held.

Because SRAM is more expensive to produce in large quantities, it is usually chosen for use only in cache memory on processor chips or as cache memory on motherboards, where the quantities used are relatively small. Over the years, hardware manufacturers have made it increasingly easy to upgrade the amount of installed RAM.

During the course of its life, dynamic RAM has undergone a number of changes and developments. Originally, individual memory chips were plugged directly into motherboards, which was an awkward task. It wasn't long before it became apparent that a more effective approach was to mount the memory chips onto a printed circuit board (PCB) and plug the PCB into a slot on the motherboard. Not surprisingly, the approach caught on. Today, the memory boards installed into PCs bear a passing resemblance to the first plug-in memory modules, but memory boards have come a long way in terms of performance, reliability, and features.

Almost without exception, RAM modules today are of the plug-in board type. They fall into one of two categories: the older and less frequently used SIMMs (single inline memory modules), and the more modern and widely used DIMMs (dual inline memory modules).

Note   The terms SIMM and DIMM refer to the physical layout of the memory, but memory still comes in different types, such as FPM (fast page mode), EDO (extended data out), and SDRAM (synchronous DRAM). SIMMs and DIMMs simply refer to the physical layout of the memory chips on the plug-in board.

Single Inline Memory Modules

Although SIMMs have generally been replaced by newer technologies, technicians will encounter the occasional SIMM in older computer systems. There are two types of SIMMs: 30-pin and 72-pin. The 30-pin units, which were introduced first, transfer data 8 bits at a time. The 72-pin SIMMs transfer data 32 bits at a time, a rate that's more in keeping with the capability of the processors used when these SIMMs were introduced. The 72-pin SIMM, apart from having 42 more pins, is 1.25 inches longer than the 30-pin SIMM, at 4.25 inches.

Dual Inline Memory Modules

The most common type of PC memory in use today is the DIMM. DIMMs are 5.25 inches in length and have two notches along the bottom edge to aid in correct installation. DIMMs have 168 pins, are installed vertically, and are secured by catches that engage the module at each end. DIMMs are usually installed directly into the PC motherboard, though some high-end systems use proprietary add-in circuit boards instead. DIMMs use a 64-bit data bus. Figure 4-9 shows a 30-pin SIMM, 72-pin SIMM, and a typical 168-pin DIMM.

 Test Smart   168-pin DIMMs use a 64-bit data bus path.

Figure 4-9 30-pin SIMM, 72-pin SIMM, and 168-pin DIMM

Note   The terms SIMM and DIMM basically define the physical appearance, or packaging, of the memory modules. This in turn dictates into which motherboards the memory can be installed.

Now that we have looked at how memory is packaged with SIMMs and DIMMs, we can look at the different types of memory in use today.

See Also   Information on adding and replacing memory modules is covered in Chapter 1.

Types of Memory

As with most things computer related, the principle of RAM is more complex than the fact that it is just memory. There are different types of RAM, and though the technological principles behind each type remain the same, the specific characteristics of each type are important when you're specifying RAM for, or installing RAM into, a computer system.

Understanding the types of available memory can be quite a challenge. Fortunately, the industry tends to embrace one or two general standards at a time, making the job of understanding the various types available somewhat simpler. In this section, we will examine some of the more common, and not so common, memory types that you might find.

Fast Page-Mode RAM

Fast page-mode (FPM) RAM came into common use in the early 1990s. It offered a 25-MHz clock rate and a maximum bandwidth of 200 Mbps. FPM RAM was an improvement over its predecessor in that it employed sophisticated (for its time) methods of locating data within RAM. Although it was fast (again, for its time), memory requirements for PC systems quickly outgrew FPM capabilities, so it has been replaced with faster technologies.

Extended Data Out RAM

Introduced in 1994, extended data out (EDO) RAM supported a clock rate of 40 MHz and a maximum bandwidth of 320 Mbps. In essence, EDO RAM is simply a sub-technology of FPM RAM rather than a new memory system. EDO RAM yields a 10 to 15 percent performance improvement over FPM RAM by eliminating the 10-nanosecond delay incurred by waiting for the memory controller to issue the next memory address. So similar are FPM and EDO RAM that a system that does not support EDO RAM can usually use EDO memory modules anyway, though there is no performance improvement. To take advantage of EDO RAM, the system into which it is installed must support it. Generally speaking, EDO RAM has been almost completely replaced by newer memory technologies.

Synchronous DRAM

Synchronous DRAM (SDRAM) provides a mechanism for synchronizing the memory with the speed at which the system bus is running. This synchronization mechanism allows SDRAM to operate in sync with the machine, and this improves performance. Before SDRAM was used, if a CPU wanted to retrieve data from memory, it had to ask for each memory block individually, which took extra time. In contrast, if SDRAM is asked for a memory block, it supplies the requested block and then starts to supply data from the next information block, and the next, and the next until the CPU tells the RAM to stop. This feature produces performance improvements if the CPU is requesting large blocks of sequential data.

SDRAM comes in a variety of speeds so that the memory can be purchased to match the speed of the system bus in which it will be installed. Currently, SDRAM is available in PC66, PC100, and PC133 versions. These versions offer the same data rates as their names, and offer 528 Mbps, 800 Mbps, and 1.1 Gbps of maximum bandwidth, respectively.

Test Smart   In most cases, you can use SDRAM that will run faster than the system speed, but not slower. For example, PC133 SDRAM will work in a PC running at a bus speed of 66 MHz, but PC66 SDRAM will not work in a system running at a bus speed of 133 MHz.

Today, it is more common to see computers using PC100 and PC133 SDRAM rather than PC66. Even though 133-MHz motherboards are now common (and fast), newer boards are always being developed to take advantage of new technologies such as DDR-SDRAM and RDRAM.

Note   PC66 SDRAM is sometimes referred to as standard SDRAM.

Double Data Rate SDRAM

One of the newest innovations in PC RAM is Double Data Rate (DDR) SDRAM. DDR-SDRAM effectively doubles the data rates of SDRAM by manipulating the way in which the data signals are sent to the memory chips. DDR-SDRAM DIMMs have 184 pins, with the extra pins being needed for the additional signaling information. DDR-SDRAM provides data rates up to a maximum of 266 MHz (133✕2) and a maximum bandwidth of 1.6 Gbps for PC100, and 2.1 Gbps for PC133. Although DDR-SDRAM is a fully developed technology, many computer systems currently still use standard 168-pin SDRAM, due mostly to compatibility and availability issues. However, as bus rates increase and more performance is demanded, systems that support DDR-SDRAM will become a more common sight. One of the biggest advantages that DDR-SDRAM has over its main competitor, RDRAM, is price, though the gap is narrowing over time. The manufacturing process of DDR-SDRAM is not unlike that of standard SDRAM, and as a result, prices are not that different than prices for traditional SDRAM.

Rambus DRAM

No discussion of RAM types would be complete without the inclusion of Rambus DRAM (RDRAM). RDRAM was brought to the PC memory market through a joint venture between Rambus and Intel. RDRAM operates at up to 800 MHz and has a maximum bandwidth of 1.6 Gbps. RDRAM achieves these very high levels of data throughput by using a system called double-clocking. One of the side effects of this electrical trickery is excess heat, which led to the inclusion of a spreader on the memory chips. The *spreader* is a metal cover that acts as a heat sink to keep the memory cool. RDRAM is provided in a RIMM (Rambus inline memory module), which can be installed only into a system that supports it.

> **Note**   As you read about memory, you may encounter the term SO-DIMM or SO-RIMM. The SO refers to Small Outline, a form of memory designed for use in mobile devices such as laptops. SO modules are easy to recognize because they are significantly smaller than their large counterparts. For more information on SO-DIMMs, refer to Chapter 1.

Although there are relatively few systems that currently accept RIMMs, that is likely to change over the coming years. That said, the industry generally does seem to be keener to pursue DDR-SDRAM rather than RDRAM, mainly due to expense and licensing issues from RDRAM's inventor, Rambus, Inc., so what the future holds for RDRAM remains unclear.

VRAM

Video RAM (VRAM) is specialized memory that is used for video cards and not as part of the system's main memory. VRAM is known as dual-ported memory because it is able to write to both of its input/output (I/O) ports at the same time. This allows it to simultaneously refresh the screen while text and images are drawn in memory. VRAM performance enhancements did not come cheaply and it was used exclusively on high-end video cards.

WRAM

Like VRAM, window RAM (WRAM) is used to enhance video performance. Also like VRAM, WRAM can be written to and read from simultaneously and is much faster than its predecessor, VRAM. The name can be a bit misleading; window RAM has nothing really to do with Windows, the operating system. Rather, the term *window* refers to how it moves data.

> **Note**   Though not specifically mentioned in the CompTIA objectives, there is another type of video memory known as Synchronous Graphic Random Access Memory. SGRAM is used on video cards to increase graphic performance.

Additional Memory Considerations

As if there were not enough to be concerned with already, there are other things to consider regarding memory.

Parity and Error-Correcting Code RAM

Generally speaking, PC memory is a reliable medium. Errors are relatively rare, particularly if good-quality RAM is purchased. Even so, errors do occur, and as you would expect, there are mechanisms in place to cope with them. Even the oldest PCs have a system called parity, which allows the system to detect an error in data held in memory and to declare it so.

The problem is that while parity is very good at detecting the error (and halting the PC to show it), it has no way of correcting the error. The demands placed on PC systems today demand a more sophisticated method of error detection and recovery. Enter ECC.

Error-correcting code (ECC) provides greater protection against errors that may develop with information stored in RAM. High-end server systems (and some desktop systems) support the use of ECC RAM. ECC RAM detects and corrects errors through the use of a mathematical calculation called a checksum. If ECC RAM detects an error, it will either correct the error or report the error, depending on the error's complexity. The extra protection that ECC-capable SDRAM provides makes it the memory design of choice for high-end servers from almost all manufacturers. ECC RAM is understandably more expensive than the non-ECC equivalent, but ECC is well worth the extra investment if the hardware platform in use supports it.

Test Smart   Parity memory detects errors in memory but ECC RAM detects and corrects memory errors.

Unbuffered vs. Buffered vs. Registered

When you investigate the memory options for a specific system, you may come across the terms unbuffered, buffered, and registered. Buffers and registers are devices that amplify the signal to ensure the integrity of the data stored in memory. In SDRAM, the device that performs this function is called a register. In EDO RAM, it is called a buffer. Registered or buffered memory is more expensive than nonregistered (or unbuffered) RAM, and the extra expense is justified by the additional technical demands of the memory device.

Memory Interleaving

Over time, memory and system manufacturers have looked for other ways to speed up RAM access, rather than just making the chips faster. One of the more popular approaches is memory interleaving.

Each time a bank of memory is addressed, it takes a very small amount of time for the bank to reset itself before it can accept any new data. Even though the amount of time, called a wait state, is very small, it still does take time and so slows down the overall memory retrieval and storage process.

Memory interleaving works by dividing the system memory banks into separate units that can be accessed independently. This allows each bank a period of time when it is not accessed. This time is used by the memory to reset and get ready to accept more data. The product of this is improved memory read and write performance.

Motherboards

The motherboard is an important component of the computer, as every other piece of system hardware either directly or indirectly attaches itself to it. This of course includes all of the major system components such as the processor, RAM, power supply, and expansion cards. As you can imagine, this makes the motherboard an important consideration when working with computer systems. Motherboards are designed with various sockets, slots, and connectors that are used to attach other computer hardware components. In this section we explore the connectors and sockets you are likely to find on modern system boards and how they are used. First, however, we can take a look at the common motherboard configurations or form factors: AT and ATX.

Motherboard—What's In a Name?   For as long as there have been computers, the term motherboard has been used to describe the computer's main circuit board but be warned, there are a few other names by which it is referred. Today, many passionate techies feel strongly that the term motherboard is obsolete and doesn't adequately describe the component, and perhaps rightly so. Originally, the term motherboard described a circuit board with no integrated components such as sound or video. In contrast, the term system board was used to describe a board with integrated components. Considering that most motherboards ship with at least some integrated components, the term is felt to be outdated. In the real world and the A+ exam, you can expect the terms system board and motherboard to be used interchangeably. Just to throw a little more jargon into the debate, you may also hear the term planar board used, which is another completely acceptable alias. Finally, if you find yourself working on an Apple computer, and many other devices such as printers for that matter, you may find that you are using the term logic board to describe the motherboard—I mean system board.

Motherboard Form Factors

Motherboards come in a variety of shapes and sizes known as *form factors*. The form factor of the motherboard dictates the size of the board, the connectors used, the location of expansion slots, and even the case it fits into. For this reason, when upgrading a motherboard, you will need to know the form factor of the motherboard used. Several form factors have come and gone over the years and today we are left with two primary ones: Advanced Technology (AT) and Advanced Technology eXtended (ATX).

Full and Baby AT Motherboards

The original AT motherboards are an older design and supported 286/386 processors. AT motherboards were introduced in 1984 by IBM and used by a then speedy 16-bit data path. AT motherboards primarily used the 16-bit ISA (Industry Standard Architecture) slots, although one or two 8-bit ISA slots were kept for backward compatibility.

> **Note** Previous to the AT form factor was the now defunct XT (eXtended Technology) form factor, which primarily used 8-bit ISA slots. Don't expect to see any XT-related questions on the A+ exam.

These AT boards did not have many integrated components, meaning that video, hard disk controllers, and the like required the addition of expansion cards. AT motherboards required AT keyboards using a DIN-5 connector. These motherboards are not popular anymore, and it's unlikely you will be working with very many of them.

The newer baby AT motherboards, shown in Figure 4-10, measure 8.5 x 13 inches and are laid out (in terms of fixing holes) exactly like the earlier AT motherboards. The screw holes and the keyboard port (5-pin DIN) are located in the same location on the motherboard, allowing any baby AT motherboard to be used in most AT cases. Though not used in modern computers, you are certainly going to come across AT motherboards when working with older Pentium-class systems. Newer computers, however, have migrated to the more advanced ATX motherboards.

 Test Smart The AT motherboards use a different form factor than the ATX motherboards and use the 5-pin DIN keyboard connector.

Figure 4-10 Baby AT motherboard

ATX Motherboard

In 1995, Intel released the ATX motherboard form factor. The ATX form factor was an open standard, meaning that anyone could freely use the design. This is in contrast to proprietary motherboard designs used by specific companies such as Apple. ATX motherboards are what you can expect to be working with today, as they are used in most modern systems. The ATX motherboards offered significant improvements over the AT motherboards in terms of both design and performance. The ATX form factor is typically larger than the baby AT motherboards and has a number of integrated components. On an ATX motherboard you can expect to see two serial ports, a parallel port, perhaps USB ports, and two mini-DIN (PS/2) connectors, one for the mouse and one for the keyboard. Recall that the AT motherboards use the 5-pin DIN connector; this provides an easy way to distinguish between AT and ATX motherboards. If you have purchased a new ATX board and are trying to fit it into an older AT case, you are going to have some difficulty; they are not interchangeable nor designed to work with each other.

One final distinction between AT and ATX motherboards has to do with power options. ATX motherboards always have a small amount of power going to them, which allows a PC technician to effectively wake up a machine from a remote location, a function known as Wake On Lan (WOL). This basically means that the system is never truly off and can be turned on using a modem or over the network. ATX power options also allow the system to power off when the operating system is shut down.

 Test Smart   ATX motherboards can be turned off via software.

Power Connectors

The motherboard can't do much of anything without power, and for motherboards, power comes from the PC's power supply unit.

As you may have guessed, power supplies, and their accompanying connectors, come in two standard varieties: AT and ATX. AT connectors are typically found on earlier computers right through to Pentium-class machines. AT connectors are recognizable by having two separate connectors needing to be plugged in side by side on the motherboard. These connectors, labeled the P8 and P9, provide the electrical connection between the power supply and the motherboard. Because of the design of the P8 and P9 connectors, you will be unable to connect them backwards but it is possible to connect them in reverse, placing P9 where P8 should go. If you are confused about how to connect these connectors, here is the rule. When connecting AT connectors, ensure that the black ground wires from each connector are beside each other. Follow this rule and you can't go wrong. Figure 4-11 shows AT connectors on an AT motherboard.

Figure 4-11 AT connectors on an AT motherboard

 Test Smart   Remember that when connecting AT connectors, the black ground wires need to be right next to each other.

ATX connectors, used with our modern-class machines, use a single 20-slot keyed connector. Known as a P1 connector, this connector uses a different socket on the ATX motherboard and fortunately cannot be incorrectly installed, at least not without a hammer and chisel. Figure 4-12 shows the P1 connector and the P1 socket on the motherboard.

Note   Some motherboards have both P1 and AT sockets to accommodate both types of power supplies.

Figure 4-12 P1 connector and P1 socket

Motherboard Features

Whether you are working with an AT motherboard or an ATX motherboard, you can expect to see some similar connectors, slots, and sockets. While their number and location may vary between motherboards, they are going to be onboard somewhere. For the A+ exam, you can expect to be required to identify the function and location of each of the various features, connectors, and slots.

Chip Sets

The chip set is an important piece of the motherboard's architecture; in fact, the chip set controls more of the system's functioning and performance capabilities than you may think. Essentially, motherboard chip sets are integrated circuits designed to perform or control certain tasks. For instance, the chip sets dictate how the CPU, the I/O devices, and the system's memory interact. In short, chip sets provide the interface between the PC and its subsystems. To learn about specific chip sets and their features, you can visit the chip set vendors' Web sites. Some of the common chip set manufacturers include Intel, ServerWorks, Via Technologies, and Silicon Integrated Systems (SIS). Figure 4-13 shows an example motherboard with the major chip set components identified.

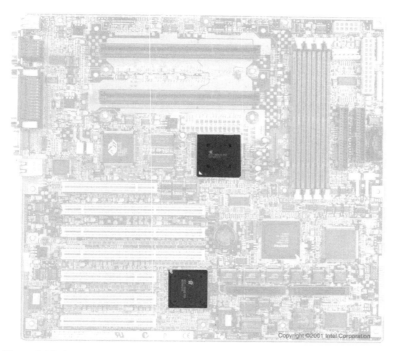

Figure 4-13 A motherboard with the major chip set components identified

CMOS Battery

On each and every motherboard there is a CMOS (complementary metal-oxide semiconductor) battery responsible for providing power to the CMOS so that it can retain the system settings when powered off. On older motherboards, the CMOS battery is fixed to the motherboard and not easily changed. Modern motherboards include an easy-to-replace 3V watch-type battery. Locating the CMOS battery on any board is not a difficult task; simply look for the flat silver disk, about the size of a quarter. Figure 4-14 shows the CMOS battery on a motherboard.

Figure 4-14 CMOS battery on a motherboard

See Also   *For more information on the function of the CMOS and CMOS battery, refer to the section "Inside the CMOS" on page 171.*

Memory Slots

All motherboards must include memory banks for the RAM to fit into. Motherboards vary on the number and the types of memory banks they provide. As mentioned earlier, SIMMs were the standard memory-bank type but have given way to the new DIMM memory banks. Some PCs offer both SIMM and DIMM slots, but today's new computers generally come exclusively with DIMMs. SIMM and DIMM slots are easily identifiable on the motherboard and, as the saying goes, a picture is worth a thousand words. Figure 4-15 shows a motherboard with DIMM memory slots identified.

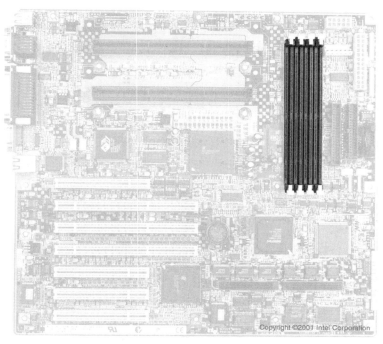

Copyright ©2001 Intel Corporation

Figure 4-15 A motherboard with DIMM memory slots

Bus Slots

Work with any computer and you will most certainly be working with expansion slots and buses. So just what is a 32-bit or 16-bit bus, and how do these relate to Industry Standard Architecture (ISA), Peripheral Component Interconnect (PCI), or Advanced Graphics Port (AGP) slots? This section explains buses, their function, and their relationship to system performance and expansion.

Essentially, a bus is all about the communication that takes place inside the computer's case. Buses are the channels that the CPU uses to communicate with other devices on the motherboard, such as expansion slots and memory modules. A close examination of a motherboard reveals numerous metallic lines that run all around the board; these lines form the basis of the computer's communication. So there we have it; a *bus* refers to the printed circuits on a motherboard that send the electronic signals to other devices attached to the computer. When we talk about bus speed, it refers to the speed at which these electronic signals pass from the motherboard to the devices. As with everything else with computers, the faster the bus, the faster data can travel.

Now, let's take a look at some of the bus types you may encounter when working with PCs.

Introducing the Bus PC bus technology can be traced back to 1981, when IBM developed a system for its XT 8088 personal computer. The slots built into the motherboard of the XT were known as 8-bit slots because expansion cards, such as video or modem cards, had 8 channels to pass data through the motherboard. To be exact, an 8-bit expansion card has 31 gold connectors on either side of the card, making 62 in total. Of these 62, 8 are used to transmit data 8 bits at a time. The expansion card is inserted into the bus slot, and the information is passed through the printed circuits. Therein lies the connection between the expansion slot and the bus.

In the mid 1980s, a new bus architecture was developed. Known initially as the AT bus, its more accepted name is the Industry Standard Architecture (ISA) bus. Though it represented a new design, it was still backward-compatible with the 8-bit bus architecture. Nowadays, we do not see the 8-bit slots, but the 16-bit ISA slots, though an older technology, are still used in modern systems. Desktop computers often still come with at least one 16-bit ISA slot, primarily to support legacy expansion cards such as modem or sound cards. For people with these older devices, there is some bad news: they are soon to be dropped completely. ISA has had a good run, but it will need to be retired to make room for new technology, such as the new universal serial bus (USB) and FireWire technology.

Micro Channel Architecture In 1987, IBM introduced its new PS/2 (Personal System 2) computers and, along with them, a new bus, the Micro Channel Architecture (MCA) bus. The MCA bus was the first to offer a 32-bit bus, but despite the increased speed MCA provided, it did not gain widespread marketplace success. The MCA bus was intended to replace the older AT-ISA 16-bit bus. Although it did improve on the 16-bit bus, MCA was made to be incompatible with ISA cards, and this perhaps was one of the reasons it never really caught on. Another factor was that MCA was a proprietary technology used only in IBM PS/2 systems.

Despite its lack of success, the pioneering MCA bus architecture paved the way to a 32-bit bus. It improved on the ISA standard by increasing speed from 8 MHz to 10 MHz, and it could transfer data by using a 16-bit path or a 32-bit path. Further, the MCA bus supported a new technology called bus mastering. Bus mastering is a technique that allows peripheral devices to transfer data to other peripheral devices without using either the CPU or system memory. This technique can significantly speed up a computer system.

Extended Industry Standard Architecture In response to IBM's MCA bus architecture, several companies joined together to design a competitive bus architecture. The result was the 32-bit Extended Industry Standard Architecture (EISA) bus. The EISA bus was designed to be compatible with the older ISA expansion cards, meaning that both the original 8-bit and 16-bit interface cards worked in the EISA slots. This single feature gave EISA an edge over IBM and the MCA bus. EISA slots were used primarily in the 80386 and 80486 computers and are not seen in our modern computers.

VL Bus Introduced in 1992 by the Video Electronics Association (VESA), the VESA local bus (VL bus) found its popularity primarily with the 386 and 486 types of computers, and it was designed for use in systems with a single processor. The VL bus enhanced the performance of high-speed devices such as video controllers. In terms of performance, running at an unprecedented 33 MHz, the VL bus represented significant improvements over the older ISA bus. For a time, most manufacturers relied on the VL bus and developed their high-end video adapters to be used with it. For a time, the VL bus was king, but the VL bus did have some major drawbacks. First among these was the fact that the VL bus did not offer bus mastering, so the CPU was involved in every data transfer from the VL bus, creating a bottleneck and degrading system performance. A second problem with the bus was that it didn't allow for the software setup of boards and it relied on jumpers. The world was going plug and play, and the VL bus wasn't up for it.

Peripheral Component Interconnect Bus Like so much of computer technology, the VL bus soon passed into obscurity, thanks in part to the development of Intel's new local bus, Peripheral Component Interconnect (PCI). The shortcomings of the VL bus created a need for a better bus, and it was Intel that took the initiative and developed the PCI bus. Intel introduced the PCI bus as direct competition for the VL bus, but it was clear early on that the VL bus was no match for it. Intel had the advantage of watching the VL bus in action and was able to overcome its shortcomings while using its strengths.

The PCI bus is used in both PC and Macintosh computers and, like the VL bus, provides a high-speed data path between peripheral devices and the CPU. The PCI bus supports 33-MHz and 66-MHz speeds and 32- and 64-bit data paths using bus mastering. Additional features of the PCI bus include support for plug-and-play devices and for the sharing of IRQs, helping to alleviate the problem of the limited number of IRQs available on a system.

The topic of IRQs as they relate to the PCI bus is quite important. Unlike ISA, which does not allow the sharing of an IRQ, the PCI bus allows several PCI devices to share a single IRQ. For example, your video card, network card, and sound card can all use IRQ 12. To avoid confusing IRQs, PCI uses its own interrupt system, often referred to as #A, #B, #C, #D. These PCI IRQs are rarely seen by the end user, but if you are interested in them, they are accessible in the system's BIOS within the PCI settings.

IRQ sharing is done automatically when the operating system (OS) supports plug and play. Though several devices are using the same resource, this situation is not registered as a device conflict within the OS—it's just part of the PCI magic. Figure 4-16 shows a motherboard with the PCI slots identified.

Note   Only Windows 95 release B and later supports IRQ sharing.

PCI Extended Bus   PCI continues to be developed, with performance enhancements along the way. The next implementation of the PCI bus is known as the PCI Extended (PCIX) bus. The PCI Extended (PCIX) bus promises to be backward-compatible with older PCI devices. Using a 64-bit data path and running at a clock speed of 133 MHz, the PCIX bus increases transfer speed from 132 Mbps to a rather impressive 1 gigabyte per second. It would seem that PCI slots will be seen in computer systems for some time to come.

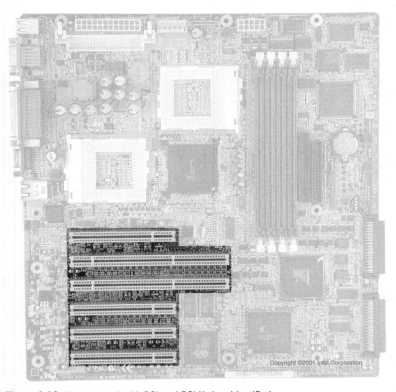

Figure 4-16 Motherboard with PCI and PCI-X slots identified

Accelerated Graphics Port   If there is one device that demands more from a bus than any other, it has to be the video card. As with many other components, it was Intel that responded with the development of the Accelerated Graphics Port (AGP), and they seemed to do it well. AGP is a local bus that can pump out video images as much as eight times faster than PCI can. The port itself provides a direct connection between the video adapter and the system's memory using a 32-bit bus. Today's computers typically come with one AGP slot, freeing up one of the PCI ports for another device. PCI slots are still used for most expansion devices, from network cards to modems, but as for video, AGP will handle that responsibility.

Test Smart   The AGP bus slot is reserved for use with video adapters; no other expansion cards use AGP.

Note   By now most of us have had some experience with USB, whether it be hooking up a digital camera or another external device, but we do not often think of USB as a bus. USB is actually an external bus that works with the system's internal PCI bus. More information on USB can be found in Chapter 1.

Table 4-2 provides a summary of the various common bus types.

Table 4-2   **Expansion Cards and Bus Connections**

Feature	XT Bus	ISA Bus	MCA	EISA	VL Bus	PCI	AGP
Speed	4.77 MHz	8 MHz	10 MHz	8 MHz	33 MHz	33 to 66 MHz	66 MHz
Bus Master	No	On one board only	Yes	Yes	No	Yes	Yes
Software Setup	No	No	Yes	Yes	No	Yes	Yes
Data Bits	8	16	32	32	32	32/64	32

Bus Slot and Expansion Card Compatibility

With the number of available expansion cards and accompanying bus slots, it can get a bit confusing trying to determine which cards and slots are compatible. For instance, you can run that old 8-bit expansion card with a 16-bit bus slot, but what about that 16-bit sound card with PCI slots? Table 4-3 identifies which expansion cards are compatible with which expansion slots.

Table 4-3 Expansion Slot Compatibility

Slot Type	8-Bit Slot	16-Bit Slot	EISA	VL Bus	PCI	PCIX	AGP
8-Bit Card	Yes	Yes	Yes	Yes	No	No	No
16-Bit Card	No	Yes	Yes	Yes	No	No	No
EISA Card	No	No	Yes	No	No	No	No
VL Bus	No	No	No	Yes	No	No	No
PCI Cards	No	No	No	No	Yes	Yes	No
AGP Cards	No	No	No	No	No	No	Yes

IDE and SCSI Connectors

On motherboards today you are likely going to see several rows of pins used to connect everything from hard disks to floppy drives to CD-ROMs. There was a time when these drive connectors were not built on the motherboard as they are today; rather, they were on an expansion card. Nowadays, floppy drive and IDE connectors are built directly on the motherboard. Most boards will typically have slots for two IDE connections, primary and secondary. The primary connection is most often used for hard drives, and the secondary is used for CD-ROMs. The floppy drive connector is usually located close to the IDE connectors. Figure 4-17 shows a motherboard with primary and secondary IDE pin connectors identified.

Figure 4-17 Motherboard with IDE connectors identified

See Also *More information on the IDE interface can be found in Chapter 1.*

You are less likely to find built-in support for Small Computer System Interface (SCSI) devices, although some of the newer and more expensive motherboards may have onboard support for SCSI devices. If you do have SCSI devices, you are most likely going to need to install an expansion card into your system. There are many ISA SCSI expansion cards floating around; however, today you are more likely to be working with a PCI SCSI expansion card.

See Also   *For more information on the SCSI interface, refer to Chapter 1.*

Taking a Closer Look

Having discussed the various components you are going to find when working with motherboards, the last piece of the puzzle we show you is how to identify these components on an actual board. To do this, you can remove the case from your system and begin to identify the various features and components on it. To get you started, refer to the motherboard in Figure 4-18 for the identified components on an AT motherboard and Figure 4-19 for the identified components on an ATX motherboard.

 Test Smart   For the A+ exam, you will be required to know the components of a motherboard. Make sure to review the following figures before taking the actual exam.

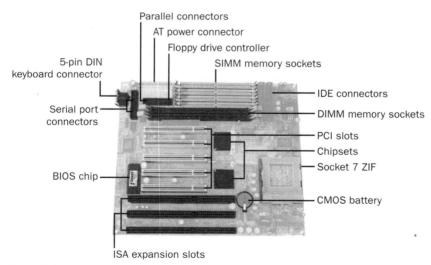

Figure 4-18 AT motherboard with identified components

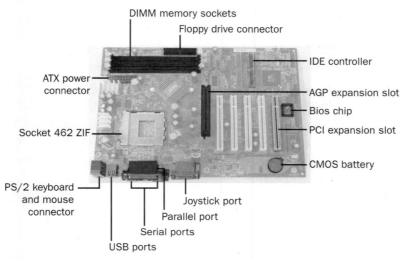

Figure 4-19 ATX motherboard with identified components

Inside the CMOS

In Chapter 1, we discussed the relationship between the system's BIOS and the CMOS. Essentially, we use the BIOS to set hardware configurations and information, and these settings have to be stored somewhere so that they can be easily accessed. The CMOS provides the storage.

The CMOS is read-only memory (ROM) that stores specific computer configurations, such as hard drive type, and keeps track of the date and time for the computer. Thanks to the CMOS battery, the CMOS maintains these settings even when the computer is turned off. On most motherboards, the CMOS battery is a coin-type battery, similar to a standard watch battery. Like all batteries, they lose power, and from time to time, these batteries may need to be replaced. The symptoms of a battery problem include losing accurate time on the computer and sometimes receiving an error message of "invalid system disk" on boot up, as the computer has lost the hard disk settings.

CMOS vs. BIOS The CompTIA objectives refer to the CMOS settings and changing those settings. In truth, this is not technically accurate, as the CMOS really has no settings. Let us explain. The CMOS is actually just a storage area for the BIOS settings. So technically speaking, we change the BIOS settings, *not* the CMOS settings. The BIOS settings are simply held in CMOS storage. This distinction may not be important for the A+ exam but in the real world, it is good to know.

Note   Many people do not consider their CMOS battery until it is too late. A good practice would be to upgrade your battery every three to five years. That way, you should be able to avoid any unwanted surprises.

Many different settings are held in the BIOS and when adding new hardware or troubleshooting a system, it is essential that technicians ensure that the settings in the BIOS are correct. Accessing the BIOS is generally done by pressing a particular key when the computer boots up. Modern computers will typically provide instructions for entering the CMOS when the system boots. Look carefully and you will see the keystroke combination for your system. For now, let's take a look at some of the settings you are likely going to need to change somewhere along your travels.

Warning   Making incorrect changes to your BIOS can cause all sorts of problems! Before making any changes, make sure you document your current settings so you can revert back to them.

■ **Printer Parallel Port**   From within the CMOS, you can change the settings for the parallel ports, and while these settings are automatically configured, they may need to be changed or modified for new hardware or to increase performance. For instance, you can change the IRQ and I/O address used by the parallel port if there is a conflict with another device. You can also set whether the system will use standard unidirectional data communication, ECP (Extended Capabilities Port), or EPP (Enhanced Parallel Port).

See Also   For more information on parallel communication, refer to Chapter 5.

■ **COM Serial Port**   As you are likely aware by now, the configuration of COM (communications) ports in newer systems is handled by plug and play. However, if you need to change the resources (IRQs, I/O ports, and so on) used by COM ports, it can be done in the CMOS...we mean BIOS. Ugh, you get it.

See Also   For more information on resource assignments for serial ports, refer to Chapter 1.

■ **Floppy Drive**   If need be, you can enable or disable support for a floppy drive in the CMOS. Most often you will have drive A enabled, but if you add a second floppy disk you need to enable support for it in the CMOS. Though not an issue as it once was, you can also set the capacity of the floppy drive. If working with an older system, you may need to do this, but it is very unlikely that this will ever need to be changed.

Note   In most BIOSs, you can select the capacity of the floppy disk installed in the system. Most restrict the choice to 720-KB or 1.44-MB 3.5-inch disks, but some older systems might also offer the choice of a 1.2-MB 5.25-inch disk. Given that almost every system shipped in the last five years or more comes standard with 3.5-inch 1.44-MB floppy disk drives, you should not need to change this option.

- **Hard Drive**   If you were to upgrade the hard drive in a computer system today, it is likely that the capacity of the hard drive would be automatically detected and installed. But this was not always the case. Hard drive settings had to be manually input into the CMOS, specifying heads, cylinders, and sector values. When troubleshooting hard drives that are not recognized by the system, a common procedure is to go into the CMOS to ensure that the hard drive has been detected. If it has not, it is likely that the hard drive has not been physically installed correctly.

Within the BIOS, there is normally a range, 46 in fact, of hard disk types defined by their heads, cylinders, and sectors. In addition, there are normally at least one or two selections in which you can manually enter drive parameters. As was mentioned a moment ago, however, nowadays you rarely need to enter drive parameters manually, as they are invariably autodetected.

Note   When installing a bootable SCSI hard disk into a system, the drive type setting in the BIOS is set to 0 or "not installed." This is because the BIOS on the SCSI controller takes care of the booting function, and therefore, the system BIOS needs to be set so that it doesn't interfere with the process.

- **Memory**   In newer systems, the amount of RAM installed will be automatically detected, or at least it should be. You might notice that after adding new RAM to your system, you are prompted to enter the CMOS. This is just to save the new configuration and you don't have to actually make any changes. Just go into the CMOS, save the settings, and exit. There are several advanced memory options that can be set in the CMOS such as RAM timings and enabling or disabling parity. These advanced settings are sometimes used by hard-core techies trying to squeeze out every last drop of performance from their RAM.

■ **Boot Sequence**   One of the settings you are likely to change at some
point is the boot sequence. The boot sequence set in the CMOS dictates in which order the system will look for the boot files. You can set
your system to boot first from a variety of sources including CD-ROM,
floppy disk, hard disk, or the network. If you have the system set to
boot from the hard disk and the disk fails, you may need to change the
boot order to boot from a floppy disk or CD-ROM to troubleshoot the
problem. Additionally, you are likely going to set the system to boot
from a CD if you are installing an operating system.

■ **Date/Time**   The date and time used by the operating system are set
in the CMOS. One thing to remember is that if your system keeps losing time or showing the wrong time, this can be an indicator that the
CMOS battery is failing.

■ **Passwords**   In most cases, there are two passwords that can be set in
the system's CMOS. The first prevents the system from booting until a
password is entered. The second password protects the CMOS itself,
which is a great idea on a shared computer. Trying to troubleshoot the
changes someone may have made to a CMOS can be a frustrating and
difficult process. If you have forgotten a CMOS password and cannot
access your system or CMOS, you will have to remove the CMOS battery to clear the settings. Alternatively, some motherboards have
jumper settings that can be changed in order to clear the CMOS. You
will need to refer to your motherboard's documentation to see how to
set the jumpers to clear the CMOS.

 Test Smart   To clear the CMOS and any forgotten passwords, you can remove
the onboard battery and reboot, or change jumpers on the motherboard.

■ **Plug and Play BIOS**   You can use the Plug and Play option in the
CMOS to configure, well, plug-and-play devices. Most often this setting
goes unchanged, as it is typically left up to the operating system to
handle plug-and-play devices. In fact, if you are using an operating
system that supports plug and play, it will override any settings within
the BIOS.

See Also   *For more information on Plug and Play, including resource assignments, refer to
Chapter 1.*

Key Points

- Processors come in different packages or form factors. Two of the more common are the SECC processor package and the PGA.

- SECC processors fit onto the motherboard using slot connectors, while PGA processors use ZIF sockets.

- L1 cache is smaller and is built into every processor. L2 cache is included in the processor package or can be mounted on the motherboard, and is larger than L1 cache.

- Processor manufacturers Intel, AMD, and Cyrix offer a variety of different processors. These processors vary in terms of speeds, caching, and features.

- Memory is packaged in two main form factors, SIMMs and DIMMs.

- There are two types of SIMMs, 30-pin and 72-pin.

- DIMMs come in a 168-pin format, with the exception of DDR-SDRAM, which uses a 184-pin format. Several types of RAM are available that use the SIMM or DIMM packaging. These include FPM, EDO, SDRAM, DDR-SDRAM, and RDRAM. VRAM, WRAM, and SGRAM are types of video memory used on video cards.

- Parity RAM can detect errors in memory.

- ECC RAM can detect errors in memory and correct certain errors.

- Two common types of motherboards are used today, AT and ATX.

- AT motherboards use a P8 and P9 connector to provide power to the board.

- The black ground wires sit side by side when connecting AT power connectors.

- ATX motherboards use a single 20-hole P1 connector to provide power to the motherboard.

- AT motherboards use a 5-pin DIN connector for the keyboard. ATX motherboards use the mini-DIN (PS/2) connector.

- The CMOS holds settings for the BIOS and is powered by a battery.

Chapter Review Questions

1   Which of the following would be considered memory packaging?

a)   SIMM

b)   SDRAM

c)   VRAM

d)   DRAM

Answer a is correct. The single inline memory module (SIMM) is a type of memory packaging. Answers b, c, and d are incorrect as these are specific types of memory and do not describe how memory is packaged.

2   Which of the following processors are designed for use in server systems? (Choose two.)

a)   Pentium II

b)   Opteron

c)   Xeon

d)   Warhammer

Answers b and c are correct. The AMD Opteron and the Intel Xeon processors are specifically designed for use in server systems. While they can be used for server systems, the Pentium II processor was designed primarily for desktop systems. There is no processor referred to as Warhammer.

3   Which of the following processors uses a socket 8 form factor?

a)   Pentium II

b)   Celeron II

c)   Pentium Pro

d)   Athlon

Answer c is correct. The Pentium Pro processors were originally developed for use in server systems and due to their enhanced capabilities required a socket 8. Answer a is incorrect as the Pentium II processors used the SECC package. Answer b is incorrect as the Celeron II processor uses PGA and SEPP packaging. Answer d, the Athlon processor, is incorrect as it uses Socket A.

4   Which type of RAM module uses a 168-pin design?

a)   DIMM

b)   SIMM

c)   EDO

d)   SDRAM

Answer a is correct. A DIMM uses a 168-pin design. None of the other answers are valid.

5 You come to work on Monday to find that someone has set a password preventing you from accessing the system's CMOS. Which of the following can you do to gain access to the CMOS? (Choose two.)

a) Reinstall the operating system.

b) Set onboard jumper settings to clear the CMOS.

c) Remove the CMOS battery and reboot the system.

d) Boot the computer using a boot disk and enter the CMOS.

Answers b and c are correct. Both of these are valid means of clearing the system BIOS. Answer a is incorrect; the BIOS is OS independent, and reinstalling the operating system will have no effect. Answer d is not valid.

6 Which of the following processors uses the SIMD technology?

a) Pentium Pro

b) Pentium II

c) Pentium III

d) All Intel processors

Answer c is correct. SIMD is effectively an extension of the MMX technology and was introduced with Intel's Pentium III processors. Answers a and b are incorrect as these processors did not yet use the SIMD technology. Answer d is not valid.

7 You have been called to troubleshoot a problem whereby the system keeps losing time and hardware settings. Which of the following is likely to correct the problem?

a) Replace the CMOS battery.

b) Replace the BIOS battery.

c) Clear the CMOS using the jumper settings.

d) Clear the BIOS using the jumper settings.

Answer a is correct. These symptoms are indicative of a failing CMOS battery. Replacing the battery would most likely cure the problem. Answers b, c, and d are not valid.

8 What is the primary function of ECC memory?

a) Faster than regular SDRAM

b) Provides error checking and correcting capability

c) Increases video performance

d) Reduces the cost of memory

Answer b is correct. ECC stands for error-correcting code, a special RAM function that makes the RAM more reliable. None of the other answers are valid.

9   You are attempting to install Windows 2000 Professional directly from the CD-ROM on a brand new system but each time the system boots, a "missing operating system" error message is displayed. Which of the following is most likely the cause of the problem?

    a)   You need to insert a formatted floppy disk with CD-ROM drivers.

    b)   The CD-ROM is corrupt.

    c)   The BIOS is set to boot from the CD-ROM.

    d)   The system is set to boot from the hard disk.

Answer d is correct. On a brand new system, the operating system must be installed before it can be used. If the boot order is configured to boot primarily from the hard disk, this would result in this error. Answer a is incorrect. Modern CD-ROM drives are bootable devices that do not need any additional driver disks. Answer b is incorrect; it is highly unlikely to be corrupt. Answer C is incorrect. If the system is configured to boot from the CD-ROM, it would most likely start and begin the installation of the OS.

10   You wish to upgrade the processor for your system. Which of the following processors use a Socket A form factor?

    a)   Pentium II

    b)   Pentium III

    c)   Athlon

    d)   Pentium Pro

Answer c is correct. The AMD Athlon processor uses a Socket A form factor to attach to the motherboard. Previous AMD processors used the socket 7 ZIF sockets. Answers a and b are incorrect as they use the Slot 1 form factor. Answer c is incorrect as the Pentium Pro processor is a PGA processor and uses a socket 8 ZIF connector.

11   Which of the following is associated with VRAM?

    a)   Sound cards

    b)   Video cards

    c)   L2 cache

    d)   Modems

Answer b is correct. VRAM is a type of video memory built into video cards and not part of the system's main memory. VRAM is not associated with any of the other components listed in the question.

12 Which of the following processors use the socket 7 design? (Choose two.)

a) K6 II

b) Athlon

c) Pentium 66

d) K6 III

Answers a and d are correct. AMD continued to use the familiar socket 7 ZIF sockets up to and including the release of the AMD K6 III. Answer b is incorrect as the Athlon processor uses the Socket A design, and answer c is incorrect as the older Pentium 66 processors used a socket 4 form factor.

13 Which of the following use ZIF sockets?

a) SIMMs

b) DIMMs

c) Processors

d) Expansion cards

Answer c is correct; ZIF sockets are used when attaching PGA processors to the motherboard. Answers a, b, and d do not use ZIF sockets.

14 What type of memory has been built directly into processors since the 486 systems?

a) L2 cache

b) L1 cache

c) SIMM

d) DIMM

Answer b is correct; L1 cache has been built into processors since the days of the 486 computer systems. Answer a is incorrect; L2 cache was once built onto the motherboard but is now included in processor packaging. Answers c and d are incorrect as SIMMs and DIMMs refer to memory packaging and are not built into any processors.

15 What is the data bus width of a regular ISA slot?

a) 8 bits

b) 16 bits

c) 32 bits

d) 64 bits

Answer b is correct. The ISA bus slot offers a 16-bit data path and although it is being phased out, it is still used to connect legacy expansion cards such as modems or sound cards. Answers a, c, and d are incorrect.

16 You want to install a 16-bit ISA card into your system. Which of the following slots on the motherboard could you use? (Choose two.)

a) EISA

b) 16-bit ISA

c) PCI

d) MCA

e) AGP

Answers a and b are correct. A 16-bit ISA expansion card can be used in standard ISA slots and it can also be used in EISA slots. None of the other answers are valid.

17 You have just finished making configuration changes in your BIOS. Where is this information stored?

a) BIOS cache

b) CMOS

c) RAM

d) CPU

Answer b is correct. Changes made in the systems BIOS are saved in the CMOS memory. The settings are held in the CMOS memory because the CMOS is powered by a battery. Answer a is incorrect; there is no such thing as the BIOS cache. Answers c and d are incorrect; the system's RAM and CPU do not hold any BIOS settings.

18 After a power supply fails in your AT system, you install a new power supply. When connecting the wires, how should they be aligned?

a) Red wires next to black

b) Black wires next to black

c) Red wires next to red

d) Black wires next to red

Answer b is correct. AT power supplies use two connectors, the P8 and P9 connectors. When attaching these connectors to the motherboard, the black ground wires should sit next to each other. None of the other answers are valid.

19 MMX technology was added to Intel processors for what reason?

a)   Enhance multimedia

b)   Increase bus-to-CPU I/O transfers

c)   Increase processor caching

d)   Increase processor speed

Answer a is correct. MMX (Multimedia Extensions) technology includes an additional 57 instructions designed to enhance sound and video performance. None of the other answers reflect the function of MMX technology.

20 What is the bus width of an AGP bus?

a)   8 bits

b)   16 bits

c)   32 bits

d)   64 bits

Answer c is correct. The AGP bus slot provides a direct connection between the video adapter and the system's memory using a 32-bit data path. AGP is used for video adapters. None of the other answers are valid.

Chapter 5

Printing and Printer Basics

In the days when PCs started making their appearance on desktops, the promise of a paper-free office came with them. Messages, documents, and manuals would all be read and transferred electronically and the forests of the world could breathe a collective sigh of relief. This never really happened, and the proof is in the printer.

Printers are the number one peripheral device and are considered by many to be less an add-on device and more a standard PC component—so much so that printers are often simply included with the purchase of a new computer system. In fact, many organizations and homes have multiple printers, collectively churning out paper by the truckload. Paper-free office? We don't think so.

Types of Printers

Over the years, many manufacturers have thrown their hats into the printer development ring. The result for us as end users has been a variety of choice for print devices, some good and some not so good. Fortunately for those of us who have to support the various types of printers out there, they basically fall into three categories: dot-matrix printers, laser printers, and ink-jet printers.

When taking the A+ exam, you might receive an equal number of questions about each of the printer types, though in the real world they are not evenly represented. For instance, dot-matrix printers were once the printer of choice for low-end printing solutions and found in all computing environments. Today, they tend to be solely in the domain of payroll, HR, and shipping departments, who use them to print multipart forms. Laser printers, on the other hand, enjoy huge success in organizations of all sizes and knowing how to support them will be part of a PC technician's daily routine. Similarly, ink-jet printers offer a low-end printing solution to homes and small businesses. As with their laser counterparts, troubleshooting ink-jet printers can be an almost daily occurrence.

Regardless of their use or popularity, for the A+ exam you will be expected to be able to support and troubleshoot each of these types of printers.

Laser Printers

Laser printers, once solely the domain of big business, can now be found in homes, small businesses, large corporations, and just about everywhere else there is a computer. As with almost every other piece of technological equipment, the cost of laser printers has fallen dramatically over the years—in the last three to five years in particular. Now, laser printers offer a viable alternative to ink-jet printers, even giving ink-jets a little competition in the choice for a home use printer. One area where laser printers have to take a backseat to ink-jet printers, though, is with color printing. It is possible to buy color laser printers, but they are prohibitively expensive in comparison to black-and-white laser and color ink-jet printers. For that reason, you are only likely to see color laser printers in corporate or specialized environments.

Laser Printer Components

Compared to the other types of printers discussed in this chapter, laser printers don't make the print process look easy. In fact, the more you learn about the laser print process, the more surprised you might be that you get a printout at all. Laser printers use many components that must work together to get that print on paper. If any of these components fails, the print job might fail or its quality will just be poor. Each of the laser printer components performs a very specific role in the print process, and you will be required to identify the functions of these components for the A+ exam.

Unfortunately, you might not be able to take the top off of your laser printer and visually identify the components discussed here. In days gone by, many of the components within laser printers were separate, but today many printer manufacturers are integrating components into the toner cartridge assembly. This approach has made replacing a single laser printer component a difficult, if not impossible, task. In a way, however, this more integrated approach makes troubleshooting a little bit easier. Instead of replacing a single component, we replace most of them at the same time. It might not be environmentally sound, but it is definitely easier. The following is an explanation of the key components the laser printer needs to function. Figure 5-1 shows a toner cartridge.

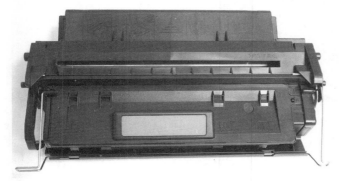

Figure 5-1 Toner cartridges come in all shapes and sizes.

- **Photosensitive drum**   The photosensitive drum (also called the electrostatic photographic drum), shown in Figure 5-2, is a key player in the laser printing process. The drum itself is simply an aluminum roller. The photosensitivity comes from the fact that the roller is coated with specialized photosensitive particles. A laser beam inside the printer shines reflected light onto the surface of the drum, creating a pattern of electrically charged, and not so charged, areas. The end result is an image on the drum to be transferred to paper. The drum is usually held inside the toner cartridge, but can be accessed in case it needs to be manually cleaned to remove excess toner. When handling or wiping the drum, use extra caution; any scratches or dents on the drum will be evident on every print job. The only remedy is to replace the drum, which normally involves replacing the entire toner cartridge.

Test Smart   If you notice a consistent pattern of unwanted ink spots on a print job, the drum might be scratched. The only remedy is to replace the drum, which in most cases means replacing the entire toner cartridge.

Figure 5-2 It is on the electrophotostatic drum that the laser "draws" the image to be printed.

- **Eraser lamp**   The eraser lamp is used to give the photosensitive drum a thorough electrical cleaning. The eraser lamp shines a light on the entire surface of the photosensitive drum, neutralizing the electrical charge. This is done to remove any remaining particles from the drum before the next print job. Not sufficiently removing the electrical charge will result in poor print quality.

- **Primary corona wire**   The primary corona is a thin wire that rests very close to the photosensitive drum, but never actually touches the drum. The primary corona wire is responsible for negatively charging the photosensitive particles on the surface of the drum.

- **Transfer corona**   The transfer corona is responsible for positively charging the paper before it reaches the toner area. To get the image from the drum onto the paper, the paper must have a positive electrical charge that will draw the toner away from the drum and onto the paper. To prevent the positively charged paper from sticking to the drum itself, a *static charge eliminator* is used to remove the charge from the paper.

- **Laser**   The laser beam is used in the writing process and creates an image of the page to be printed on the photosensitive drum. The photosensitive drum holds an electrical charge when not exposed to light. Because it is completely dark within the toner cartridge, when the laser hits areas on the drum, the drum discharges in the areas hit by the laser, leaving the image.

- **Toner**   It is sometimes assumed that toner is simply powdered ink, but it is a bit more complex than that. Printer toner is a powder composed of plastic and iron particles that cling to the surface of the drum after the primary corona wire provides an electrical charge to the drum. The transfer corona applies an electrical charge to the paper, and the toner is transferred from the drum to the paper where it is melted onto the paper by the fuser.

■ **Fuser**   If you were to touch a printed piece of paper after it leaves the laser printer, you would notice that it is warm, (unless you are wearing gloves). This is a result of the fusing process. When the toner initially transfers from the drum to the paper, it is only held there by an electrical charge. The fuser effectively melts the toner to the paper. When working inside a printer, care should be taken to avoid contact with the fuser because it gets very hot.

■ **Printer controller**   One of the components not held in the toner cartridge is the printer controller circuitry. The controller is a motherboard equivalent for laser printers; it converts the signals and messages from the computer to signals for the various components within the printer. Essentially, the controller is a circuit board that holds the printer's memory and communicates with the PC.

Test Smart   Knowing what the various components do in the print process is important because it helps in the troubleshooting process. When a print job fails or has poor quality, we can use our knowledge of the components to help identify which one has failed.

Like we said, there is a lot going on in that laser printer, and many components at work. No wonder we need to spend our time troubleshooting them.

The Electrophotographic Print Process

All most end users need to know about the laser printing process is that you put blank paper in and paper with text on it comes out. As technicians, we need to know what happens in between the paper going in and the paper coming out. The process by which a laser printer creates printed output is broken down into six separate steps: cleaning, charging, writing, developing, transferring, and fusing. You can expect to be quizzed on these steps in the A+ exam, so we will look at each of them independently.

Test Smart   Be prepared to identify the steps involved in the laser print process. If it is handy, use a mnemonic. For instance, classic rock lovers might say "Creedence Clearwater Was Definitely Top Five." Food-focused folks might come up with "Cold Cola With Doritos Taste Fabulous." We have a few others of our own, but you should try and come up with one that works for you. Hey, who says studying for an A+ exam can't be fun?

Cleaning Phase   To work correctly, laser printers need a clean slate, or in this case a clean drum, to begin with. To do this, two things must happen, a physical and an electrical cleansing. The physical cleaning is accomplished by a rubber blade that effectively scrapes off the excess toner from the drum, similar, in a way, to a wiper blade scraping your windshield. The extra toner is collected in a toner receptacle inside the toner cartridge. The amount of excess toner is extremely small as is the receptacle. The extra toner will just sit there until the toner cartridge is replaced.

With the rubber blade taking care of physically cleaning the drum, we also need a method of electrically cleaning the drum to remove the electrical charge. To do this, an eraser lamp shines on the drum, causing it to lose all of its electrostatic charge. In essence, this wipes out the particles on the drum, making sure that there are no residual particles from the previous charging.

If the drum is not being effectively cleaned, the result is poor print quality, which would manifest itself as residue on the printout from previous printed pages. In some cases, if it happens a lot, the drum might need to be changed, or the eraser lamp replaced.

Conditioning/Charging the Drum   The second step in the laser printing process is the conditioning or charging of the drum. In this phase, a special wire, known as the *corona wire*, applies a negative charge to the photosensitive drum. This negative charge typically ranges between 600 and 1000 volts.

Writing   In this phase, the laser beam goes to work. The laser beam flashes on and off as directed by the information sent to it as a print job. The beam reflects off of mirrors to hit the drum. Wherever the laser beam hits the photosensitive drum, the negative charge is reduced from its 600-volt plateau to −100 volts, creating an image on the drum.

Developing   After the laser light does its job, the drum holds an electrical representation of the image to be printed. The next job is to transform the image into something that can be written to the paper. To do this, toner must be applied to the areas on the drum exposed to the laser light. Inside the toner cartridge is the *developing roller* that uses a magnet and electrostatic charges to attract the iron particles in the toner to itself. When the developing roller rotates and the toner is between the developing roller and the photosensitive drum, the toner is attracted to the areas that have been exposed to the laser. The end result of the development stage is that the photosensitive drum has toner stuck to it wherever the laser had written.

Transferring   In this phase, the image is transferred from the drum to the paper. To do this, the transfer corona gives the paper a positive charge that attracts the negatively charged toner from the surface of the drum to the positively charged paper. In effect, the toner leaps from the drum to the paper. The image, however, is only held on the paper by a weak static charge. To fix it more securely, it needs to be fused to the paper.

Note   Not all printers use a transfer corona. Some use a transfer roller, but the effect is the same.

Fusing   During the fusing stage, the toner, which contains a special chemical, is melted, causing it to stick (or fuse) to the paper. To make the toner melt, the paper is passed through one or more rollers, which are called fuser rollers. These rollers are heated to a very high temperature by a fuser lamp. Both of these components reach very high temperatures (plenty hot enough to burn you), so you should exercise caution when working inside a laser printer that has recently been used (or even powered on).

Forget RPM, This Is PPM

Although the process we have just described seems long and complex, today's laser printers are able to perform the entire process in just a few seconds. Modern high-performance laser printers can turn out upward of 32 *pages per minute*, or PPM. If you figure it out, that means the laser printer is going though the six-step process in a little under two seconds. Think about it—that's one one thousand, two one thousand, done.

 Test Smart   Before taking the A+ exam, be sure you know the six steps in the laser printing process and what occurs at each step.

Dot-Matrix Printers

If you were to walk down to your local computer reseller hoping to buy a dot-matrix printer, you are likely to return home empty handed. Dot-matrix printers are all but extinct in most environments; however, there are a few of those loud and clunky dinosaurs in use, particularly in environments like payroll and shipping where multipart stationery is required.

Dot-matrix printers are perhaps the simplest of the three types of printers discussed here. The basic principle of a dot-matrix printer is that a collection of pins, typically 9 or 24, organized in a rectangular shape, are pressed against a ribbon, which in turn presses against the paper. Behind the paper is something called a platen. The platen is a cylinder roller that guides the paper through and also provides a backstop for the printing mechanism to bang into. The platen is most often made of a hard rubber or rubber-like material. As far as dot-matrix print quality is concerned, the higher the number of pins the higher the print quality.

Note Though dot-matrix printers were available in 9 and 24 pins, 24-pin dot-matrix printers were the standard. 24-pin dot-matrix printers were designated as letter quality (LQ), 9-pin as near letter quality (NLQ).

 Test Smart Dot-matrix printers use *pins* to create the print on paper.

Dot-matrix printers typically come in two sizes; 80-column dot-matrix is the type used with "normal" paper widths like those accommodated by most laser or ink-jet printers. You can also get 132-column dot-matrix printers that can accommodate wider paper formats, which makes them suitable for applications where this width is required. Good examples of this might be the printing of pay slips, invoices, or delivery waybills. Because there are fewer situations now that demand the extra width, you are far more likely to encounter 80-column dot-matrix printers than 132. Figure 5-3 shows an example of an 80-column dot-matrix printer. A 132-column printer is quite a bit wider than the 80-column printer. This makes it easy to identify what kind of printer you are working on.

Figure 5-3 At one time, 80-column dot-matrix printers like this were used for a wide variety of printing tasks.

Dot-matrix printers often use a tractor feed mechanism to transfer paper through the printer. To use a tractor feed, the holes in the sides of the specialized continuous feed paper must be aligned with the feed mechanism on the printer. Depending on the printer, this can be kind of a tricky task and if you do not get it exactly right, the paper will jam the printer or the printout will be crinkled. The tractor feed mechanism is one of the reasons why dot-matrix printers fell out of favor.

 Test Smart   Dot-matrix printers offer slower printing than ink-jets or lasers. The speed of dot-matrix printers is measured in *characters per second*.

Ink-Jet Printers

Most of us have had at least some experience with ink-jet printers, whether our own or trying to fix someone else's. Ink-jet printers, also known as bubble-jet printers, have become commonplace and are found in all computer environments from homes to large corporations. Their ability to print cheaply in color adds to their popularity. Figure 5-4 shows an ink-jet printer.

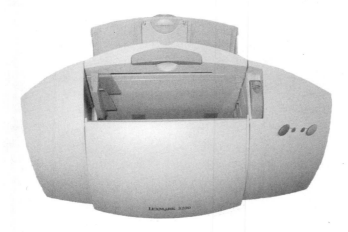

Figure 5-4 Ink-jet printers have become a common sight in homes and businesses.

Ink-jet printers spray ink onto the paper to form images or text. This might sound a little too random to produce good-quality print jobs, but actually it is very efficient. Most ink-jet devices today work by heating the tiny ink bubbles that form on the 300 to 600 tiny nozzles on each ink-jet print head. Once these tiny ink droplets heat to their boiling point, they burst and an electrically charged plate deflects the ink onto the paper. The print head moves across the paper horizontally while the paper feed mechanism pulls the paper through the printer.

 Test Smart   For the A+ exam, remember that most ink-jet printers are thermal, requiring ink drops to boil on the nozzle and then be deflected onto the paper using electrically charged plates.

As with laser printers, the quality of print jobs for ink-jet printers is measured in dots per inch (dpi); the higher the dpi, the better the print, but the more ink is used. When printing text, ink-jets will typically require a dpi of 150; true photo-quality prints will require 1200 dpi and higher. As with laser printers, the speed of ink-jets is measured in pages per minute (PPM). When choosing a printer, one of the things to keep an eye on is the PPM rating for the printer.

To provide high-quality printing, the nozzles on the print head are very small, about the size of a human hair. While allowing a clear and precise print job, this also means that the nozzles themselves can become clogged. This is a common problem with older ink-jet printers, but less a concern with the newer models. Even so, it can still be an issue, which is why practically all ink-jet printers offer a cleaning function. Figure 5-5 shows an example of the cartridges used in an ink-jet printer.

Figure 5-5 Ink-jet cartridges come in a variety of shapes and sizes.

Note   Ink-jet printers are referred to as nonimpact printers because unlike dot-matrix printers, the print mechanism never actually comes into contact with the paper.

The Darker Side of Ink-Jet Printers In terms of initial outlay, ink-jet printers are an attractive option. For very little investment you can buy a printer that will provide you with crisp black print and full-color capabilities. There are, however, hidden costs associated with ink-jet printers namely, the ink cartridges. Depending on the ink-jet printer you purchase, the ink cartridges can represent a huge cost over time. For instance, to replace one color and one black cartridge, you might pay half the cost of the ink-jet printer. To make this even more of a consideration, many color ink-jet printers have more than one cartridge, and in some cases might even have four—black, yellow, magenta, and cyan. Because of the ongoing costs of ink-jet cartridges, some people are looking for alternatives. For this reason, it is becoming increasingly common for people to refill the ink in cartridges. Some people believe this is a good strategy, while others maintain that using the old print cartridges is a bad idea because of the wear and tear on the print heads.

Connecting Printers

Printers vary, not only in terms of design and manufacturer, but also in the methods used to connect and access them. Some of these connection methods are more common than others, but as a PC support technician you will need to be able to identify and manage each of these connection methods. In this section, we look at the various connection methods, starting with arguably the most common method of all—parallel.

Parallel

Connecting a printer through the parallel port continues to be one of the most popular methods of connecting a printer to a computer. Many other technologies such as USB and network connections have reduced the use of parallel port connections, but it will be some time before it is gone altogether, if ever.

To connect a printer to the computer, a cable with a DB-25 connector is used to attach to the PC and a Centronics 36 connector on the printer. Once connected, you have four different parallel modes to choose from. These modes dictate the speed at which the parallel ports operate. These modes are usually set in the system's BIOS and include unidirectional, bidirectional, enhanced parallel port, and extended capabilities port.

Unidirectional Parallel Ports

The unidirectional port is the "standard" parallel port offering very little in terms of performance. Unidirectional parallel ports only allow data transfer out from the computer; that's why it's called unidirectional—one-way—communication. Unidirectional parallel ports have been with us since the time of those early XT and AT IBM computers. A standard unidirectional parallel port is restricted to speeds of 150 kilobytes per second (KBps) and a maximum transmission distance of 15 feet.

Bidirectional Parallel Ports

Bidirectional ports offered a huge advantage over the unidirectional ports—bidirectional communication. This feature allows the port to both transmit and receive data; however, the two-way communication cannot happen simultaneously. The benefit of two-way communication is that it allows the printer and the operating system to "talk to each other."

Enhanced Parallel Ports

The speed offered by a bidirectional parallel port was okay for a time, but as we began to add other devices to parallel ports such as external hard disks, scanners, and CD-ROMs, more speed was needed. To meet this need, the Institute of

Electrical and Electronics Engineers (IEEE) developed a new parallel port standard, called IEEE 1284, designed to provide greater transfer speeds. The enhanced parallel port (EPP) is one implementation of the IEEE 1284 standard. The EPP protocol allows for two-way communication between devices and transfer speeds of between 600 KBps and 1.5 megabytes per second (MBps). Although two-way communication is offered, it allows for only one way at a time, known as half-duplex communication.

Enhanced Capabilities Port

Another implementation of the IEEE 1284 standard is the enhanced capabilities port (ECP). The ECP port is specifically designed to offer high-speed transfer rates and uses a direct memory access (DMA) channel and buffer to increase printing performance.

 Test Smart   Switching between the various parallel port modes is normally done in the system's BIOS.

Standardize This!   Previously, we made reference to a gang of folks calling themselves the Institute of Electrical and Electronics Engineers (IEEE). In the computer world, the IEEE is a very well-known organization, responsible for defining standards for a range of networking and connectivity related technologies. For example, they are the body that defines Ethernet networking standards, serial and parallel communication, and even network management and data security standards. For more information on the IEEE, visit *www.ieee.org*.

Network Connected Printers

In many environments, more than a single user needs to access a printer. In such cases, we use network printers to allow several users access to a single printer. There are two main ways of accessing printers over the network: through a network share, or by connecting the printer directly to the network.

Printer Sharing

As you might already know, you can connect a printer directly to your PC, and if you are on a network, you can allow other users on that network to access your printer. Effectively, when you share a local printer to the network, the computer becomes a print server and other network systems go through that computer to access the printer. The print server controls who can and who cannot access the printer over the network by using permissions.

Connecting Printers Directly to the Network

In many corporate and business environments, it is better to connect a printer directly to the network rather than to use a shared printer. This is because true networked printers are easier to manage and several networked printers can be managed from a central location rather than from individual computer systems. Network printers connect to the network using a network interface card and network cabling. Network printers are often configured from a display panel on the printer or from specialized software on the server. One of the biggest advantages of connecting a printer directly to the network is that it can be placed in the most convenient location, nearest to the users who need it. In some cases, rather than using a network interface card to connect a printer to the network, a box called a standalone print server is used. The box is connected to the network, and then the printer is connected to the box. Print jobs are sent to the box, which forwards them on to the printer. This configuration works if the printer doesn't support network printing through a network interface card.

USB

In terms of printer connectivity, USB is the new kid on the block. Increasingly, though, printers are being made available with both a parallel and a USB port. Some printers even come with just a USB port, which can create a problem if you are trying to connect it directly to an older system that does not have USB ports. This is generally not a problem with newer systems, but some older systems and even some modern servers do not come with USB ports.

The advantages of having a printer connected via USB are the same as with any other USB device. The printer can be plugged into the computer while the system is turned on, and in most cases the connection of the printer will be automatically recognized by the computer and it will "plug and play."

One of the interesting things about connecting a printer via USB is the speed. USB has higher data transmission rates than those provided by a parallel port. One last note about USB—it is a bidirectional interface, which means that you can have all of the advantages that bidirectional communication brings.

Serial

Connecting a printer through the serial port is not done much anymore simply because the serial port does not offer the speed that other technologies such as parallel and USB can provide. Because of this, you are unlikely to come across very many of them in your travels. Serial printers connect to the PC through one of the system's serial ports using a cable with either a DB-9 or DB-25 female connector.

Infrared

Cabling of any sort can be an eyesore and in some instances can even be impractical. One notable option we have that allows us to move away from traditional printer cabling is using wireless infrared transmission. Infrared transmission is a wireless medium that uses the infrared range of the electromagnetic spectrum. Many modern operating systems and laser printers provide infrared transmitters and receivers that allow for wireless infrared communication between devices to occur. This is particularly useful for devices such as personal digital assistants (PDAs), which often rely on infrared as their primary means of connection.

Upgrading Your Printer   It used to be that upgrades were the domain of desktop computers but today you are also likely to find yourself upgrading your printer. Though often overlooked, upgrading a printer can increase its long-term usefulness and reduce the number of printers that find their way to local landfills. Some of the more common printer upgrades include memory, hard disks, and network cards. Some of these components, such as memory, often must be specifically designed for the printer you are upgrading. The process of performing the actual upgrade follows the same basic procedures as any desktop upgrade. In addition to upgrading the hardware components, many printers allow you to upgrade other components such as printer trays, staplers, and fax devices. Of course not all printers have the option to upgrade; to see what upgrade options are available for your printer, refer to the manufacturer's Web site.

Troubleshooting Printers and Print Quality

Troubleshooting printers is just one of the necessary evils of the PC technician's world. Unlike other less demanding PC components, printers have many moving parts, and in the world of PCs, moving parts represent potential failure points. No matter what type of printer you find yourself supporting, there are many things that can go wrong with it. One important thing to remember when troubleshooting printers is to look for the easiest solutions first. Move to more complex solutions only after the easy ones have been ruled out. In this section, we explore some of the more common printer errors you are going to encounter.

Note   Like many other computer components and peripherals, printers can have firmware updates designed to enhance the functionality of the printer or correct errors. It is a good idea to periodically check the printer manufacturer's Web site to see if a firmware upgrade has been released for your printer.

Troubleshooting Dot-Matrix Printers

As mentioned earlier, dot-matrix printers are simple devices, and in terms of troubleshooting, this simplicity makes them easier to work with. Table 5-1 highlights some of the hotspots when troubleshooting a dot-matrix printer. Keep in mind that the manufacturer's manual that ships with a particular printer is often better for specific troubleshooting problems. The ones presented in the table are general procedures and practices aimed at getting you through the A+ exam.

 Test Smart   Keep an eye on the common printing problems listed in the following tables. Questions on troubleshooting printers are sure to appear on the exam.

Table 5-1   Troubleshooting Dot-Matrix Printers

Problem	Potential Solution
Printer will not turn on	No power is getting to the printer; check that the power cable is plugged in.
Power is getting to the printer but it does not print	Verify that the printer is online and not out of paper. If LEDs are flashing, cross-reference flashing LEDs with the manual that accompanied the printer.
Printer will not go online	Verify that there is paper in the printer and the printer ribbon is in place.
Paper does not feed correctly	Ensure that the paper is inserted into the tractor feed mechanism correctly. If the paper is not correctly aligned, the paper will wrinkle or jam as it goes through the printer.
Text split across two sheets of paper	This will often occur when the paper is not correctly placed in the tractor feed mechanism. Replace the paper, ensuring that it is correctly aligned.
Paper is crinkled after the print job	Realign the paper in the tractor feed mechanism.
Print head moves across the paper but does not type on the paper	This often happens if the ink ribbon is installed incorrectly or it is out of ink.
Writing on paper is faint	This is typically because the ribbon needs to be replaced.
Text is garbled	Ensure that the correct driver is being used for the printer and that the printer is using the correct settings.
Text is faint or inconsistent	This is most certainly due to a worn ribbon. Replace the ink ribbon.
Printed text is dark on one side and light on the other	This was a common dot-matrix problem, most often caused by a faulty ribbon or misaligned platen (the roller against which the print head presses).

Test Smart   Because dot-matrix printers are simple devices, the solution to most of your printing problems is often to realign the paper in the feed mechanism or to replace the ink ribbon.

Troubleshooting Ink-Jet Printers

Ink-jet printers are everywhere; there might even be one on your desk right now. Each and every one of these ink-jet printers might be one print job away from needing a little troubleshooting magic. Fortunately, in terms of troubleshooting at least, if you have seen one ink-jet printer you have seen them all. This makes troubleshooting ink-jets from various manufacturers that much easier. Table 5-2 shows a few things to keep in mind when troubleshooting ink-jet printers.

Table 5-2   Troubleshooting Ink-Jet Printers

Problem	Potential Solution
Printer will not turn on	No power is getting to the printer; check that the power cable is plugged in.
Power is getting to the printer but it does not print	Verify that the printer is online and not out of paper. If LEDs are flashing, cross-reference flashing LEDs with the manual that accompanied the printer.
Printer will not go online	Verify that there is paper in the printer and that the ink cartridge(s) is installed properly.
Paper does not feed correctly	Friction feed rollers might need to be adjusted, more paper might need to be added to the paper tray, or a lighter weight paper might need to be used.
Print head moves across the paper but does not type on the paper	The ink cartridge might be empty or low or the ink might be dry. Try replacing the ink cartridge.
Print quality is faint	Ink is old or running out; replace the ink cartridge.
Ink speckles on printout	Sometimes the ink within a printer can find its way onto other components by which the paper passes. As it does, it is transferred to the paper. To correct the problem, clean the inside of the printer with a damp cloth to remove unwanted ink stains.
The printout has the wrong colors	Verify that the ink cartridge is full and that it is not clogged. To do this, clean the ink-jet according to the manufacturer's documentation. In printers that have more than one color cartridge, also make sure that the cartridges are in the correct slots.
Text is garbled	Ensure that the correct driver is being used for the printer and that the printer is using the correct settings.

Test Smart   Many printers come with an alignment utility that you can run after the new cartridge is installed. This utility is normally available with the software that came with the printer and is used to ensure that the letters are printed in correct alignment.

Troubleshooting Laser Printers

Laser printers can be more difficult to troubleshoot than the other types of printers discussed here. However, once you get the hang of troubleshooting them, it is not difficult to isolate the cause of a printing error. Table 5-3 provides a quick look at some of the more common problems you will encounter with laser printers.

Table 5-3   Troubleshooting Laser Printers

Problem	Potential Solution
Light ghost images appear on printout	Ghost images are caused by residue from a previous print job. This is often caused by too much toner on the drum, and the drum not being sufficiently discharged and picking up toner from a previous print job. Replace the toner cartridge or drum. If the problem still exists, take the printer to an authorized service shop.
Dark ghosting appears on print jobs	Dark ghosting can be caused by a damaged drum. Replace the drum or toner cartridge.
Random spots or streaks appear on the print job	The drum is not clean; residual particles are still on the drum. Either clean the drum or replace the eraser lamp.
Consistent marks appear on every print page	This is often caused by a damaged drum; the drum will need to be replaced.
Print quality is too light	Check the toner. This error can be caused when toner is running low. Some printers also have a "darkness" or intensity setting that you should check.
Print jobs appear patchy	This can be caused when the toner is running low. A shake of the toner cartridge might be enough to get a few more print jobs out of the printer, but you will need to replace the toner cartridge in the very near future.
Laser printer prints a blank page	This could be a result of a failed transfer corona. If the transfer corona does not positively charge the paper, the toner will not be transferred from the drum.
Print smudges or streaks after printed out	The fuser roller might not be correctly fusing the toner onto the paper. It might be necessary to replace the fuser roller or fuser assembly.

General Printing Considerations

Having looked at some specific problems for the three different types of printers, we can look at some of the general considerations you have to think about when troubleshooting printers.

Printer Drivers Have you ever seen a print job that looked more like Egyptian hieroglyphics than a standard document? Unless the intended task was to print hieroglyphics, the garbled and unreadable text is a result of the incorrect printer driver being installed. Every printer has to have a printer driver installed to communicate with the operating system. If the wrong driver is used, there is a communication breakdown and the result can be unreadable print jobs. To correct the problem you can go to the manufacturer's Web site and download the latest drivers for your printer. Ensure that you download the drivers that exactly match the model number of your printer.

Feed and Output

Printers use two different types of feed mechanisms, the tractor feed method used by the dot-matrix printers and the friction feed mechanisms used by dot-matrix, ink-jet, and laser printers. Tractor feed printers provide us with numerous headaches because if the printing paper isn't properly aligned, the print jobs will be wrinkled or jam the printer. Such errors were commonplace with dot-matrix printers. Despite the issues with tractor feed mechanisms, it was easy to troubleshoot them and isolate the cause of the problem.

Friction feed printing mechanisms are more commonly associated with laser and ink-jet printers. Effectively, the paper is fed between rollers and wound through the printer. One common problem associated with friction feed printers is when pages stick together and more than a single sheet is fed through the printer. On some printers, the rollers used to force paper through the printer can be adjusted when this happens. On others, devices called separator pads, used to separate the paper coming in from the paper tray, might need to be replaced. When separator pads fail, multiple sheets are fed through the printer. Another common problem with friction feed mechanisms is when no paper is picked up by the rollers, often caused by dust from poor-quality paper getting stuck on the rollers. This is often corrected simply by cleaning the rollers. If time is at a premium, placing more paper in the print tray also often does the trick.

 Test Smart   When friction feed rollers do not pick up paper from the tray, the solution might be as simple as adding more paper in the tray. If multiple pages are retrieved from the tray, replace the separator pad(s).

Common Errors

A multitude of errors can occur in the printing process. Most of these printer errors are displayed on the printer's console using text error messages or LEDs. You might need to refer to the manufacturer's documentation to discover exactly what these error codes mean. Some common printer errors include the following:

- **Paper out** A printer cannot print without paper. One of the more common errors is simply that the printer is out of paper. This could mean the entire printer is out of paper or a specific tray in the printer is empty. To correct the problem, add paper to the paper tray following the manufacturer's guidelines.

- **Low ink/toner** Regardless of the type of printer used, there is only a finite amount of ink or toner we can use before it needs to be replaced. Replacing ink or toner in most printers is a straightforward process, but in some it might be necessary to refer to manufacturer documentation to see how the procedure is correctly accomplished.

- **Incorrect port mode** This error message indicates that the printer is using the wrong parallel port mode. Recall from earlier in the chapter that parallel printer communication can be unidirectional, bidirectional, EPP, or ECP. To correct the problem, you will likely need to enter the system's BIOS and change the parallel port settings.

- **No default printer selected** If you try to print from within a Windows environment and receive this error, the system has not been informed as to the default printer to use. This can be because either a default printer has not been selected, or the system does not detect a printer to print to. The solution to this problem is to ensure that the OS recognizes a printer and that it is selected as the default printer for the system.

- **Input/output error** When you receive an I/O error, you can assume one thing: the printer and the computer are not communicating. This problem can be as easy to fix as ensuring that the printer is turned on and that it is physically cabled correctly. Once any physical cause has been ruled out, you might need to verify that the correct drivers for the printer are being used and that there are no resource conflicts between the printer and another device.

Paper Jams

It seems like a PC technician cannot go a whole day without having to hear about a paper jam. Paper jams are an all too often occurrence and can be caused by faulty printer components or user error. Whichever one it is, the result is the same—there is a paper jam.

When you are faced with the task of removing a paper jam, the thing to do is find the paper that is jammed (bet you didn't need a book to tell you that one). And gently remove it. On some printers, it is tricky to find and remove a paper jam; with others, finding the offending paper is easy. Wherever the jam is, it is best to remove the paper in the same way that it travels through the printer. Pulling paper in the opposite direction it is intended forces the rollers and other internal components to travel in a direction they were not designed to.

If a printer continues to jam, it might be that the printer is attempting to feed through paper that is too thick. You can try to use a lighter weight paper to see if the problem is corrected. If not, it might be that the printer needs to be serviced.

Note   The documentation that came with the printer is sure to identify the correct location and method for accessing paper jams. Before attempting to get to a paper jam, read the manual to find the shortest and easiest method to do so.

Safety Precautions

Many safety precautions when dealing with printers fall into the realm of common sense. For instance, it is not a good idea to let long hair, jewelry, ties, or other such dangling things come too close to the feed rollers. Doing so might allow you to experience the six stages of the laser print process firsthand.

When working with laser printers, be careful working around the actual laser, because it is possible for it to cause eye damage. In addition, keep away from that fuser; it is very hot and can give you a significant burn. For this reason, it is always best to let the printer cool down a bit before working inside of it. Also worthy of note is the primary corona wire, which carries a very high voltage and should thus be avoided.

Preventative Maintenance

Like every other PC component and peripheral device, printers last longer the more we look after them. There are a few things we need to maintain to ensure that printers last as long as they were designed to.

One of the best and simplest ways to ensure printer longevity is to simply keep it clean. Dust, small pieces of paper, and other foreign objects are enemies to printers. For printer-specific preventative solutions, consider the following.

Laser Printers

- Laser printers produce ozone gas and use a special ozone filter to manage ozone emissions. Replace or clean the ozone filter periodically.

- Use compressed air to blow out dust and small paper residue.

- Use a PC vacuum to remove any excess toner from within the printer.

- Carefully clean the transfer corona with denatured alcohol.

Dot-Matrix Printers

▣ Inspect printer ribbon and replace if necessary.

▣ Use compressed air to blow out dust and small paper residue.

▣ Ensure that the platen is correctly aligned.

▣ Clean the print head using denatured alcohol.

Ink-Jet Printer

▣ Remove ink cartridges and wipe excess ink from the metal plates.

▣ Inspect the inside of the printer. Wipe away any excess ink from the interior with a lint-free cloth.

▣ Use compressed air to blow out dust and small paper residue.

▣ Use new and good-quality cartridges.

▣ Use the printer's built-in cleaning function to periodically clean the print heads.

Note   In your travels, you might hear the term *print consumables*. Print consumables refer to those items that are consumed by the printer and must be periodically replaced. Print consumables include such things as ink, toner, and paper.

Key Points

▣ There are three main types of printers used in today's computer environments: dot-matrix, ink-jet, and laser printers.

▣ Laser printer components include the photosensitive drum, eraser lamp, primary corona wire, transfer corona, laser, toner, fuser, and printer controller.

▣ The laser print process includes six steps: cleaning, charging, writing, developing, transferring, and fusing.

▣ Dot-matrix printers use a tractor feed mechanism, while ink-jet and laser printers use a friction feed paper mechanism.

▣ Ink-jet and laser printers measure print speed in pages per minute, while dot-matrix printers measure print speed in characters per second.

▣ There are several parallel port modes, including EPP, ECP, unidirectional, and bidirectional.

■ ECP parallel ports offer the fastest transmission speeds of any parallel port mode.

■ Printers can connect to a PC using several different methods including USB, parallel, serial, network, and infrared.

■ When troubleshooting dot-matrix printers, make sure that the platen is correctly aligned, that the ink ribbon is OK, that the correct printer drivers are being used, and that the paper is correctly installed in the tractor feed mechanism.

■ When troubleshooting ink-jet printers, ensure that the ink cartridges have ink, that the inside of the printer is free from splattered ink, that the correct print drivers are being used, and that the paper tray has the correct weight and sufficient supply of paper.

■ When troubleshooting laser printers, inspect the drum for scratches or other imperfections, and ensure that there is enough toner, that the correct drivers are being used, and that the system is cleaned periodically.

■ Common printer errors include low toner/ink, out of paper, input/output communication errors, and incorrect parallel port being used.

■ When troubleshooting any computer, verify that the correct printer driver is being used. The most recent printer drivers are available from the manufacturer's Web site.

■ Periodic maintenance for laser printers includes cleaning or replacing the ozone filter.

Chapter Review Questions

1 Which of the following paper feed mechanisms is associated with a dot-matrix printer?

   a)   Friction feed

   b)   Impact feed

   c)   Tractor feed

   d)   Dual feed

Answers a and c are correct. Dot-matrix printers use tractor feed and friction feed mechanisms to weave the paper through the printer. Answers b and d are not valid paper feeding mechanisms.

2   Which of the following represents how the speed of ink-jet printers is measured?

a)   Characters per second

b)   Inches per minute

c)   Lines per second

d)   Pages per minute

Answer d is correct. Ink-jet printers and laser printers measure the speed of print jobs in pages per minute (PPM). Answer a is incorrect; dot-matrix printers measure speed in characters per second. Answers b and c are invalid.

3   When using a dot-matrix printer, which of the following makes contact with the paper to create the print?

a)   Corona wire

b)   Pins

c)   Electrically charged plates

d)   Nozzles

Answer b is correct. Dot-matrix printers are impact printers, meaning that the print head requires contact with the ribbon, which in turn contacts the paper. Answer a is incorrect. The corona wire is a component found in laser printers. Answers c and d are incorrect. Ink-jet printers make use of electrically charged plates and nozzles in the printing process.

4   You are troubleshooting a dot-matrix printer that splits text across two continuous-feed sheets. What is the likely cause of the problem?

a)   Friction feed mechanism is misaligned

b)   Low toner

c)   Paper not correctly inserted in the tractor feed

d)   Broken ribbon cartridge

Answer c is correct. If the paper is not correctly inserted into the tractor feed mechanism, the text might run onto the second page of the continuous-feed paper. Answer a is incorrect; friction feed can only be used to print a single page at a time. Answers b and d are incorrect. Low toner and a broken ribbon cartridge will not cause the problem identified in the question.

5   You are working with a laser printer. Which of the following components presents the greatest risk to the technician?

a)   Fuser

b)   Refuser

c)   Corona wire

d)   Drum

Answer a is correct. When working with laser printers, the device most likely to cause injury is the fuser. The fuser is used to melt the toner onto the paper and gets quite hot in the process. Touching this will certainly give you a burn. Answer b is not a valid component, and answers c and d do not offer a great threat to technicians.

6   You have just installed a new printer, but when you use it, only garbled text is printed. Which of the following is most likely the cause?

a)   Ink needs to be replaced

b)   Corona wire not functioning

c)   Transfer corona not working

d)   Wrong printer drivers

Answer d is correct. If a printer is using incorrect or outdated printer drivers, the result is often garbled and unreadable text. The solution is to ensure that you are using the latest print drivers. Answers a, b, and c would not cause garbled and unreadable text to print out.

7   You need to change the parallel mode for your computer system. Which of the following modes are valid? (Choose two.)

a)   STP

b)   TCP

c)   EPP

d)   Bidirectional

Answers c and d are correct. EPP and bidirectional are both parallel port modes. Answers a and b are not valid parallel port modes.

8   During which of the following stages is the toner melted onto the paper?

a)   Fusing

b)   Cleaning

c)   Striping

d)   Writing

Answer a is correct. During the fusing stage, the toner, which is only held on the paper with a weak electrical charge, is permanently fused to the paper. Answer b is incorrect. During the cleaning phase, the drum is physically cleaned with a rubber blade and electrically cleaned using the eraser lamp. Answer c is not a valid laser printing step. Answer d is incorrect. During the writing phase, reflected laser light applies an image to the drum.

9   While troubleshooting a laser printer, you notice several sheets are fed through simultaneously. Which of the following might explain the reason? (Choose two.)

a)   Worn separation pad

b)   Wrong paper

c)   Incorrect printer drivers

d)   Faulty tractor feed

Answers a and b correct. Laser printers use a separation pad to help feed only a single piece of paper through the rollers at a time. If the separation pad becomes worn, several pages might feed through simultaneously. If you are trying to feed through a weight of paper that the laser printer was not designed to be used with, it might also cause multiple pages to be fed through the rollers. Answer c is incorrect; the wrong printer drivers would not cause multiple pages to feed through the printer. Answer d is incorrect; laser printers do not use a tractor feed.

10 Which of the following are the correct steps in the laser print process?

a)   Cleaning, charging, writing, developing, transferring, fusing

b)   Cleaning, charging, writing, developing, transferring, fusing, rendering

c)   Charging, cleaning, writing, developing, transferring, fusing

d)   Cleaning, charging, writing, fusing, transferring, developing

Answer a is correct. The correct steps in the laser printing process are cleaning, charging, writing, developing, transferring, fusing. None of the other answers are valid.

11 Which of the following represent methods of connecting a printer to a computer? (Choose three.)

a)   Infrared transmissions

b)   Shared network access

c)   Serial port

d)   IEEE 1450 port

Answers a, b, and c are correct. There are many methods to connect a printer to the computer. These include using infrared transmissions, shared network access, and even older serial ports are sometimes used. Answer d is not a valid port.

12 You are troubleshooting a dot-matrix printer using multipart forms. The printout is visible on all pages of the multipart stationery except the top page. Which of the following components are you likely to replace?

a)   Primary corona

b)   Print head

c)   Ribbon

d)   Fuser assembly

Answer c is correct. If a dot-matrix printout is visible on all pages except the top one, the problem is most likely that the ribbon has run out of ink. The impact of the print head will still push on the paper and make the printout visible on the other pages, but nothing will appear on the top page. Answers a and d are incorrect. These components are associated with a laser printer. Answer b is incorrect. Because the text appears on the other pages of the multipart stationery, the print head would appear to be working correctly.

13 Which of the following components is responsible for transferring toner from the drum to the paper?

a)   Fuser

b)   Transport corona

c)   Transfer corona

d)   Development wire

Answer c is correct. The transfer corona in laser printers puts a positive charge on a piece of paper, forcing the toner on a negatively charged drum to transfer to the paper. Answer a is incorrect; the fuser is used to permanently place the toner on the paper. Answers b and d are not valid laser printer components.

14 You are troubleshooting a laser printer that displays ghosted images in the print job. Which of the following causes ghost images?

a)   Damaged reflector coil

b)   Damaged fuser

c)   Low toner

d)   Drum is not being sufficiently cleaned

Answer d is correct. If during the cleaning phase the drum is not being physically and electrically cleaned, ghost images can appear on subsequent print jobs. It might be that the rubber blade or eraser lamp is not doing the cleaning job. Answer a is not a valid answer. Answer b is incorrect; a damaged fuser will not sufficiently melt the toner on the page, not cause ghosting. Answer c is incorrect; low toner would not cause ghosting.

15 Which of the following components charge the drum after it has been cleaned?

a)   Transfer corona

b)   Multiplier

c)   Primary corona

d)   Conditioning wire

Answer c is correct. The primary corona wire applies a negative charge to the drum after it has gone through the cleaning phase. Answers a is incorrect; the transfer corona charges the paper to draw the toner away from the drum. Answers b and d are not valid.

16 Which of the following are required steps in the ink-jet printing process? (Choose two.)

a)   Boiling the ink

b)   Cleaning the drum

c)   Discharging ink drops using electrically charged plates

d)   Charging the drum

Answers a and c are correct. On most ink-jet printers, the ink drops on the print head nozzles are heated to a boil, burst, and then are dispersed on the paper using electrically charged plates. Answers b and d are printing steps associated with laser printers.

17 You are hooking up a device to the parallel port and require the highest speed possible from the port. Which of the following parallel port modes offers you the fastest data transfers?

a) EPP

b) ECP

c) Unidirectional

d) SCSI

Answer b is correct. The ECP parallel port mode offers bidirectional communication between the computer system and the printer. ECP ports also use advance buffering and a DMA channel to increase their efficiency. Answers b and c are incorrect; these parallel port modes do not offer the transmission speeds of an ECP port. Answer d is incorrect; SCSI is not a parallel technology.

18 You are troubleshooting a laser printer. The laser successfully creates an image on the drum but pages print out blank. What is the most likely cause of the problem?

a) Low toner

b) Printer driver problem

c) Transfer corona failure

d) Eraser lamp failure

Answer c is correct. If the transfer corona were to fail, it would not positively charge the paper and therefore would not take the toner from the drum. Answer a is incorrect; even if the toner were low, something would still be printed on the paper. Answer b is incorrect. The wrong printer driver might cause garbage text to print, but would not necessarily cause blank pages to be printed. Answer d is incorrect because the failure of the eraser lamp would not cause the printing of blank pages. More likely the printout would have ghost images due to improper cleaning.

19 A single user on a network has a printer connected to their USB port. Another user on the same network would like to print to that printer. What is the easiest way to allow both people to print to that printer?

a) Install a multiaccess printer driver.

b) Share the printer over the network.

c) Install a new dedicated network printer.

d) Attach both computers to the printer using a USB cable.

Answer b is correct. The easiest method of allowing others to access a printer connected to a local computer system is to share it over a network. Access to the printer is controlled by permissions on the computer that is connected to the printer. All the other answers are invalid.

20 Several users printing to a network printer complain that the print quality is poor; there are several consistent marks or ink spot patterns on their printouts. Which of the following could explain the problem?

a)   Scratched or damaged drum

b)   Wrong toner being used

c)   Ink ribbon is worn out

d)   The ozone filter needs to be replaced

Answer a is correct. If a laser printer's drum becomes scratched or damaged, each subsequent print job will shows the effects of the damage on the printout. This creates a consistent pattern of ink marks on the paper printouts. None of the other answers provided will cause a consistent pattern of ink spots on the printed page.

Chapter 6

Introduction to Networking

Walk into any business, school, and even many homes, and you are very likely to see a computer network. Given the popularity of computer networks today, it's hard to imagine that it wasn't too long ago when computer networks were the exception rather than the rule. Even as recently as seven or eight years ago, most offices and workplaces had proprietary standalone computer systems, and if you wanted to transfer a file to another person in the office, you would need to put the files on a floppy disk and physically take the files to the other computer. This early "network" came to be affectionately known as a *sneakernet*—get it?

Before networking became widespread, printing was also a problem as each system either needed a printer connected directly to it, or the files to be printed had to be manually copied to a system that had a printer attached. There was some experimentation with printer-sharing devices but typically the result was too many printers, too much walking, and too many floppy disks.

Thankfully, those days are behind us, and today networks are a familiar sight in businesses of all sizes. The old sneakernet has been replaced with a more efficient, centralized approach to file and print access (which some say is a shame as the sneakernet never needed upgrading and never crashed).

Understanding what networks were originally designed for can take some of the mystery and complexity out of them. Fundamentally, when you strip it right down, the function of any network is to share files and other resources with other people. They also allow us to communicate using applications such as e-mail and instant messaging (IM).

Before we begin our discussion of networking, we should probably point out that it is a very broad topic and although identified as an objective for the A+ exam, the coverage of networking concepts and technologies is, to say the least, introductory. The actual A+ exam will require general networking knowledge and an understanding of fundamental networking terms and concepts but nothing more. If this brief introduction to networking perks your interest, other certifications, such as CompTIA Network+, probe a little deeper into the networking world and are a good way to expand your networking knowledge. For now, however, let's just stick to the basics and the information you'll need for the A+ exam. To begin with, let's take a brief look at what a network is and some of its key components.

See Also   *This chapter focuses on network-related hardware and design. Discussions of the software end of networking such as protocols and operating systems is covered in Chapter 10.*

Networking Hardware

A network can be as simple as two computers connected to share a printer or as complex as several thousand computers sharing a database between several cities or even countries. In either case, whether large or small, networks all share some common hardware, features, and designs. In this section we introduce some of the hardware used to create networks and what it takes to configure them.

Network Interface Cards

One of the first pieces of networking hardware to consider is the *network interface card (NIC)*. The function of the network card is to provide the physical connection to the network, that is, to connect your local computer system to a network. For instance, if you are connected to the Internet right now using a high-speed connection, you likely have a network card installed in your computer, which provides the physical connection to the Internet.

Network cards today are typically internal expansion cards that fit into one of the motherboard's expansion slots. Network cards have traditionally been add-in devices, but increasingly with the popularity of networks, network cards are being integrated onto motherboards. Integrated network cards are particularly popular with laptop systems, but for those laptops that do not have a built-in network interface card, a PCMCIA card is often used. Figure 6-1 shows an expansion NIC for a desktop system and Figure 6-2 shows a PCMCIA NIC for a laptop system.

Figure 6-1 An expansion NIC

Figure 6-2 PCMCIA NIC

NIC Considerations

As a computer technician, you can expect at some point to be installing, upgrading, or replacing a network card in a system. For the most part, the procedure is straightforward, but there are a few key points to consider before popping the case off the computer.

■ **Drivers** To get the NIC to work with the operating system, it will need the correct software drivers. These drivers would have likely shipped with the network card, but if not, you can download the latest drivers from the network card, manufacturer's Web site. To do this, you will need to use another computer or have a dial-up connection or some other means to access the manufacturer's Web site. Remember, when it comes to drivers, the most recent ones will often not be the ones that ship with the device but rather will be those that are listed on the manufacturer's Web site.

■ **System resources**   All add-on expansion cards require certain system resources. Network cards must be assigned a unique interrupt request (IRQ) address and memory I/O address. If your network card is plug and play, these should be configured automatically. If not, you will have to set these resources manually. To do this you will need to refer to the documentation for the network card.

See Also   *For more information on installing and configuring network cards, refer to Chapter 1. For more information on configuring software for network cards, refer to Chapter 10.*

■ **Available expansion slot**   Most systems today have several available expansion slots. Before buying that card, you will likely want to confirm that you have one available and that the slot is of the correct type. For instance, you will need to confirm that a PCI slot is available if you are using a PCI NIC. If you are using an old ISA NIC, you'd best be extra cautious; many modern motherboards do not include the older ISA slots.

■ **NIC speed**   Not all network cards operate at the same speed. Many smaller networks today still use network cards that function at 10 megabits per second (Mbps), so if you want to get 100 Mbps out of a network that uses 10-Mbps hubs, you are out of luck. Similarly, if you install a 10-Mbps NIC into a network functioning at 100 Mbps, it will work, but only at 10 Mbps. In some cases, it may not even work at all, as some 100 Mbps networks are not backward-compatible.

■ **Cabling**   A final consideration is the cabling used on the network. Cabling is discussed later in this chapter; however, it is important to make sure that the network card can accommodate the type of cabling used on the network. In the real world, this consideration is less a concern than it once was. This is simply because UTP (unshielded twisted-pair) cable and RJ-45 connectors have become the network media of choice. Still, it is worth mentioning.

Legacy Cards and Jumper Settings

It is always easier to deal with new, out-of-the-box hardware, but this is not always possible. At some point you will be working on an older system and, therefore, an older network card. Configuring the network cards of yesterday is a bit more involved than in our modern plug and play era. One of the main differences between the old and the newer NICs is the need to configure the older card's jumper settings. Jumpers are tiny plastic and metal on/off switches that configure how the card is set up and the system resources it will use. For instance, if you wanted an older network card to use IRQ 5 and a specific I/O address, you would set the jumpers on the card to configure it as such. Manually setting jumpers to use system resources was once a necessary evil and when not done correctly often caused a difficult-to-troubleshoot hardware malfunction. System technicians breathed a collective sigh of relief when resource allocation became automatic. Figure 6-3 shows configuration jumpers on a network card.

Jumper blocks

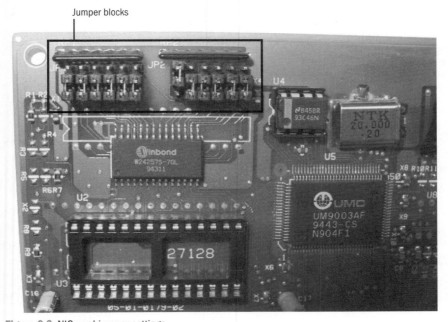

Figure 6-3 NIC card jumper settings

Test Smart   Ensure that you know the function of jumper settings for the A+ exam.

MAC Address   Each and every network card (or any other type of network interface for that matter) ever made has a unique identifier known as the *Media Access Control (MAC)* address burned onto it. The MAC address is often referred to as the *hardware address* **because it is physically embedded on a chip within the card or interface**. A MAC address is a 6-byte address used to identify the card on the network and forms the basis of network communication. This is why each card has to have a unique MAC address; duplicate addresses would undoubtedly cause communication problems on the network. An example of a valid MAC address would be 00-04-E2-1C-7B-5A. While this number address looks rather hieroglyphic, there is a method to the madness. The first three bytes (00-04-E2) represent the manufacturer of the card. The second three bytes (1C-7B-5A) are referred to as the Universal Local Area Network MAC address. Basically, they are used to make the NIC's address unique. To find out the MAC address of the NIC you are using, the following commands can be used according to your operating system:

- ifconfig—Linux/some UNIX
- ipconfig—Microsoft Windows NT/2000/XP
- winipcfg—Microsoft Windows 9x/Me

Installing the Network Card

Once you are convinced you have everything you need to install the network card, you are ready to pop off the case and do so. The actual physical installation of a NIC follows the same basic procedures for installing any other expansion card such as a sound card, video card, or internal modem. The basic procedure is to power off the computer system, and while observing ESD best practices, remove the case and install the NIC into an available expansion slot, making sure to secure it in place. If you are installing a network card into a system that uses an ATX power supply, you should also remove the power connector from the motherboard. Figure 6-4 shows the installation of the network card.

> **Tip**   Before jumping in and starting to remove and handle the network card in your system, you may want to review some of the safe hardware-handling procedures covered in Chapter 3. Pay special attention to the section on electrostatic discharge (ESD).

With the network card physically installed in the computer, the next step is to put the cover back on and start up the system. If your card supports plug and play, the system will attempt to install the correct driver and configure system resources. You may be prompted to supply the drivers, which likely came with the NIC when purchased, or you will have downloaded the latest version of the driver from the manufacturer's Web site.

Figure 6-4 NIC installation

If you are using a Windows system and want to confirm that the network card installation has been successful, you can view a newly installed network card in Windows
Device Manager, as shown in Figure 6-5. If your new NIC is not shown in Device Manager, it either has not been recognized by the system or the wrong drivers were used. For
more information on installing devices, refer to Chapter 1 and look for the section on
adding and removing field-replaceable modules.

It is certainly not difficult to find old NICs lying around, and you may find yourself
trying to install one of these older cards. When installing older, legacy NICs, the installation can become a bit more difficult as it might be necessary to manually configure the
network card if plug and play is not supported. Manually configuring the network card
involves setting jumpers and unique IRQ and I/O addresses for the card. If there are no
jumpers on the card, it might be that the card is "jumperless" and will need to be configured through a software utility supplied by the manufacturer. Before installing a legacy
NIC in your system, you will need to see if this software and the latest drivers are available
from the manufacturer's Web site. But be warned, out-of-date hardware is well hidden on
the Internet and it might take some digging around to find the drivers and configuration
software that you are looking for.

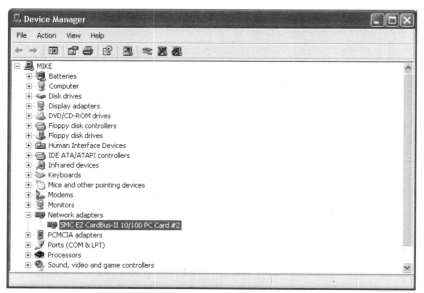

Figure 6-5 NIC installation in Device Manager

Note   The CompTIA objectives weigh heavily in the corner of the Windows operating system. The physical installation of network cards follows the same physical procedures regardless of the OS.

Duplex Modes

One final consideration to keep in mind when configuring your network card is something called the duplex settings. As far as network cards are concerned, there are two modes of duplexing to be aware of: *full duplex* and *half duplex*. These duplex modes simply refer to the way communication is handled between devices. We say devices because duplexing does not always refer to network cards. It also describes everything from modems to microphones and even regular telephones. The duplex setting defines the device's ability (or lack thereof) to send and receive data at the same time. In the realm of network cards, this means a NIC configured in full duplex mode is able to send and receive data simultaneously. Network cards configured in a half duplex mode can send *or* receive but not at the same time. This has a huge impact on the speed of the link established by the NIC. For instance, a 100-Mbps NIC using half duplex mode sends and receives data at 100 Mbps. However, the same card configured in full duplex mode can send and receive data at up to 200 Mbps. That is a considerable performance benefit.

You may be wondering why you have never had to adjust the duplex setting for your network card. Nowadays we rely upon the network card driver configuration to manage our duplex settings. While it is necessary for computer technicians to understand the concept of duplexing, in real-world applications we rarely have to concern ourselves with it. Having said that, a common strategy when troubleshooting a network card problem is to change the duplex setting as some hardware configurations (hub/switch and network card) don't seem to work well together. The basic strategy is to use full duplex first and then switch to half duplex if you encounter problems. Most modern networks have built-in support for both full and half duplex modes and offer an easy way to switch between modes.

Test Smart   Before taking the A+ exam, be sure you understand the difference between half duplex and full duplex communication.

Note   There is another mode called *simplex*, which allows for one-way communication only. An example of this would be a television that allows the signal to pass in only one direction. This is not discussed here, as network connections do not use simplex.

Network Cable Characteristics

Having discussed network interfaces in detail, we can now look at the different types of cables commonly used in today's networks. Some of these cable types have fallen out of favor in recent years and are not widely implemented, but they might still be found in some legacy networks, so a knowledge of them is important. The cable types you can expect to see on the A+ exam include:

- Coaxial
- Twisted-pair
- RS-232
- Infrared
- Fiber-optic

Each of these four cabling types has its own unique characteristics, advantages, and disadvantages. These advantages and disadvantages make them well suited for some network environments and completely impractical in others. It is up to network administrators to know the difference.

Cabling or Media? This is as good a time as any to clear the air on a little lingo controversy. Throughout this chapter and in accordance with the CompTIA objectives, we have used the term *cabling* to define the physical connections between computer systems. In truth, this term is no longer relevant to modern networks. For instance, network technologies such as wireless can be used to create network connections but are certainly not cabling in the traditional sense. Because of this, network technicians will commonly refer to all copper-based, fiber–optic, and wireless technologies as *network media*. At the end of the day, cabling is used by CompTIA but between you and us...media is the correct terminology.

Coaxial Media (We Mean Cable)

For many years, coaxial (coax for short) cable was the cable of choice for most networks, mostly because there was not a viable alternative. It was cheap, easy to install, and *if* implemented correctly, stable. Today, the popularity of coaxial cable has given way to other network cabling, but people who work with networks are still likely to encounter a network using coaxial somewhere along the way.

Two types of coaxial cable are commonly used in computer networks: thin coax (RG-58) and thick coax (RG-62), both of which are described next.

Thin Coaxial

Thin coaxial was the network cable of choice a few years ago. Thin coax, which resembles ordinary television cable, consists of an outer cover, a copper wire or aluminum shielding, insulation, and a conducting core, as shown in Figure 6-6. The transmission signal flows along the conducting core. The shielding protects the core from interference, and the insulation layer keeps the core isolated from the shielding.

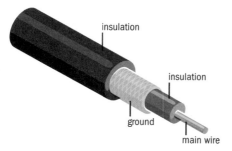

insulation

insulation

ground

main wire

Figure 6-6 The composition of coaxial cable

In actual network implementation, thin coax runs from computer to computer, connecting directly to each device without the need for a hub or other network equipment. As the name suggests, the cable is thin, lightweight, and easy to install, connecting to each computer using devices called *British Naval Connector (BNC) T connectors*. At each end of a thin coax network segment, which can be up to 185 meters in length, are 50 Ohm terminators that soak up the signal once it has reached the end of the cable. Examples of BNC connectors and terminators can be seen in Chapter 1. In common network implementations, thin coax is limited to a speed of 10Mbps.

Thick Coax

As you may have guessed, thick coax cable is a thicker form of coaxial cable. Thick coax is over 1 cm in diameter and fairly inflexible. The inflexibility makes thick coax cable difficult to work with, but the cable thickness does offer some unique advantages, namely, thick coax has a greater resistance to interference and greater conductivity. Thick coax has a signal capacity of 500 meters (1,640 feet), making it ideal for use as a network backbone. A *backbone* is the term given to a segment of cable that acts as a connector for multiple segments. For example, you might have a thick coaxial backbone running between floors of a building, but the networks on each floor will use another type of cable.

Like thin coax networks, each of the physical ends of the cable must be terminated to prevent signal reflection. If there is a break in the cable, the entire network will fail.

Thick coax is, however, very expensive and slow, having a maximum transfer speed of 10 Mbps with common networking standards. This is often far too slow for today's speed-hungry networks. Furthermore, unlike thin coax, which can connect directly to the network device, thick coax requires the use of other equipment to attach devices to the network cable. These devices, called *vampire taps*, pierce the outer casing of the cable and make a direct connection to the wires inside. Special cables and connectors, called *Attachment Unit Interface (AUI)* connectors, are then used to connect to the network cards. These relatively expensive devices add considerably to the overall cost of building a network with thick coax. The high cost, low speed, and installation restrictions mean that other cabling systems, such as fiber optics, are now chosen instead of thick coax.

Twisted-Pair Cable

Twisted-pair cabling has replaced coaxial as the cable of choice for many networks. This is due in part to the increased speeds that twisted-pair cabling can accommodate, and because it is easier to install and manage than its coaxial counterparts. There are two types of twisted-pair cable: unshielded twisted-pair (UTP) and shielded twisted-pair (STP). By far, the most commonly used is UTP.

UTP has become the most popular network cable due primarily to its low cost and easier installation. The current standard for UTP allows for speeds of up to 100 Mbps, but new technologies allow even faster speeds using regular UTP. UTP cables connect to network devices through the use of small plastic RJ-45 connectors, as shown in Figure 6-7. More pictures of RJ-45 connectors are found in Chapter 1.

Figure 6-7 An RJ-45 connector used on UTP cabling

Just to throw a little confusion into the mix, there are different categories of UTP cable, each with different applications, capabilities, and characteristics. Table 6-1 summarizes the categories of UTP cable.

Table 6-1   The Categories of UTP Cable

Category	Description
Category 1	Is the older UTP telephone cabling, which can carry voice signals but not data.
Category 2	Can transmit data at up to 4 Mbps, but because of its slow speed is rarely seen in the network environment.
Category 3	Can transmit data at up to 16 Mbps. UTP networks that have been in place for some time might use Category 3 cabling.
Category 4	Has a maximum transfer rate (bandwidth) of 20 Mbps.
Category 5	Has a maximum bandwidth of 100 Mbps. Category 5 has been the standard for network cabling for a number of years. In a very large percentage of UTP environments, Category 5 (or Cat5, to give its common name) is the cable type in use.
Category 5e	Has a maximum bandwidth of 1000Mbps. The category 5e standard replaces category 5.
Category 6	Ratified in June 2002, Category 6 has a maximum bandwidth of 1000Mbps. Category 6 cable has more stringent construction standards than Category 5e cable and better resistance to outside interferences such as crosstalk and EMI (electromagnetic interference).

Regular UTP does have its detractors, namely that it is highly susceptible to interference and attenuation. It is not recommended for UTP cable to exceed 100 meters (328 feet).

The inexpensive nature of UTP and its ability to transmit at high speeds means that these shortcomings, such that they are, are often overlooked.

Beyond Category 6 The funny thing when writing about networking is that after every fact, there is some technician somewhere ready to throw a "Yeah but..." into the mix. As a preemptive measure, here is the "Yeah but..." as far as UTP cable categories are concerned. Category 6 is, at the time of writing, the highest standard of UTP cabling as assigned by the Telecommunication Industry Association/Electronic Industries Association (TIA/EIA) who ratify such things. The truth is, the standards makers are one step behind the cable manufacturers, who are developing faster UTP implementations as we speak. On the horizon are Category 6a and even Category 7. These UTP cables are designed to run as fast as 350 Mbps! The bottom line is if you are at a party and someone is debating with you on what the highest category of UTP cable is...go talk to someone else.

Test Smart UTP cable has a maximum transfer speed of 100 Mbps and can be run no more than 100 meters.

Shielded Twisted-Pair Cable

As the name implies, the difference between UTP and STP cable is in the shielding. STP cable, which can be used up to a maximum of 90 meters, uses a copper jacket inside the outer sheath to reduce attenuation and a foil wrap around each individual wire within the cable, which prevents crosstalk. All of this makes STP less influenced by EMI and other sources of interference. However, you will have to pay for the benefits that STP cabling provides. Due to its construction, it is considerably more expensive than UTP, and in environments where money is the bottom line, STP cannot compete with UTP. In environments where it is necessary to use a more EMI-resistant cable, money will have to take a back seat.

Crossover Cables When working with UTP cables, you will most certainly run into crossover cables. Crossover cables are specially constructed cables in which the 1 and 3, and 2 and 6 cables are crossed. What this does is put the transmission line from one device on the receive device of the other and vice versa. Using crossover cables enables certain specific connections to be achieved, such as directly connecting two PCs or connecting two network hubs or switches. Most network connections can be achieved with non-crossover cables, called *straight-through cables*, as the intermediate network devices (hubs and switches) make the necessary wire crossing internally. For this reason, it is far more common to use straight-through cables than it is to use crossover cables.

Network Cabling and Data Threats

Regardless of the type of computers, network design, or network architecture used, each computer on a network has to be connected using some form of network cabling. Common network implementations use copper-based cable, fiber cable, and even wireless technologies such as radio waves. However, the increasing availability of wireless technology means that computers are breaking free of the traditional network attachment methods. That said, today, only a very small percentage of organizations use wireless networking. Before we jump into describing more of the various cables used to create today's networks, we thought it wise to first review some of the terms and considerations you will have to know about when discussing network cabling. We'll start by discussing one of the most common terms, bandwidth.

Bandwidth

Bandwidth is one of those terms that is thrown around a lot in the computer world—usually, in the form of a complaint about not enough of it. As it relates to cabling, *bandwidth* basically refers to the transmission capacity or throughput of the cable. You are most likely going to hear bandwidth speed measured in megabits per second (Mbps), meaning that a cable with a bandwidth of 10 Mbps can transmit 10 million bits per second. Sound fast? At one point it may have been, but in today's demanding network environments, it isn't. Today's networks typically transmit at speeds of 100 Mbps, which is still too slow for many organizations.

The need for speed has created the pursuit of technologies to increase bandwidth. Some strategies commonly used to increase bandwidth include replacing hubs with switches (discussed in the Ethernet section later in this chapter) and replacing traditional copper-based networking cable with fiber-optic solutions. Although there is some debate as to what the actual maximum speed of fiber optic cable is, it is generally accepted that the maximum is 100 gigabits per second (Gbps), which represents a staggering 100 billion bits per second. But as you might expect, the faster you go, the more you have to pay. Technologies such as fiber optics are often out of the reach of many businesses; there is a fine line between performance and finances.

Attenuation

Network cabling can only be of a certain length before the data signals that pass through them weaken. The degradation of data signals as they pass through a particular network cable is referred to as *attenuation* and it is a major consideration when designing or troubleshooting a network.

Distance is one of the factors that defines what types of cabling can be used for a particular network. For example, in environments where a cable must run great distances, fiber-optic cable can be used up to 50 km, depending on frequency, before the data signal weakens, which is longer than any other physical cable. Other network cabling, such as the widely used unshielded twisted-pair, can only be run in distances of 100 meters before the data signal fades.

Tip   In the networking world, there is an exception to pretty much every rule. In this case, the maximum distance for a cable can be increased using devices called *repeaters,* which regenerate data signals as they pass along the network media. With the signals regenerated, the set distance limits no longer apply.

Interference

Attenuation is one of the threats to the integrity of data signals on network cabling, but there is another common one. As signals pass through twisted-pair or coaxial network cables, they can be subjected to particular interference known as *electromagnetic interference (EMI).*

There are many devices in and around an office that can cause EMI, including computer monitors, fluorescent lighting units, and even refrigerators. EMI can weaken the signal within the cable and make it unreadable by the receiving device. Some cable types are more susceptible to EMI than others, and as you might expect, the more money spent on cabling, the better the resistance to EMI. In terms of EMI resistance, fiber-optic cable is completely resistant as it uses light instead of copper as a transmission medium.

In addition to EMI, another type of interference known as crosstalk can cause problems. *Crosstalk* refers to the interference from other wires around or within the cable. For example, if two wires are run very close together, the signals in both wires may interfere with each other. Crosstalk is typically combated by twisting the wires within the cable. If you ever have the opportunity to look inside some cable, such as UTP network cable, you will see that the wires are twisted around each other. This twisting helps prevents crosstalk.

 Test Smart   Before taking the exam, be sure you understand the three common threats to data signals: attenuation, crosstalk, and EMI.

RS-232

Before reading the CompTIA objectives, had you ever heard of RS-232 cable? As in "Hey Mike, pass me a section of that RS-232." Probably not because it doesn't exist. The CompTIA A+ objectives include RS-232 in the cabling category, but in reality, RS-232 is not cabling at all. Actually, *RS-232 (Recommended Standard-232)* is a TIA/EIA standard for serial transmission between computers and peripheral devices such as modems, mice, and keyboards. In the real world, referring to serial communication as RS-232 is a little like referring to Sting as Gordon Sumner; it may be technically accurate, but no one will know who or what you are talking about.

Note   Serial connections send data over the cable one bit at a time. It is a simple way to send information in or out of the computer, but it's not as fast as other ways the computer can communicate. Parallel communication is faster than serial because it sends several bits at a time in parallel instead of single bits in sequence, as with serial communication. Parallel communication is often associated with printers or removable storage devices, which need faster speeds.

The RS-232 standard was introduced way back in the 1960s, and is still the most widely used communication protocol in use today. It is simple, inexpensive to implement, and though relatively slow, more than adequate for most simple serial communication devices such as keyboards and mice. RS-232 commonly uses a 25-pin DB-25 or 9-pin DB-9 connector, such as with a serial mouse. Wireless technologies can also use RS-232 serial communication. In a normal environment, RS-232 has a limitation of 50 feet and offers slow data rates of 20 Kbps.

Infrared

Infrared communication is not foreign to any of us who have used a TV or stereo remote control, but in terms of networking, infrared technology has been largely ignored. This is likely a result of the emergence of other, faster technologies such as the newer radio wave–based 802.11b wireless Ethernet networking standard. Infrared is often referred to as IrDA, named after the Infrared Data Association, which holds the responsibility for developing standards for wireless infrared transmissions.

The function of IrDA is to provide cable-free communication for a range of devices including laptops, PDAs, keyboards, mice, digital cameras, printers, and so on. Basically, if something works over a wire/cable connection, it will work over the IrDA infrared data link. The convenience of not having to work with cables has a downside, and that is performance. IrDA transmissions are limited to 115 Kbps, depending on the device. This slow speed is due partly to the fact that IrDA uses a half duplex communication method. There are developments under way and IrDA 2.0, the latest version, boasts speeds of 4 Mbps—OK, but too slow for many of today's data transfers. You could grow old waiting to get all of the high-resolution pics out of your digital camera. As a comparison, consider that your USB 2.0 devices can transfer at speeds up to 480 Mbps and IEEE 1394 (FireWire) gets as high as 400 Mbps. Considering the speed difference, a cable here and there is a reasonable trade-off.

In addition to the speed being a problem, the fact that IrDA is a point-to-point technology can also be an issue. Point-to-point communication works in the same way your TV remote would; you need to point the device directly at the other device to have it function. Ever try to change the channel when someone is standing in the way? The same effect happens when the transmission is interrupted between computer components; put your bag of Doritos in the wrong spot and you lose your connectivity. In addition, the maximum distance between the sending and receiving devices for an infrared data transmission is normally limited to between 1 and 3 meters. Given the transmission speeds, the line-of-sight requirement, and distance restrictions, infrared does not make for an ideal network connectivity solution. Why is it included in the A+ objectives under networking hardware? We will leave that one to you to try and figure out.

Note   IrDA communication uses half-duplex communication. This means it is able to send and receive data but not at the same time.

IrDA is supported across several platforms; it is very much integrated with newer Windows platforms and has been available since Windows 95. Infrared is also supported by the mainstream Linux distributions as well as Macintosh systems. Support from these operating systems usually makes setting up IrDA devices a painless process.

Fiber-Optic Cable

There is a constant demand for faster networking speeds, and fiber-optic cable was introduced to help meet this need. Compared with the other types of cabling discussed here, fiber-optic cable is a relative newcomer to the world of corporate networking. Unlike the other transmission types, fiber-optic cable uses light instead of electrical signals and so is not susceptible to interference as is copper wire. Fiber-optic cable has a central glass core, which is surrounded by a glass cladding and protected by an outer sheath. Although the cable is designed to be durable and easy to work with, special attention is needed when you're working with fiber-optic cabling. In many cases, special tools and skills are required for installing fiber optics, though as the technology becomes more popular, simplified methods are being introduced. Figure 6-8 shows an example of fiber-optic cabling.

Black polyurethane outer jacket
Strength members
Buffer Jacket
Cladding (silica)
Core (silica)
Silicone coating

Figure 6-8 Fiber-optic cable

Because it transmits light, fiber-optic cable is capable of transmitting long distances at very high speeds. In terms of performance, fiber-optic cable has no match, being able to transfer data at speeds of 100 Mbps to beyond 1Gbps. However, when it comes to cost and difficulty of installation, fiber-optic cable becomes less attractive.

Test Smart   If you need to run network cable over long distances or require high speeds and increased resistance to EMI and crosstalk, fiber-optic cabling is your best choice.

Media Characteristics Summary

Understanding the basic characteristics of network cable types is an important skill for anyone working with or supporting networks. Table 6-2 summarizes the cable types discussed in this section.

Table 6-2   Summary of Cable Types

Cable Type	Susceptibility to Interference	Transmission Speed	Maximum Distance	Installation Difficulty
Thin coax	Low	10 Mbps	185 meters	Low
Thick coax	Very low	10 Mbps	500 meters	Difficult
UTP	High	10 to 100 Mbps	100 meters	Easy
STP	Low	10 to 500 Mbps	90 meters	Moderate
RS-232	N/A	20 Kbps	50 Feet	N/A
Infrared	High	115 Kbps-4 Mbps	1 meter	Easy
Fiber-optic	None	100 Mbps to 1Gbps and beyond	Up to 30 miles	Difficult

See Also   *Pictures and descriptions of the connectors used with the various cables can be found in Chapter 1.*

Hardware Protocols

The term hardware protocols can be a little misleading, but they are essentially standards used to dictate the entire infrastructure of the network. In addition to the types of cabling that can be used, they define how data is placed onto the network, how fast the data can be transmitted, how errors are detected and corrected, and what physical connections are required for devices. In this section, we will look at the two most common network architectures or standards in use today: Ethernet and token ring.

Ethernet

Of the handful of standards used in local area networks, Ethernet is by far the most popular. Although no definite figures are available, some estimates put Ethernet's market share somewhere in the region of 90 to 95 percent.

Originally developed by two scientists at Xerox's Palo Alto Research Center, Ethernet was based upon a network access method developed at the University of Hawaii in the 1960s. The first version of Ethernet was designed to connect 100 computers on a single 1-km cable segment at a speed of 2.94 Mbps. The commercial possibilities for this amazing technology did not escape the powers that be at Xerox, and they quickly teamed up with some of the other technical innovators of the day, Digital Equipment Corporation and Intel, to develop a standard for a 10-Mbps Ethernet. Today, this internationally recognized standard connects millions of PCs, servers, and other network devices all over the world.

CSMA/CD Network Access

Ethernet transmissions are made possible through a media access system known as *Carrier Sense Multiple Access with Collision Detection (CSMA/CD)*. When a device on an Ethernet network wants to transmit to another device, the first device checks to see if the line is clear and then transmits. The only problem is that if two devices perform this action at the same time, they will both "think" the line is clear and so will both attempt to transmit. Ethernet can accept only one signal at a time, so the two transmissions will collide with each other. These collisions damage the data packets on the network. To avoid another collision, each system will wait a period of time, known as the backoff, before retransmitting the data. If the data collides again, the delay before retransmission is increased and the data is sent again. This process continues until eventually the sending node gives up and reports an error.

The more devices that are connected to an Ethernet network, the more likely it is that there will be collisions on the network. In other words, the more devices you add to an

Ethernet network, the slower, exponentially, the network will become. This decrease in performance has driven improvements in the structure of Ethernet networks. Improvements include the substitution of older hubs with new, high-performance, Ethernet switches (discussed later in this section). With that out of the way, we can look at some of the specific Ethernet standards.

10Base2

The 10Base2 Ethernet standard uses thin coaxial (RG-58) cable and suffers from the shortcomings of this particular medium. 10Base2 has a maximum length of 185 meters (607 feet) and because of its composition offers a fair amount of resistance to interference. There are a few very good reasons why thin coax has fallen out of favor; one of the more important is that it is limited to transfer speeds of 10 Mbps. This speed limitation reduces its effectiveness in many network environments.

10Base5

The 10Base5 standard uses the thick coaxial (RG-62) cable and, as you can gather from the name, has a transfer speed of 10 Mbps and runs over distances of 500 meters. The 10Base5 standard specifies a true bus topology, meaning that computers attach to the network cable itself using special cables and connectors—it does not use additional networking equipment.

If you ever find yourself in the unique situation where you are connecting computer systems in a 10Base5 network, you will likely notice that thick coax is marked every 2.5 meters. This is because network devices in a 10Base5 network must be connected with a minimum distance of 2.5 meters between each other to prevent noise on the cable.

10Base-T

Although there is no such thing as "standard Ethernet," it is generally accepted that a "normal" Ethernet network is one that operates at 10 Mbps and has the name 10Base-T. This may sound fast, and to many users it may seem fast, but nowadays more and more organizations are looking for even faster ways to connect their Ethernet devices. 10Base-T can operate on Category 3, 4, and 5 UTP cable and is limited to distances of 100 meters.

Test Smart   Ensure that you familiarize yourself with the characteristics of 10Base-T before taking the A+ exam.

The need for speed has led to developments in networking hardware and improvements in the Ethernet specification. Now, Fast Ethernet, which is 10 times faster than standard Ethernet, is commonplace, and organizations looking for even more bandwidth are turning to Gigabit Ethernet, which is 100 times faster than the original Ethernet standard. Separate discussions of these technologies are included next.

Ethernet Standard Naming The names that are given to networking standards, such as 10Base2, are not just arbitrary—they actually describe the networking standard and its characteristics. Consider, as an example, 10Base-T. The "10" denotes the speed—10Mbps, the "Base" indicates that the medium is baseband (able to carry only one signal at a time), and the "T" defines the type of cable used—in this case, twisted-pair.

There are exceptions to this naming structure. For example, 10Base2 and 10Base5 use numbers associated with the distances over which they can be used instead of the cable type, but in almost all other cases the naming scheme works as described.

Fast Ethernet—100Base-T

Fast Ethernet, or to give it its proper name, 100Base-T, is a 100-Mbps networking standard based on the principles of standard Ethernet. A number of standards fall under the Fast Ethernet banner; the most commonly implemented is 100Base-TX, which uses Category 5 (or higher) UTP cabling. The following sections describe the Fast Ethernet standards.

- **100Base-FX**   This is the standard for running Fast Ethernet over fiber-optic cable. Due to the cost of implementation, this is rarely used. One of its largest advantages is its distance capabilities: 100Base-FX can reach an impressive 10,000 meters.

- **100Base-T4**   100Base-T4 can use category 3, 4, and 5 cable to reach speeds of 100Mbps. With regard to distance limitations and other characteristics, 100Base-T4 is comparable with 100Base-TX.

- **100Base-TX**   This is the Fast Ethernet standard of choice on today's networks. 100Base-TX is most often implemented with UTP cable, but it has been known to be used with STP. 100Base-TX operates at speeds of 100 Mbps and offers a maximum transmission distance of 100 meters. The difference between TX and T4 is that T4 uses all four pairs of wire within the UTP cable. TX only uses two pairs.

The following table summarizes the characteristics of the various Ethernet standards.

Note   On the fringe of Ethernet standards are relatively new technologies that provide 1000-Mbps transfer speeds over UTP and fiber-optic cabling. Gigabit Ethernet is designated as 1000Base-T over UTP cabling and as 1000Base-F over fiber-optic cabling. Gigabit technologies fall outside the scope of the A+ objectives but are interesting nonetheless.

Characteristic	10Base2	10Base5	10Base-T	100Base-FX	100Base-T4	100Base-TX
Maximum Distance	185 meters	500 meters	100 meters	100–10,000 meters	100 meters	100 meters
Transfer Speed	10 Mbps	10 Mbps	10 Mbps	100 Mbps	100 Mbps	100 Mbps
Cable Used (minimum)	Thin coax	Thick coax	Category 3, 4, 5	Fiber-optic cable	Category 3, 4, 5	Category 5

 Test Smart   For the A+ exam, you will be expected to identify the characteristics of Ethernet standards. Pay close attention to the information provided in Table 6-3.

Token Ring

Token ring technology was introduced in the mid-1980s and quickly became the network design of choice for many organizations. Nowadays, token ring networks account for only a small percentage of the networks in use, though many organizations that invested heavily in token ring technology in the past continue to use the system to preserve their investments. One of the disadvantages of token ring networks is that the devices used to construct the networks are relatively expensive. Also, there are fewer people with experience in maintaining token ring networks, and this can make it harder for organizations to find suitable support personnel.

Unlike Ethernet, token ring networks employ a method called *token passing* to achieve network communication. The system is relatively maintenance-free and works like this: on a token ring network, the first computer to log on to the network creates a special frame called a *token*. This token circles around the network looking for a computer that has data to transmit. When a computer has the token, the computer attaches its message to the token, and the token travels around the network until it gets to the destination computer. A computer on a token ring network can transmit data only when it has this token, and a token ring network can have only one token on it at any one time. Figure 6-9 shows a token ring network.

After reaching the destination computer, the token returns to the sending computer and confirms with the sending computer that the data was delivered successfully. Although the token process sounds complicated, it is actually quite efficient. Unlike the popular Ethernet networks, which can have collisions between data packets, token ring networks don't have collisions because only one computer can transmit at a time.

Despite the efficiency of the token ring design, it suffers from a major disadvantage: lack of speed. Early implementations of token ring networks could pass data at 4 Mbps, and today's token ring networks can work at speeds of 16 Mbps. Although this is faster than Ethernet, it is much slower than Fast Ethernet.

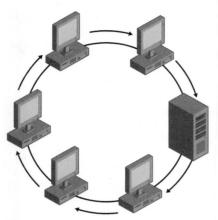

Figure 6-9 A token ring network

Note   A token ring network can run at 4 or 16 Mbps, but all devices on the network must run at the same speed.

Network Topologies

Network topology simply refers to how the network is laid out. There are three main network topologies used on today's networks: bus, star, and ring, although you may well see networks that employ more than one of these topologies, in which case they are referred to as being hybrid networks. Each of these different topologies has enjoyed a measure of success in the networking world, but over time, one has emerged as the leader—and it's the design you are most likely going to encounter when working with networks—the physical star.

Star Topology

In a *star topology*, all computer systems on the network connect to a centralized device called a *hub* or *switch*. Each computer system connects to the hub or switch using its own length of cable, meaning that systems can be added to or removed from the network without disrupting the network for any of the other systems. This is an important distinction and one of the star topology's biggest advantages. As you will see with the other topologies, adding computers to the network is not so easy and can disrupt the entire network.

One of the biggest potential concerns with the star topology is that because systems connect to a centralized device, if that device were to fail, every computer connected to it would be unable to access the network. This means that when a hub or switch fails, a large number of network users will be left in the cold. Fortunately, hubs and switches are not complex devices and have very few moving parts, so failure of such devices is infrequent. Hubs and switches are discussed later in this chapter.

The star topology is most often associated with Ethernet networks and connects devices to the hub using standard UTP cable. Figure 6-10 shows an example of a star topology. Table 6-3 summarizes the features of the star topology.

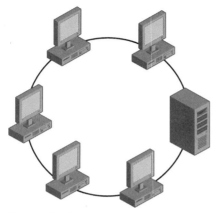

Figure 6-10 Star topology

Table 6-3   **Summary of the Star Topology**

Key Features	Advantages	Disadvantages
Most commonly implemented network topology used today.	Computer systems can be added or removed from the network without disrupting network users.	Centralized device (hub/switch) causes a single point of failure.
Uses individual cables to connect each device to the network.	A cable failure affects only the network device connected to it.	Because each device requires its own length of cable, more cable is required than in a bus topology.
Problem isolation is straight-forward.	When a device fails in a star topology, it can be easier to trace the location of the problem.	Additional network equipment such as the hub or switch is needed to make the network connection.

Bus Topology

A few years ago, the physical bus topology was what you were most likely to see when walking into a networked environment. Those days are gone. In a *bus topology*, all devices on the network are connected using a single length of cable—in most cases, coaxial cable. Figure 6-11 shows the layout of the bus topology.

Bus networks suffer from a unique problem known as signal reflection. When data is sent along the wire on a bus network, it may reflect back onto the wire after it reaches the end of the cable. This signal reflection can cause all sorts of problems as the reflecting signals can disrupt the data flow of the network. To work around this problem, special devices called *terminators* are placed at the physical ends of the cable. These terminators are simply resistors designed to soak up the signal as it reaches the ends of the bus and prevent signal reflection. Troubleshooting a bus network will most certainly involve ensuring that the physical ends of the cable in a bus network are correctly terminated.

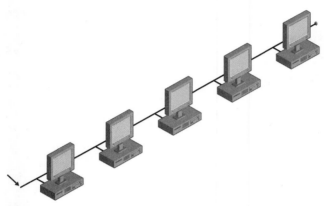

Figure 6-11 Bus topology

One of the biggest drawbacks of the bus topology, and the reason why the star topology is more popular, is that a single break in the cable in a bus network will render the entire network unusable. So when a computer system is being added or the cable breaks, network use will be disrupted. In corporate environments where downtime is measured in dollars, this is not an attractive feature. Table 6-4 summarizes the features, advantages, and disadvantages of the bus topology.

Table 6-4 Summary of the Bus Topology

Key Features	Advantages	Disadvantages
Uses a single length of cable to interconnect network devices.	No additional network devices are required to make the network.	Adding or removing devices on the network will disrupt the entire network.
Uses terminators to dampen signal reflection at the ends of the cables.	A bus network is fairly cheap and easy to implement.	Commonly uses coaxial cable, which is prone to cable breaks. This will disrupt network use.
Network devices connect directly to the cable.	Less physical cable is required to make the network.	Given a cable break, troubleshooting a bus network can be a difficult process.

Ring Topology

In a *ring topology*, all devices are connected to a cable segment that has no start or end, as depicted in Figure 6-12. The advantage to this layout is that data can run on the cable in both directions. The downside is that the ring must be complete to function, a requirement that makes it necessary to use specialized networking equipment. If there were to be a problem at some point on the ring, the system can automatically move data around the ring in the opposite direction to avoid the problem area.

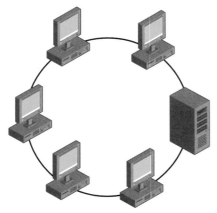

Figure 6-12 Ring topology

The most common implementation of the ring topology is actually something called the *star ring*. In this configuration, all devices connect to a centralized device similar to a hub, called a *Multistation Access Unit (MSAU)*. Although it may appear like a hub, its actual function is quite different. The role of the MSAU is to create an internal ring function within the device instead of an external ring made with actual cabling.

When using the ring topology in its purest form, a single break in the cable will prevent users from accessing the network. When using a star ring configuration, the failure of the MSAU will cause network failure, but at least computer systems can be added to the network without disrupting network service. Table 6-5 summarizes the features, advantages, and disadvantages of the ring topology.

Table 6-5   Summary of the Ring Topology

Key Features	Advantages	Disadvantages
Devices are connected in a ring formation.	When not used in a star ring configuration, additional network devices, MSAUs, are not needed to complete the network.	Disruption in the loop disrupts the entire network.
A star ring uses an MSAU to form the ring function internally.	Devices in a star ring configuration can be added and removed without network disruption.	The MSAU in a star ring provides a single point of failure.

Mapping Ethernet Standards to Topologies

Having discussed the various Ethernet standards and topologies, we can now identify which standards are associated with which topology. Though you may have already pieced that information together while reading through this chapter, we have decided to leave little doubt, as the A+ exam will require you to know which topology is associated with the various Ethernet standards. So without further delay, Table 6-6 provides a look at the relationship between topologies, cabling, and Ethernet standards.

Table 6-6   Mapping Ethernet Standards to Topologies and Cable Types

Ethernet Standard/ Hardware Protocol	Topology Used	Cable
10Base2	Bus	Thin coax
10Base5	Bus	Thick coax
10Base-T	Star	UTP/STP
100Base-X	Star	UTP/STP/fiber

Test Smart   Be ready to identify which topologies are used by the various networking standards. In other words, memorize the info in the preceding table.

Networking Devices

Before concluding our discussion on networking hardware, we think it's a good idea to explain some of the network hardware devices mentioned in this chapter. A detailed knowledge of these devices is not required for the A+ exam, but you can expect to need a general knowledge of what they are and what they are designed to do.

Repeaters

Though not widely used anymore, at least as separate devices, repeaters are used to regenerate data signals as they pass through a network cable. For instance, we know that the distance limit for 10Base-T is 100 meters. If we use repeaters, we can amplify the signal and the 100-meter limit can be increased. While the function of repeaters is as important now as it always was, the signal repeating function is now commonly built into devices such as hubs and switches.

Hubs and Switches

Hubs and switches are common sights in today's networks. Modern networks that use UTP cable use hubs and switches to interconnect network devices. Each device connects to a port in the hub or switch. In larger networks, hubs and switches can be connected together to accommodate more devices.

Hubs and switches come in a variety of configurations. The smaller ones used in homes or small offices typically have 4 to 12 ports, while larger hubs and switches can have as many as 48. Each port on the hub or switch is capable of having a single device plugged into it, which can either be a computer system, printer, or another hub or switch to accommodate more network devices. Figure 6-13 displays a 24-port switch.

Figure 6-13 24-port switch

The Difference Between a Hub and a Switch

By now, you might be curious to know what the difference is between hubs and switches, especially considering that when you look at them side by side, it's hard to tell them apart. At first glance, a hub and a switch are identical, but each functions in a very different manner.

Of the two, hubs are the older technology and on a very basic level, simply allow communication between connected devices. The hub is not really a very intelligent device and does not manage the data in any way. Although hubs can create network connectivity, they do so in an inefficient manner. For example, when a computer plugged into the first port of an eight-port hub wants to send data to a system on port eight, the data is forwarded to all of the ports on the hub, even though six of the ports don't need the data. In other words, all the hub does is provide an electrical pathway between the devices plugged into it.

As you can appreciate, sending data to all devices connected to a hub, whether the information is destined for them or not, is an inefficient way of doing business. This is where a switch comes in. A switch, as the name implies, functions by switching data between the ports on the switch as needed. Using the same example as before, if a device plugged into port one of the switch wants to send data to a device connected to port eight, the data is received by the switch on port one and forwarded to port eight. No other ports get the data, as they don't need it. This simple little improvement significantly increases the performance of the entire network and is a good, cost-effective strategy for upgrading a network. As you might expect, switches cost a little more than regular hubs, but they are worth the cost.

Multistation Access Units

The last piece of network equipment we touch on in this chapter is the MSAU. MSAUs are often thought of as the hub equivalent for star ring networks. While often similar in appearance to a hub or switch, the similarity ends with appearance, as they function entirely differently. The function of the MSAU is to form the internal ring function of the network. MSAU devices are used in a star ring topology. In real-world applications, token ring networks are rarely seen anymore, so the chance that you'll encounter an MSAU is unlikely, but still possible.

Key Points

■ Network Interface Cards (NIC) are used to provide the physical connection to the network. Legacy network cards use jumper settings to assign resources; newer cards are typically plug and play devices. Network interfaces can be found in any device that connects to the network including printers, DSL modems, etc.

■ NICs are installed into a computer system in the same was as any other expansion card and are available in both PCI and ISA versions.

■ Network cards can communicate in either full-duplex or half-duplex mode.

■ As data travels along a network cable, its signal strength weakens—this is called attenuation. The signal can also be disrupted by outside influences including crosstalk and EMI.

■ Types of commonly used network media include coaxial cable, twisted-pair cable, and fiber optic.

■ Coaxial cable comes in two types—thin coax and thick coax. Thin coax is typically used for Ethernet bus networks. Thick coax is more likely to be used for backbone purposes.

■ Twisted-pair cabling comes in two versions—unshielded twisted-pair (UTP) and shielded twisted-pair (STP). UTP cable is categorized to define its function and purpose.

■ RS232 is a TIA/EIA standard for serial communication between computers and peripheral devices.

■ Fiber-optic cable uses light instead of electrical pulses to carry information. This makes it capable of transmitting over greater distances, and at greater speeds, than copper-based media such as UTP.

■ Ethernet is the most common network standard in use today. There are many versions of the standard, including 10Base2 (Ethernet over thin coax cabling), 10Base5 (Ethernet over thick coaxial cabling), 10Base-T (10Mbps Ethernet over UTP cabling), and Fast Ethernet (100Mbps Ethernet over UTP and fiber-optic cable).

■ Token ring is a token passing network architecture implemented in a logical ring, physical star topology. Token ring is relatively uncommon nowadays, with Ethernet being the network standard of choice.

■ Common network topologies include star, ring, and bus. In some environments, more than one topology is used, giving rise to the term hybrid.

Chapter Review Questions

1 You have been called to troubleshoot a 10Base5 network and suspect the cable length may be the problem. What is the maximum cable distance of 10Base5 networks?

a)   100 meters

b)   185 meters

c)   500 meters

d)   1000 meters

Answer c is correct. The maximum cable length specified by the 10Base5 standard is 500 meters. If the cable is run farther than this, then the data signals may lose their strength and become unreadable to the receiving device. Answer a is incorrect; 100 meters specifies the maximum distance of UTP cable used with 10Base-T and 100Base-T networks. Answer b is incorrect as 185 meters is the maximum cable distance specified by 10Base2 networks. Answer d is not a valid answer.

2 What is the topology associated with 10Base2 networks?

a)   Ring

b)   Star ring

c)   Bus

d)   Star

Answer c is correct. The 10Base2 Ethernet standard uses a bus topology where each network device attaches directly to the network cable without the need for additional network hardware. Answer a is incorrect; the ring network is associated with a token ring network topology. Answer b is incorrect as a star ring topology is associated with a token ring network that uses an MSAU to form the network's ring function. Answer d is incorrect. The star topology is associated with 10Base-T and 100Base-T networks and is commonly implemented using standard UTP cable.

3 You are installing a new 10Base-T network. Which of the following network cables will you use?

a)   Thin coax

b)   UTP

c)   Thick coax

d)   RG-58 cable

Answer b is correct. When implementing a 10Base-T network, it is most likely that you will be using regular UTP cable. 10Base-T networks can be implemented with category 3, 4, and 5 UTP. Answers a and c are incorrect. Thin coax is associated with 10Base2 networks, and thick coax is associated with 10Base5 networks. Answer d is wrong as RG-58 is another way of describing thin coax.

4 You are a technician working with a 10Base2 bus network. Which of the following is required to connect the computers to the cable?

a) BNC connectors

b) BNC connectors and a hub

c) BNC connectors and an MSAU

d) Thin coax cable and RJ-45 connectors

Answer a is correct. BNC connectors are used to connect the computer system to the network cable. Pictures of BNC connectors can be seen in Chapter 1. Answer b is incorrect as hubs are not needed in a 10Base2 network design. Answer c is incorrect as an MSAU is also not used on a 10Base2 network. Finally, answer d is invalid because thin coax cabling does not use RJ-45 connectors.

5 Which of the following topologies is associated with a 100Base-T network?

a) Ring

b) Bus

c) Star ring

d) Star

Answer d is correct. 100Base-T networks use a star topology. 100Base-T is commonly implemented using UTP cabling and a hub or switch. Answers a and c are incorrect as both are associated with a token ring network and not 100Base-T networks. Answer b is incorrect as a bus topology network is associated with 10Base5 or 10Base2 networks.

6 What is the maximum transfer distance of a 10Base2 network?

a) 185 meters

b) 500 meters

c) 100 meters

d) 50 km

Answer a is correct. 10Base2 networks are implemented using thin coax cable, which has a distance limit of 185 meters. Answers b, c, and d are incorrect. 500 meters is the cable limitation associated with 10Base5, 100 meters the distance limitation of UTP, and 50 km is a limitation of fiber-optic cable.

7 A company has called you asking for a recommendation on network cable. They need to run the cable through an elevator shaft where there is a lot of electrical interference. Which of the following cables is most resistant to electrical interference?

a) STP

b) Dual-shielded coaxial

c) Fiber-optic

d)   10Base2 ThinNet

Answer c is correct. Because fiber-optic cable uses light as a transmission medium and not copper, it is resistant to the effects of EMI. This makes it well suited to be used in environments where traditional copper-based cable may be ineffective. Answers a, b, and d are incorrect. While all of these cables offer varying degrees of resistance to electrical interference, they do not compare to fiber-optic cable.

8   The network card in your system is configured to send and receive data but cannot do both at the same time. Which of the following duplex settings is being used?

a)   Half duplex

b)   Full duplex

c)   Simplex

d)   Bowflex

Answer a is correct. When network cards are configured to send and receive data but not simultaneously, they are configured in half duplex mode. Answer b is incorrect as full duplex communication allows for two-way simultaneous communication. Answer c is incorrect; simplex allows for only one-way communication. Answer d is incorrect as a Bowflex is actually an exercise machine.

9   Which of the following describes the weakening of data signals as they travel down a particular network cable?

a)   Crosstalk

b)   Attenuation

c)   EMI

d)   Bandwidth

Answer b is correct. Network cables all have a specified length that they can be run without regenerating the data signal. The weakening of data signals as they traverse a network cable is known as attenuation. Answer a is incorrect. Crosstalk refers to the interference that occurs between wires within a particular cable or when two cables are placed in close proximity to each other. Answer c is incorrect; EMI is the interference from electrical devices such as fluorescent lights. Answer d is not a valid answer.

10 On a bus network, where should terminators be located?

a)   On both physical ends of the coaxial cable

b)   On a single physical end of the coaxial cable

c)   On the physical connection of each networked device

d)   Terminators are not used on bus networks

Answer a is correct. When working on a bus network, you need to ensure that each of the physical ends of the cable is terminated. If both are not terminated, the network will not function properly. Answers b, c, and d are invalid.

11 Which of the following is an advantage of the star network topology?

a) Additional networking hardware such as hubs are not needed.

b) Star networks use less physical cable than other topologies.

c) Computers and other network devices can be added or removed from the system without disrupting network access for other users.

d) Star networks do not have a single point of failure.

Answer c is correct. On a star network, each device on the network is connected using its own length of cable. This means that devices can be easily attached and removed without disrupting current network users. Answers a, b, and d are not true about star networks.

12 You have been asked to upgrade your network hubs to switches. What is the advantage of using switches over hubs?

a) Switches are cheaper.

b) Switches are easier to install.

c) Switches are more efficient than hubs.

d) Switches can maintain more connected ports simultaneously.

Answer c is correct. Upgrading hubs to switches is a common strategy to increase the network's overall performance. Switches manage incoming data more efficiently than hubs. Answers a, b, and d are not true of switches.

13 A network user has complained about slow network access. She is currently using a 10-Mbps network connection in half duplex mode. If you were to configure her network card in full duplex mode, what would the speed of the link be between the network card and the network switch?

a) 10 Mbps

b) 20 Mbps

c) 30 Mbps

d) This cannot be done.

Answer b is correct. In full-duplex mode, network cards are able to send and receive information simultaneously. This would allow a 10-Mbps card to transfer at 20 Mbps. Answer a is incorrect as a half-duplex configuration allows for a 10-Mbps data transfer rate using a 10-Mbps NIC. Answers c and d are invalid.

14 You are installing a 10Base-T network. Which of the following UTP categories could you use? (Choose 3.)

a) Category 2

b) Category 3

c) Category 4

d)   Category 5

Answers b, c, and d are correct. 10Base-T networks can be designed over three different UTP cable categories, 3, 4, and 5. Answer a is incorrect as 10Base-T cannot function over Category 2 cable.

15 You are working on a 100Base-T network and want to connect two network systems using UTP cable, but the systems are over 100 meters apart. Which of the following network devices could you use to complete the connection?

a)   Extender

b)   Multiplier

c)   Repeater

d)   MSAU

Answer c is correct. When you need to extend the distance at which a signal can be sent through a particular cable, you can use a repeater to regenerate the data signal. Answers a and b are not valid networking devices. Answer d is wrong, as an MSAU is a device used in a star ring network.

Check Yourself

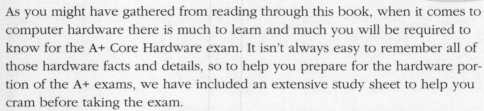

(before you test yourself)

As you might have gathered from reading through this book, when it comes to computer hardware there is much to learn and much you will be required to know for the A+ Core Hardware exam. It isn't always easy to remember all of those hardware facts and details, so to help you prepare for the hardware portion of the A+ exams, we have included an extensive study sheet to help you cram before taking the exam.

The study sheet is organized by the CompTIA domains, with each of the six A+ Hardware domains represented in order. If upon reading the study sheet you find a spot you need to brush up on, you can refer back to where that information was covered in the book.

A+ Core Hardware

Domain 1.0 Installation, Configuration, Upgrading

System Components

System Board

- The system board, also known as the motherboard, but sometimes referred to as the mainboard, is the primary circuit board into which all of the other components connect.

- The two most common types of motherboards used today are the older Advanced Technology (AT) motherboards and the AT Extended (ATX) motherboards.

- ATX motherboards use PS/2 keyboard connectors.

- AT motherboards use DIN-5 connectors.

Power Supply

- Power supplies are necessary because, in practical terms, a computer power supply takes the AC voltage supplied through the cable connecting it to the wall, converts it to DC, and drops the voltage to a fraction of what was supplied.

■ There are two primary types of power supplies: AT power supplies, which have unique connectors to fit on an AT motherboard, and ATX power supplies designed to work with ATX motherboards.

■ AT power supplies use P8 and P9 connectors to attach to the motherboard.

■ ATX power supplies use a 20-pin P1 connector to attach to the motherboard.

■ A power supply has numerous plastic connectors that can be used to plug in peripherals such as hard drives, floppy drives, and so forth.

■ The connectors used for hard drives and CD-ROMs are called Molex connectors. The connectors for floppy disk drives are called Berg connectors.

Processor/CPU

■ CPUs provide the processing power for the computer system.

■ Processors come in a variety of shapes and sizes, and the type of processor used must be compatible with the board into which it is to be plugged.

■ Processors generate a significant amount of heat and use heat sinks and fans to move the hot air away.

■ Common processor formats include PGA and SECC.

Memory

■ RAM stores information temporarily so that it can be used and accessed by the components of the system.

■ There are two basic types of RAM: static RAM (SRAM) and dynamic RAM (DRAM).

■ Static RAM is so named because it holds data in a different way than does dynamic RAM. Static RAM can hold data until the system is powered down, whereas DRAM must be continually refreshed to make sure the data is held.

■ Memory comes in two main form factors, SIMMs (single inline memory modules) and DIMMs (dual inline memory modules).

■ The terms SIMMs and DIMMs are used to refer to the physical layout of the memory, but memory still comes in different types, such as FPM (fast page-mode), EDO (extended data out), and SDRAM (synchronous DRAM).

Storage Devices

■ Storage devices include hard drives, CD, CD-R, and CD-RW drives, DVD drives, floppy drives, Zip drives, tape drives, and external hard drives.

■ There are three basic types of storage: magnetic, optical, and silicon.

■ Magnetic storage media would include hard disks, floppy disks, and proprietary formats like tape and Zip disks.

■ Optical storage would include all of the CD- and DVD-based media.

■ There is an increasing trend toward static RAM storage devices like USB memory sticks and memory cards such as those used in digital cameras. These storage devices use silicon as the storage medium.

Monitor

■ Computer monitors are the means by which we interact with the computer system.

■ A computer can function without a monitor, and in fact some systems are intended to be used in this "headless" method, but in general a PC has a monitor.

■ Monitors come in different types. Traditional cathode-ray tube (CRT) monitors are the most common, but there is an increasing trend toward liquid crystal display (LCD) screens, which are also called flat-panel displays.

■ There are many video standards defined, but the most common ones are Video Graphics Array (VGA) and Super Video Graphics Array (SVGA).

■ SVGA is more common nowadays but if you find yourself working with an older computer system, you might find yourself staring at a VGA monitor.

Modem

■ Modems translate the digital signals sent from your computer into analog signals that can be transferred over a conventional phone line.

■ External modems are housed in a box and normally require an external power supply. Connectivity to the PC can be achieved via a serial or USB port. Internal modems are installed in an expansion slot inside your computer.

Firmware

■ Firmware is a program that is stored on a chip but it is neither hardware nor software. In other words, it is between hardware and software—in between soft and hard comes firm.

■ Firmware is upgraded periodically in a process known as flashing.

BIOS

■ The basic input/output system (BIOS) is a firmware program that passes information to the PC as it boots up.

■ The BIOS firmware is stored in the CMOS.

■ BIOS settings include the parameters for the hard disks, the boot order, and the enabling and disabling of on-board devices.

■ The process of upgrading the BIOS is referred to as flashing. The BIOS can be flashed to provide additional functionality or to correct a problem with the current version of the BIOS.

CMOS

■ The complementary metal-oxide semiconductor, or CMOS, is a chip that stores the settings for the BIOS.

■ The CMOS has a battery associated with it that supplies it with the small amount of power needed to retain the settings while the PC is off.

Field-Replaceable Modules

When replacing FRMs, consider the following:

■ Replace with a similar component. Whenever possible, replace the failed component with a similar or identical one.

■ When replacing electrical components, use proper ESD preventative procedures.

■ Replace the correct component. Before taking the old component out and replacing it with the new one, follow the troubleshooting steps to make sure that you are replacing the correct component.

■ Ensure functionality. After replacing the FRM, test it for functionality. If it's a new component, you must ensure that it works with the current hardware configuration.

■ Put the system back to normal. As a matter of courtesy, after replacing a component, return everything back to its original state.

Working with System Resources

I/O Address

■ All devices require a unique I/O address to communicate in the system.

■ Some core components have I/O addresses reserved for them; other devices that we add on, such as printers, need to have I/O addresses assigned.

Table A-1 lists the most common devices and their standard I/O addresses.

Table A-1 Standard I/O Address Assignments

I/O Address	Device
1F0–1F8	Hard disk controller
200–207	Game I/O
278–27F	Parallel port (LPT2)
2F8–2FF	Serial port (COM2)
320–32F	Hard drive controller, 8-bit ISA
378–37F	Parallel port (LPT1)
3B0–3BF	Monochrome graphics adapter
3D0–3DF	Color graphics adapter
3F0–3F7	Floppy drive controller
3F8–3FF	Serial port (COM1)

IRQs

■ Every device that wants to communicate with the CPU must use an IRQ.

■ Unless IRQ assignments are handled by the OS, devices should not share an IRQ address; if they do, one or both devices will fail to function.

■ In modern systems, Plug and Play manages the assignment of IRQ addresses, which greatly reduces the chances of conflicting IRQ addresses.

Table A-2 lists the standard IRQ assignments for various devices.

Table A-2   Standard IRQ Assignments

IRQ Address	Device
IRQ 0	System timer
IRQ 1	Keyboard
IRQ 2/9	Open (cascades to IRQ 9)
IRQ 3	Default IRQ for COM2 and COM4
IRQ 4	Default for COM1 and COM3
IRQ 5	LPT2 (often used with audio cards)
IRQ 6	Floppy drive
IRQ 7	LPT1
IRQ 8	Real-time clock
IRQ 9	Redirect to IRQ 2
IRQ 10	Open
IRQ 11	Open
IRQ 12	Open (often used with PS/2 mouse)
IRQ 13	Math coprocessor
IRQ 14	Primary hard drive controller
IRQ 15	Secondary hard drive controller

DMA

- Direct memory access (DMA) is a method used by peripheral devices to access the system's main memory and store data without having to use the CPU.

- Operating systems today assign DMA channels through Plug and Play; however, some legacy devices require that DMA channels be set using jumper settings.

Table A-3 lists the default DMA channels for various system devices.

Table A-3   Default DMA Channels

DMA Channel	Device
0	DRAM refresh
1	Sound card
2	Floppy disk drive
3	ECP parallel port
4	DMA controller
5	Open (sound card)
6	Open
7	ISA hard disk controller

Table A-4 lists the standard IRQ and I/O addresses of PC serial and parallel ports.

Table A-4 Resources Used by Communication Ports

Port	IRQ	I/O Address
COM1	IRQ 4	3F8h
COM2	IRQ 3	2F8h
COM3	IRQ 4	3E8h
COM4	IRQ 3	2E8h
LPT1	IRQ 7	378–37Fh
LPT2	IRQ 5	278–27Fh

Peripheral Ports, Cabling, and Connectors

DB-9/DB-25

- DB-9 connectors are used for serial communication ports. Some PCs will have one DB-9 and one DB-25 connector for serial ports. Serial ports are male.

- The most common application for a DB-25 connector is a parallel port. Parallel ports are female.

- DB-25 connectors are also used with some external SCSI implementations.

Figure A-1 shows examples of DB connectors.

Figure A-1 DB connectors are commonly used to attach peripheral devices to the PC.

- Serial ports transfer data 1 bit at a time. They are most often used for mice and external modems.

- Serial ports can use asynchronous or synchronous communication.

RJ-11/RJ-45

■ The RJ-11 connector is used for telephone cables. In a PC environment, the RJ-11 connector can accommodate up to six wires, but in telephone cable applications only two and sometimes four wires are used.

■ RJ-45 connectors are used with twisted-pair network cabling. They can accommodate up to eight wires.

Figure A-2 shows RJ-11 and RJ-45 connectors.

Figure A-2 RJ-11 connectors are shown on the left, and RJ-45 connectors on the right.

BNC

■ BNC connectors are used in networks that use thin coaxial cabling. BNC connectors have a kind of twist-and-lock system that uses locating pins on the receptacle. Figure A-3 shows an example of a BNC connector.

Figure A-3 BNC connectors are used with thin coaxial network cabling.

PS/2 Mini-DIN

■ PS/2 connectors are used with newer ATX motherboards. The term mini-DIN is used because the connectors are smaller than the standard DIN keyboard connector. Figure A-4 shows an example of a mini-DIN connector and plug.

DIN-5

■ The 5-pin DIN connector is used with AT motherboards to attach keyboards. Figure A-4 shows a DIN-5 connector.

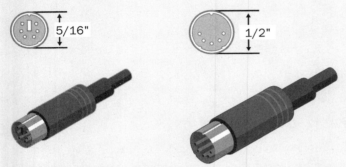

Figure A-4 The mini-DIN connector is shown on the left. The DIN-5 connector, on the right, is used to attach keyboards to AT motherboards.

USB

■ USB has two types of connectors associated with it. A small flat connector is defined as the host or hub connector. A smaller squarer connector is defined as the peripheral connector. Figure A-5 shows an example of a typical USB cable.

Type A (host or hub)   Type B (peripheral)

Figure A-5 USB connectors are used to connect a variety of peripheral devices to the PC.

■ USB ports transfer data at speeds up to 12 Mbps. USB 2.0 supports speeds of up to 480 Mbps.

■ All devices on a USB port share the same IRQ—that which is occupied by the USB controller.

IEEE 1394/FireWire

■   IEEE 1394, or FireWire as it is more commonly known, is an interface used for external devices including hard disk drives, digital cameras, and MP3 players.

■   Devices on a FireWire bus share the same IRQ—that which is occupied by the FireWire controller.

■   FireWire supports speeds of up to 400 Mbps.

Parallel

■   There are two parallel connectors associated with PCs. The DB-25 male connector is used for the PC end of a parallel printer cable. The 36-pin Centronics connector is used for the printer end of the connection.

■   Parallel ports transfer data 8 bits, (1 byte), at a time.

Installing and Configuring IDE/EIDE Devices

■   Modern motherboards include two IDE connectors on the motherboard, known as the primary and secondary controllers; each of these allows two devices to be attached.

■   IDE devices can only be attached internally; IDE does not support the connection of external devices such as printers, scanners, or external hard drives.

■   To differentiate between devices using the same IDE channel, each device needs to be designated as either a master or a slave.

■   When the jumpers are set to cable select, the cable connectors determine master and slave status. The master device will be the one at the end of the IDE cable and the slave will be the one using the middle IDE cable connector.

■   The ATA/IDE interface uses two communication methods or, as they are known, transfer modes. The two modes are Programmed Input/Output (PIO) and the more recent direct memory access (DMA) mode.

■   ATA-100 and ATA-66 use the latest DMA transfer modes and require an 80-conductor, 40-pin cable.

■   Pin 1 on an IDE cable is typically marked with a red stripe. Position 1 of the cable must align with the correct pin on the drive when installing.

Installing and Configuring SCSI Devices

■ Always ensure that both ends of the SCSI chain are terminated with the correct termination method.

■ Ensure that each of the devices connected to the SCSI chain has a unique SCSI ID.

■ Verify that the SCSI host adapter is using the correct system resources.

■ Match cabling with the SCSI devices and needs.

■ Ensure that cabling does not exceed recommended lengths.

■ If possible, install one SCSI device at a time to test the configuration as you go along.

■ Always use good cabling purchased from a reputable manufacturer.

SCSI Standards

Table A-5 lists the various SCSI standards and some characteristics of each.

Table A-5   SCSI Standards

Standard	Maximum Transfer Rate	Maximum Number of Devices
SCSI-1	5 MBps	8
Fast SCSI-2	10 MBps	8
Fast/Wide SCSI-2	20 MBps	16
Ultra SCSI	20 MBps	8
Ultra Wide SCSI	40 MBps	16
Ultra2 SCSI	40 MBps	8
Wide Ultra2 SCSI	80 MBps	16
Ultra3 SCSI (Ultra160)	160 MBps	16
Ultra 320	320 MBps	16

Installing and Configuring Peripheral Devices

Monitor/Video Card

■ Video cards are physically installed like any other expansion card, except that some video cards use video-specific bus interfaces like AGP and VESA local bus.

■ Video cards use on-board processors and RAM to alleviate these tasks from the main system processor and RAM.

■ Video cards must have the right software drivers to operate in the correct manner.

■ Monitors that are Energy Star compliant have power-saving features that can save electricity.

■ Monitors are rated as to the maximum resolution they can support. Commonly supported resolutions include 640×480 (VGA), 800×600 (SVGA), and 1024×768 (XGA). Other resolutions are also supported.

■ The maximum resolution is governed by the video card and its driver and the limitations of the monitor.

■ Refresh rates define the speed at which the screen is "redrawn." They are measured in hertz (Hz). The higher the refresh rate, the clearer the picture.

■ Setting the refresh rate beyond the capabilities of the monitor can at best cause the picture to not be displayed, and at worst irreparably damage the monitor.

■ People differ in their susceptibility to noticing flickering on a monitor. It might be that some people can see a flicker when others cannot. Increasing the refresh rate can reduce flickering.

Modem

■ Modems can be either internal or external. External modems require a power supply.

■ External modems can connect to the PC by either a serial cable or a USB connection.

■ Modems include two ports—one for connection to the wall socket, the other for plugging in a phone. Both of these connections are RJ-11.

■ The speed of a modem is measured in bits per second (bps).

USB Peripherals and Hubs

■ All devices in a USB chain must be within 5 meters of each other.

■ You can have up to 127 devices on a USB channel, although this is unlikely in practical applications.

■ Most systems come with at least two USB ports. USB hubs are available if you wish to add more devices.

- USB version 1 supports speeds of 12 Mbps. USB 2.0 supports speeds up 480 Mbps.

- USB hubs can be linked together, or daisy chained, to provide greater capacity.

- USB hubs can be powered via USB or through a separate power supply.

IEEE 1284

- The IEEE 1284 standard defines parallel communication, which is most commonly used between PCs and printing devices. It can also be used for interfacing with a scanner and other devices such as external CD-ROMs.

- The IEEE 1284 specification dictates that data is passed in blocks of 8 bits—that is to say, 8 bits at a time.

IEEE 1394

- IEEE 1394 (FireWire) supports up to 63 devices on a single bus.

- Like USB, FireWire is a plug-and-play technology. Also, it can provide power to devices.

- FireWire has a maximum speed of 400 Mbps.

External Storage

- External storage devices are generally SCSI, USB, or IEEE 1394 compliant devices. They can include CD-R/RW, DVD, hard disks, or memory cards.

- Most external storage devices require power to be supplied separately from the system though there are exceptions.

- Whether the external storage device will be plug and play depends on the interface being used, rather than the device.

Infrared Devices

- Infrared communication uses light to communicate between devices.

- Infrared communication can accommodate speeds of up to 4 Mbps.

- Most infrared devices require a clear path between the sending and receiving device. This is known as line of sight.

Upgrading System Components

Memory

- The most common reason today for a RAM upgrade is to accommodate software demands.

- Increasing the RAM often brings immediate improvements in system performance.

- Before buying new RAM, ensure that you have purchased the correct RAM for your system.

- When installing RAM, make sure you align the notches on the RAM with the connector on the motherboard.

- Always observe ESD best practices when installing RAM. It is extremely sensitive to ESD damage.

- Most PCs will automatically detect the increase in the RAM. If the newly installed RAM is not recognized by the BIOS, confirm compatibility and correct installation.

Hard Drives

- The new drive should remain in its antistatic bag until it is ready to be installed.

- Handle the drive by the corners or sides, keepings your hands off of the circuitry.

- Do not apply undue pressure to the top of the hard drive.

- Make sure all system power is off before installing the new drive.

- Make sure to use the correct screws when mounting the hard drive.

- When installing or upgrading SCSI devices, confirm device compatibility, SCSI IDs, and termination.

- When installing IDE devices, confirm master/slave configurations.

CPU

- Before installing a new processor, take the time to review the documentation that came with the new processor.

- The ability to support a higher level of processor will depend on the physical configuration on the board, the capabilities of the board chip set, and the system BIOS. In some cases, the BIOS might need an update to accommodate the new processor. Often, a new processor was not designed to be used with some boards and you might find yourself replacing the processor and motherboard at the same time.

Troubleshooting a CPU Upgrade

■ If the system fails to start after the processor upgrade, ensure that the processor is properly seated in the slot. If it is, ensure that no pins on the processor were bent during the upgrade.

■ Confirm any jumper settings for the processor. Also determine whether a BIOS upgrade is required.

■ When upgrading a processor, it is recommended that the new processor be installed with a new fan and heat sink combination. Typically, new heat sinks and fans are included with the processor when purchased.

Upgrading the BIOS

■ An upgradeable BIOS can be updated through a process known as flashing. When upgrading a BIOS is mentioned, it refers to the process of flashing the CMOS chip to update its programs.

■ Flashing can be a dangerous process. If the upgrade flash process is disrupted, for example by a power outage, or the computer shuts down unexpectedly, the BIOS chip can be damaged.

■ Make sure you are using the correct BIOS flashing program for your system. Some manufacturers make intelligent programs that can sense a mismatch, others don't.

Working with Portable Systems

Battery

■ Most portable batteries are either nickel metal hydride (NiMH) or lithium (LiIon).

■ The laptop power adapter recharges the battery when the portable is plugged into a wall socket.

■ The battery is typically located on the bottom of the laptop for easy access.

Type I, II, and III Cards

■ Three types of PC Cards are used with portable systems, Type I, II, and III.

■ Type I cards are 3 ½ mm thick, use one row of sockets, and are sometimes used to add RAM to the system

■ Type II cards are 5 ½ mm thick, use two rows of sockets, and are used to add devices such as modems and NICs to the system.

■ Type III cards are 10 ½ mm thick, use three rows of sockets, and are often used to install hard drives and adapters for devices such as CD-ROMs or tape drives.

Memory

■ Portable systems typically use the SO-DIMM memory form factor.

■ Memory upgrade slots are typically found under the keyboard or on the undercarriage.

Docking Stations

■ Portable systems can plug into docking stations to access desktop PC components such as printers, monitors, keyboards, and so on.

■ Docking stations sometimes provide expansion slots for adding additional devices to the systems to allow more functionality.

■ Most laptop computers now integrate devices, so docking stations are not so widely used.

Port Replicators

■ Port replicators are similar to docking stations, though they are intended to replicate ports on the notebook or laptop computer rather than to provide additional functionality.

■ Use of a port replicator makes it unnecessary to continually plug and unplug keyboards, mice, printers, and so forth into ports on a laptop or notebook computer.

Domain 2.0 Diagnosing and Troubleshooting

Troubleshooting Cables

- **Bent or damaged cables**   Bends or crimps in the cable could indicate damage to the cable. Better to replace the cable and eliminate this as a potential problem than to assume it is OK.

- **Loose connectors**   Not all cables are equal, and some are simply not as durable as others. Test the ends; if they are loose, they might not be making an adequate connection.

- **Cable length**   There are standards that specify how long certain types of cables can be. These maximum cable lengths are quite adequate for most cable types, but they can be surpassed. Be aware of your cable's length requirements.

- **Cable location**   Signal integrity can be compromised depending on where the cable is located. Cables near air conditioners, motors, or large electrical devices might cause interference. This does not apply to fiber-optic cable.

BIOS/CMOS

- A loss of system settings or time indicates a failed or failing CMOS battery. Replace the battery to correct the problem.

- An indicator that the CMOS battery might be going is the CMOS checksum error. This error is often displayed on boot-up when the CMOS battery begins to fail.

- If new hardware, such as a new hard drive, is not correctly identified in the BIOS, the BIOS might need to be upgraded. Updating the BIOS is referred to as flashing the BIOS.

POST Errors

- A complete POST check is performed only from a cold boot of the system. A warm boot will run through portions of the POST process such as the memory check, but not the entire routine.

- Each and every POST process must verify the processor, video, and memory.

- One beep at the end of the POST process indicates that the POST process has completed successfully.

POST Numeric Error Codes

■ Older PCs use numeric codes during the POST process to indicate an error.

Table A-6 lists the classes of numeric error codes.

Table A-6   Numeric Error Code Classes

Error Code Class	Description
100–199	Motherboard errors
200–299	Memory or RAM errors
300–399	Keyboard errors
400–499	Monochrome video errors
500–599	Color video errors
600–699	Floppy drive errors
1700	Hard drive errors

Table A-7 includes a sampling of the most common error codes.

Table A-7   Specific Numeric Error Codes

Error Code	Description
161	Dead CMOS battery
201	Failed or incorrectly installed memory
301	Keyboard not plugged in or is faulty
601	Floppy drive or floppy drive controller has failed
1101	Serial card is faulty
1701	Hard disk drive controller is faulty

■ In modern systems, POST error codes are reported with text messages such as "HDD controller failure" or "Floppy drive failure."

Power Supplies

■ Common symptoms of a failed power supply include a system that will not boot or one that spontaneously restarts.

■ If a fan in a power supply fails, it is best to replace the entire power supply and not try to fix the failed fan. The power supply contains capacitors that hold an electrical charge that can injure a technician.

■ If you suspect that the power supply is not operating correctly, the power output can be tested with a multimeter.

Slot Covers

■ Always replace slot covers. Although they might seem not to have a purpose other than cosmetic, slot covers must be in place to prevent dust from entering the case and to maintain proper airflow in the case.

Front Cover Alignment

■ The front cover of a computer case must be aligned correctly. If it is not, devices such as recessed floppy disk drives or CD-ROM drives may become inaccessible. In addition, incorrect cover alignment can affect correct air flow and increase exposure to dust.

Storage Devices and Cables

Floppy Drive

If the floppy is having difficulty reading disks, clean the floppy drive heads using denatured alcohol. Common floppy drive failure symptoms include:

■ **Floppy drive light stays on**   This is often a result of the floppy drive cable being attached incorrectly. Verify that the floppy drive cable is aligned with the correct pins on the floppy drive.

■ **Floppy drive light does not come on**   This indicates that the drive is not getting power. Check the power connections to the floppy drive.

■ **System halts, saying a floppy drive cannot be located**   The BIOS cannot detect the floppy drive. Enter the BIOS and input the floppy drive settings and verify that the floppy drive has been physically installed correctly.

■ **Error message when accessing the floppy drive**   If you are working within the operating system and attempt to use the floppy drive, you might get an error indicating that the disk in the drive is not formatted or the device cannot be accessed. If this happens with a single floppy disk, it might simply be a faulty disk and not the floppy drive itself. If the same error message occurs with several disks, it is more likely that your floppy drive has failed. Sometimes cleaning the floppy drive heads will correct the problem, or the floppy drive needs to be replaced.

Troubleshooting SCSI Devices

As with all troubleshooting procedures, when you're working with SCSI systems, be sure to make only one change at a time. Making multiple changes confuses the issue and prevents you from knowing what the exact remedy to the problem was:

- **Termination**   Each of the physical ends of a SCSI bus must be terminated to prevent signal reflection.

- **SCSI IDs**   Each device on a SCSI bus must have a unique ID. When troubleshooting your SCSI configuration, ensure that each of the devices has a unique ID assigned to it.

- **Cable connections**   Ensure that all of the SCSI cables, internal and external, are correctly and securely attached.

- **Cable length**   Verify that none of the cables being used exceed their recommended length.

Troubleshooting IDE Devices

- Ensure that pin 1 of the cable is aligned correctly to pin 1 of the IDE channel.

- Verify that the master/slave jumpers are correctly set.

- Confirm that the IDE disk is getting power and the power connector is securely attached.

- Check the IDE cable to ensure that it has not become disconnected from the motherboard.

- Sometimes the IDE cable itself might be faulty. To determine if this is the case, swap it out with a known working one.

- To verify that the hard drive is installed and recognized by the computer system, you can go into the system's BIOS settings and confirm that it detects the hard drive. Modern BIOSs automatically detect the presence of a new hard drive and add the settings for it. Older BIOSs might require that you do this manually.

- If the hard disk is detected but is shown as the wrong size, it is often not a problem with the physical installation, but means that the BIOS needs to be updated to accommodate the size of the new hard disk(s).

Hard Disk Failure Symptoms

■ Files are missing or corrupt.

■ You hear a clunking or grinding noise, caused by the read/write heads coming in contact with the platters.

■ The hard drive does not run or is unable to execute a program.

■ The system does not boot, and indicates an error such as a missing operating system or the inability to find Command.com.

■ In most cases, problems with CD, CD-RW, DVD, and DVD-RW drives can be cured by making sure that media is clean and that the drives themselves are also clean.

■ Tape drive problems can often be cured by using a cleaning tape. Use of a cleaning tape should be considered routine maintenance.

Cooling Systems

■ Fans and heat sinks are used to move hot air away from processors, which generate a significant amount of heat as they operate. Additional fans are used in the power supply and computer case to ensure heat dissipation.

■ Because the amount of heat generated by processors is surpassing the cooling abilities of heat sinks and fans, liquid cooling systems are being introduced that are able to move more heat away from the processor more quickly.

■ Many PCs and components have heat sensors that can alert users to temperatures that could be damaging to the system. Configuration of these sensors is often done through the BIOS.

Processors

■ Verify that the processor was correctly installed.

■ Verify that the processor fan is working and that the heat sink is installed and functioning properly.

Memory

■ If you have newly installed RAM, confirm with the manufacturer's Web site that it is compatible with your current configuration.

- Depending on the motherboard, it might be necessary to match equal capacity memory modules in available banks.

- Sometimes a memory problem is nothing more than a poorly seated module. When troubleshooting memory, it's a good idea to carefully remove the RAM and reinsert it.

- If your system is freezing periodically and you suspect memory is the cause, a good strategy is to swap out the RAM and see if the problem is corrected.

- If the memory in your system is old or the inside of the case is particularly dirty, the contacts and connectors might need to be cleaned.

Troubleshooting Display

Monitors

- Verify that there is a connection between the monitor and the video card; look for the LEDs on the front of the monitor.

- Verify that the cable is correctly attached to the video card in your system. Loose cables might cause display problems and color errors.

- Verify that the settings have not been changed on the monitor; if the brightness setting was changed, the display might just be too dark to see.

- Swap out a monitor with a known working one to help isolate the cause of the problem.

Video Card

- Verify the installation and that the video card is correctly seated in one of the system's expansion slots.

- Verify that the latest drivers are being used for the video card. This simple procedure can fix a number of display anomalies. To get the latest drivers for the video card, go to the manufacturer's Web site.

- Verify the settings on the monitor. New monitors allow you to make very specific settings—adjusting these settings will change how the monitor displays information on the screen.

- Fuzzy on-screen images can often be corrected by degaussing the monitor.

■ The symptom of a bad monitor cable is a display with a blue, red, or green tint to it.

Keyboard

■ If you are called to fix a keyboard that continually beeps even after the system is restarted, you have a stuck key or there is something pressing down on a key.

■ When troubleshooting a keyboard problem, reseat the cable connection at the back.

■ Swap out a malfunctioning keyboard with a known working one to see if the problem is with the keyboard or the keyboard controller.

Mouse Errors

■ To correct erratic cursor movement on the screen or unresponsive cursor movement, clean the mouse ball and rollers.

■ Verify that the mouse cable has not become unplugged.

■ Ensure that there is not a resource conflict between the mouse and another device.

■ A serial mouse can also be involved in a resource conflict. If your serial mouse is connected to COM1 or COM3, it will be using IRQ 4; if it's connected to COM2 or COM4, your mouse will be using IRQ 3. Ensure that no other devices are using these resources.

Touch Screens

■ Touch screens are used with special applications such as point of sale (POS) and information kiosk services. Touch screens have an additional connection to a normal monitor in order to carry the "touch" information back to the system. Systems with a touch screen accept the input either through the serial port or via a special card installed in the system.

Network Interface Cards (NIC)

■ **I/O settings** If any new NIC has been added, check to see if there is an I/O address conflict. Use the specific hardware reviewing tools to see if this is the case.

■ **Network card drivers** An incorrect driver might make a card work improperly. Even if the driver installed is assigned by the operating system, visit the manufacturer's Web site to get the most recent driver available.

- **IRQ conflicts**   Verify that the network card has an IRQ address and that it is not in use by another system component.

- **Card settings**   Make sure all of the card's network settings are correct. One wrong setting and the card might not work at all.

- **Network card LED**   Most modern network cards have an LED on them (link light), which is used to tell if there is an active connection to the network. If you cannot access a network, check to see if the LED is lit. If it is not, there might be problem with the network card installation or setup.

Sound Card

- Like any other card, you must ensure that the correct system resources are assigned to a sound card and that the appropriate drivers are installed. Also ensure that the input or output devices are connected to the correct port on the sound card as the connections are often identical.

Modems

Table A-8 lists some common modem problems and their possible solutions.

Table A-8   Summary of Modem Troubleshooting

Symptom	Possible Solution
The modem stops working.	If the modem stops working, check whether new hardware has been added that might be causing a resource conflict. If new software was added, verify that the modem settings have not changed.
The modem keeps hanging up after making a connection.	Verify that the modem settings are correct. Also, you might need to download and install the latest modem drivers.
The modem is not connecting at the correct speed or is operating slowly.	If a modem is connecting more slowly than it should, verify that you have the latest drivers installed. The problem can also be a result of poor phone line quality, which is something you cannot do very much about.
The modem makes a connection but you cannot authenticate.	This is often caused by the wrong user name/password combination. Verify that you are inputting the correct settings.
The operating system cannot find the modem on a COM port.	This can often be fixed by moving the modem onto another COM port or checking the configuration of the port to make sure it's correct.
The modem dials but cannot connect.	Ensure that the correct phone number is being dialed.
The modem gives an error that it cannot make a connection to the server.	Verify that the protocol settings are correctly configured to access the server.

Modem Commands

■ When working with and troubleshooting modems, we often use something called the AT command set, to help in the process. The AT commands are used from a communications application, such as the HyperTerminal utility in Windows, and talk directly to the modem. Table A-9 lists some common AT commands and what they do.

Table A-9 Sample of the AT Command Set

Command	Result
ATA	Sets the modem to auto answer.
ATH	Hangs up an active connection.
ATDT *phone number* or ATDP *phone number*	Dials the specified *phone number* using tone (T) or pulse (P) dialing.
ATZ	Resets the modem.
AT13	Displays the name and model of the modem.
ATX	Resets the modem to a predefined state.

IEEE1394/FireWire

■ Troubleshooting IEEE 1394 connections is often related to ensuring that the physical connections are correct and that the correct drivers are installed. If an external hub is being used then you must ensure that the hub is correctly connected and powered.

Infrared

■ In addition to correct hardware and software configuration, when troubleshooting infrared connections you must also ensure that there is a direct line of sight between the sending and receiving device. Also ensure that the devices are no more than a few feet apart. If necessary, move the devices very close together to make sure that the distance is not an issue.

USB Troubleshooting

■ **Installation**   For the most part, USB devices will install easily. If they do not, you will need to check in Windows Device Manager to be certain that the USB root hub is functioning correctly. If the root hub is displayed with an exclamation point in a yellow circle, it is not functioning and USB devices cannot be used on that system. The problem can often be corrected in the system's BIOS. From within the BIOS, verify that the root USB controller is being assigned an IRQ address.

- **Device drivers**   Operating systems supporting plug and play will automatically try to install the drivers for your USB device. When the OS cannot find the drivers, you will be prompted to supply the necessary drivers. Ensure that you are using the correct and most recent drivers from the manufacturer's Web site.

- **Firmware**   If a USB device does not function or functions erratically, the firmware for the USB device might need to be upgraded.

- **Power**   Some USB devices require external power to operate. An example of such a device is an external hard disk. Other devices that require very little power will plug directly into the system, drawing the power from the system itself. When troubleshooting, ensure that devices that require external power are in fact receiving it.

Troubleshooting Tools

POST Cards

- POST diagnostic cards work with any operating system and display detailed information on the POST process. POST cards are expansion cards that are plugged into the system, and once the system is restarted, error messages are reported via on-board LEDs.

Hardware Loopback Plug

- Hardware loopback plugs, also known as hardware loopback connectors or loopback adapters, redirect outgoing data signals back into the system. This causes the system to believe that it is both sending and receiving data. The loopback plug is used in conjunction with diagnostic software that will test the incoming and outgoing signal.

- Hardware loopback plugs test a port to see if it is sending and receiving information correctly.

Multimeter

- A multimeter is used for troubleshooting or testing power-related issues in the system. It's used to test four key power areas: AC voltage, DC voltage, continuity, and resistance. The multimeter itself uses two connector probes, one negative and one positive, an analog or digital display, and a switch to select the type of power test you want to perform.

■ Looking for a defective or broken cable is done by setting the multimeter to test for continuity, and testing power supplies and batteries is done by testing the voltage.

Tone Generator and Locator

■ A tone generator is a troubleshooting tool used in a network environment. The tone generator makes a signal on one end of a network cable and the tone locator finds it at the other end. This is often used when trying to find the ends of a network cable.

Troubleshooting Process

■ **Determine the severity of the problem**   Determine how serious the problem is and whether there is a threat to the data. Problems that might lead to a loss of data take precedence over most others. Problems that fall into this category are malfunctioning backup devices, corrupt hard disks, or virus activity.

■ **Gather information necessary to isolate the problem**   Before attempting to fix a problem, first gather information necessary to help isolate the problem. Information comes from three key sources: from the computer user, from system-generated errors and error logs, and from your own senses.

■ **Determine the potential cause or causes**   After gathering the information, you can isolate the potential cause of the problem. Keep in mind that in the midst of a seemingly complex problem, the easiest solution is often the right one.

■ **Fix the problem**   After isolating the cause you can try your fix. Remember to try only one thing at a time. If your solution does not fix the problem, you will need to identify another potential cause and try again.

■ **Review and document**   When documenting a troubleshooting procedure, be sure to write down each step you took and the result. Make sure that the steps you took can be followed by someone else.

Domain 3.0 Preventative Maintenance

Cleaning Compounds

- **Water**   A damp cloth and a little soapy water are used for cleaning plastic and metal surfaces, but water should never be used on internal electric components.

- **Denatured alcohol**   Denatured (isopropyl) alcohol is often used for cleaning the inside of some components such as floppy drive heads. The cleaning solution is typically applied with a lint-free swab directly to the heads.

- **Regular glass cleaner**   Glass cleaner has limited application for cleaning computer equipment. Its use should be restricted to cleaning the display screen of a CRT monitor. Glass cleaner should never be used to clean an LCD screen; it can eat right through it.

- **Compressed air**   Compressed air is sold in cans and used to blow off dust and debris from inside components or the computer case itself. Compressed air is well suited for cleaning fans, power supplies, and other hard-to-reach places.

- **Non-static vacuums**   Non-static vacuums are seen in most PC repair shops and are used for sucking the dust out of the computer case, keyboard, power supplies, and even peripheral devices. Non-static vacuums are specifically designed for use with computers. Regular vacuums actually create a storm of static electricity and can damage the components you are trying to clean.

Cleaning Common Components

Mouse

- A damp cloth can be used to wipe off the mouse ball. This should be enough to get it clean, and smooth off the surface.

- A can of compressed air is often used to blow out dust from inside a mouse.

Keyboard

- Keyboard surface areas can be cleaned with distilled water.

- Spills such as cola or coffee that can leave your keys sticky and non-functioning might require that the keyboard be soaked in distilled water.

- A keyboard, like any other component, must be completely dry before reconnecting it to the computer.

Monitor

- Stains or spills on the glass can be cleaned using regular glass cleaner.

- It's best not to spray the cleaner directly onto the monitor. Instead, first squirt it onto a lint-free cloth and then use that.

- Warning: Do not clean the monitor while it is plugged in! Be sure the monitor is disconnected from the PC and unplugged from the electrical outlet before cleaning.

LCD Monitor

- If you notice moisture on your screen, wipe it off gently with a soft cloth before powering on your monitor.

- Never use regular glass cleaner to clean an LCD display.

Floppy Drive

- The best way to clean floppy drive read/write heads is to use a cleaning diskette or some denatured alcohol on a swab.

- To remove the dust from inside a floppy drive, you might have to use a non-static vacuum and/or compressed air.

Power Threats

- **Sag** A drop in power supply that only lasts a short period. A sag is generally the most common type of power anomaly.

- **Brownout** A drop in supply voltage that lasts more than a few seconds.

- **Spike** A sharp and very sudden increase in line voltage that pushes the supply voltage above an acceptable threshold.

- **Surge** An unacceptably large increase in supply voltage that lasts longer than a spike. This condition is also known as a swell.

■ **Noise**   Interference can cause the supply voltage to be inconsistent.

■ **Blackout**   Complete failure of the power supply.

Uninterruptible Power Supplies (UPS) and Surge Suppressors

■ The function of the UPS is to power the computer in case of a power outage, and to provide sufficient time to allow a computer user to properly shut the system down and prevent data loss.

■ UPS systems can be either intelligent—that is, interface with the system via a data cable—or dumb, which means there is no communication between the UPS and the system to which it supplies power.

■ By protecting a system from a "dirty" shutdown, an intelligent UPS can prevent hardware damage, increase availability, and decrease potential data loss.

■ With an offline UPS, when the power fails or does not meet requirements, the battery supplies power to the equipment connected to the UPS.

■ Online UPS systems are more suited to use with sensitive equipment because they always supply power to connected equipment through the batteries.

■ The more components that rely on the UPS, the shorter the time the battery can keep all of the equipment live.

■ Devices that require a lot of power such as laser printers should not be plugged into a UPS system.

■ Surge suppressors are designed to help filter out power spikes.

■ One big power spike can wipe out your surge suppressor. In case of an electrical storm, the surge suppressor might not be able to protect the system.

Storing Components for the Future

■ Wherever possible, the safest way to store components such as memory, motherboards, or processors is to return them to their original packaging.

■ In lieu of the original packaging, components should be sealed inside antistatic bags. These bags will prevent the effects of ESD on stored components.

- Once inside the ESD bag, it is best to store components in a cool, dry place. Too much heat and too much moisture can be a problem because you are more likely to get electrostatic build-up in these conditions.

Handling High-Voltage Equipment

- If you ever work with high-voltage equipment, make sure that the device you are working on is unplugged and that you are not wearing antistatic straps. High-voltage equipment doesn't really concern itself with ESD and the straps could actually attract voltage from high-voltage devices.

- Monitors use capacitors that retain a charge even after the device is unplugged.

- Like CRT monitors, power supplies use capacitors that maintain a charge long after they have been unplugged. Even if only the power supply fan fails, it is best to replace the entire unit than try to repair the power supply.

- You should not attempt to repair high-voltage equipment like power supplies and monitors unless you have been specifically trained to do so.

Disposing of Unwanted Equipment

- **Monitors (CRTs)**   Check to see if there is somewhere to donate the monitor or search for a hazardous waste program that can assist you by taking your old monitor.

- **Batteries**   Computer batteries should not be thrown out in a landfill site. To properly dispose of batteries, you need to follow local hazardous waste guidelines and most often take the batteries to a recycling depot. UPS batteries are of a particular concern and must be carefully disposed of.

- **Toner kits/cartridges**   Wherever possible, refill toner and ink cartridges and reuse them. Many local print shops and even the manufacturer will often buy back or at least take used print cartridges and resell them. This is often the easiest method to get rid of them. Another option is to dispose of them according to local hazardous waste guidelines.

- **Chemical solvents and cans**   Dispose of chemicals as you would any other hazardous household product. Many local communities sponsor hazardous waste drop-off sites. These are ideal for disposing of old computer chemical solvents.

- **Material Safety Data Sheet**   An MSDS is a detailed document that contains instructions for handling, transporting, and disposing of particular products.

Electrostatic Discharge (ESD)

- ESD is an electrical charge that can damage electronic circuitry and computer components.

- A component damaged by ESD might not fail immediately but might degrade over time until it fails.

- Dust and other debris inside your computer case can cause a hidden ESD effect. Over time, the dust can hold a small electric charge and this will eventually begin to degrade the performance of internal components.

ESD Protection Devices

- **ESD wrist strap**   Antistatic wrist straps are designed to filter out static charges and safely discharge them. An ESD wrist strap has a strap that fits around your wrist and an attached cable. The cable attaches to an earth ground such as the grounding wire of a wall outlet. The cable uses a 1 megohm resistor to negate the effects of ESD.

- **Antistatic mat**   When you use an antistatic mat, the component you are working on is placed right on top of the mat. The function of the mat is to dissipate the charge of anything that might come into contact with it. Like ESD wrist straps, ESD mats use a cable to attach to a grounding source. A variation on the antistatic mat is the antistatic floor mat. A technician would be required to stand on a floor mat to prevent ESD.

- **Antistatic spray**   The function of antistatic spray is to remove the static effect from clothing. Antistatic spray is not as effective as antistatic mats or wrist straps.

- **Antistatic bag**   When not working with components, it is always best to leave them in their antistatic bags.

Domain 4.0 Motherboard/Processors/Memory

Processor Packaging

■ The most commonly used processor form factors are the pin grid array (PGA) processor packaging and the Single Edge Contact Cartridge (SECC).

■ PGA processors plug directly into the motherboard using zero-insertion-force (ZIF) sockets.

■ SECC cartridges are mounted into an integrated circuit board or "slot" on the motherboard.

Intel Processors

■ MMX was introduced with the Pentium processor and consists of 57 processor instructions geared specifically toward the improvement of sound and video processing. Table A-10 lists additional characteristics of Intel processors.

Table A-10   Summary of Intel Processors

Processor	Form Factor	Voltage	Speeds	L1 Cache (KB)	L2 Cache (KB)	Socket
Pentium	273- or 296-pin PGA	3.3 or 5	60–233 MHz	16	256–512 (On motherboard)	Socket 4, 5, or 7
Pentium Pro	387-pin PGA	3.1 or 3.3	150–200 MHz	16	256–1 MB (Integrated cache)	Socket 8
Pentium II	242-pin SEC	3.3	233–400 MHz	32	512 (Integrated cache)	Slot 1
Pentium III	242-pin SECC or 370-pin PGA	1.3–2.05	450 MHz–1.3 GHz and higher	32	256–512 (Integrated cache)	Slot 1 or PGA 370
Celeron	SEPP or 370-pin PGA	1.3–2.05	Up to 2.2 GHz	16–32	0–512	Socket 370, Slot 1
Pentium 4	478-pin or 423-pin PGA	1.1–1.8	1.7–2.8 GHz	8	256–512	PGA 478 or PGA 423
Itanium	Slot M	1.7	733–800 MHz	32	96	Slot M

AMD Processors

- **K6-II**   Are available in a variety of clock speeds up to 550 MHz. The K6-II provided support for 3DNow! and used a Socket7/Super7 motherboard interface. All K6-II processors use 3.3 volts.

- **K6-III**   Offers 64-KB L1 cache and a full-speed 256-KB L2 cache. Designed to fit into a Socket7/Super7 motherboard, the K6-III supports a 100-MHz bus speed and comes with 3DNow! support.

- **Duron**   The Duron processor is currently available in speeds up to 1.3 GHz. The Duron includes a 128-KB L1 cache and a 64-KB L2 cache, which is synchronized to the processor speed and supports 3DNow! and SIMD instruction sets, providing increased capabilities in graphic and audio applications.

- **Athlon**   The Athlon utilizes Socket A motherboard connections. The Athlon has 128 KB of L1 cache and 256 KB of L2 cache, all of which runs at full CPU speed.

- AMD processors, all the way to the recent AMD K6-III, continue to utilize the original socket 7 form factor.

Cyrix Processors

- The 6x86-P Cyrix processors ranged from 120 to 200 MHz, and functioned at roughly the same speeds as the Pentium equivalents. Cyrix still makes a few lower-end CPUs such as the Cyrix M-II, which like the AMD processors, uses a socket 7 form factor. Another Cyrix processor, the VIA C3, uses a Socket 370 ZIF socket.

Memory Form Factors

- There are two types of SIMMs: 30-pin and 72-pin. The 30-pin units, which were introduced first, transfer data 8 bits at a time. The 72-pin SIMMs transfer data 32 bits at a time. The 72-pin SIMM, apart from having 42 more pins, is 1.25 inches longer than the 30-pin SIMM at 4.25 inches.

- Most DIMMs have 168 pins, are installed vertically, and are secured by catches that engage the module at each end. DIMMs use a 64-bit data bus. DDR SD-RAM uses 184-pin DIMMs.

Memory Types

■ **Fast page-mode RAM**   FPM uses a 25-MHz clock rate and a maximum bandwidth of 200 Mbps. FPM RAM employs sophisticated methods of locating data within RAM.

■ **Extended data out RAM**   EDO RAM supports a clock rate of 40 MHz and a maximum bandwidth of 320 Mbps.

■ **Synchronous DRAM**   SDRAM comes in a variety of speeds so that the memory can be purchased to match the speed of the system bus in which it will be installed. Currently, SDRAM is available in PC66, PC100, and PC133 versions. These versions offer the same data rates as their names, and offer 528 Mbps, 800 Mbps, and 1.1 Gbps of maximum bandwidth, respectively.

■ **Double Data Rate SDRAM**   DDR-SDRAM DIMMs have 184 pins, with the extra pins being needed for the additional signaling information. DDR-SDRAM provides data rates up to a maximum of 266 MHz (133 * 2) and a maximum bandwidth of 1.6 Gbps for PC100, and 2.1 Gbps for PC133.

■ **Rambus DRAM**   RDRAM was brought to the PC memory market through a joint venture between Rambus and Intel. RDRAM operates at up to 800 MHz and has a maximum bandwidth of 1.6 Gbps. RDRAM achieves these very high levels of data throughput by using a system called double-clocking.

■ **VRAM**   Video RAM (VRAM) is specialized memory that is used for video cards and not as part of the system's main memory. VRAM is known as dual-ported memory because it is able to write to both of its input/output (I/O) ports at the same time. This allows it to simultaneously refresh the screen while text and images are drawn in memory.

■ **WRAM**   Window Ram (WRAM) is used to enhance video performance. Also like VRAM, WRAM can be written to and read from simultaneously and is much faster than its predecessor, VRAM.

■ **SGRAM**   Synchronous Graphics Ram (SGRAM) is used on video cards to increase graphics performance.

Parity and Error-Correcting Code RAM

■ Parity is a mechanism by which errors can be detected in RAM.

■ ECC RAM detects and corrects errors through the use of a mathematical calculation called a checksum. If ECC RAM detects an error, it will either correct the error or report the error, depending on the error's complexity.

AT Motherboards

■ AT boards did not have many integrated components, meaning that video, hard disk controllers, and the like required the addition of expansion cards.

■ AT motherboards require AT keyboards using a DIN-5 connector.

■ Newer Baby AT motherboards measure 8.5 x 13 inches and are laid out (in terms of fixing holes) exactly like the earlier larger AT motherboards. The screw holes and the keyboard port (5-pin DIN) are located in the same location on the motherboard, allowing any baby AT motherboard to be used in most AT cases.

■ AT power supply connectors are recognizable by having two separate connectors needing to be plugged in side by side on the motherboard. These connectors, labeled the P8 and P9, provide the electrical connection between the power supply and the motherboard.

■ When connecting AT connectors, ensure that the black ground wires from each connector are beside each other.

Figure A-6 shows an AT motherboard and identifies its major components.

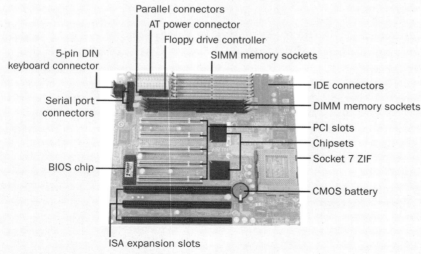

Figure A-6 An AT motherboard with components identified.

ATX Motherboards

- The ATX form factor is typically larger than baby AT motherboards and has a number of integrated components.

- On an ATX motherboard you can expect to see two serial ports, a parallel port, perhaps USB ports, and two mini-DIN (PS/2) connectors, one for the mouse and one for the keyboard. Recall that AT motherboards use the 5-pin DIN connector; this provides an easy way to distinguish between AT and ATX motherboards.

- ATX motherboards can be turned off via software.

- ATX power supplies, used with our modern-class machines, use a single 20-slot keyed connector.

  Figure A-7 shows an ATX motherboard and identifies its major components.

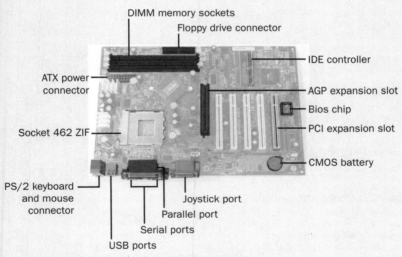

Figure A-7 An ATX motherboard with components identified.

Motherboard Bus Slots

- **Micro Channel Architecture (MCA)** The MCA bus was the first to offer a 32-bit bus and was intended to replace the older AT-ISA 16-bit bus. Although it did improve on the 16-bit bus, MCA was made to be incompatible with ISA cards, and this perhaps was one of the reasons why it never really caught on.

- **Extended Industry Standard Architecture (EISA)** The EISA bus was designed to be compatible with the older ISA expansion cards, meaning that both the original 8-bit and 16-bit interface cards worked in the EISA slots. EISA slots were used primarily in 80386 and 80486 computers and are not seen in our modern computers.

- **VL bus**   The VESA local bus (VL bus) was used primarily with the 386 and 486 types of computers, and it was designed for use in systems with a single processor. The VL bus enhanced the performance of high-speed devices such as video controllers. In terms of performance, running at an unprecedented 33 MHz, the VL bus represented significant improvements over the older ISA bus.

- **Peripheral Component Interconnect (PCI)**   The PCI bus is used in both PC and Macintosh computers and, like the VL bus, provides a high-speed data path between peripheral devices and the CPU. The PCI bus supports 33 MHz and 66 MHz speeds and 32- and 64-bit data paths using bus mastering. Additional features of the PCI bus include support for plug-and-play devices and for the sharing of IRQs, helping to alleviate the problem of the limited number of IRQs available on a system.

- **PCI Extended (PCIX) bus**   The PCIX bus promises to be backward compatible with older PCI devices. Using a 64-bit data path and running at a clock speed of 133 MHz, the PCIX bus increases transfer speed from 132 Mbps to a rather impressive 1 gigabyte per second.

- **Accelerated Graphics Port (AGP)**   The AGP bus slot is reserved for use with video adapters; no other expansion cards use AGP.

Bus Slot and Expansion Card Compatibility

Table A-11 lists the types of expansion slots and their characteristics.

Table A-11   Expansion Slot Compatibility

Slot Type	8-Bit Slot	16-Bit Slot	EISA	VL Bus	PCI	PCIX	AGP
8-Bit Card	Yes	Yes	Yes	Yes	No	No	No
16-Bit Card	No	Yes	Yes	Yes	No	No	No
EISA	No	No	Yes	No	No	No	No
VL Bus	No	No	No	Yes	No	No	No
PCI Cards	No	No	No	No	Yes	Yes	No
AGP Cards	No	No	No	No	No	No	Yes

CMOS

■ The complementary metal-oxide semiconductor (CMOS) provides the storage for the BIOS settings.

■ The CMOS is read-only memory (ROM) that stores specific computer configurations, such as hard drive type, and keeps track of the date and time for the computer.

■ Using an on-board battery, the CMOS maintains these settings even when the computer is turned off. On most motherboards, the CMOS battery is a coin-type battery, similar to a watch battery.

■ The symptoms of a battery problem include losing accurate time on the computer and sometimes receiving an error message of "invalid system disk" on boot-up, because the computer has lost the hard disk settings.

Common BIOS/CMOS Settings

■ **Printer parallel port**   From within the CMOS, you can change the settings for the parallel ports. You can change the IRQ and I/O address used by the parallel port if there is a conflict with another device. You can also choose whether the system will use standard unidirectional data communication, ECP (Extended Capabilities Port), or EPP (Enhanced Parallel Port).

■ **COM Serial Port**   The configuration of COM ports in newer systems is handled by plug and play. However, if you need to change the resources (IRQs, I/O addresses, and so on) used by on-board COM ports, it can be done in the BIOS.

■ **Floppy Drive**   Floppy drive support can be enabled or disabled in the BIOS. Support for a second floppy drive will need to be enabled in the BIOS.

■ **Hard Drive**   Settings for the hard disk are maintained in the CMOS. If you were to upgrade the hard drive in a computer system today, it is likely that the capacity of the hard drive will be automatically detected and installed, but in some systems it might still need to be entered manually. Manually inputting hard disk settings into the CMOS includes specifying heads, cylinders, and sector values.

- **Memory**   If new memory is added to a system, the settings will have to be recognized by the BIOS. This might be done automatically or you might have to enter the CMOS and exit to make the memory change.

- **Boot Sequence**   The boot sequence set in the CMOS dictates in which order the system will look for the boot files. You can set your system to boot first from a variety of sources including CD-ROM, floppy disk, hard disk, or the network.

- **Date/Time**   The date and time used by the operating system is set in the CMOS. One thing to remember is that if your system keeps losing time or showing the wrong time, this can be an indicator that the CMOS battery is failing.

- **Passwords**   In most cases, there are two passwords that can be set in the system's CMOS. The first prevents the system from booting until a password is entered. The second password protects the CMOS itself. If you have forgotten a CMOS password and cannot access your system or CMOS, you will have to remove the CMOS battery to clear the settings. Alternatively, some motherboards have jumper settings that can be changed in order to clear the CMOS.

- **Plug and Play BIOS**   You can use the Plug and Play option in the CMOS to configure plug-and-play devices. Most often this setting goes unchanged, as it is typically left up to the operating system to handle plug-and-play devices. In fact, if you are using an operating system that supports plug and play, it will override any settings within the BIOS.

Domain 5.0 Printers

Laser Printer Components

- **Photosensitive drum**   The photosensitive drum is an aluminum roller coated with specialized photosensitive particles. A laser beam inside the printer is used to shine reflected light onto the surface of the drum, creating a pattern of electrically charged, and not so charged, areas. The drum is held inside the toner cartridge but can be accessed in case it needs to be manually cleaned to remove excess toner.

- **Eraser or erasure lamp**   The eraser lamp is a light used to give the photosensitive drum a thorough electrical cleaning. The eraser lamp shines light on the entire surface of the photosensitive drum, neutral-

izing the electrical charge. This is done to remove any remaining particles from the drum for the next print job.

- **Primary corona wire**   The primary corona wire is responsible for
  negatively charging the photosensitive particles on the surface of the
  drum.

- **Transfer corona**   The transfer corona is responsible for positively
  charging the paper before it reaches the toner area. To get the image
  from the drum onto the paper, the paper must have a positive electrical
  charge that will draw the toner away from the drum and onto the
  paper. To prevent the positively charged paper from sticking to the
  drum itself, a static charge eliminator is used to remove the charge
  from the paper.

- **Laser**   The laser beam is used in the writing process and creates an
  image of the page to be printed on the photosensitive drum. The photosensitive drum holds an electrical charge when not exposed to light,
  because it is completely dark within the toner cartridge. When the laser
  hits areas on the drum, the drum discharges in the area hit by the laser,
  leaving the image.

- **Toner**   Printer toner is a powder composed of plastic and iron particles that cling to the surface of the drum after the primary corona wire
  provides an electrical charge to the drum. The transfer corona applies
  an electrical charge to the paper and the toner is transferred from the
  drum to the paper, where it is melted onto the paper by the fuser.

- **Fuser**   When the toner initially transfers from the drum to the paper,
  it is only held there by an electrical charge. The fuser effectively melts
  the toner onto the paper. When working inside a printer, care should
  be taken to avoid contact with the fuser, as it gets very hot.

- **Printer controller**   The controller is a motherboard equivalent for
  laser printers. It converts the signals and messages from the computer
  to signals for the various components within the printer. Essentially,
  the controller is a circuit board that holds the printer's memory and
  communicates with the PC.

Laser Printing Process

- **Cleaning phase**   A rubber blade wipes away extra toner from the
  drum, and the eraser lamp shines on the drum, causing it to lose all of
  its electrostatic charge.

- **Conditioning/charging the drum**   A special wire, known as the *corona wire*, applies a negative charge to the photosensitive drum. This negative charge typically ranges between 600 and 1000 volts.

- **Writing**   The laser beam reflects off of mirrors to hit the drum. Wherever the laser beam hits the photosensitive drum, the negative charge is reduced from its 600-volt plateau to −100 volts, creating an image on the drum.

- **Developing**   Inside the toner cartridge is the *developing roller* that uses a magnet and electrostatic charges to attract the iron particles in the toner to itself. When the developing roller rotates and the toner is between the developing roller and the photosensitive drum, the toner is attracted to the areas that have been exposed to the laser. The end result of the development stage is that the photosensitive drum has toner stuck to it wherever the laser had written.

- **Transferring**   The transfer corona gives the paper a positive charge that attracts the negatively charged toner from the surface of the drum to the positively charged paper. In effect, the toner leaps from the drum to the paper.

- **Fusing**   During the fusing stage, the toner, which contains a special chemical, is melted, causing it to stick (or fuse) to the paper. To make the toner melt, the paper is passed through one or more rollers, which are called fuser rollers. These rollers are heated to a very high temperature by a fuser lamp.

Troubleshooting Laser Printers

Table A-12 describes some common printing problems with laser printers and their possible solutions.

Table A-12   Troubleshooting Laser Printers

Problem	Potential Solution
Light ghost images on printout	Ghost images are caused by residue from a previous print job and often caused by too much toner on the drum.
Dark ghosting appears on print jobs	Dark ghosting can be caused by a damaged drum. Replace the drum or toner cartridge.
Random spots or streaks on the print job	The drum is not clean, residual particles are still on the drum.
Consistent marks on every print page	This is often caused by a damaged drum. The drum will need to be replaced.
Print quality is too light	Check the toner level. This error can be caused when toner is running low.

Table A-12   Troubleshooting Laser Printers

Problem	Potential Solution
Patchy print jobs	This can be caused when the toner is running low. A shake of the toner cartridge will often be enough to get a few more print jobs out of the printer.
Laser printer prints a blank page	This could be a result of a failed transfer corona. If the transfer corona does not positively charge the paper, the toner will not be transferred from the drum.
Print smudges or streaks after being printed out	The fuser roller might not be correctly fusing the toner onto the paper.

Dot-Matrix Printers

■ The basic principle of a dot-matrix printer is that a collection of pins, typically 9 or 24, organized in an oblong shape, are pressed against a ribbon, which in turn presses against the paper.

■ The platen is a roller that guides the paper through and also provides a backstop for the printing mechanism to bang into.

■ Dot-matrix printers often use a tractor feed mechanism to transport paper through the printer. To use a tractor feed, the holes in the sides of the specialized continuous feed paper must be aligned with the feed mechanism on the printer.

■ Print speed with dot-matrix printers is measured in characters per second.

Troubleshooting Dot-Matrix Printers

Table A-13 describes common problems with dot-matrix printers and possible solutions.

Table A-13   Troubleshooting Dot-Matrix Printers

Problem	Potential Solution
Printer will not turn on	No power is getting to the printer; check that the power cable is plugged in.
Power is getting to the printer but it does not print	Verify that the printer is online and not out of paper. If LEDs are flashing, cross-reference flashing LEDs with the manual that accompanied the printer.
Printer will not go online	Verify that there is paper in the printer and the ribbon is in place.
Paper does not feed correctly	Ensure that the paper is inserted into the tractor feed mechanism correctly. If the paper is not correctly aligned, the paper will wrinkle or jam as it goes through the printer.
Text split across two sheets of paper	This will often occur when the paper is not correctly placed in the tractor feed mechanism. Replace the paper, ensuring that it is correctly aligned.

Table A-13   Troubleshooting Dot-Matrix Printers

Problem	Potential Solution
Paper is crinkled after the print job	Realign the paper in the tractor feed mechanism.
Print head moves across the paper but does not type on the paper	This often happens if the ink ribbon is installed incorrectly or it is out of ink.
Text is garbled	Ensure that the correct driver is being used for the printer and that the printer is using the correct settings.
Text is faint or inconsistent	This is most certainly due to a worn ribbon. Replace the ink ribbon.
Printed text is dark on one side and light on the other	This is a common dot-matrix problem, most often caused by a faulty ribbon or misaligned or worn platen.

Ink-Jet Printers

■ Ink-jet devices today work by heating the tiny ink bubbles that form on the 300 to 600 tiny nozzles on each ink-jet print head. These tiny ink droplets heat to a boil, then burst, and an electrically charged plate deflects the ink onto the paper.

■ The quality of print jobs for ink-jet printers is measured in dots per inch (dpi); the higher the dpi, the better the print but the more ink is used.

■ The speed of ink-jet printers is measured in pages per minute (PPM).

Troubleshooting Ink-Jet Printers

Table A-14 describes common problems with ink-jet printers and possible solutions.

Table A-14   Troubleshooting Ink-Jet Printers

Problem	Potential Solution
Printer will not turn on	No power is getting to the printer; check that the power cable is plugged in.
Power is getting to the printer but it does not print	Verify that the printer is online and not out of paper. If LEDs are flashing, cross-reference flashing LEDs with the manual that accompanied the printer.
Printer will not go online	Verify that there is paper in the printer and the ink cartridge is in place.
Paper does not feed correctly	Friction feed rollers might need to be adjusted, more paper might need to be added to the paper tray, or a lighter weight paper might need to be used.
Print head moves across the paper but does not print on the paper	The ink cartridge might be empty or low or the ink might be dry. Try replacing the ink cartridge.
Print quality is faint	Ink is old or running out; replace the ink cartridge.

Table A-14   Troubleshooting Ink-Jet Printers

Problem	Potential Solution
Ink speckles on printout	Sometimes the ink within a printer can find its way onto other components by which the paper passes. As it does, it is transferred to the paper. To correct the problem, clean the inside of the printer with a damp cloth to remove unwanted ink stains.
The printout has the wrong colors	Verify that the ink cartridge is full and that it is not clogged. To do this, clean the ink-jet according to the manufacturer's documentation.
Text is garbled	Ensure that the correct driver is being used for the printer and that the printer is using the correct settings.

Connecting Printers

■ **Parallel ports**   To connect a parallel printer to the computer, a parallel cable is employed with a DB-25 connector on one end to attach to the PC and a Centronics 36-pin connector on the other end to attach to the printer. The different parallel port modes set in the system's BIOS include unidirectional, bidirectional, Enhanced Parallel Port, and Extended Capabilities Port.

- Unidirectional parallel port: Unidirectional parallel ports allow data transfer only out from the computer. That is why they are called unidirectional, one–way, communication. A standard unidirectional parallel port is restricted to speeds of 150 KBps and a maximum transmission distance of 15 feet.

- Bidirectional parallel ports: Bidirectional ports offer bidirectional communication. This feature allows a bidirectional port to transmit and receive data but not simultaneously.

- Enhanced Parallel Ports: The Enhanced Parallel Port (EPP) was one implementation of the IEEE 1284 standard. The EPP protocol standard allows for two-way communication between devices and transfer speeds from 500 KBps to 2 MBps. Although two-way communication is offered, it allows for only one way at a time, known as half-duplex communication.

- Enhanced Capabilities Port: The ECP port improves on the EPP port by allowing two-way simultaneous full-duplex communication between the PC and device connected to the ECP port. The ECP port is specifically designed to offer high-speed transfer rates and uses a direct memory access (DMA) channel and buffers to increase printing performance.

■ **Printer sharing**   You can share a local printer to the network and
secure it using permissions. When sharing a local printer to the network, the computer becomes a print server and other network systems
go through the computer to access the printer.

■ **Connecting printers directly to the network**   Network printers
connect to the network using a network interface card and network
cabling. Network printers are often configured from a display panel on
the printer or from specialized software on the server. One of the biggest advantages of connecting a printer directly to the network is that
it can be placed in the most convenient location, nearest the users who
use it, rather than having it connected to a computer system.

■ **USB**   The newest type of printer connection is USB. The printer can
be plugged into the computer while the system is turned on, and in
most cases, the connection of the printer will be automatically recognized by the computer and it will "plug and play." USB is a bidirectional interface, which means that you can have all of the advantages
that bidirectional communication brings.

■ **Infrared**   Infrared transmission is a wireless medium that uses the
infrared range of the electromagnetic spectrum. Many modern operating systems and laser printers provide support for infrared transmitters
and receivers that allow for wireless infrared communication between
the two devices to occur. This is particularly useful for devices such as
personal digital assistants (PDAs).

■ **Serial ports**   Connecting printers using a serial connection offers
slow speeds. Serial printers connect to the PC through the system's
serial port using a DB-9 or DB-25 female connector.

Common Printer Errors

■ **Paper out**   One of the more common errors is simply that the printer
is out of paper. This could mean the entire printer is out of paper or a
specific tray in the printer is empty. To correct the problem, add paper
to the paper tray following the manufacturer's guidelines.

■ **Low Toner**   Replacing ink or toner in most printers is a straightforward process but in some it might be necessary to refer to manufacturer documentation to see how the procedure is correctly
accomplished.

- **Incorrect Port Mode**   This error message indicates that the printer is using the wrong parallel port mode. Parallel printer communication can be unidirectional, bidirectional, EPP, or ECP. To correct the problem you will need to enter the system's BIOS and change the parallel port settings.

- **No Default Printer Selected**   This is an error that appears in the operating system print subsystem. The system has not been informed as to the default printer to use. This can be because either a default printer has not been selected or the system does not detect a printer to print to.

- **Input/output error**   The printer and the system are not communicating. Ensure that the printer is turned on and that it is physically cabled correctly.

Printer Preventative Maintenance

Laser Printers

- Laser printers produce ozone gas and use a special ozone filter to manage ozone emissions. Replace or clean the ozone filter periodically.

- Use compressed air to blow out dust and small paper residue.

- Use a PC vacuum to remove any excess toner from within the printer.

- Clean the transfer corona with denatured alcohol.

Dot-Matrix Printers

- Inspect the printer ribbon and replace it if necessary.

- Use compressed air to blow out dust and small paper residue.

- Ensure that the platen is correctly aligned.

- Clean the print head using denatured alcohol.

Ink-Jet Printer

- Remove ink cartridges and wipe excess ink from the metal plates.

- Inspect the inside of the printer. Wipe away any excess ink from the interior with a lint-free cloth.

- Use compressed air to blow out dust and small paper residue.

- Use new and good-quality cartridges.

- Use the printer's cleaning utility to periodically clean and align the print heads.

Network Cabling

■ There are three types of network cable commonly used with networks: coaxial, twisted-pair, and fiber-optic.

■ Coaxial cable used to be very popular but has now been largely replaced by twisted-pair.

■ Two types of coaxial cable are used in networking: RG58, also known as thin coaxial, and RG8, known as thick coaxial. The latter can be used over greater distances and is less susceptible to interference.

■ In common network implementations, thin coaxial cable is limited to 10 Mbps.

■ Traditionally, cables are covered with a PVC coating, but cables that are to be run in confined spaces such as within suspended ceilings are coated with a special fire-retardant covering and referred to as "plenum grade" cable.

■ Twisted-pair cable comes in two varieties, unshielded twisted-pair (UTP) and shielded twisted-pair (STP). Of the two, the latter is more resistant to outside interference by virtue of the shielding that is enclosed in the cable.

■ Twisted-pair cable is rated by category. There are currently seven defined categories. The categories define the appropriate use for the cable as well as the maximum speed at which they can operate.

Table A-15 lists the categories of UTP cables and their characteristics.

Table A-15   The Categories of UTP Cables

Category	Description
Category 1	Is the older UTP telephone cabling, which can carry voice signals but not data.
Category 2	Can transmit data at up to 4 Mbps, but because of its slow speed is rarely seen in the network environment.
Category 3	Can transmit data at up to 16 Mbps. UTP networks that have been in place for some time might use Category 3 cabling.
Category 4	Has a maximum transfer rate (bandwidth) of 20 Mbps.
Category 5	Has a maximum bandwidth of 100 Mbps. Category 5 has been the standard for network cabling for a number of years. In a very large percentage of UTP environments, Category 5 (or Cat5, to give it its common name) is the cable type in use.

Table A-15 The Categories of UTP Cables

Category	Description
Category 5e	Has a maximum bandwidth of 1000 Mbps. The Category 5e standard replaces Category 5.
Category 6	Ratified in June 2002, Category 6 has a maximum bandwidth of 1000 Mbps. Category 6 cable has more stringent construction standards than Category 5e cable and better resistance to outside interferences such as crosstalk and EMI.

■ Fiber-optic cable is becoming increasingly popular because it offers greater distance and vastly improved resistance to outside interference.

■ There are two types of fiber-optic cable used in networking. Single mode is capable of carrying a single signal over great distances. Multi-mode cable can carry more than one signal but over shorter distances.

■ Bandwidth refers to the transmission capacity or throughput of the cable.

■ Network cabling can only be of a certain length before the data signals that pass through them weaken. The degradation of data signals as they pass through a particular network cable is referred to as attenuation.

■ As signals pass through twisted-pair or coaxial network cables, they can be subjected to a form of interference known as electromagnetic interference (EMI). EMI is caused by such things as computer monitors and fluorescent lighting units.

■ Some cable types are more susceptible to EMI than others, and as you might expect, the more money spent on cabling, the better the resistance to EMI. In terms of EMI resistance, fiber-optic cable is completely resistant because it uses light instead of copper as a transmission medium.

A summary of cable types and characteristics is shown in Table A-16.

Table A-16 Summary of Cable Types

Cable Type	Susceptibility to Interference	Transmission Speed	Maximum Distance	Installation Difficulty
Thin Coax	Low	10 Mbps	185 meters	Low
Thick Coax	Very low	10 Mbps	500 meters	Difficult
UTP	High	10 to 1000 Mbps	100 meters	Easy
STP	Low	10 to 1000 Mbps	90 meters	Moderate
RS-232	N/A	20 Kbps	50 feet	N/A

Table A-16   Summary of Cable Types

Cable Type	Susceptibility to Interference	Transmission Speed	Maximum Distance	Installation Difficulty
Infrared	High	115 Kbps to 4 Mbps	1- to 3 meters	Easy
Fiber-Optic	None	100 Mbps to 1 Gbps and beyond	Up to 30 miles	Difficult

■ Using crossover cables enables certain specific connections to be achieved, such as directly connecting two PCs or connecting two network hubs or switches.

Network Interface Cards

■ The function of the network interface card (NIC) is to provide the physical connection to the network; that is, to connect your local computer system to a network.

■ To get the NIC to work with the operating system, it will need the correct software drivers. You can download the latest drivers from the network card manufacturer's Web site.

■ All add-on expansion cards require certain system resources. Network cards must be assigned a unique interrupt request (IRQ) address and memory I/O address.

■ Each and every network card ever made carries a unique identifier known as the Media Access Control (MAC) address.

■ NICs configured in full-duplex mode are able to send and receive data simultaneously. Network cards configured in a half-duplex mode can send and receive but not at the same time.

■ Network cards have LEDs on them to indicate the connection state of the card as well as the operating status of the card. For example, an LED may indicate the speed of the connection or the duplex state of the connection. The exact LED information depends on the card.

■ Network protocols define the rules and methods for communication between devices on the network at a software level.

■ There are four protocols used on networks today: the Transmission Control Protocol/Internet Protocol (TCP/IP), Internetwork Packet Exchange/Sequenced Packet Exchange (IPX/SPX), NetBIOS Extended User Interface (NetBEUI), and AppleTalk. Of these protocols, TCP/IP is now by far the most prevalent.

■ Nowadays, network cards generally only come with a single cable connection although it is possible to get cards with more than one connection (UTP, coax, and so on). These multiple-connection cards are often referred to as combo cards.

Network Models

■ Two network models are used on networks, peer-to-peer and client/server.

■ In a peer-to-peer network model, each of the systems on the network can serve as both a server and a client, accessing other resources on the network and offering services of its own.

■ Administration on a peer-to-peer network can become impractical if there are too many systems on the network. The generally accepted maximum number of systems on a peer-to-peer network is 10.

■ Client/server networks use a centralized administration model, which makes it easier to manage larger number of systems. Client/server networks often use specialized hardware and software to perform the server function.

Infrared

■ Infrared is a wireless communication method that offers speeds of up to 4 Mbps over short distances.

■ Infrared is more popular as a means of communication between devices such as a PDA and a desktop computer than as a networking method.

Wireless

■ Wireless networking offers speeds of up to 11 Mbps with many speed improvements on the way.

■ The IEEE 802.11 standard set defines the specification for wireless networking. Currently the 802.11b standard is the most widely implemented.

■ In addition to the 802.11b standard, manufacturers can also voluntarily conform to a standard called Wi-Fi. The Wi-Fi standard is designed to guarantee compatibility between devices from different vendors.

■ Concerns about wireless networking are centered around security and the currently expensive nature of wireless networking equipment. It is expected that both of these issues will be addressed in the near future.

■ To create a wireless network you will need at least two wireless network cards in two devices, or one network card and a wireless access point (WAP) that is wired to the network.

Internet Connectivity

■ Internet access has become an almost universal requirement for home and business computer users alike. There are a number of methods of accessing the Internet.

■ Access to the Internet via a LAN has become popular in business environments and home networks. Typically the actual connection to the Internet is established through a single system and then that connection is shared with other users on the network. Sometimes special software called proxy servers are used to manage and control Internet access and usage.

■ DSL is an Internet access method that uses standard phone lines to deliver high-speed, always-on access. The main consideration with DSL is that it is not offered in all areas and users must be within a certain distance of the telecommunications company's exchange in order to use it.

■ Many cable television companies now offer Internet access through the same physical connection as the TV signal. Cable Internet access is an always-on access method that offers high-speed access at a reasonable price. Availability depends on the location.

■ Integrated Services Digital Network (ISDN) is a dial-up Internet access method that can offer between 128 and 1.544 Mbps of bandwidth (depending on the version used). ISDN connections require special networking equipment. ISDN connection use channels within the connection that are either used for signaling information or carrying data.

■ Internet access via modem is referred to as dial-up because the connection must be dialed each time a connection to the Internet is required. Dial-up access is simple and inexpensive because the only requirements are a modem, a phone line, and an account with an Internet Service Provider (ISP). The downside is that the speed is limited to 56 Kbps.

- In areas where other high-speed Internet access methods such as cable and DSL are not available, satellite Internet access is used. One-way satellite access requires that requests are sent via modem and responses downloaded via the satellite link. Two-way satellite uses special equipment to establish a two-way direct link with the satellite.

- Wireless Internet access is becoming popular in populated areas and in confined areas such as airports, coffee shops, schools, and universities. Areas that offer wireless Internet access are referred to as "hotspots."

Part II

A+ Operating Systems

Now that we have discussed the hardware used in today's PCs, it's time to take a look at the operating systems that run on them.

In this, the second section of *Faster Smarter A+ Certification*, we cover the information related to the Operating Systems Technologies part of the A+ exam. Remember, to become A+ certified you will need to pass both the Core Hardware and the Operating Systems Technologies exams. As in the Core Hardware section of this book, this part is broken down into chapters that correspond to the CompTIA specified domains for the Operating System Technologies exam.

In view of the fact that most widely-used operating systems are from Microsoft, the focus of the Operating Systems Technologies exam is Microsoft operating systems. Specifically, you will need to demonstrate an understanding of Microsoft Windows 9x, Me, 2000 and XP. Although the exam will not require that you exhibit an in-depth knowledge of all these operating systems, you will need to demonstrate a thorough understanding of basic concepts such as configuring the user interface, using basic troubleshooting and configuration commands, and configuring the operating system for connection to the network.

Chapter 7

Introducing the Operating System

Up to this point in the book, we have dealt almost entirely with hardware issues. The second part of this book deals with software issues, covering the objectives for the A+ operating system technologies exam. The objectives focus on the Windows operating systems, specifically Windows 9x, NT, 2000, and XP. In light of that, we will limit our discussions to the operating systems that are going to be covered in the actual exam. Remember, 30% of the exam questions come directly from the OS Technologies CompTIA domain. Ensure that you have a good understanding of the material presented in this chapter before moving to the next.

What Has an OS Done for You Lately!

Before we start looking at some of the specific objectives relevant to the A+ exam, we thought we would take a few paragraphs just to look at what an operating system does. The problem is that describing the major functions of the operating system in a few short paragraphs is simply not an easy thing to accomplish. Operating systems are actually quite complex and provide a wide range of services to us as users. In its most basic form, the operating system provides an interface through which we can interact with the computer system. Without the OS, we would just sit at the desk staring at hardware. Some of the core services that an operating system offers are

- **Security**   Nowadays, perhaps more than ever, the need to make sure that our data is kept away from prying (and often unseen) eyes is paramount. Today's modern operating systems offer a variety of ways to make sure that our information does not fall into the wrong hands.

- **Access to storage**   Operating systems provide the means by which we can store data—one of the most fundamental computing requirements. By providing drivers to access storage devices, file systems to organize our data, and programs to access it, the OS not only makes storage possible, it also makes it practical.

- **Access to printing**   The need to turn our electronic thoughts into printed matter is also one of the core computing requirements. Operating systems provide printer subsystems and drivers so that we can print to a multitude of different printing devices. They also provide the means by which we can manage, manipulate, and control our print jobs after they have been sent to print.

- **Network access**   Today, more than ever, the need to access a network has become a fundamental requirement for many PC users. Whether that network is a small home network of a few computers, a corporate network of a couple thousand computers, or a network that encompasses millions of computers (the Internet), the foundations for the access are provided via the OS.

Any operating system we choose to use, whether it is just plain MS-DOS, or Windows, or one of the many others out there, provides us with the ability to create, manage, and organize our data, and thus our work and lives. Hurrah for the OS.

What OS Are You Running?   You might think that asking what operating system you are running is an odd question. After all, you probably know. Right? On your home PC this might be the case, but what if you are working as a technical support rep for a large company with over a thousand users running a variety of operating systems? That makes things a little more complicated.

At first glance, nearly all Windows operating systems look the same, so just looking at the screen is not enough to determine which OS is installed. In most versions of Windows, the quickest way to determine which OS is installed is to click Start. The left side of the menu will have the name of the OS version written vertically. For a more detailed, and hence more accurate, version of the information, right-click My Computer and select Properties, or access the System Properties dialog box by double-clicking the System icon in Control Panel.

Contrasts Between Windows 9x/Me, Windows NT, Windows 2000, and Windows XP

Windows 9x/Me, Windows NT, Windows 2000, and Windows XP are widely used operating systems and although they share some similar features and functions, under the hood they are different. This is because they are designed for different purposes. Windows NT and Windows 2000 are more expensive operating systems and designed for use in a business environment as is Windows XP Professional. Windows 9x/Me and Windows XP Home Edition are designed as home-use operating systems and designed more for compatibility than performance.

When working with Windows-based operating systems, you will be expected to know the difference between these operating systems in terms of functionality and how to support them. In this section, we take a quick look at each of these operating systems including some of their key characteristics and utilities.

Windows NT

Windows NT 4 was introduced by Microsoft as an upgrade to Windows NT 3.51. The two products are similar, with the most visible difference being that Windows NT 3.51 used the same graphical user interface as Windows 3.x, whereas Windows NT 4 adopted the Windows 9x style of interface. Microsoft designed the Windows NT products as operating systems for business and included such features as high security and increased levels of fault tolerance.

Windows NT 4 was available in two versions: Windows NT Workstation and Windows NT Server. The workstation product, while obviously designed for use as a workstation operating system, includes networking functionality and is particularly popular in peer-to-peer network configurations. In terms of file-sharing capability and logon security, both products share the same characteristics.

Although Windows NT 4 has now been superseded by Windows 2000, the number of installed sites using Windows NT 4 remains very high, and you stand a much better than average chance of working with a Windows NT system.

Supported File Systems

Windows NT uses two file systems: FAT (file allocation table) and NTFS (NT file system). FAT is the familiar file system used with Windows 95 and Windows 98, and although it can be used in Windows NT, it is not recommended. The drawback of the FAT file system is that it offers no file- or folder-level security; NTFS does, making it a better file system in any system where security is an issue. NTFS also offers performance advantages over FAT on larger disk partitions. FAT, however, has one major advantage over NTFS: it can be read by a variety of operating systems, including OS/2, Windows 9x, MS-DOS, and, of course, Windows NT, Windows 2000, and Windows XP. NTFS volumes can be read by only Windows NT, Windows 2000, and Windows XP. This can cause problems if Windows NT 4 is installed in a dual-boot configuration on the same system as, say, Windows 98. If you format a partition with NTFS for Windows NT 4, when you boot into Windows 98, you will not be able to see that partition. Another thing worthy of note is that Windows NT 4 does not support FAT32, which means that if a Windows 98 partition is formatted with FAT32, Windows NT 4 will not be able to see it. So, the only common file system that the two share is good ol' FAT.

 Test Smart   Windows NT 4 does not support FAT32.

NTFS is a more advanced file system, designed specifically for Windows network operating systems. When you're working with Windows NT, it's important to know that FAT can be converted to NTFS, but after a hard disk partition has been set as NTFS, it cannot be changed back to FAT.

 Test Smart   Converting from FAT to NTFS can be done at the command line with the Convert.exe command. There are only two parameters. The first is the drive to be converted, the other is the specification of the file system to convert to, which is a little odd because there is only one choice, NTFS. So, to convert the D: drive to NTFS, you would use the command `convert d: /fs:ntfs`. Remember also that it is a one-way conversion—you cannot convert the file system back.

Note   A common strategy during the Windows NT installation is to divide the system files and the boot files into separate partitions. Be aware, however, that Windows NT puts its own twist on the naming of these partitions; the Windows NT system partition holds the Windows NT boot files, and the boot partition holds the system files. How confusing is that?

Managing Disk Drives

Hard drive management in Windows NT is done with the Disk Administrator tool, located in the Administrative Tools (Common) folder on the Start menu. The Disk Administrator tool provides a central location from which you can do a variety of hard disk maintenance and configuration tasks. The tasks typically performed here include formatting disks and partitions, deleting partitions, creating extended partitions, and checking for partition errors. Figure 7-1 shows the Disk Administrator window.

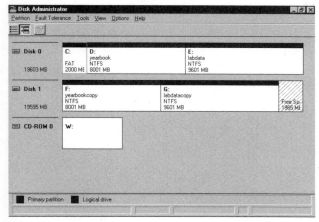

Figure 7-1 The Disk Administrator utility is used to manage disk drives.

User Management Basics

A basic understanding of user accounts and account management is required when you're working with the Windows NT platform. Though a detailed explanation is not provided here, we'll give you enough information to get started.

In Windows NT, account management tasks, including changing passwords, adding users, and deleting users, are all done in the User Manager utility. Figure 7-2 shows the User Manager window.

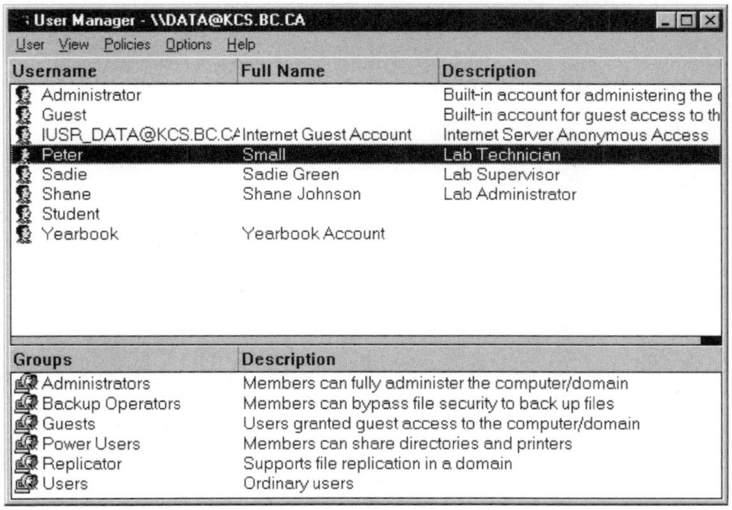

Figure 7-2 User accounts are managed through the User Manager utility.

In the Windows NT 4 environment, one user account ranks higher than the rest. The Administrator account is king, and access to this account should be restricted to only those people who need it. The Administrator account has no restrictions on it, allowing full control over file access, user and account management, security policies, and print resources. Because of this, caution should be exercised regarding who does and who does not have access to the Administrator account.

Monitoring and Performance Tools

When managing a Windows NT system, there are a few monitoring and performance tools commonly used by administrators. Two of the more popular utilities are Performance Monitor and Network Monitor. Together, these tools can provide a comprehensive view of life on the Windows NT system.

Performance Monitor   As the name suggests, monitoring performance on a Windows NT system is done through the Performance Monitor utility. Performance Monitor enables you to analyze specific hardware components or programs by using a dynamic display. Performance Monitor is used to determine if the system is experiencing any problems or bottlenecks due to insufficient or malfunctioning hardware. Figure 7-3 shows a sample Performance Monitor screen in Windows NT.

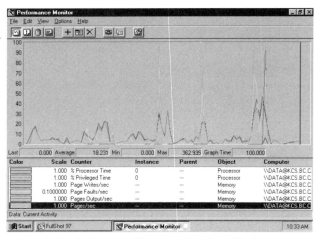

Figure 7-3 The Performance Monitor tool is a key utility in system management.

Network Monitor   Network Monitor is the tool used to capture and analyze a range of network-related statistics. The Network Monitor tool is one of the key utilities to use for network troubleshooting and capacity planning. Depending on the environment, you might be actively involved in the monitoring of networks to diagnose problems, gather network data, and monitor network usage.

Windows 2000 Basics

Windows 2000, the successor to Windows NT 4, provided many enhancements to the services already offered by Windows NT 4. Windows NT and Windows 2000 function the same in some respects, but in many others, they are vastly different. From a usage perspective, however, if you can use one, you can use them both. Without doubt the biggest difference between the two operating systems is the addition of Active Directory, a standards-based directory services system that provides much-improved user account management capabilities. In addition, many tasks have been streamlined, and additional wizards are available to assist in administrative tasks.

Note   New to Windows 2000 is Active Directory, the new approach to user and account management on Windows systems in a server-based environment. Active Directory is a cornerstone concept for Windows 2000 because it significantly affects the layout and makeup of a Windows 2000–based network. Active Directory is such a complex subject that we could devote the entire book to that one subject. Rather than do that (which won't help you with A+ certification), check out the information about Active Directory at *http://www.microsoft.com/windows2000*.

File System

The file systems available in Windows 2000 are somewhat different from those offered with Windows NT 4. Windows 2000 supports the FAT16, FAT32, and NTFS file systems, whereas Windows NT 4 offered only FAT16 and NTFS. The difference between FAT and FAT32 is that FAT32 is designed to work with larger disks.

Along with the ability to use FAT32, Windows 2000 introduces a newer version of NTFS, sometimes referred to as NTFS5, which provides more capabilities and increased security options. Remember that Active Directory and other security-related features are available only on NTFS partitions. In Windows 2000, converting from FAT16 or FAT32 to NTFS uses the same command as with Windows NT, the Convert.exe command.

The New NTFS

The NTFS version included with Windows 2000 offers some key advantages over the NTFS version that was offered with Windows NT. Two of these improvements are encryption and disk quotas.

■ **Encryption**   You might want some of the files or folders on your system to be reserved for your eyes only. In such circumstances, Windows

2000 allows you to encrypt individual files and folders. Once a file or folder is encrypted, only those who have encrypted it and special users defined as Data Recovery Agents can access it. It does this through a feature called the Encrypting File System (EFS).

■ **Disk quotas**   Disk quotas are a means to restrict the amount of space that a user can is given to save files on the system. Any Windows 2000 NTFS partition can support disk quotas.

Monitoring and Performance Tools

Windows 2000 has improved on the monitoring and performance tools that were available with Windows NT 4, making them more user friendly and more powerful. Of the tools that are available, you need to be aware of a handful of them for the A+ exam. These are covered in this section.

> **Note**   The Microsoft Management Console (MMC) is a common interface used to centralize the location of Windows 2000 performance and administrative tools. These management tools, referred to as snap-ins, are added to the MMC to manage the hardware, software, and networking components of the server. They include Windows Event Viewer, Device Manager, Computer Management, Performance Logs and Alerts, System Information, and Services.

Event Viewer   Event Viewer is a Windows utility that maintains and displays logs of important system activities. The Windows 2000 version of Event Viewer enhances the features that Windows NT 4 offered. In addition to the Application, System, and Security logs present in the Windows NT 4 version, Windows 2000 Event Viewer tracks directory service events, DNS events, and file replication events, if those services are installed. For the most part, it is the System log that you will want to keep a close eye on. The System log tracks events related to hardware components. There is a more detailed discussion of Event Viewer later in this chapter.

> **Note**   The Application log and System log can be viewed by any user; the Security log can only be viewed by using an account with administrative privileges.

Task Manager   Present in Windows 2000 is the familiar Task Manager. As with Windows NT, the Task Manager in Windows 2000 provides a quick look at the programs and processes running on the computer. CPU and memory usage can be viewed, and processes and programs can be shut down if needed.

> **Note**   As with Windows NT 4, the Windows 2000 system can be secured by pressing Ctrl+Alt+Delete and selecting Lock Computer.

Managing Disk Drives

Windows 2000 drops the Disk Administrator tool of Windows NT and replaces it with the Disk Management utility found in the Computer Management console. Like its Windows NT cousin, Disk Management is used to create volumes, delete volumes, format disks, and create fault-tolerant configurations. In addition to these standard features, common to both Windows 2000 and Windows NT, the new Disk Management tool allows the configuration of *dynamic disks*, which allow you to make changes to a disk without rebooting, and network disk management, which allows you to manage the disks on other Windows 2000 systems on the network. Figure 7-4 shows the Computer Management console with the Disk Management pane.

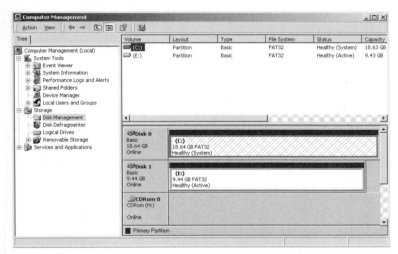

Figure 7-4 The Disk Management utility is used to manage disk drives.

User Management Basics

Windows NT 4 administrators looking for the User Manager For Domains tool to manage user accounts will not find it in Windows 2000. User Manager For Domains has been retired. On a Windows 2000 Professional system, where you can only create local users and groups, use the Computer Management tool instead, found in Control Panel, Administrative Tools, Computer Management. On Windows 2000 Server systems that use Active Directory, use the Active Directory Users And Computers MMC snap-in, also accessed through the Administrative Tools folder.

Note   On a Windows 2000 Professional system, you can only create local user accounts and groups. These accounts and groups can be applied to resources on the local system but not on other systems. In contrast, accounts created through Active Directory in Windows 2000 Server can be applied to systems within the directory.

Although the look of the screen is somewhat different, the basic functions of creating, adding, and deleting user accounts remain the same as in Windows NT. There are a few more bells and whistles and some additional template groups in Windows 2000, but if you are comfortable in Windows NT, it won't take you long to understand basic procedures in Active Directory Users And Computers. As with Windows NT, in Windows 2000 the Administrator account is king; care must be taken when using this account, and its privileges should not be given to anyone except those people who need to perform administrative tasks on the system.

Windows XP Basics

Windows XP is the latest offering for workstation operating systems from Microsoft. There are two versions: Windows XP Home Edition is designed to be a replacement for Windows 9x/Me, and Windows XP Professional is designed as a replacement for the business-oriented Windows 2000 Professional. Although the two look very similar, the Professional product has many enhancements that make it more suited to a business environment, including increased security and enhanced network connectivity.

Note   One of the things that is very different in Windows XP is product activation. Whereas before all you had to do to install a product was to enter a serial number, now the product must be registered with Microsoft, and the registration is PC specific. If the product is not activated within a certain time from the installation, you'll no longer be able to use the operating system.

Although many aspects of Windows XP are the same as with other versions of Windows, there are some distinct differences. First of these is that enhancements have been made to the multi-user aspects of the operating system.

Microsoft, realizing that a PC in a home environment is often going to be used by more than one person, has made the process of creating and accessing the user accounts defined on the system much more straightforward, even going as far as displaying the defined users on the initial screen when the system has booted. This makes it simple for users to access the system as the correct account and have personalized settings and configurations. If a Windows XP

Professional system is configured to connect to the network, it offers the more traditional user name and password dialog box rather than the flashy new Welcome screen.

Note Windows XP has a more "rounded" feel to it than the traditional Windows interface. As with most things aesthetic, people tend to either love it or hate it. If you fall into the latter group, Windows XP provides an option to revert to a more classic Windows interface.

It's the Same, but Different

Many of the aspects of Windows XP Professional are borrowed from Windows 2000. For example, you can still use the Computer Management utility to manage the system and pressing Ctrl+Alt+Delete still brings up the Task Manager. Yet, all of the utilities have been tweaked slightly to make them more visually appealing and usable.

The same is true for Windows XP Home Edition. Many of the utilities and aspects of the system are the same as with Windows 9x; they just look slightly different.

File System Support

One thing that both Windows XP Home Edition and Windows XP Professional have in common is that they support FAT16, FAT32, and NTFS. If you are looking for security, you should opt for NTFS.

The Differences

Having talked about both versions, it's time to take a quick look at why they are different. In simple terms, Windows XP Professional is more powerful than the Home Edition. Table 7-1 details some of the features that Windows XP Professional includes that Windows XP Home Edition does not.

Table 7-1   Selected Features of Windows XP Professional Not Included in Windows XP Home Edition

Feature	Description
Multiprocessor support	Windows XP Home Edition supports only one processor. Windows XP Professional supports two.
Domain logon	If you need to log on to a Microsoft network domain, you'll need Windows XP Professional.
Remote Desktop	Allows you to access your Windows XP Professional system from another Windows system and use it as if you were sitting at it. Very cool!

Table 7-1   Selected Features of Windows XP Professional Not Included in Windows XP Home Edition

Feature	Description
Encrypting File System	By using NTFS, Windows XP Professional can offer the EFS feature to protect files. Although Windows XP Home Edition offers support for NTFS, it does not provide EFS support.
Roaming user profiles	Roaming profiles are used when a system is connected to the network. It makes sure that the user's environment is consistent no matter what computer they log on from.
Group Policy	Another network feature, Group Policy allows network administrators to apply settings to a system over the network based on the role of the PC and the user logging on to it.

As you can see, many of the features included in Windows XP Professional are geared toward a networked environment and "power users."

Managing the System

Windows XP Professional uses the Computer Management utility, as featured in Windows 2000, for the management of the system. Through this tool you can also manage the local users and groups and perform disk management tasks.

Getting to Know Windows 9x *(Briefly)*

Now that we have reviewed Microsoft's Cadillac operating systems, we can move on to the Windows 9x operating systems. Windows 9x is no longer shipped with new systems, but it is still used on a countless number of older systems. This means you will likely be called upon to support them. Most people, particularly PC technicians, have spent time working with Windows 9x systems, so we won't dwell on them here for very long.

Windows 9x–Supported File Systems

The Windows 9x world supports only two file systems, FAT16 and FAT32. FAT16 was the original file system but the release of Windows 95 OSR2 (Operating System Release 2) gave us the option to use the FAT32 file system. One of the key advantages of FAT32 is its support for larger hard disks. Today, most of the hard disks we use are too large for the FAT file system, which means you will use FAT32 far more in the real world.

> **More Info** A discussion of the various file systems is presented later in this chapter.

System Management and Configuration

System management of Windows 9x is generally confined to using the tools provided in Control Panel and via registry editing. The specific tools used for this purpose are discussed in more detail later in this chapter.

Major Operating System Components

As we have discussed, an operating system is a complex combination of many elements and parts. Even so, there are specific components within an operating system that provide the foundation for all of the other functions. These could be defined as the major operating system components. Specifically, the CompTIA A+ objectives pinpoint the registry, virtual memory, and file system as key components in this category.

Registry

Since Windows 95, the architecture of Windows has changed somewhat. Instead of the old text files of Windows 3.x, Windows 95 introduced a single hierarchical database that holds the system's hardware and software settings. This database, known as the registry, is the central location where all of the system configurations are kept. In truth, you will rarely need to access the registry directly to make changes. Instead, you'll use the utilities in Control Panel and other system utilities to make the changes. When you do need to access the registry and make changes manually, you can use tools called registry editors to do so. The two registry editors are called Regedit.exe and Regedt32.exe. The former is used on Windows 9x systems and Windows XP systems, the latter is used on Windows NT 4 and Windows 2000 systems. How and when these editors are used is discussed later in this chapter.

When you look at the registry using an editor, it almost looks like what you might see when navigating around Windows Explorer. As mentioned, the registry is structured into a hierarchical tree-like structure and divided into groups called keys. You will not need to know the keys or their functions for the A+ exam, but for example purposes, on a Windows 98 system you would find the following keys:

- HKEY_CLASSES_ROOT
- HKEY_CURRENT_USER
- HKEY_LOCAL_MACHINE

■   HKEY_LOCAL_USERS

■   HKEY_CURRENT_CONFIG

■   HKEY_DYN_DATA

If you double-click on one of these keys, several subkeys will open, displaying various cryptic values. Figure 7-5 shows the Windows registry from a Windows 98 system viewed through Regedit.

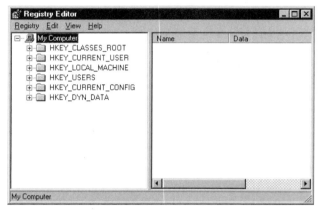

Figure 7-5 You can see the Windows registry and its six main keys in the Regedit utility.

Virtual Memory

Virtual memory is the name given to an area of space on the hard disk that is used by the operating system as if it were normal physical memory. Virtual memory is the reason that, when you look at the available memory in Windows through some utilities, it appears to be much larger than it actually is. Although use of virtual memory is now practically mandatory, too much of it and not enough physical memory can be a bad thing. Virtual memory is much slower than physical memory and so excessive reliance on virtual memory can make a system run slower than it really should. You can either let Windows handle the assignment of swap space automatically, or configure it yourself. On a Windows 98 system, this is done through the Performance tab of the System utility. On a Windows 2000 system, from the System utility select the Advanced tab and click the Performance Options button.

Test Smart   The area of a hard disk that is used as virtual memory is referred to as the swap ●
file.

The virtual memory area is actually a file, commonly referred to as the swap file. Virtual memory is a great thing because it makes it possible for the system to operate with more RAM than it actually has installed, but as with so many things in life, along with the benefits come a few issues.

Disk Thrashing—It's Not a Good Thing Disk thrashing occurs when the system has to pull memory data from disk too often. The disk ends up spending more of its time performing this task and not enough satisfying other requests. The result is that the disk will appear to be constantly in use (which it is).

The only real way to get around the disk-thrashing problem is to add more physical RAM to the system.

In the same way that problems can occur with physical RAM, the swap file itself can be corrupted. The good thing about problems with the swap file is that replacing the swap file, unlike replacing RAM, doesn't cost anything.

A problem with the swap file might be obvious, in that you will receive a message that tells you of the fact, or it might be subtle. As with physical RAM errors, you might find that the system freezes or hangs, or that a program generates errors during use. Given the simplicity of replacing the swap file, it is certainly something you should consider as a troubleshooting step.

Replacing the Swap File

The process of replacing the swap file depends on which operating system you are using. On a Windows 2000 system, the swap file is re-created each time the system boots. In Windows 9x, you must manually delete the swap file, which is located in the root directory and is called Win386.swp. You will need to restart the system in MS-DOS mode to do this; otherwise, it is very likely that the swap file will be in use.

Note If you are experiencing repeated corrupt swap files, there might well be something wrong with the hard drive in the system. You should run ScanDisk or Chkdsk to determine if your hard drive is having problems.

On a Windows 2000 system, in a default configuration, the swap file is located in the root directory and called Pagefile.sys. The file is flagged as a hidden and system file. Fortunately, because Windows 2000 re-creates the page file each time the system is restarted, you will not need to locate it and delete it manually as you might have to do with Windows 9x.

Managing Swap File Size

Another consideration that comes with using a swap file is managing its size. Windows 9x actually has a setting that lets the OS handle all aspects of virtual memory sizing, and unless you have a very good reason for not using this feature, you should just leave it be. If you do want to configure virtual memory on a Windows 9x system, you can do so. Figure 7-6 shows the Virtual Memory dialog box in Windows 9x that allows you to configure virtual memory.

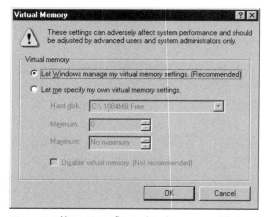

Figure 7-6 You can configure virtual memory settings or have Windows manage them for you automatically.

The Windows 2000 configuration for swap files is slightly more advanced than in Windows 9x, though like Windows 9x you can specify both a minimum and maximum size for the file. You should be wary of setting the initial size of the file too small because Windows will only have to increase it "mid flow," which can create performance issues. Another interesting problem can occur if there is not enough disk space available for the operating system to expand the file toward its upper limit as required. In some cases, this will cause the system to slow down noticeably, and in others, it can actually cause the system to crash. The moral of this story is to always make sure that there is enough free disk space to allow the swap file to expand to its maximum size. You can see the Virtual Memory dialog box in Windows 2000 in Figure 7-7.

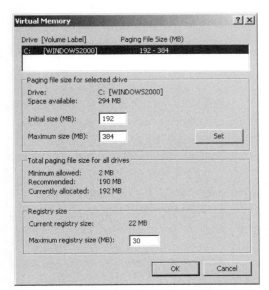

Figure 7-7 Windows 2000 virtual memory settings can be set in the Virtual Memory dialog box.

Note One way of improving performance on a Windows 2000 system is to split the page file across multiple drives. So, for example, if you had a Windows 2000 system with two drives, you could place one half of the page file on one drive and half on another. You will almost certainly get some level of performance improvement, though how much depends on your disk configuration. Keep in mind that there is no benefit to having the page file split between two partitions on the same drive, however.

File System

File systems are the means by which data (in the form of files) is organized on storage devices such as hard disks and CDs. The characteristics of a file system define such things as the maximum file name length, the permissible characters for file names, and the organization of the files within folders. There is a detailed discussion of the file systems used on Windows systems and their various characteristics later in this chapter, in the section titled "Managing Disks, Directories, and Files."

Major Operating System Interfaces

When you power up a Windows-based computer system, there are some familiar characteristics that you can expect to see. All of the versions of Windows being discussed here provide an easy-to-navigate graphical user interface (GUI) that you can navigate through using the keyboard and mouse. When Windows starts, you are taken directly to what Microsoft calls the desktop, which is simply the main area from which you work. By default, the desktop contains several icons that are shortcuts to often-accessed Windows programs. Shortcuts to other frequently accessed programs can easily be added to the desktop to provide quick access to them. Figure 7-8 shows an example of the Windows 2000 desktop.

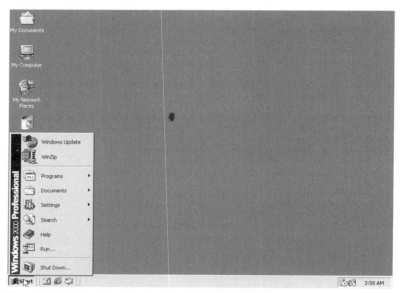

Figure 7-8 The Windows 2000 desktop screen provides a good example of the typical Windows GUI.

Notice the Windows taskbar at the bottom of the screen. The taskbar is fully customizable to include program shortcuts and also includes icons of the programs that are currently running on the system. The taskbar also holds the system Start button from which most programs and utilities can be executed.

In the following sections we explore some of the interface components you are likely to use on a frequent basis.

Windows Explorer

As a PC technician supporting any Windows operating system, you are going to have to become more than familiar with Windows Explorer. Windows Explorer shows all of the drives connected to the system; by clicking on any of these drives you can see the files and folders held within the drive. Figure 7-9 shows Windows Explorer in a Windows 2000 system.

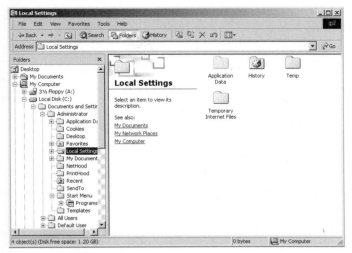

Figure 7-9 Windows Explorer allows you to see the contents of the disk drive.

Besides navigating through files and folders, Windows Explorer allows you to see all of the installed programs and the files they use. You can also manually remove files and folders from within Windows Explorer. Finally, Windows Explorer gives you a method of easily copying and moving files and folders around the system. For example, you can move files from the floppy drive to the hard disk.

Note   To view hidden files in Windows 2000 or Windows XP, you can select Folder Options from the Tools menu in Windows Explorer.

My Computer

The My Computer icon has been placed on the Windows 9x and Windows 2000 desktops by default. When you select the My Computer icon, the My Computer window opens, which displays all of the installed system drives and shortcuts to some of the commonly accessed Windows utilities. Selecting any of the drives in the My Computer window will open that drive and display the contents of that drive. Figure 7-10 shows the My Computer window on a Windows 2000 system.

Figure 7-10 The My Computer window displays installed drives and shortcuts to Windows utilities.

Control Panel

Windows Control Panel is one of those areas that PC technicians will definitely have to know their way around. Control Panel provides access to the areas you need to perform the installation, management, and configuration of hardware and software on Windows-based systems. To access Control Panel, click Start, Settings, and then click Control Panel. Figure 7-11 shows the Control Panel window.

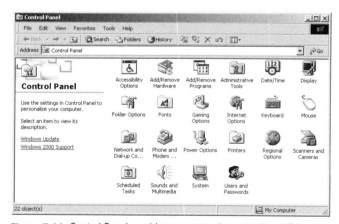

Figure 7-11 Control Panel provides access to the system's configuration and management utilities.

Test Smart   Many questions on the A+ exam will require that you know which utility in Control Panel is used to do what. Before taking the exam, spend some time working in Control Panel in Windows 9x, Windows 2000, or Windows XP (or all of them) and familiarize yourself with what is where. In particular, focus on the System, Network, Display, and Add/Remove Programs utilities, but don't ignore any of the others either.

When Control Panel is displayed, several icons, or utilities, can be accessed. The number of utilities and the names of these utilities vary somewhat between Windows versions, but look hard enough and you will find everything you need to configure the system.

As an A+ technician, you will need to know what each of the utilities in Control Panel does. For the A+ exam, however, there are only some key ones we need to concentrate on. Listed next are some of the key Control Panel utilities.

■ **Add/Remove Programs**   When you add new programs to the operating system, the preferred method of installing programs is to use the Add/Remove Programs utility in Control Panel. When removing a program, it is recommended to use the Add/Remove Programs utility to cleanly remove the program from the system. This is in contrast to manually erasing the program in Windows Explorer, for example. The Add/Remove Programs utility is also used to create a Windows startup disk.

■ **Add New Hardware**   When new hardware is added to the system that is not detected by Plug and Play, you can use the Add New Hardware utility to add devices to the system. When the utility is selected, a wizard starts, guiding the process of a device installation. When using the Add New Hardware feature, you might need to have the device drivers on hand for the device because you will be prompted for them during the installation process. You can also use the Add New Hardware utility to troubleshoot an existing device.

■ **Display**   The Display utility is used to customize the display settings for the system. Using the Display utility, you can change everything from the screen saver used, the background and the color scheme of the desktop, various desktop themes, and picture resolution, and view the characteristics of the video adapter being used. In the Advanced Display settings you can also change the system's refresh rate and hardware acceleration settings.

■ **Printers**   Most systems today have a printer connected to them, whether it is directly connected to the system or connected over the network. The Printers utility in Control Panel is used to add, remove, and configure the printers connected to the computer system. With the Printers utility you can also stop and restart print jobs that you have sent to the printer.

■ **System**   The System utility is one that technicians will access frequently. Once selected, the System utility will open the System Properties dialog box, which provides the technician with valuable system-wide information as well as some advanced configuration settings. Some of the key areas accessed through the System Properties dialog box include Device Manager, which shows the installed hardware in the system and its status; Hardware Profiles, which enables you to establish different hardware profiles on your computer, a setting typically used with laptop systems; and Performance Options, which allows you to optimize program response and change the system's virtual memory.

■ **Network**   The Network utility in Control Panel is where you go to configure the network. This includes adding and removing protocols, configuring network cards, and enabling file and printer sharing.

Computer Management Console

Introduced in Windows 2000 and now also included in Windows XP Professional is the Computer Management console. The Computer Management console provides access to many different system utilities and allows you to perform a variety of administrative tasks including disk management, configuring user accounts (if the system is not a domain controller), viewing and installing hardware devices, and monitoring system activities. In short, just about any administrative task you can think of can be accessed directly from the Computer Management console. Figure 7-12 shows the Computer Management console.

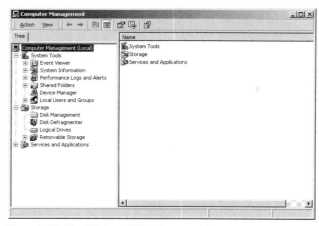

Figure 7-12 The Windows 2000 Computer Management console is used to perform system-wide administrative tasks.

Accessories/System Tools

The Accessories/System Tools program group is significant because it's where you can find many of the tools that you use to configure and manage a system.

The exact tools included depends on the version of Windows that you are using. For example, a Windows 2000 system has shortcuts in the System Tools program group for System Information, Backup, and Disk Cleanup, to name but a few.

There are also a number of tools in the Accessories program group that, while not being directly associated with management of the system, you might find yourself using on a regular basis. These include the text editor Notepad, Calculator, and the Command Prompt. The Accessories menu is also where you can find the Games program group!

Command Line

The command line can be accessed from the Accessories group or by invoking a command interpreter (Command.com in Windows 9x and/or Cmd.exe in Windows NT/2000/XP) from the Start, Run command. There are many actions you can perform from the command line and many utilities that you can use to perform those actions. Some of the more commonly used commands are discussed later in this chapter in the section "Using Command-Line Functions and Utilities."

Network Neighborhood/My Network Places

It is through the Network Neighborhood/My Network Places utility that you can access the network and subsequently other systems on it. On Windows 9x and Windows NT systems the utility is called Network Neighborhood. On Windows 2000 and Windows XP systems it is called My Network Places.

What you see when you start the utility will depend on how your system is configured, whether you are connected to a network, and how the network is configured. If you are connected to a network and your system is configured appropriately, you might be able to browse the network to see what services are offered. With the necessary permissions you will also be able to connect to and use resources such as shares and printers on other systems. There is a more detailed discussion of using Network Neighborhood/My Network Places to connect to and use network resources in Chapter 10.

Taskbar/Systray

The taskbar is the bar that appears, by default, at the bottom of the screen. The color of the bar will depend on the color scheme being used. When a program is started, a box for that program is placed on the taskbar. The size of the box depends on how many programs you have loaded at the time. Programs with a box on the taskbar can be maximized by clicking on the corresponding box, and minimized by doing the same. The taskbar can be dragged to any position on the edge of the screen—that is, left, right, top, or bottom. You can also increase the size by dragging the top edge of it or cause it to be hidden by dragging the top edge off the screen. A typical taskbar is shown in Figure 7-13.

Figure 7-13 The taskbar has a box for each program that is open on the system.

The system tray or systray is the name given to the "recessed" area of the taskbar, which, by default, is on the right-hand side of the taskbar. Programs loaded in the system tray are typically those that run in the background like instant messaging applications and virus checkers. For most programs in the system tray, you can activate them or bring up an options menu by double-clicking them. Figure 7-14 shows the system tray on a Windows 2000 system.

Figure 7-14 The system tray is typically used for programs that run in the background.

Start Menu

Introduced by Microsoft with great fanfare when they released Windows 95, the Start button is now almost an icon of the twentieth century. In a default location, the Start button is nestled down in the bottom left corner of the screen and clicking it brings up the now familiar Start menu.

The Start menu has some options that are fixed, such as the Shut Down and Help options, and the top portion of the menu has options that can be added and removed as necessary. If an option on the menu has a submenu, which many do, a small black triangle appears next to that menu option indicating the fact.

Note   Windows operating systems provide a quick and easy way to execute a program by using the Run command. The Run command is accessed by choosing the Start button and then the Run option. In the Run dialog box, you can simply type the name of the program you wish to execute and it will run on the system. The Run dialog box also includes a Browse button, so if you do not remember the name of the executable file you wish to run, you can easily search for it.

The Start menu can be made to disappear in the same way as you made it appear, by clicking the Start button.

Device Manager

When administering a computer system, you need to have a utility that shows you what hardware is installed in a system and whether that hardware is functioning within the operating system. In a Windows OS environment, the utility used to do this is Device Manager. Using Device Manager, you can easily see what hardware has been detected by the system, the resources used by the device, and whether the device is currently functioning. If a resource conflict is shown in Device Manager, you can manually change resources to correct the conflict.

 Test Smart   Device Manager uses small icons to display the current status of a device. Devices that are not recognized by the system or are incorrectly configured will be displayed with a yellow question mark or a yellow exclamation point. A red *X* indicates that the device has been disabled.

To access Device Manager, right-click the My Computer icon and then select Properties. Alternatively, you can access Device Manager by selecting the System utility in Control Panel. Figure 7-15 shows Device Manager in a Windows 98 system.

Figure 7-15 Windows Device Manager is used to view detected hardware devices.

Note   In Windows 9x, if a device is loaded through Config.sys, it might still run correctly yet not appear in Device Manager. This is normal.

Identifying Major System Files

Knowing an operating system involves knowing the files that make it tick. There are literally hundreds of files used by each of the operating systems being discussed, both in the boot process and after the system has successfully started. Thankfully, you do not really need to know what they all do—at least not for the A+ exam. There are, however, a handful of key files and utilities you must be aware of. As far as the A+ exam is concerned, you need to focus on those files used in the boot process and those used in troubleshooting procedures. In this section, we take a tour through the major Windows 9x and Windows NT/2000 files and the key features you need to review for the A+ exam.

Windows 9x—Specific Files

In computing terms, Windows 9x could now be considered an "old" operating system. In its time, though, it broke new ground not just with a new interface, but with a new approach to configuration. The following are some of the files that you might find yourself working with on a Windows 9x system.

Test Smart   Ensure that you are familiar with the files listed in the following section and what they are intended for.

Io.sys

The Io.sys file is a key file and is used in the initial stages of the boot process. The Io.sys file is located in the root directory (C:) and is responsible for loading other system files and verifying their settings. It also provides a mechanism that allows low-level communication between hardware and the operating system.

Msdos.sys

This file provides basic operating system functionality such as routines for opening and closing files and other system-related tasks. Msdos.sys also contains the multiboot configuration for Windows 9x systems. An interesting point about Msdos.sys is that it must be at least 1024 bytes (1 KB) in size. For that reason, the file is often padded with comments and text so that it does exceed the 1-KB threshold. Like Io.sys, Msdos.sys can be found in the root of the C: drive.

Autoexec.bat

The Autoexec.bat file is used during the boot process and contains the program and environment settings. For example, if you want to launch a particular program during the boot process, such as Mscdex for the CD-ROM, you reference the program in the Autoexec.bat file and it will be executed during the start phase. Programs can be added and removed from the Autoexec.bat file using the Edit command or Sysedit from within Windows. The Autoexec.bat file is found in the root of the C: drive.

Test Smart   The bottom line concerning the Autoexec.bat file is this: if the command can be executed from the command line within MS-DOS, it can be included in the Autoexec.bat file.

Some of the common entries you might find in an Autoexec.bat file are

- **path=c:\;c:\dos; c:\data**   The Path statement tells the operating system where to look for a command that is executed from the command line. By default, the OS will first look in memory and then in the current directory. If the command cannot be found, the OS starts working through the Path statement in order. If the command cannot be found in one of the directories discussed in the Path statement, it will return a "Command not found" error.

- **c:\path\driver.exe**   The loading of drivers for devices is commonly performed through the Autoexec.bat file.

- **prompt pg**   The Prompt command customizes how the DOS prompt will appear. This example gives us the ever popular C:\> prompt format.

Command.com

This file provides the command interface for the user. Basic commands such as Dir, Copy, and Cd are built into Command.com. The Command.com file can be found in the root of the C: drive.

Config.sys

The Config.sys file is often used in conjunction with the Autoexec.bat file, but instead of handling the loading of programs, the Config.sys file is responsible for the loading of the device drivers and the configuration of the system's memory. As with the Autoexec.bat file, though not needed by Windows 9x, the Config.sys file is still used for backward compatibility for those legacy programs running within Windows 9x that do need to access a Config.sys file to operate. Device drivers loaded into the Config.sys file are added with the line Device= or Devicehigh= followed by the device driver name. The Devicehigh option loads the devices into upper memory. Some examples of commands found in the Config.sys file include

- **files=xx**   Defines how many files DOS can have open at one time.

- **buffers=xx**   Defines how many memory buffers should be reserved for memory-to-hard-disk transfers.

- **dos=high,umb**   Specifies that the DOS kernel should be loaded into upper memory, thereby freeing up conventional memory.

■   **device=himem.sys**   The Device= lines are used to load device drivers into memory. In this example, the Himem.sys driver enables access
to extended memory.

Note   When editing text files like Config.sys, Autoexec.bat, and Win.ini, it's a good practice to
insert comments explaining any changes you have made. This enables someone else to understand why something is configured a certain way. Adding a comment is simple; all you have to do
is start the line with a semicolon (;) or the word "Rem." As the file is processed, these lines are
ignored by the operating system. These can also be useful for excluding a line from executing. So,
for example, if there is a driver that you do not want to load, but you don't want to remove the line
from the file, you can just add the semicolon or Rem and the line will be ignored. Some techies
refer to this as "remming out a line."

Himem.sys

This is an extended memory driver—it makes the memory area above 1 MB
available for use by the operating system. Modern operating systems can access
memory through built-in drivers, so you will only encounter Himem.sys when
working with DOS (or DOS mode programs through Windows).

Emm386.exe

Emm386 is a memory manager that works by deceiving the processor into thinking that it is storing data in extended memory when in fact it is using a special
type of memory called expanded memory. As a side task, Emm386 also makes
it possible for programs to use the upper memory that could otherwise only be
used by the OS and drivers.

Windows 9x and Windows NT 4 support the use of memory drivers like
Himem and Emm386 for backward compatibility purposes only. They do not
actually require them to operate.

Win.com

This is the startup file for Windows 9x. It is located in the root of the directory
in which Windows is installed. There are a number of switches that can be used,
but one of the most useful is /d, which causes Windows to start in safe mode.

System.ini

The System.ini file is also held in the Windows root directory and is included
with Windows 9x and Windows 2000 for backward compatibility. The Sys-
tem.ini file stores data about the system's hardware for MS-DOS programs used
with Windows. It is included with later Windows versions to allow older programs that use and reference the System.ini file to work in modern Windows
versions.

Win.ini

The Win.ini file is left over from the days of Windows 3.x and is not a required file for Windows 9x or Windows 2000. However, both of these operating systems can use the Win.ini file in their boot process. The Win.ini file holds program settings and personalized settings such as fonts, screen savers, and display settings. The Win.ini file is included for backward compatibility only and is found in the root of the Windows directory.

Registry Data Files

Since Windows 95, the majority of hardware and program settings are stored in one large database known as the registry. This registry is made from two primary files, System.dat and User.dat.

- **System.dat** The System.dat file is essential for Windows to run and includes the settings for the system's hardware, including resource allocation, device drivers, and hardware configurations. System.dat is an essential file and, as a safety measure, a backup copy of the file is made every time the computer is turned off. The backup file, System.da0, is held in the Windows folder and will be used by the system in the event that the System.dat file fails.

- **User.dat** The other side of the registry equation is the User.dat file. This file holds only user-specific information such as passwords, personalized color settings, and installed programs. Like the System.dat file, the User.dat file is automatically backed up each time the computer is shut down. The backed up file is named User.da0. The backup file is used if the original User.dat file becomes corrupt.

Test Smart Be sure you remember that the System.dat and User.dat files have an automatic backup file made, System.da0 and User.da0.

Windows NT/2000/XP Key Files

When working with Windows 2000, there are some key files that you need to be aware of. Most of the files reviewed here are used in the boot process, and while a Windows system uses only a handful of files in the boot process, it is necessary to know what they are designed to do. The following is a summary of the Windows boot files for an Intel-based system and the files you are likely going to see on the A+ operating system exam.

More Info There is a more detailed discussion of these files in Chapter 8.

- **Boot.ini**   This file defines the location of the Windows NT system files.

- **Ntldr**   This file is responsible for loading the operating system.

- **Ntdetect.com**   This file is responsible for detecting hardware and building a hardware list.

- **Ntbootdd.sys**   This file is used only when the system boots from a SCSI device that does not have a BIOS installed.

- **Bootsect.dos**   The Bootsect.dos file holds the boot sector information of any other operating systems that are loaded on the system.

Note   Windows 2000 does not offer the level of backward compatibility of Windows 9x and does not use the System.ini or Win.ini files. There are Autoexec and Config files in Windows 2000 but they are named Autoexec.nt and Config.nt and by default are installed in the C:\Winnt\System32 directory.

Ntuser.dat

The Ntuser.dat file contains configuration information specific to each user defined on the system. Each user that successfully logs on to the system will have an Ntuser.dat file created in the C:\Documents and Settings\Username folder. When the user logs on to the system, the information in the Ntuser.dat file is placed in the HKEY_CURRENT_USER subtree of the registry.

Registry Data Files

As with the Windows 9x registry discussed earlier, the Windows NT/2000 registry has a set of hives that hold the registry information. Each of these hives has a corresponding file that contains the information for the hive. In an installation that uses default folder locations, these files can be found in the C:\Winnt\System32\Config directory.

Using Command-Line Functions and Utilities

Even though the majority of work will be done from within a Windows graphical interface, a PC technician will still need to know how to work with the command prompt. In this section, we take a whirlwind tour through some of the basic commands you will need to be familiar with. Besides reading their descriptions here, to prepare for the actual A+ exam we would certainly recommend that you try out each of these commands and use the help facility built into almost all commands to determine what switches are available for the command. When it comes to working on the command line there is no substitute for some hands-on experience.

Note Command-line commands are referred to as both internal and external commands. Internal commands are primary commands and built into the Command.com or Cmd.exe file. Internal commands include Dir, Cls, Copy, and Delete. External commands are not included in the Command.com file and are supplied as separate program files. Such commands include Xcopy, Attrib, and Edit.

Dir

The Dir command is one that you will use with great frequency. In the days before Windows Explorer and a graphical method of accessing files and folders, the Dir command was used to list the contents of various directories. For example, if you needed to look inside the Windows directory from a DOS prompt, you would enter **dir windows.**

There are many switches that are used with the Dir command; perhaps two of the more common are /p and /w. As in the preceding example with the Windows directory, many directories have several hundred individual files in them. The /p and the /w commands help to see the files. The Dir /p command pauses after each screenful of listed files. This allows you to see each of the files at your own speed. The Dir /w command uses a wide list format for files instead of a single-column list. This allows more files to be seen on the screen at once, though with less detail. To see the available switches for the Dir command, type **dir /?** at the command prompt for a full list.

 Test Smart Help for practically all DOS commands can be obtained by typing the command followed by the /? switch.

Aces Are High and Asterisks Are Wild! When working with DOS commands, you can use wildcards to work with multiple files at once. They're very useful.

There are two wildcard characters you can use. The question mark (?) is used to denote a single character. For example, if you wanted to view all of the .bat files in the current directory that started with A and were three characters long, you would type the command **dir a??.bat**. The other permissible wildcard character is an asterisk (*), which is used to denote a group of characters. For example, if you wanted to view all of the .bat files in the current directory, you would type **dir *.bat**.

The wildcards can be used consistently across nearly all DOS utilities, but should be used with care. For example, now that you know what an asterisk does, it doesn't take a genius to figure out what the command Delete *.* does.

Now, where did that backup tape go?

Attrib

The Attrib command is used to view and modify the attributes of a file. File attributes include hidden (h), system (s), read-only (r), and archive (a). File attributes are discussed in detail later in this chapter.

You can view the attributes of an individual file by typing **attrib** followed by the file name. To add or remove the attributes from that file, use the + and - characters. For instance, if you want to make a file called Comptia.bat a hidden and read-only file, you would type the following:

attrib +h +r comptia.bat

The Attrib command is often used to view hidden system files from a DOS prompt.

Ver

The Ver command is an internal DOS command used to identify which version of DOS is being used on the system. From the command prompt, type **ver** and press Enter. This command is available on Windows platforms but must be run from the command prompt.

Mem

In the old days of Windows, knowing exactly how your memory was being allocated was a key consideration in the management of the system. The Mem command is used to view the available memory included in conventional, extended, and expanded memory. To view the available options with the Mem command, type **mem /?** at the command prompt.

ScanDisk

ScanDisk is a widely used Windows 9x utility that is used to detect and correct file problems and errors on hard disks and floppy disks. During the ScanDisk operation, the hard disk is examined for physical errors that will be marked as "bad" so that no new data can be stored in that location. ScanDisk will also detect and correct cross-linked files.

DOS 6 and later versions included a version of ScanDisk that was run from the command line. ScanDisk can also be run from inside the graphical interface. To check a drive for errors using ScanDisk, right-click on the drive and select Properties from the menu. In the properties dialog box that opens, select the Tools tab and click the Check Now button. Once selected, the ScanDisk utility will be displayed, as shown in Figure 7-16.

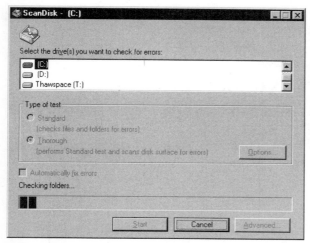

Figure 7-16 The ScanDisk utility is used to detect and correct errors on the hard disk.

Note   As shown in Figure 7-16, the ScanDisk utility can perform a standard and thorough inspection of the hard drive. The Standard option checks only the files and folders for errors, and the Thorough option also scans the hard disk itself for errors. If you select the Thorough option, get comfortable; it is a very lengthy process.

Defrag

Defragmenting the hard disk is all about organization. The function of this utility is to rearrange the files on the disk in a contiguous fashion. Essentially over time files are saved onto the hard disk and often written to different areas on the disk. In addition, files are deleted, leaving empty spaces all over the drive. When you run the defragmentation utility, all of these files are organized on the hard disk, increasing the performance of the hard disk. One error many make is assuming that the Defrag utility is used to correct hard disk errors; Defrag is only used to rearrange and organize the files on the computer.

Note   When using Defrag, you should really try to leave the system alone so that it can do its thing. Also, programs like virus checkers and screen savers can cause delays in the Defrag process because they use valuable system resources.

Edit

In the days before the graphical interface, the Edit command was widely used as a text editor to modify the key system files and even create batch files. Issuing the Edit command will open a simple text editor and allow you to edit, save, and print files. Figure 7-17 shows the Edit screen in DOS.

Figure 7-17 The Edit utility is just one of the tools that can be used to edit text-based configuration files.

Xcopy

The Copy and Move commands are certainly useful and even mandatory for the PC technician to use, but they have one significant limitation: they can only copy or move files from one directory at a time. To assist in those times when you need to copy more than a single directory at a time, Microsoft developed the Xcopy command. The /s switch for the Xcopy command enables you to copy the files in the specified directory as well as its subdirectories.

More Info The CompTIA A+ objectives list the Format and Fdisk commands in this section, but they are also included in the objectives for Domain 8. These commands are discussed in Chapter 8.

Copy

There is really no mystery as to what the Copy command does—it copies a file from one location to another. For those of you who have gotten used to the ability to simply drag files to where you want them from within Windows, the DOS-based Copy command can certainly seem like a lot of work. Basically, the Copy command is issued followed by the file you wish to copy and then the destination for the file. The following example shows the process of copying a file called Test.txt from the floppy drive, A: to the hard disk, C:.

copy a:\test.txt c:

The only way to really get the hang of copying files around the system is to actually practice it for a while. For additional help on the Copy command, type **copy /?** at the command prompt.

Note Another DOS command, the Move command, is designed to move files between locations instead of copying them. Both commands function similarly, and if you can use one, you can use both.

Format

The Format command is used to prepare a disk for use. Specifically, it is used to create a file system and a root directory on the disk so that it can be used. There is a detailed discussion of the Format command in Chapter 8.

Fdisk

The Fdisk utility is used in the first stage of disk preparation. Fdisk is actually used to create the partitions on the disk. Once the partitions are created, they can be formatted for use. As with the Format command, there is detailed discussion of Fdisk in Chapter 8.

Setver

Though listed here in the CompTIA objectives, the Setver command is not one you will use on a regular basis, but it is one that PC technicians should know about. The Setver command is used to manually set the DOS version reported to a program. This is typically done for backward compatibility. For example, older programs might not recognize a more recent version of DOS and by using the Setver command you can trick the program into thinking the DOS version is older than it actually is.

Scanreg

The Scanreg utility was included with Windows 98. This utility is used to make a backup copy of the system's registry. Scanreg actually works in the background to make a backup copy of the registry files each time the computer is started. However, you can also manually perform the registry backup using the Scanreg /backup command. If the registry becomes corrupt and you need to manually restore the backup files, you can run the Scanreg /restore command from a DOS command line. Another useful Scanreg command is Scanreg /fix, which can be used to repair a corrupted registry.

MD/CD/RD

The MD, CD, and RD commands are grouped together in the CompTIA objectives, but are actually used for very different purposes. However, they all have something to do with directories.

- ■ **MD**   MD is short for Make Directory and is used to do exactly that. The basic syntax for the command is md dirname.

- ■ **CD**   The CD command is used to change to a different directory within the structure. The basic syntax for the command is cd newdir. It is possible to change to a directory more than one level down by listing the path of the directory you wish to change to, for example, cd \newdir\olddir\olddata. This command would take you immediately from your current position in the file system to the \newdir\olddir\olddata directory. As with the other commands described in this section, the backslash (\) is used to denote the root of the file structure. In fact, a very commonly used CD command is CD \, which will take you immediately to the root directory of the drive.

■ **RD**   The RD command is used to remove a directory. The basic usage of the command is rd dirname. The RD command will work only if the directory is empty of both files and subdirectories. If you have the need to remove a populated directory or a directory with subdirectories, you will find it easier to use the more powerful, and more dangerous, Deltree command.

Delete/Rename

As the name suggests, the Delete command is used to delete files from the system. The basic usage for the Delete command is as follows: delete filename. As with many of the other commands discussed in this section, the Delete command can be used with wildcards to make the deletion of multiple files simpler.

The Rename command is used to rename a file. The basic usage of the command is as follows: ren oldfile.txt newfile.txt.
Again, wildcards can be used to simplify the process. For example, the command ren oldfile.txt newfile.* would have the same effect as the original command.

Note   Like many other commands, both the Delete and Rename commands can be used in a shortened version—Del for Delete and Ren for Rename.

Deltree

The Deltree command is a very useful, and yet very dangerous, command that can be used to removed an entire directory structure. Rather than deleting all files in a directory and then removing the directory itself, Deltree allows you to perform the action in one swift command. The basic usage for Deltree is: deltree directoryname.

After confirming that you do indeed want to delete the directory and all its sub-directories, the system does exactly that.

Type

The Type command can be used to view the contents of a file at the command prompt. It should be noted that only text files are properly viewable through the Type command, and even then formatting within the file can make it difficult to read. If you really need to view a text file, it's probably best to use a utility such as Edit. If you have to use Type as a command of last resort, the usage is simple: type filename.

Echo

The Echo command is used most often in batch files where it can cause a string of text or the result of a command to be sent to the screen. For example, if you were to type **echo Good Morning** and press Enter, the text *Good Morning* would appear on the screen. By default, Echo is on. Therefore, it is common to start batch files with the echo off command so that each command and its result will not be displayed on the screen.

Set

The Set command is used to view the environment variables that have been con-figured on the system. There are two common uses of the command—the first is to view the current configuration of certain system settings. To do this you just type the command and a list of settings will be displayed.

The second use is that of actually configuring the aforementioned systems settings, in which case, as well as knowing how to use the Set command, you will also need to understand what system parameters you are setting and to what. In reality, you can create any environment variable you want. For exam-ple, you could say Set winner=yes.

Then, when you use the Set command to view the variables, the line *winner=yes* would appear. There is no harm done and if in the unlikely event some program or other asked the environment for the value of *winner* it would reply with *yes*. The potential harm comes from changing or removing one of the preexisting variables that is integral to the workings of the system. The bottom line with environment variables is that unless you have a specific reason for changing them, they are best left alone.

Ping

The Ping command is used to test connectivity between two systems that are running the TCP/IP protocol suite. Ping is a particularly important troubleshooting tool and an important one for PC technicians to understand. There is a detailed discussion of the Ping utility in Chapter 10.

Managing Disks, Directories, and Files

Data management is a critical task for PC technicians, and so an understanding of how data is stored on systems, and the configuration of hard disks, is an essential skill.

Disks

By now you should be fairly comfortable with disks and their use in PC systems. The bottom line is that a PC will have at least one, but perhaps multiple, hard disks installed in it. Generally speaking, as long as the BIOS recognizes the hard disk, you will generally find that the OS does not have very many problems accessing it. Of course, there are always exceptions to this, particularly if you are using unusual hardware or trying a new installation of SCSI devices. Once a drive is installed, you can then partition the drive—the first step in preparing a disk for use.

Partitions

Partitioning refers to the process of dividing a disk up into areas that can be used for different purposes. There are different types of partitions that you can use depending on your needs. For more information on the types of partitions and their uses, refer to Chapter 8.

Note   Because the most common circumstance in which you partition a disk is during an installation, CompTIA also includes preparation of the disk in the Installation, Configuration, and Upgrading Domain of the Operating System Technologies objectives. Because it is logical to discuss disk preparation in that context, refer to Chapter 8 for detailed coverage on partitioning drives.

File Systems

There are only a handful of file systems used with Windows operating systems. They are discussed in the following sections.

FAT (FAT16)

FAT16 was the original Windows file system for hard disks and served us well for many years. As larger hard disks were introduced, FAT16 lost some of its luster. The FAT16 file system will only recognize partitions up to 2 GB. Nowadays, hard drives far exceed 2 GB, forcing FAT16 users to partition their hard disks into many smaller portions. Another limitation of FAT is in its security. The FAT file system offers no local security on files and folders, making it unsuitable for use on any system where file confidentiality is important.

Perhaps the greatest advantage of the FAT16 file system and the reason it is still used on some systems today is that it is a universal file system. FAT16 partitions can be read and accessed by DOS, Windows 3.x, Windows 9x, Windows NT, and Windows 2000. In terms of compatibility, this makes FAT16 the clear winner.

FAT32

FAT32 was introduced with Windows 95 OSR2, and offers some significant improvements over its predecessor, including more efficient use of hard disk space and support for larger hard disks up to 2 terabytes. Windows 2000 and Windows 9x operating systems, since the release of Windows 95 OSR2, support FAT32. It should be noted, however, that Windows NT 4 does not support FAT32.

Despite the advantages over FAT16, FAT32 still suffers from some significant drawbacks in comparison to the alternative file system, NTFS. First among these would have to be that it does not offer local security for files and folders. This means that anyone who sits down at a system using FAT32 can access any file. As you might imagine, this is not always a desirable feature. A second drawback for FAT32 is that it does not support disk compression, though with today's larger hard disks the need to rely on disk compression to conserve space is not as important as it once was.

NTFS

The NT file system, NTFS, was developed for the Windows NT operating system and offers significant improvements over FAT16 and FAT32 used in Windows 9x systems. In fact, for most applications, it is recommended that NTFS be used on Windows NT and Windows 2000 systems instead of FAT16 or FAT32. NTFS cannot be used on Windows 9x systems.

Some of the main characteristics and features of NTFS include

- **Security**   Unlike FAT file systems, NTFS offers file- and folder-level security. This means that it is possible to restrict access to files and folders on the local system. FAT partitions offer no local security.

- **Volume size**   NTFS allows for a theoretical maximum volume size of up to 2 TB.

- **Logging**   NTFS offers the ability to log system activities, and in case the system goes down, you can review those logs to help determine the cause of the shutdown.

- **Disk performance**   NTFS offers a higher level of performance than FAT, particularly with larger files.

- **Compression**   NTFS offers the ability to compress, on the fly, files on the drive, thus saving hard disk space.

NTFS5

The latest version of NTFS, NTFS5, was introduced with Windows 2000 (the version of NTFS in Windows NT is referred to as NTFS4). In addition to offering the same performance and security benefits of its predecessor, NTFS5 introduces some new features into the mix. Two of the more significant improvements are disk quotas and encryption. Each of these were discussed earlier in the chapter.

 Test Smart   It is important to remember that if files are backed up from an NTFS partition and restored to a FAT partition, the NTFS-specific characteristics such as permissions, encryption, and compression will be lost.

HPFS   The High Performance File System, HPFS, was introduced with an operating system known as OS/2. In its day, HPFS was quite impressive with its ability to support 2-terabyte volumes, a 2-gigabyte file size, and names up to 255 characters. HPFS was not widely used in the Windows world, and while Windows NT can read HPFS volumes, no other Windows OS offers support for HPFS.

Note   One file system that is often overlooked is one that is supported by all of the Windows-based operating systems, CDFS. The CD-ROM File System is similar to FAT and is the standard format used by data CDs. CDFS is termed as a read-only file system, as it is generally associated with read-only media.

Directory Structures

To work effectively with files and folders on a system, you will need an understanding of how the directory structure of the file system is formed, and how to navigate it.

The very top of a directory structure is referred to as the root. The root is designated as a backslash (\) for short. So, when you are referring to a folder and are describing the path from the root, you include the backslash to denote this. For example, the path \folder1\folder2\folder3 denotes that you are referring to the path from the root. If you were to cite the same example without the first backslash, you would be referring to the path from your current position, which might or might not be the root of the drive.

Any folder that is created under the root folder is considered a subfolder, and any folder created under that is considered a subfolder of that subfolder.

Creating Folders

Managing data files on your local computer system will require a knowledge of how to create folders to organize those files. A folder is basically a container for all those files and it is used to organize files and make them easier to find when you need them.

There are two primary methods for creating folders in Windows, Windows Explorer and My Computer. When Windows Explorer is displayed, the current folders in a drive are listed in the left pane with the contents of those folders displayed in the right pane. To create a new folder in the directory tree of a drive, choose File from the menu bar, point to New, and click Folder. Once selected, the new folder will appear and you will be required to give it a name. Alternatively, you can right-click in a blank area of the right pane and select New Folder from the shortcut menu. Figure 7-18 shows the creation of a new folder in Windows Explorer.

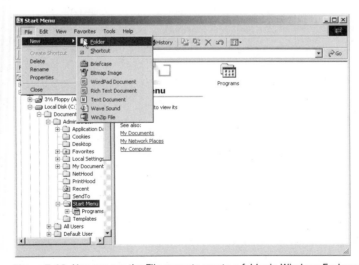

Figure 7-18 You can use the File menu to create a folder in Windows Explorer.

Creating a folder using My Computer follows the same basic procedures as in Windows Explorer. First, click on the drive you wish to create the folder in. Then, choose File from the menu bar, point to New, and select Folder.

Note   It is also common to create folders from the command line. The command for creating directories is MD (make directory). To create a directory called Test, the command would be *md test*.

Navigating the Directory Structure

To navigate between the folders, you can use a graphical utility such as Windows Explorer or you can use command-line utilities such as Change Directory (CD). This command and its usage were discussed in the previous section.

Files

You will certainly not get very far working with and supporting a Windows-based operating system without having a thorough knowledge of files and folders and how to navigate through them. The A+ exam will expect you to have a working knowledge of files and how they are managed in a Windows environment.

More Info   The two primary tools used to navigate through files and folders in Windows 9x and Windows 2000 are Windows Explorer and the My Computer utility. A discussion of both of these tools was provided earlier in the chapter.

Creating Files

In most cases, files are created through programs when we save our work. For example, if you are typing a letter in Microsoft Word and you choose Save, after supplying a file name, the program creates a file of that name and saves the data into it.

It is also possible to create files manually should the need arise. Perhaps the easiest way to do this is to right-click within a directory in Windows Explorer and then select New. A submenu will appear with the different types of files that can be created in this way. The exact options that appear on the menu will depend on what programs you have installed on the system.

File-Naming Conventions

It used to be that you could only use eight characters and a three-letter extension when naming your files and folders. This led to some creative, albeit cryptic, names being used, often making it difficult to find files once they were saved to the hard disk. The introduction of long file names with Windows 95 changed the rules for the naming of files. Today, names for files and folders can be up to 255 characters long. It is hard to imagine why anyone would need a file name that long.

Test Smart File names cannot include certain characters, including \ / ? * : " < > |.

Each file name you create is accompanied by a file name extension, which is used to associate the file with its parent program. For example, a file called Test.doc is associated with Microsoft Word, and when the file is double-clicked, it will automatically be opened with the parent program. Table 7-2 shows some common file name extensions you can expect to see when working in a Windows environment.

Table 7-2 Common File Name Extensions

File Name Extension	Associated Program or Function
.exe	Identifies an executable program. Examples of such files include Setup.exe and Install.exe.
.bat	Identifies an executable batch file. Batch files are used to run specific programs or sets of commands.
.com	Used to identify a command file. An example of a command file is Command.com.
.bmp	Identifies a graphic (bitmap) file.
.jpg	Identifies a graphic (JPEG) file.
.ini	Identifies an initialization file for a program. Examples of .ini files include Win.ini and System.ini. These are text files and typically edited with the Sysedit utility.
.sys	Used with system files.
.doc	The file extension associated with Microsoft Word documents.
.txt	Documents saved in a text format.

Test Smart File with certain file names suggest that they are executable, that is, they can be run from the command line. Executable file name extensions include .bat, .exe, and .com.

File Attributes

In the Windows world, there are four attributes that can be assigned to individual files and folders: read-only (r), archive (a), system (s), and hidden (h). When working with files and folders, you need to know what each of these attributes does and how they affect files and folders. Table 7-3 shows each of the attribute options and a description of each.

Table 7-3   File and Folder Attributes

Attribute	Description
Read-only (r)	The read-only attribute is applied to a file or folder to help protect it from being modified, renamed, or accidentally deleted. When you wish to modify a read-only document, the original will not be written over; rather, you will need to save the new document as a separate file with a different name.
Archive (a)	When the archive attribute is applied, the file or folder will be marked for backup. Windows backup utilities can be set to back up files with the archive attribute set. By default, all files are assigned the archive attribute when they are changed or created but folders will have to be done manually.
System (s)	The system attribute is automatically assigned to key Windows and DOS files. System files are often also assigned the hidden attribute as an extra level of precaution.
Hidden (h)	Files and folders assigned the hidden attribute will not be visible by default from within Windows or DOS.

Test Smart   When removing attributes the minus (–) sign is used, and when adding attributes the plus (+) sign is used.

As mentioned earlier, file attributes can be viewed and modified in DOS using the Attrib command. In Windows, you can view and modify the attributes for files simply by right-clicking on the file and choosing the Properties option from the shortcut menu. Figure 7-19 shows a file's properties dialog box and its assigned attributes.

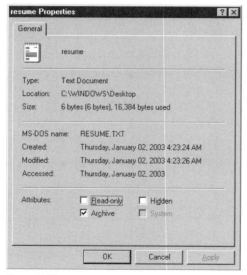

Figure 7-19 Files can be assigned four attributes: read-only, system, hidden, and archive.

File Compression

Originally, the rise in popularity of file compression was brought about by our need to store ever-increasing amounts of data on expensive, low-capacity hard disks. Today, where hard disk space is cheaper than real estate in Chernobyl, the need for file compression has all but disappeared.

Note Back in the days when a 40-MB drive was considered big, Microsoft provided tools that could be used to compress the disk, thereby fitting more data on it. First there was DoubleSpace, and then came DriveSpace. Nowadays, with 40-GB and larger drives commonplace, no one worries too much about compressing their disk drives, so the chances of encountering DriveSpace in your travels is reasonably slim.

On a Windows NT, Windows 2000, or Windows XP system, you can use file compression as long as you have NTFS partitions. It can be enabled on a single file, or a folder and all the files and subfolders. In essence, this allows you to compress the entire drive. It used to be that compression systems used to slow file access down slightly because each file that was retrieved needed to be uncompressed before it could be read. Nowadays, the compression algorithms are so efficient, and PCs so powerful that performance is rarely an issue. Even so, if you are thinking of compressing files just for something to do, it is worth considering.

Note In this discussion, we are talking about compressing files while they are on the disk. This is different from using a program like WinZip to place files into an archive so that they can be copied or e-mailed. This reason for compression is still alive, very well, and very necessary.

File Encryption

Whereas file compression is becoming largely unnecessary on a PC hard disk, the need for encryption is growing all the time. File encryption is a mechanism by which files are encoded so that only the intended users are able to view them. Now, you might think that passwords provide the same level of protection but encryption takes the protective process one step further, by actually scrambling the data in the file.

Although third-party encryption systems have been around for some time, encryption became available to the masses when Microsoft included the Encrypting File System (EFS) with Windows 2000. Although the configuration of EFS is beyond the scope of the A+ objectives, it is important to know two things. One is that EFS is a feature that was introduced with Windows 2000. The other is that you need to be using NTFS in order to access the EFS functionality. No surprise there.

File Permissions

File permissions are attributes that can be set on a file that govern what can, and cannot, be done to the file by a given user. File permissions are very useful because they allow you to exercise control over files on the system. On stand-alone systems, which are the main focus of the A+ exam, file permissions are a useful feature. On server systems, file permissions are an absolute necessity.

Whether or not security through file permissions is available to you depends on the file system that you are using, which depends in part on the operating system you are using. For example, Windows 9x only supports FAT and FAT32 file systems, which do not have file permission features. However, Windows NT, Windows 2000, and Windows XP Professional support NTFS, which does indeed provide file permission functionality.

There are six basic permissions that can be assigned to a user, or a group of users. These permissions are detailed in Table 7-4.

Table 7-4　**NTFS File Permissions**

Permission	Description
Full Control	Allows full access and control over the file including changing the permissions and ownership.
Modify	Allows the user to see, change, and delete existing files. If applied to a folder, also allows the creation of new files.
Read & Execute	Allows the user to see the file and its contents. If the file is an executable, the user can also execute that file.
List Folder Contents	Allows the user to see the files in a folder and their attributes but not to actually open the file.
Read	Allows the user to see the files in a folder and to open, but not make any changes, to the files.
Write	Allows a user to create new files and make changes to the contents of existing files. It does not allow the user to delete a file.

NTFS permissions are cumulative—that is, the permissions assigned to a user and a group, if the user is a member of that group, combine. The exception to this rule is when a user or group is denied a certain permission. In that case, the permission is removed whether it was derived via the user or the group.

File Types (Text vs. Binary Files)

Two types of files can exist on a PC—text and binary files. To put it simply, if the file is not a text file then it's a binary file.

Text files are those that are created using, well, text—as in numbers and letters. They can be viewed and edited in an editor such as Edit or Notepad. Although it might be possible to open a binary file in an editor, it most likely will just look like a bunch of hieroglyphics. Inserting even a single space in the file might render it useless.

Major Operating System Utilities

In particular, CompTIA identifies disk management, system management, and file management tools as being of particular importance. These three classifications and some of the tools that fall into each category are discussed in the following sections.

Disk Management Tools

Disks hold the most valuable asset related to the PC—the data. While other parts can be replaced as needed, the hard disk is more than just a field-replaceable unit. It might hold many times its value in terms of information assets. For that reason, technicians should care for and nurture hard disks in their care with just a little more diligence than any other component in the system. Fortunately, there are a number of tools that are available to help.

Defrag.exe

When an operating system writes files to disk, it does so in a progressive manner, using areas of space on the disk as they appear. This can mean that even moderately sized files end up getting written in chunks that are spread across the disk. The upside of this approach is that space on the disk gets used efficiently. The downside is that this fragmentation can cause the system to run slowly as the hard drive has to read data from several locations on the disk to retrieve a single file.

Fragmentation of the disks is a double whammy—not only does it slow the system down because the hard disk has to work harder to retrieve the files, the increased workload can literally wear the hard disk out quicker than it would do otherwise. So, defragmenting your hard drives does more than just speed the system up—it could literally mean that it lasts longer.

The Defrag utility works by looking at the disk and literally reordering the files so that they are placed contiguously on the drive.

Fdisk.exe

Fdisk is the utility used to partition the hard disk. A hard disk has to have at least one formatted partition to hold the operating system. This partition can be created by Fdisk or by the Windows Setup program when it is booted from the CD-ROM drive. For more information on the Fdisk utility, refer to Chapter 8.

Backup/Restore Utility

One of the primary things technicians need to know when working with any system is how to back up and restore data. Each and every operating system provides a method of backing up and restoring files. Some utilities are better to use than others, which has led some technicians to purchase third-party backup software. In the A+ exam, you will be expected to know the backup utilities that are available in Windows and the different types of backup strategies you can use.

Windows NT   By today's standards, the Backup utility included in Windows NT 4 is somewhat limited. You can launch the Windows NT Backup utility by choosing Backup on the Administrative Tools menu. The Windows NT Backup utility allows you to choose entire drives or specific files or folders that you want to have backed up.

One of the biggest shortcomings of the Windows NT 4 Backup utility is the lack of an integrated scheduler, meaning that jobs can be run only with the technician at the console or by using a separate scheduling program.

Windows 2000 Backup   Microsoft engineers had definitely been reading the messages in the suggestion box when they revamped the Backup utility for Windows 2000. Although the basic functionality is the same as in Windows NT 4, the addition of a scheduling feature and the provision for backing up to a file on the disk make it pretty much all the backup software that most companies will ever need. The Backup utility is accessed by choosing Start, Programs, Accessories, System Tools, Backup. Figure 7-20 shows the Windows 2000 Backup utility.

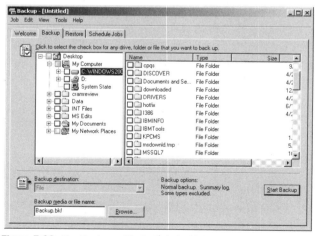

Figure 7-20 The Backup utility included with Windows 2000 offers improvements over the version included with Windows NT 4.

Windows XP Backup   The Backup utility supplied with Windows XP is basically the same as that provided within Windows 2000, with the exception that it has a slightly different wizard and the whole thing looks "XP-like." Apart from that, there are really no major differences between the Windows XP and Windows 2000 versions. To access the Windows XP Backup utility, click Start, All Programs, Accessories, System Tools, Backup.

Windows 9x Backup   Windows 9x includes a utility appropriately named Backup. The Windows 9x utility allows you to back up to a variety of sources such as floppy disks or external drives. There is actually a wizard that guides you through the process of creating a backup. You can decide which files to back up and which ones not to. To choose the files you wish to back up, you can scroll through Windows Explorer to find them and save them to an external drive. The Backup utility is also used to restore the backed-up files.

Backup Strategies

When it comes to backing up, there are several techniques used. The specific ones used will often depend on the nature of the data and the needs of the organization. The basic criterion that governs the type of backup chosen is time. To use an example, if the data that needs to be backed up can be written in the period between 1:00 A.M. and 5:00 A.M. when there is no one working, then a full backup of your data on a nightly basis is a practical and wise option. If, on the other hand, you are trying to squeeze your backup into a narrow time slot, one of the other backup methods combined with a periodic full backup might be a more practical solution.

When it comes to choosing a type of backup, there are three primary choices: full, incremental, and differential backups.

Full Backup   As the name suggests, a full backup saves all directories and files from the hard disk. Of course, a full backup is the best option, but there are some reasons why doing a full backup is not always possible.

As discussed, many organizations have data that is very dynamic and changes at a rapid pace, and this type of dynamic data has to be saved frequently. Depending on the size of the data, backing up can take a very long time. Because of the time full backups can take, they are often restricted to weekly or monthly use, though the increasing speed and capacity of backup media is making nightly full backups a much more realistic proposition even for those with gigabytes of data.

Test Smart   The clear benefit of the full backup is that it only takes a single tape, or set of tapes, to restore the backup.

Incremental Backup   An incremental backup provides a much faster method than a full backup. During an incremental backup, only the files that have changed or been created since the last full or incremental backup are included. Because of this, the time it takes to do the backup might be a fraction of the time it takes to do a full backup. To determine whether a file has changed since the last full backup, the backup software looks at the archive bit setting on the file. When a file is changed in any way or copied from one area of the disk to another, the archive bit is set to indicate that, at the next time of backup, the file needs to be copied or archived. Once the file has been backed up, the incremental backup process clears the archive bit.

Test Smart   For the A+ exam, be sure that you understand the role that each backup type plays, and how and what files it backs up.

Differential Backup   Differential and incremental backups often get confused but there is a clear distinction between the two. While an incremental backup backs up the changed or created files since the last full or incremental backup, differential backups provide a middle ground, backing up the files that have changed since the last full backup. Restoring differential backups is a faster process because only two tapes are needed, the last full backup and the latest differential, but over time the amount of differential data that needs to be backed up will increase (compared to incremental backups). Like incremental backups, the differential backup uses the archive bit to determine what files need to be backed up. Unlike the incremental backup, however, it does not clear the archive bit. Therefore, the file is repeatedly backed up until the archive bit is reset by the next full or incremental backup.

ScanDisk

As we discussed earlier, ScanDisk is a widely used utility that is used to detect and correct file problems and errors on hard disks and floppy disks. For more information on ScanDisk, refer to the earlier section "Using Command-Line Functions and Utilities."

Chkdsk

Chkdsk, short for CheckDisk, is a command-line utility that you can use to check the state of the file system. Chkdsk reports disk usage as well as indicates whether or not there are any issues with the drive.

To use Chkdsk, simply type the command at the command prompt. If the result of the command shows that there are problems with the drive, you can then run the command again, this time using the /f switch, which instructs Chkdsk to fix any errors it finds. As with the other tools discussed in this section, it is a good idea to run the Chkdsk utility periodically to ensure that your disks are kept in tip-top condition.

Disk Cleanup

Disk Cleanup was a feature introduced with Windows 98 that searches for files on your hard disk that might be able to be deleted without affecting the running of the system. Files that might be included in the cleanup process include temporary Internet files and temporary files. You can access the Disk Cleanup feature in Windows by clicking Start, Programs, Accessories, System Tools, Disk Cleanup. Figure 7-21 shows the Disk Cleanup dialog box with a report of how much disk space is being used by each type of file.

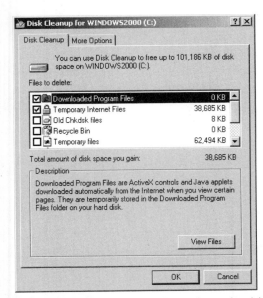

Figure 7-21 The Disk Cleanup utility can be used to delete temporary files from your disk.

Format

As we discussed earlier, the Format command is used in the final stages of preparation of a disk. Now, while that might make it seem like a tool that is only used when installing a new system, Format is also used when it becomes necessary to format a specific drive on a hard disk while leaving the drive that the operating system is on intact. Although it is not a difficult operation, the key here is to be very, very careful and make sure that you are formatting the correct drive. Also, because it is very difficult, if not impossible, to retrieve data from a drive that has been formatted, you should ensure that you have a complete backup of the drive, or better yet, the entire system, before you start.

System Management Tools

A variety of tools are used in the day-to-day management of a system running Windows. Some of the more commonly used, and useful, tools are discussed in the following sections.

Device Manager

As we discussed earlier in this chapter, Device Manager is a utility that can be used to view and change the configuration of the hardware devices installed on your system. For more information on Device Manager, refer to the section titled "Major Operating System Interfaces" earlier in this chapter.

Computer Manager

As we discussed earlier, on a Windows 2000/XP Professional system, management of the computer is performed through the Computer Management console. The console can be accessed by selecting Control Panel, Administrative Tools, Computer Management. Here you can perform tasks like viewing the Event Viewer logs, configuring local user accounts, and performing disk management tasks.

Msconfig.exe

The Msconfig utility, introduced with Windows 98, is similar to the Sysedit utility; however, the Msconfig utility is far more versatile. The Msconfig utility allows you to safely modify legacy Windows files without making permanent changes. It allows you to customize these files, determining which of the legacy files Windows is to use.

Regedit.exe

You make changes to the registry mainly through the utilities found in Control Panel. However, there are times when you need to directly modify the system's registry. In such cases, you need a registry editor such as Regedit. The Regedit utility allows you to navigate through the registry, viewing the settings. It also allows you to search through and modify values in the registry, and to manually export the entire registry to create a backup. In fact, before making any changes to the registry, it is recommended that you first back it up in case something goes wrong. Changes to the registry are dynamic, meaning that as soon as they are applied, they are in effect. There is no margin for error when working with the registry. Another way of taking a backup is with the Scanreg utility, which was discussed earlier in this chapter. The Regedit utility can be found in the C:\Windows directory.

Regedt32.exe

Regedt32 is a registry-editing tool used in Windows NT 4 and Windows 2000. As well as being a 32-bit program, Regedt32 is able to recognize and work with some of the special features of the registry unique to Windows NT 4 and Windows 2000. The Regedt32.exe file can be found in the System32 directory under the Windows installation directory.

Test Smart   When editing the registry, you usually use Regedit in Windows 9x and Windows XP and Regedt32 in Windows NT 4 and Windows 2000. Where possible, you should always try to configure the system through Control Panel, which is a safer method than using a registry editor.

Sysedit.exe

There are many legacy files still included in Windows such as the System.ini and the Win.ini files. These files are text files and often modified in programs such as Notepad; however, there was a built-in utility in Windows used to edit them, the Sysedit utility. The Sysedit utility allows you to edit the legacy system files simultaneously including the Autoexec.bat, Win.ini, System.ini, Config.sys, and Protocol.ini files.

Scanreg

As was discussed earlier, Scanreg is a utility used to repair, back up, and restore the registry. For more information on Scanreg, refer to that section earlier in this chapter.

Event Viewer

In Windows NT 4 and Windows 2000, perhaps the first place to look when you're searching for anomalies or information on the functioning of the system is Event Viewer. If Windows NT/2000 records an error in the system or in a program, the error is recorded in the Event Viewer logs. The information is recorded in three separate log files: the Security log, the Application log, and the

System log. The Security log contains such information as both successful and unsuccessful logon attempts; the Application log contains information logged by programs; and the System log records information pertaining to components or drivers in the system.

Task Manager

Press Ctrl+Alt+Delete while using a Windows NT 4, Windows 2000, or Windows XP system, and you will open a Windows Security dialog box that provides a button to start the Windows Task Manager utility. Alternatively, you can press Ctrl+Shift+Esc or run the command Taskman from the Run dialog box.

The Task Manager provides a quick look at what is going on in a system, and it is often the first place to look if you are having a problem. The Task Manager has three tabs showing different information: the Applications tab shows which programs are currently running; the Processes tab shows which processes are running and their approximate memory and CPU usage; and the Performance tab shows overall system resource usage. The Task Manager provides a quick reference for technicians to see what the system is doing or, in some cases, not doing. Figure 7-22 shows the Performance tab of the Task Manager.

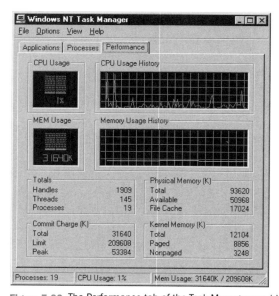

Figure 7-22 The Performance tab of the Task Manager provides information on how the system is performing.

File Management Tools

Working with files is an almost daily occurrence for almost all PC technicians, and understanding the tools you can use to work with files is very important.

Fortunately, many of the tools used for file management have already been discussed in this chapter, so included here are only very brief explanations. For a more in-depth look at the tools, refer to the appropriate section in this chapter.

Attrib.exe

The Attrib command is used to change the attributes on a file. As we discussed earlier, there are four file attributes (r, a, s, h) that can be applied to or removed from files as needed. From a file management perspective, this is important because you might find it necessary to change the attributes of a file in order to work with the file or to delete it. Likewise, you might decide to alter the attributes so that the file cannot be deleted or so that it gets included in the next backup. For more information on the use of the Attrib command, refer to the section earlier in this chapter, "Using Command-Line Functions and Utilities."

Extract.exe

If you have ever looked through a Windows 9x CD, you might have noticed special files known as cabinet (.cab) files. These are compressed files, which are typically automatically extracted during the installation process. However, if you need to manually extract files, you can use the Extract utility. The extract utility must be run from the command line. To extract a compressed file, simply type **extract** followed by the file you wish to decompress. Extract allows you to retrieve a single file from a Cab utility, which can be useful if a user deletes an important file by accident.

Edit.com

As we discussed earlier, Edit.com is a rudimentary text editor that runs from a command prompt. Its role in file management is limited to editing existing files and creating new text files.

Windows Explorer

Finally, as we have already seen, Windows Explorer makes a powerful file management tool, and is quite frequently the tool of choice for PC technicians.

Key Points

- Control Panel provides access to system configuration utilities that modify the system registry.
- Use the Add/Remove Programs utility to cleanly remove a program from the system and, in Windows 9x, create a boot disk.

- The Add New Hardware utility is used to add devices to the system and modify the device drivers used by hardware.

- The Advanced Display settings are used to change the system's refresh rate and hardware acceleration settings.

- Some of the key areas accessed through the System Properties dialog box include Device Manager, Hardware Profiles, and Performance Options.

- Windows versions since Windows 95 use a single hierarchical database called the registry that holds the system's hardware and software settings.

- In Windows 9x, the registry is composed of the User.dat and System.dat files.

- The registry is edited using registry editors called Regedit.exe and Regedt32.exe.

- Windows NT uses the FAT16 and NTFS file systems.

- Windows 2000 can use the FAT16, FAT32, and NTFS file systems.

- All versions of Windows 9x can use FAT16 and versions since Windows 95 OSR2 can use the FAT32 file system.

- Windows 2000 introduced Active Directory and the use of dynamic disks.

- The newer version of NTFS used with Windows 2000 allows for file- and folder-level encryption and disk quotas.

- Windows 2000 boot files are hidden. To access them, you need to enable the ability to view hidden files in Windows Explorer.

- Windows 2000 supports three primary RAID configurations: mirroring, spanned volumes, and a specialized RAID configuration known as RAID 5.

- The Autoexec.bat file is used optionally during the Windows 9x boot process and contains program and environment settings.

- The Config.sys file used optionally during the Windows 9x boot process is responsible for the loading of the device drivers.

- Virtual memory is the name given to an area of space on the hard disk that is used by the operating system as if it were normal physical memory.

- Himem.sys is an extended memory driver.

- The Dir command is used to list the contents of various directories.

- The Attrib command is used to view and modify the attributes of a file.

- The Edit command is used as a text editor to modify the key system files.

- Each file name we create can be associated with its parent program through its file name extension.

- Three backup types are full, differential, and incremental.

- The FAT16 file system will only recognize partitions up to 2 GB but can be recognized and read by all Windows operating systems.

- FAT32 offers more efficient use of hard disk space than FAT16 and support for larger hard disks.

- ScanDisk is a widely used utility that is used to detect and correct file problems and errors on hard disks and floppy disks.

- The Extract utility is used to decompress Windows installation files.

- The Defrag utility is used to organize the files on the hard disk, increasing the performance of the hard disk.

- FAT16 can be converted to FAT32 using the Cvt1.exe command. FAT32 cannot be converted to FAT16.

- FAT16 and FAT32 can be converted to NTFS using the Convert.exe command. NTFS cannot be converted to FAT16 or FAT32.

Chapter Review Questions

1   Which of the following two files comprise the system's registry on a Windows 9x system?

   a)   User.ini

   b)   System.ini

   c)   System.dat

   d)   User.dat

Answers c and d are correct. The registry on a Windows 9x system is stored in the System.dat and User.dat files. Answer a is incorrect. There is no standard Windows file called User.ini. Answer b is incorrect. System.ini is one of the standard Windows startup files.

2   Which of the following commands would successfully reveal a hidden file called Test.doc?

   a)   attrib +h test.doc

   b)   attrib –h test.doc

   c)   attrib –s test.doc

   d)   attrib +a test.doc

Answer b is correct. The Attrib command is used to change the attributes on a file or directory. In this case, the -H switch is used to remove the hidden file attribute from the file Test.doc. Answer a is incorrect. This command would add the hidden attribute to the Test.doc file. Answer c is incorrect. The –S switch would remove the system attribute from a file. Answer d is incorrect. The +A switch would add the archive attribute to a file.

3   Which of the following backup strategies backs up all of the files that have been changed or created since the last full backup?

   a)   Differential

   b)   Incremental

   c)   Marginal

   d)   Lateral

Answer a is correct. A differential backup copies all files that have been changed or created since the last full backup. Answer b is incorrect. An incremental backup backs up files that have been changed or created since the last full or incremental backup. Answers c and d are incorrect. These are not accepted terms used to describe a type of backup.

4   You are installing Windows 2000 on a new system. Which of the following file systems can you choose from? (Choose two.)

a)   NTFS

b)   FAT32

c)   HPFS

d)   CDFS

Answers a and b are correct. Windows 2000 supports both NTFS and FAT32. Answer c is incorrect. Although Windows NT 4 supported HPFS for read-only purposes, it is no longer supported in Windows 2000. Answer d is incorrect. Although Windows 2000 supports CDFS, you cannot specify that a partition be formatted with CDFS during the installation. It is a file system associated with read-only media.

5   You want to edit the startup files for Windows 98. Which of the following utilities could you use to do this? (Choose two.)

a)   Sysedit

b)   Regedit

c)   Edit

d)   Regedt32

Answers a and c are correct. The Windows startup files are text files. They can be edited through the Windows 9x utility Sysedit or through any text editor including Edit. Answer b is incorrect. The Regedit utility is used for editing the registry; it cannot be used for editing the startup files. Answer d is incorrect. Not only can't the Regedt32 utility be used for editing the Windows 9x startup files, it is designed for use on 32-bit versions of Windows such as Windows NT 4 and Windows 2000.

6   You want to copy the contents of a directory and all its subdirectories to another drive. Which of the following commands would you use?

a)   dir /s

b)   Sysedit

c)   copy /s

d)   xcopy /s

Answer d is correct. The Xcopy command, when used with the /s switch, can be used to copy a directory and all its subdirectories. Answer a is incorrect. The Dir command is used to get a listing of files in the current directory, not to copy files. Answer b is incorrect. The Sysedit utility is used to edit system files on a Windows 9x system. It is not used to copy files. Answer c is incorrect. Although the Copy command is used to copy files, it cannot be used to copy subdirectories.

7   Which of the following commands can be used to configure environment variables?

a)   Varset

b)   Set

c)   Setvar

d)   CD

Answer b is correct. The Set command can be used to change environment variables. Answers a and c are incorrect. These are not valid commands. Answer d is incorrect. The CD command is used to change to another directory.

8   Which of the following are valid wildcard characters? (Choose two.)

a)   &

b)   ?

c)   *

d)   #

Answers b and c are correct. The question mark is used as a wildcard to denote a single character. The asterisk is used to denote a group of characters. Answers a and d are incorrect. These are not valid wildcard characters.

9   Which of the following files is *not* automatically opened by Sysedit?

a)   Config.sys

b)   System.ini

c)   System.dat

d)   Win.ini

Answer c is correct. The System.dat file is associated with the Windows 9x registry and is not opened by Sysedit, which is only used for editing text files. Answers a, b, and d are all incorrect. All of these files are automatically opened by Sysedit.

10 Which of the following operating systems uses dynamic disks?

a)   Windows NT 4

b)   Windows 2000

c)   DOS

d)   Windows 98

Answer b is correct. Windows 2000 uses both basic and dynamic disks. The latter are able to provide enhanced features such as spanning, striping, and RAID. All of the other answers are incorrect.

11 Which of the following commands would you use to attempt to fix a corrupted registry?

a) scanreg /restore

b) scanreg /regfix

c) scanreg /fix

d) scandisk /regfix

Answer c is correct. The /fix switch of Scanreg can be used to attempt to fix a corrupted registry. Answer a is incorrect. This command would attempt to restore the registry from a backup. Answer b is incorrect. There is no /regfix switch for Scanreg. Answer d is incorrect. The ScanDisk utility is used to test and repair problems with the hard disk, not the registry.

12 While editing the Msdos.sys file, you notice that there are rows of commented out characters with apparently no purpose. Why are they there?

a) They are padding characters to make sure that the file is at least 1024 bytes in size.

b) They contain the checksum for the file.

c) They contain the license key for the OS in encrypted form.

d) They contain a list of error codes in encrypted form.

Answer a is correct. The Msdos.sys file must be a minimum of 1024 bytes (1 KB) in size. Because the contents of the file do not always make it this big, padding characters are used. All of the other answers are incorrect.

13 Which of the following Control Panel utilities would you use to configure virtual memory?

a) System

b) Memory

c) Performance

d) Virtual Memory

Answer a is correct. The virtual memory settings are configured through the System utility in Control Panel. Answers b, c, and d are incorrect. Control Panel does not have utilities named Memory, Performance, or Virtual Memory.

14 Which of the following commands could you use to view memory usage statistics? (Choose two.)

   a)   Sysedit

   b)   Memshow

   c)   Mem

   d)   Taskman

Answers c and d are correct. Both the Mem command and the Task Manager can be used to view memory usage statistics. Answer a is incorrect. The Sysedit utility is used to edit the Windows 9x configuration files. It cannot be used to view memory usage statistics. Answer b is incorrect. Memshow is not a recognized DOS or Windows command.

15 Which of the following is *not* an NTFS permission?

   a)   Read

   b)   Read & Execute

   c)   Open

   d)   Modify

Answer c is correct. Open is not a valid NTFS permission. All of the other answers are incorrect.

16 Which of the following tools can you use to edit the registry on a Windows 98 system?

   a)   Sysedit

   b)   Regedt32

   c)   Regedit

   d)   Scanreg

Answer c is correct. The Regedit tool is used on Windows 9x systems to edit the registry. Answer a is incorrect. The Sysedit utility is used to edit the Windows 9x startup files. Answer b is incorrect. The Regedt32 utility is used to edit the registry on Windows NT 4 and Windows 2000 systems. Answer d is incorrect. The Scanreg utility is used to back up, restore, and fix the registry. It is not used to edit it.

17 What name is given to the feature of NTFS5 that allows the amount of disk space available to a user to be controlled?

a)   Disk management

b)   Disk space allocation

c)   Disk space control

d)   Disk quotas

Answer d is correct. The disk quota feature of NTFS5 allows the amount of space available to a user to be controlled and monitored. All of the other answers are incorrect.

18 Which of the following files is *not* associated with the Windows NT boot sequence?

a)   Boot.ini

b)   Win.ini

c)   Ntbootdd.sys

d)   Ntldr

Answer b is correct. The Win.ini file is a Windows 9x startup file. All of the other answers are incorrect.

19 Which of the following file names would you type at the command prompt to start Windows 95?

a)   Win.ini

b)   Win.bat

c)   Win.exe

d)   Win.com

Answer d is correct. The file used to start Windows 95 from the command prompt is Win.com. Answer a is incorrect; Win.ini is one of the configuration files used by Windows during startup. Answers b and c are incorrect. Although these are both valid names for executable files, they are not the files used to start Windows.

20 Which of the following commands might you find in an Autoexec.bat file?

a)   dos=high,umb

b)   prompt pg

c)   device=c:\himem.sys

d)   files=20

Answer b is correct. The Prompt statement is used to configure the appearance of the command prompt and is found in the Autoexec.bat file. Answers a, c, and d are all incorrect. These are statements that you might find in the Config.sys file.

Chapter 8

Installing the Operating System

In Chapter 7, we outlined some of the characteristics of various Windows operating systems. Now that we have a better understanding of the different operating systems available in the Windows family and what they are designed to do, we can look at the process of installing an operating system and some considerations before the installation. By now, many of you have experience installing a Windows operating system, perhaps numerous times, and are familiar with the basic procedures and steps to follow. If not, or if it has been a while since your last install, we recommend that part of your A+ exam preparation include installing a Windows operating system. A little hands-on experience might be just what you need for the actual exam.

Hands-on experience aside, this chapter focuses on the key points you need to know when installing, or preparing to install, a Windows operating system. The installation procedures presented in this chapter are by no means intended to be a comprehensive tutorial on installing an OS; we just target the areas you need to know for the A+ exam. Further, despite the number of different Windows flavors, they all have some similar general installation procedures and best practices. It is these that are more likely to appear on the A+ exam than OS-specific procedures.

Pre-Installation Procedures

It is only natural when holding any new software package to become impatient and immediately want to unwrap and install it. While this approach is the most widely implemented, it is most certainly not the recommended way to install software, particularly an operating system. The preferred course of action is to take your time and do a little legwork before the actual installation. The term we use for this legwork is *pre-installation procedures*, and although they are largely ignored, they are quite important. In the next section, we take a look at a few items to keep in mind before installing an OS.

Hardware Requirements

It might sound obvious, but before installing an OS on your computer it is a good idea to verify that the system you are installing onto meets the hardware requirements for the OS. You do not want to start the installation only to find that the hard disk is too small or the system doesn't have enough memory. So how do you know if the hardware requirements are met? Microsoft maintains a list of the minimum hardware requirements for each OS on their Web site. Be warned, however, these are the minimum requirements; put a few applications on that system and you will find that the minimum requirements just don't cut it.

Verifying Hardware Compatibility

One often overlooked but important pre-installation step is to verify that the hardware you intend to use is compatible with the OS. Windows-based OSes have had a good track record with hardware compatibility, which is not to suggest that hardware verification is not an important consideration—far from it. In fact, do not be surprised if the exam includes questions pertaining to hardware verification and when, why, and how to use Microsoft's hardware compatibility list (HCL).

The HCL is not unique to Windows; all of the major OS vendors provide an HCL, which can normally be found on their respective Web sites. The HCL is, quite simply, a list of the hardware that has been tested and verified to work with an OS. Microsoft provides only tested drivers for the devices listed on the HCL, which means that it will guarantee support only for those devices. This doesn't mean that you can't use hardware that's not on the HCL because you might still be able to obtain the appropriate device drivers directly from the manufacturer. What it does mean is that if something is not working between that device and Windows, in terms of support, Microsoft won't necessarily be there for you.

Microsoft maintains an HCL for all of the Windows family operating systems on their Web site at *www.microsoft.com/hcl*. The HCL on this site is the most up-to-date list of hardware compatibility, and whenever possible you should make this your first stop for hardware verification. To verify your hardware for compatibility with Windows, type in the type of hardware you are looking for, for example, modems, and then scroll through the list of modems to see whether your modem is supported.

Installation Type

Of the many decisions you will be faced with during the installation of the operating system, one is the type of installation you will choose. You will have different installation options depending on the version of Windows you are using, but three of the common installation types include typical, custom, and compact.

The typical installation type is the most common. During the installation, Windows will install the OS along with some of the more popular programs and utilities such as Notepad, WordPad, and other system-monitoring tools. Many users do not use all of the programs installed with a typical installation and that is where a custom installation comes in. A custom installation gives the person installing the OS more control over what is installed on the system. If a user does not require all of those utilities and programs, a custom install is the key. Alternatively, if a user requires additional Windows components not installed during a typical installation, they can be added.

Finally, the compact installation option is designed for systems with limited hard disk capacities and sometimes laptop systems where all of those extra Windows components are simply not needed. Given today's larger hard disks, it is not an often-used option, but at least you have the choice.

Choosing a File System

For certain operating systems including Windows NT/2000/XP, during the installation, you can select the file system you want for your installation. It is recommended to use NTFS when the system will maintain sensitive data. If you elect to use FAT partitions and change your mind, they can be converted to NTFS after the installation. Before starting the installation, you will certainly want to have some idea of the file system you will use. File systems are discussed in more detail later in this chapter as well as in Chapter 7.

Network Configuration

If you are installing an OS on a system that is to be part of a network, the pre-installation might include finding any network settings you will need for the installation. If you do not know these settings, you might need to get the information from the network administrator.

Starting the Installation

One thing you can expect when working as a PC technician is that you will be forever installing and upgrading operating systems and therefore will need to know the easiest way to get the operating system up and running on that PC. Starting the installation of an operating system is certainly not rocket science but there are a few things you will need to know.

PC technicians will often find themselves installing an operating system on a hard disk that is not bootable. In days of old, this was not much of a problem. Operating systems were installed from a series of floppy disks, and starting the installation was as easy as placing the first floppy disk in the drive and running the installation files. Times have changed. Since the original version of Windows 95, which was available on floppy disk and CD, Windows operating systems can no longer be installed entirely from floppy disks. This leaves CDs, which means that during the installation of an operating system on a nonbootable hard disk, there must be a method of accessing the CD-ROM drive.

There are two ways to access the CD-ROM drive on a nonbootable system. The first method is to use a bootable floppy disk with CD-ROM drivers on it. The disk will take the system to the point where you can access the CD-ROM drive from a command prompt. Windows versions since Windows 98 have included a method of creating a bootable floppy disk that will take you to the command prompt with CD-ROM access, or will enable you to automatically start the Windows installation. To make a bootable floppy disk, refer to the documentation for the Windows version you are using.

See Also   *Creating startup disks and the files required on them is covered later in this chapter.*

The second option when installing an OS onto a nonbootable system is to boot directly from the CD-ROM drive. For the last few years, it has been possible to set the BIOS to boot directly from the CD-ROM drive. This allows you to put the installation CD, such as Windows 2000, into the CD-ROM drive and boot from the CD. The installation of the OS will begin automatically. Most Windows versions since the original Windows 95 CD allow you to boot from the CD-ROM.

Test Smart   If you have a bootable CD in the CD-ROM and the system halts with a "No Operating System Found" error message, ensure that the BIOS is set to boot from the CD.

Partitioning the Hard Disk

Even when you know how to start the installation, there are a few things you need to do before the installation actually begins. One such procedure involves the partitioning of the hard disk. New hard disks must be partitioned before they can be formatted and used by the operating system. When you partition a hard disk, you can divide the hard disk up into several partitions or make the entire hard disk a single partition. Either way, the hard disk must have at least one partition before you can install the operating system.

If a hard disk is partitioned into two or more parts, it gives the appearance of having more than a single physical drive. For instance, there might be only a single physical hard drive in the system but you might see a C:, D:, and E: on your system. To understand how this works, you need to know a little something about primary and extended partitions.

A Little Something about Primary and Extended Partitions

The concept of partitioning drives can at first seem confusing, but once you get your head around it, it is straightforward, and for those installations where the entire hard disk will be left as a single partition, C:, then you needn't worry about it at all. However, there will most certainly come a time when you need to work with several partitions.

To be able to boot from the hard disk, you must have at least one primary partition; this partition stores the operating system and is the one you actually boot from. In the Windows world, the name of the primary partition on the primary controller is always C:. A hard disk can only contain up to four primary partitions. This is not a restriction of the operating system but rather a restriction of PC architecture. To be more specific, the restriction is a limitation of the computer's master boot record; there is no getting around the four-primary-partition limit. For example, if you were using a 100-GB hard drive, you could partition the drive into four 25-GB primary partitions, but even these 25-GB partitions might be too large for your needs. That's where extended partitions come into play.

Extended partitions provide the means to slash the partition sizes to whatever you want them to be. To create an extended partition, you can take some space away from the primary partition to create the extended partition, using a program called Fdisk. Extended partitions act as if they were actually independent drives; however, they do not actually get a drive letter. Instead, the extended partitions are divided down further into *logical drives*. Logical drives do get a drive letter and give you the ability to reduce that 100-GB hard drive into very small sections. The number of logical drives you can use is limited by the number of letters in the alphabet. Logical drives are not bootable, so they will not contain an operating system. Figure 8-1 shows some examples of partition strategies.

Test Smart   Primary partitions are bootable, whereas logical partitions are not.

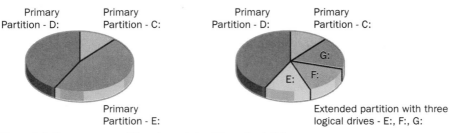

Figure 8-1 There are many different ways to partition a hard disk.

Note   Before installing Windows, it is important to determine the partitioning strategy you will be using. Some people choose to install one OS on their system, meaning that the entire hard disk can be used for a single OS. However, another common strategy is to make separate partitions to install multiple operating systems, for instance, having both Linux and Windows installed on the system.

Partitioning with Fdisk

One of the primary programs used for partitioning hard disks is the Fdisk utility. Fdisk is a command-line utility used to create partitions, delete partitions, display partition information, or mark a partition as being active. The active partition is one that can be booted from—a system must have an active partition and there can be only one.

Note   In the Fdisk utility, you also have the option to delete non-FAT partitions. This is handy if you need to remove an NTFS partition from the system.

Test Smart   The system must have one partition designated as the active partition in order to boot.

When in the Fdisk utility, you can first create the primary partition and if you have left enough room, create other partitions. You can create an extended partition to create logical drives. Once you have made changes with the Fdisk program, the system will need to be rebooted for the changes to take effect. Figure 8-2 shows the main screen of the Fdisk utility.

Note   Though not widely used, the /mbr switch can be used with the Fdisk utility to repair a damaged master boot record.

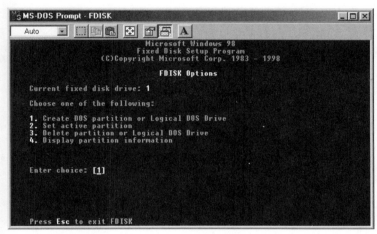

Figure 8-2 Fdisk is used to create, manage, and delete partitions.

One final consideration worth mentioning about Fdisk is using large disk support. The version of Fdisk included with Windows versions since Windows 95 OSR2 includes the option of choosing FAT16 or FAT32. As shown in Figure 8-3, when Fdisk is first enabled, it asks whether you want to enable large disk support. If you select Yes, you will be using FAT32. If not, you will be using FAT16.

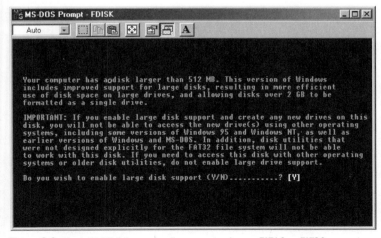

Figure 8-3 The initial Fdisk screen allows you to choose FAT16 or FAT32.

In addition to Fdisk, Windows 2000 and Windows XP users have another partition utility available after the installation of the OS. The Windows Disk Management utility is a graphical utility that allows you to fully configure the partitions on your system. It not only allows all of the functionality of the Fdisk utility, but the graphical interface makes it much nicer to use. Windows NT includes a similar utility but in the Windows NT world it is called Disk Administrator.

Formatting the Hard Drive

After creating the partitions on the hard disk, the partitions must be formatted before they can be used by the operating system. Formatting the hard disk has two key functions—it creates a root directory and a file allocation table (FAT). The root directory provides the basis for a structure by which you can later create files and folders, and the FAT is responsible for keeping track of where data is stored on disk.

The actual formatting of a drive is a relatively simple process and can be done from the command line using the Format utility. The exact syntax for this command is *format* drive letter:, where *drive letter* is the letter of the drive you wish to format. If you need to format anything other than the primary partition, C:, you can do so from within any of the Windows operating systems, as long as Windows itself is not installed on the drive to be formatted.

 Test Smart   When formatting a drive, the correct syntax is `format` followed by the drive letter.

Installation Commands

Many of the OS installations performed today do not require you to manually start the installation process. Instead, you will boot from the CD and the process will begin automatically. However, as a PC technician, when things do not work as they should, or when you're working with older technology, you need to know the commands used to start the installation, and, in addition, the commands used to customize the installation.

Things are real easy in the Windows 9x world. To manually start the installation of the OS, simply use the Setup program. Windows NT and Windows 2000/XP have two installation programs and the one used depends on the OS you are installing from. Winnt.exe is used if you are installing from a Windows 9x system or from MS-DOS. Winnt32.exe is used to start an installation from a Windows NT or Windows 2000 system. Both Winnt and Winnt32 have a number of switches that can be used to customize the installation. Table 8-1 shows some of the more commonly used options for the Windows 2000 Winnt program, and Table 8-2 shows the available options for the Windows 2000 Winnt32 program.

Table 8-1   Commonly Used Winnt.exe Options

Option	Description
/s:path	Specifies the location of the Windows 2000 installation files
/u:file	Allows you to specify the location of the answer file that is used in unattended installations
/a	Enables accessibility options

Table 8-2   Commonly Used Winnt32.exe Options

Option	Description
/s:path	Specifies the location of the Windows 2000/XP installation files
/checkupgradeonly	Performs a test on a Windows NT system for upgrade compatibility

Note   The Windows NT 4 version of the Winnt program had a switch, /ox, that allowed you to create a set of boot disks from which you could start the installation. Microsoft removed the /ox switch in Windows 2000, probably due to the fact that most PCs now support bootable CDs.

Installation Methods

As we all know, the most common method of installing an operating systems is using the CD or floppy disks and then staring at the wall while waiting for the software to install. For the most part all we must do is boot directly from the CD-ROM and when prompted fill in a few blank spaces. Most of the modern PC systems in use today support the ability to boot from the CD-ROM by simply changing the boot order in the system's BIOS.

If your system doesn't support booting from the CD-ROM, you will need to make a bootable floppy disk with CD-ROM support. You can then start the computer with this boot disk and run the appropriate setup command, Winnt, Winnt32, or Setup.

Installations over the Network

Installing from a CD-ROM is okay if you are installing the OS onto a single computer, but what if you needed to install the same OS to hundreds of computers? That's where you can use the network install. Network installations require more administrative effort than installations using the CD-ROM or floppy disks but are often used in larger networks and where the CD-ROM device is not available.

For a network installation, the installation files must be accessible on the network. In Windows NT/2000/XP, for instance, the I386 folder holds the files you need. These files are typically placed on a network file server. This file server, which is referred to as the distribution server, must be accessible to the client system on which you want to install the OS. From the client computer you can then access the distribution server and the installation files. Those who have performed network installs will certainly know that this is an oversimplified description, but in theory at least, it's this easy.

> **Note**   Running multiple installations over the network can have a negative impact on the perfor-mance of the entire network. Quite often, the best course of action is to perform a network instal-lation during times of slow network usage.

If It Just Won't Install...

Most of the installations you perform are likely to proceed without incident, par-ticularly if you have paid close attention to the pre-installation procedures. How-ever, despite your best efforts, things might still run afoul and you can expect that at some point you will find yourself troubleshooting a failed installation. Table 8-3 outlines some of the installation problems you might encounter and some of their potential solutions.

Table 8-3   **Common Installation Problems and Potential Solutions**

Error	Possible Solution
Corrupted media on CD or floppy	If the files on the CD or the floppy disks cannot be read during the installation, the media might be corrupt. In the case of an OS CD, you can try the CD in a different CD-ROM device. If the problem persists, you might need to obtain a replacement CD from Microsoft. If the floppy disks are the problem, make a new set of installation disks.
OS doesn't recognize the CD-ROM	In the rare occurrence that the CD-ROM device is not recognized, you might need to perform an alternate installation method such as mak-ing boot floppies to start the installation or installing over the network. Alternatively, you can make a boot disk with CD-ROM drivers and boot from the disk, and then run the install commands.
Insufficient hard disk space	OK, let's be honest, if you have done the pre-installation procedures, you will not run into a problem. Still, if you run into a shortage of space, you might need to resize a partition or reformat a partition to allow for the installation.
Windows does not start after installation	If during the install, or after the installation, the OS fails to start, there might be a hardware compatibility problem. Verify that all of your hard-ware is on the Windows HCL. For Windows 2000/XP, you might need to run the winnt32.exe /checkupgradeonly command to list incompat-ible hardware.
Installation keeps freezing part way through	This is sometimes caused by damaged media but also hardware fail-ure. Verify that the hard disk does not have bad sectors or that the memory is not faulty.

Note   Just because you have finished installing the OS doesn't mean you are finished. After the installation, it's time to download and install all of those patches, service packs, and updates. This is an important consideration because such updates are designed to fix bugs in the OS that have appeared since its initial release. Each and every OS has these updates and fortunately they are free for download from the Microsoft Web site.

Upgrading the Operating System

When new operating systems are released, they include many new features and functions you'd probably like to have, so you might choose to upgrade your operating system to the new one. The main benefit of upgrading an operating system, in comparison to performing a new installation, is that when you upgrade you get to keep many of your settings and programs. If you choose not to upgrade, you'll need to start from scratch and recreate all settings and reinstall all programs. In this section, we look at some of the procedures used for upgrading the various operating systems.

General Upgrade Considerations

Before we get into the specific OS upgrades, we thought it a good idea to first review some general upgrade considerations and procedures. Such tips can save not only time and money but a whole lot of unnecessary headaches.

- **Hardware requirements**   Having the software to upgrade your system is one thing, having the hardware to support that software is another. Before performing the upgrade, make sure that the current hardware meets the minimum hardware requirements for the new OS. Pay special attention to hard disk space and memory.

- **Hardware compatibility**   Operating systems have a hardware compatibility list (HCL). The HCL is a list of the hardware tested and proven to work with the OS. If you want the upgrade to go as smoothly as possible, you will want to verify that the hardware works with the new OS. To verify your hardware's compatibility when upgrading to Windows 2000, you can use the **winnt32 /checkupgradeonly** command.

- **Software compatibility**   We all have programs that we rely on and can't do without. Before upgrading the OS, it would be a good idea to verify that these programs will work with the new OS. Windows XP includes a compatibility mode designed to allow you to use legacy programs but it doesn't always work. Better to be safe than sorry!

■   **Backups**   We would be remiss if we did not include a reminder about backups. You might find out that the upgrade did not go as planned and you have lost everything. When performing backups, ensure that both the data and key system files, such as the .ini and registry files, are saved somewhere safe.

■   **Check the disk**   You will want to know that your hard disk is error free and finely tuned before the upgrade process. To ensure this, it is a good idea to run Disk Defragmenter and ScanDisk on the hard disk.

■   **Virus scan**   It is always a good idea to perform a quick virus scan on the system before the upgrade. Afterwards, it is important to disable the virus checker for the upgrade because it can cause an error and halt the system during the upgrade process.

■   **Verify upgradeability**   It might sound obvious, but you might want to ensure that the OS you have can be upgraded to the one you want. For the most part, upgrading within the Windows family is possible with a few exceptions. Windows 3.*x* won't make the leap to Windows 2000 but Windows 9x and Windows NT 4 will.

Test Smart   To upgrade to Windows 2000 from a Windows 3x system, you will first need to upgrade to Windows 98 or 95.

Upgrading Windows 95 to Windows 98

When Windows 98 first came out, it was with great fanfare and almost every-body wanted to see what the big deal was. For those working as PC technicians at the time, it became commonplace to be upgrading those Windows 95 systems to Windows 98.

In most cases, the upgrade from Windows 95 to Windows 98 is straightfor-ward and most likely the easiest upgrade you will be involved with. Windows 98 actually shipped in two versions: one was an upgrade CD and the other was designed for a clean install of Windows 98. To upgrade the Windows 95 system, simply put the Windows 98 upgrade CD in the CD-ROM drive from within Win-dows 95 and, if AutoRun is enabled, you will be asked if you would like to upgrade your system to the newer Windows 98 operating system. If a setup pro-gram did not instantly start when the CD was placed in the CD-ROM drive, you can manually start the upgrade using the Setup.exe program on the CD.

The upgrade from Windows 95 to Windows 98 typically kept all of the set-tings and programs intact, and in addition, most of the drivers used with Win-dows 95 worked with Windows 98. This meant that there was a good chance the hardware and software all worked after the upgrade. This certainly cannot be said of all upgrades.

Upgrading from Windows NT Workstation 4 to Windows 2000

Windows NT Workstation and Windows NT Server served us well for many years, but as technologies such as wireless, remote access, and the like became more commonplace, Windows NT began to show cracks. The release of Windows 2000 was welcomed by system administrators and the advancements it brought provided considerable improvements over its Windows NT counterparts.

For the most part, the upgrade process from Windows NT to Windows 2000 is not very difficult. In our experience, however, while many of the programs carried over, there were many hardware devices that required more attention. Finding drivers for some hardware devices was a challenge in the past, but now it is not so hard. For the most part, the upgrade is straightforward and most configurations such as network settings and users and groups are migrated in the upgrade.

Replacing Windows 9x with Windows 2000/XP

Windows 9x operating systems were most popular in homes and small offices. Windows 9x offers neither the stability nor security of Windows 2000/XP, making it an inappropriate choice for many environments. As a result, many people were dissatisfied with Windows 9x versions and chose the upgrade path to Windows 2000/XP.

Windows 2000/XP and Windows 9x are architecturally very different, making upgrading to Windows 2000/XP more troublesome than other upgrades. Many programs, such as games and utilities, will not work after the upgrade, and you will need to hunt down new device drivers for much of your hardware.

You can run the Windows 2000 setup from within Windows 9x and you will be asked if you would like to upgrade. Choose Yes and the process will begin. Keep in mind, however, that the process is one way. Windows 2000/XP does not have an uninstall feature to return to Windows 9x.

 Test Smart   Upgrading from Windows 9x to Windows 2000/XP is done from within the current operating system. The setup program should begin automatically.

Upgrading to Windows Me

When Windows Me was released, we had two choices: buy the Windows Me upgrade disc designed to upgrade Windows 95 and 98 to Windows Me, or buy an installation CD designed to install Windows Me on a system without an OS. As an added incentive, the upgrade CD was available at a discounted price. With that deal, who wouldn't want to upgrade to Windows Me? It turns out, quite a few.

As with any other upgrade, there are a few considerations before upgrading to Windows Me. The most important step here is to ensure that your hardware is compatible with Windows Me, and that the hardware is up for it. Windows Me has a higher hardware requirement than Windows 95/98, a fact that caught a few upgraders by surprise. One other consideration is that if you have older hardware that requires a DOS driver, you could be in for a surprise, because Windows Me does away with real-mode DOS. This caused problems for a number of software titles.

Note   As a reminder, be sure to get the latest driver software for any scanners, modems, or peripheral devices attached to your computer. To get this information, consult the hardware documentation or visit the manufacturer's Web site.

Upgrade Paths

Windows Me was really designed to replace Windows 95/98 and not much more. To begin with, to upgrade successfully, make sure you have the proper version of Windows Me. If you have Windows 3.x or no previous version of Windows, you will need the Full version. You cannot upgrade from Windows 3.x. Windows 95, 98, and 98 SE users could use the Upgrade version, place the CD in the drive, and the installation should begin automatically.

As an upgrade option from Windows 95/98, Windows Me is a good choice, but Windows Me doesn't have much upgrade use beyond that. Which is to say, it is unlikely that anyone would want to upgrade (downgrade) from Windows 2000/XP to Windows Me. Further, the OSes are architecturally different, so it isn't going to happen.

Upgrading to Windows XP

Backward compatibility with existing software was a key concern for Microsoft during the development for Windows XP, and for that reason, Microsoft assembled a group of application specialists, developers, and project managers to painstakingly test various programs' compatibility with Windows XP. The results of their efforts proved positive for those of us satisfied with our legacy software who don't want to spend the money upgrading software unnecessarily. The bottom line is this: Windows XP Professional is designed to work with both the most current programs and those programs commonly used in days gone by, and yes, this includes games. Such versatility does not bode well for earlier Windows operating systems that made a clear distinction between the two.

Nothing is perfect and while most programs are supported by Windows XP, there are those that are still a bit quirky and do not run smoothly under Windows XP Professional. To use these programs, Windows XP uses different compatibility modes that in effect "trick" the application into believing it is running under its native OS such as Windows 3.*x* or Windows 98. This magic happens in the background, and the user is unaware of it.

Note   If you are purchasing new software for your Windows XP system, look for the XP-Ready logo on the software. This indicates that the software is supported and tested to work with Windows XP.

While Microsoft did their best to accommodate backward software compatibility, there are exceptions. Most of us not only have programs on our systems, we also have *utilities* designed to manage, maintain, and monitor our systems. Unlike programs such as word processors or games, utility programs such as virus checkers or hard disk management utilities work at a deeper level. What this means is that older virus-checking utilities from vendors such as McAfee and Norton might not work with Windows XP. The same holds true for the older disk partitioning, defragmenting, and other such utilities.

Note   Windows XP has a new built-in feature called AppsHelp designed to protect itself from programs that might compromise the system integrity. If you attempt to run such a program, Windows XP will block it.

Windows XP Upgrade Rules

Most newer versions of Windows can be upgraded directly to Windows XP Professional while older Windows versions such as Windows 3.*x*, Windows 95, and Windows NT 3.*x* require some additional considerations. Once the hardware has been verified to meet the minimum recommended requirements and once the hardware has been verified with the HCL, you can begin the upgrade process. Table 8-4 summarizes the upgrade requirements for the various Windows platforms.

Table 8-4   Windows XP Upgrade Requirements

Operating System	Upgrade
Windows 95	Upgrade to Windows 98, and then to Windows XP Professional
Windows 98	Upgrade directly to Windows XP Professional
Windows Me	Upgrade directly to Windows XP Professional
Windows NT 3.*x*	Upgrade to Windows NT Workstation first, and then to Windows XP Professional
Windows NT Workstation 4	Upgrade directly to Windows XP Professional
Windows 2000 Professional	Upgrade directly to Windows XP Professional

Dual-Booting Windows

In a dual-boot configuration, the computer system has two working operating systems and, during the boot process, you will be able to decide which of the operating systems you will boot into. In a dual operating system configuration, the operating systems are completely separate and will each need their own configuration and programs installed.

Wherever possible, it is recommended that each of the operating systems be installed in a separate partition but this is not always possible. When using a dual-boot configuration, you will have to be mindful of the file systems you are using. For example, if you are booting with a Windows 98 machine using FAT32 and you have Windows 2000 installed using NTFS, you will be able to boot into Windows 98 but will not be able to see the NTFS partition. Windows 2000 will, however, be able to recognize the FAT32 partition.

Where installing operating systems in separate partitions is not possible, they can be placed on the same partition. The rules for which operating systems can be installed together are dictated by the file system supported by the OS. For example, you can install Windows NT to dual-boot with Windows 2000, but only using the FAT16 file system, because Windows NT does not support FAT32 and the NTFS versions used with the two are different. Similarly, you can dual-boot with Windows 2000 and Windows 98 in the same partition, but only using the FAT32 or FAT16 file system.

 Test Smart   For the A+ exam, be aware of the file system restrictions for dual-booting operating systems. If you are dual-booting and cannot see the other OS, it is likely that the file system is not recognized. File system compatibility was covered in Chapter 7.

Giving the OS the Boot

Most of the time, your systems will boot without incident and you will be gently guided into the comforting glow of your familiar desktop. Unfortunately, no OS is bulletproof and at some point they will stubbornly refuse to boot. In such cases, PC technicians must have an understanding of what is happening during the boot process to help isolate the problem, and they must have a knowledge of the tools and procedures to use to try to get back to that desktop.

Windows versions have different boot procedures, boot files, and methods for repairing the system. In this section, we look at some of the things you can do in Windows 9x and Windows 2000 systems to get the system back up and running.

Windows 9x

Though many of the Windows 9x systems have now been upgraded and new computers are no longer shipping with Windows 9x versions, there are still countless computers out there in many different environments. What this means is that there are plenty of Windows 9x systems out there that you will be called upon to support. With that in mind, you need to know the fundamentals of the Windows 9x boot process.

Startup Disk

One utility you will find yourself using often when working on Windows 9x systems is the startup disk. These startup disks are a must-have when trying to troubleshoot a failed Windows 9x system, and fortunately they are not difficult to make. The procedure for making a startup disk in Windows 9x systems is as follows:

1   Click the Start button, point to Settings, and then click Control Panel.

2   Select Add/Remove Programs in Control Panel to open the Add/Remove Programs Properties dialog box.

3   In the Add/Remove Programs Properties dialog box, select the Startup Disk tab, as shown in Figure 8-4. Click the Create Disk button to create the Windows 9x startup disk.

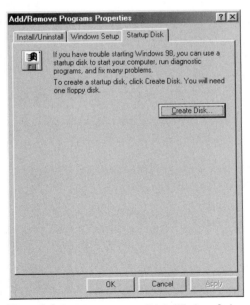

Figure 8-4 Creating a startup disk in Windows 9x is a simple process.

One thing we should point out is that Windows 95 does not include CD-ROM drivers on the startup disk. This is a real nuisance if you need access to the CD-ROM drive, which is where the Windows 95 CD actually is. To get around this limitation, you have to manually modify the Windows 95 boot disk to include the support for the CD-ROM drive. Mscdex.exe is the primary driver that enables CD-ROM support. The Mscdex.exe file is referenced in the Autoexec.bat file and will then be loaded automatically in the boot process.

 Test Smart   Mscdex is the driver used to enable CD-ROM support and is referenced in the Autoexec.bat file.

The startup disk you make in Windows 98 has no such limitations and will be created with CD-ROM drivers. Of course, you can also boot directly from the Windows 98 CD, making the boot disk unnecessary. You can also, if need be, use the boot disk created within Windows 98 to boot a Windows 95 system.

Now that we have outlined the graphical way to create the boot disk, we should point out that it can also be done from the command line using the familiar Format command. The correct syntax is *format a: /s*. The /s switch signifies that the system files are to be copied to the floppy disk. When the switch is not used it will just perform a regular format on the disk.

It is probably most common to make a bootable system disk using the Format command but it can also be done using the Sys command. If a floppy drive or a hard disk has already been formatted, you can make it bootable using the Sys command. Once the Sys command is issued, the Io.sys, Msdos.sys, and Command.com files are transferred to the disk and it will be bootable.

 Test Smart   Both the Format and Sys commands can be used to make a floppy disk bootable.

Windows 9x Boot Modes

In a perfect world, our Windows 9x systems would boot into normal operation each time we need them to. While this is most often the case, you can certainly expect at some point to be managing a system that simply will not boot. In such a case, you have a variety of boot modes to choose from to try to get back into the system. Two of the primary boot options are safe mode and MS-DOS mode.

Safe Mode

Safe mode is truly one of the best friends of anyone supporting a Windows 9x system. It is not that uncommon in the Windows 9x world to have something go wrong with the system that keeps it from booting. This is often caused by a virus, the installation of a new program, or the addition of new hardware and drivers. To access Safe Mode and the other boot modes, press F8 during system startup.

By booting into safe mode, you are booting into Windows loading only necessary device drivers. This means that only the device drivers for the keyboard, mouse, and VGA display are loaded. If the cause of the system failure is not hardware related, the system should boot by bypassing most of the files at startup. As you can guess, you will not have the same system functionality in safe mode that you enjoy in normal mode. For instance, you will not be able to access those devices you have come to rely on such as the CD-ROM, network, and other peripheral devices.

Once you are in safe mode you can begin to look around for whatever is causing the system not to boot. Any recent changes to the system, such as the addition of software or driver changes, might be at the root of your problems. You will know that you are in safe mode because the words *Safe Mode* will appear in every corner of the display.

Note Safe mode does not load the Config.sys and Autoexec.bat files.

MS-DOS Mode

Booting into MS-DOS mode was once a very popular option. When you boot into MS-DOS mode, only those drivers needed to get DOS going are loaded, including the Config.sys and Autoexec.bat files. MS-DOS mode was often used for troubleshooting by those familiar with DOS, and some early games required the system to use MS-DOS mode.

No Mouse—No Problem When you boot into safe mode, or when the mouse isn't working, you might find yourself sitting at a screen wondering how to move the cursor. Seasoned IT veterans wouldn't even wince at such an occurrence, but those who have grown attached to the mouse might have more trouble. The good news is that even without the assistance of the mouse, you can still navigate through the Windows graphical interface. All you need is a keyboard and a whole lot of patience.

The basic keys used in keyboard navigation are the Tab key, which can be used to move around between elements on the page or buttons in a dialog box, and the arrow keys, which can be used to move between icons on the desktop. The Alt+Tab combination also allows you to switch between running programs.

If your keyboard has a Windows Start key, great. If not, you can bring up the Start menu by pressing Ctrl+Esc. You can then navigate the menus with the arrow keys.

Finally, the Alt+F4 combination is particularly useful because it can be used to close programs, and if you are at the desktop, it also brings up the Windows Shutdown dialog box.

Other Windows 9x Boot Options

While safe mode and MS-DOS mode are two of the more common boot options, there are a few other ones you need to be aware of for the A+ exam. Table 8-5 shows the different boot options for Windows 9x systems.

Table 8-5   Boot Options for Windows 9x

Boot Option	Function
Logged Mode	Windows will try to load normally and then create a log file of the boot activities. The log file is named Bootlog.txt.
Safe Mode With Networking	This works much the same way as the Safe Mode boot option; however, the network drivers are loaded, providing you with access to the network.
Step-By-Step Confirmation	The step-by-step feature allows you to say yes or no to the loading of each device specified in the Autoexec.bat and Config.sys files.
Command Prompt Only	This option is sometimes used when the system will not even get into safe mode. This option gets you to a command prompt.

Windows NT and Windows 2000/XP

In the Windows operating system world, Windows NT, Windows 2000, and the more recent Windows XP are the OS workhorses. They are designed with reliability in mind, but even the most robust operating systems will have their times of failure. In this section, we look at some of the key files in Windows NT and Windows 2000/XP and some basic procedures to follow when the system won't start.

Startup Disk

One of the things a PC technician should have on hand or at least be able to make in a hurry is a start-up disk. The process of making startup disks is not complicated, at least not after you've done it a few times. There are two primary ways of making a startup disk, one for Windows NT and one for Windows 2000/XP.

In Windows NT, the most common method of making the startup disk is to format a floppy in Windows NT and then manually copy the boot files onto the floppy disk. The files you will need to copy include Ntldr, Boot.ini, and Ntdetect.com. This startup disk is the first step in getting back into your system.

 Test Smart   When making a boot disk with Windows NT, ensure that you copy the three files, Ntldr, Ntdetect.com, and Boot.ini.

Another option you have is to re-create the Windows installation disks. In Windows 2000, four installation disks are required to boot the machine. Disk sets can be created with the Makeboot command. The Makeboot command is located on the Windows 2000 CD.

When a system is booted using these disks, you will have the option to attempt to repair a Windows 2000 installation. This is done by using an automated emergency repair process or by using the Recovery Console. The Recovery Console is a feature that allows you to access the system's hard drive and perform commands to attempt to correct the problem.

Test Smart   Windows NT 4 boot files are hidden; to access them, you will need to use the Attrib command at a command prompt.

Windows NT 4 and Windows 2000/XP Boot Options

In most cases, your operating system will boot in normal mode and all drivers and programs will be loaded and installed with no problem. However, there will be those times when the system will refuse to boot. Fortunately, Windows NT and Windows 2000/XP have numerous boot-up options that can help you get back into your system. As a PC technician, you will definitely need to know the different boot options and how these are used to get back into the OS.

Windows 2000/XP Boot Options

Windows 2000/XP offers numerous recovery options. If you have a Windows 2000/XP system that has failed to start, these might become your best friend. Press F8 during the boot-up process to access the Windows 2000/xp recovery boot options. These options are

- **Safe Mode**   Similar to safe mode in Windows 95/98, this safe mode starts the system with minimal files and drivers, including those for mice, keyboard, base video, and mass storage. If the system fails to start in safe mode, your next step is likely to be using an Emergency Repair Disk.

- **Safe Mode With Networking**   This option starts the system with minimal drivers, as with safe mode, but includes network connections.

- **Safe Mode Command Prompt**   Things are not looking promising if you are using this option. This option starts the system with minimal drivers and goes directly to a command prompt, not to the Windows desktop.

- **Enable Boot Logging**   When you're booting into Windows, this option logs the services and drivers that were loaded on startup. To help determine the exact cause of the boot problem, you can review the log. The log is named Ntbtlog.txt and is located in the C:\Winnt directory by default.

- **Enable VGA Mode** Similar to the VGA mode available in Windows NT, this option starts Windows with a basic VGA driver.

- **Last Known Good Configuration** When this option is used, the system attempts to start by using the information saved when Windows was last shut down.

- **Directory Services Restore Mode** Used only on Windows 2000 domain controllers, this option attempts to restore the Active Directory service on a domain controller.

- **Recovery Console** The Recovery Console is new to Windows 2000, and for those of you who like to work from the command line, this one's for you. Using the Recovery Console, you can do administrative tasks such as start and stop services or format disks. The Recovery Console is used primarily to recover from a failed computer. If the computer refuses to boot, you can start the Recovery Console from the Windows 2000 setup disks, from the Windows 2000 CD, or from the system itself if the utility is installed. If the Recovery Console is installed, it will appear as a boot option in the start-up menu screen. With this utility taking up only 7 MB of space, it's worthwhile to have it installed. To install the Recovery Console, refer to the help files accompanying Windows 2000. The basic procedure is to access the Windows 2000 CD, go into the i386 file folder, and type **Winnt32.exe /cmdcons**.

Test Smart To access the different boot options for Windows 2000, you need to press the F8 key when prompted during the boot process.

Windows NT 4 Boot Options

While Windows NT 4 does not offer as many boot options as does Windows 2000, there are some key ones that can be lifesavers in getting you back into the system.

- **Last Known Good Configuration** If you change the configuration of your Windows NT system or install a piece of hardware that prevents the system from booting correctly, all is not lost. Among its other recovery tools, Windows NT provides the Last Known Good Configuration option, though it is perhaps less effective than it could be.

Essentially, every time you manage to boot the server successfully, a copy of the most recent successful boot information is stored. The theory is that the next time you reboot, if the server has trouble booting, you can elect to use the Last Known Good Configuration—the configuration information from the last time you successfully booted. This strategy does have some practical uses, such as recovering from a severe device driver problem that prevents a system from booting, or finding that an essential driver is accidentally disabled and thus preventing the server from starting. The Last Known Good Configuration option is no good at recovering from corrupt or missing files or drivers.

■ **Windows NT VGA Mode**   Video-related problems seem to appear with some frequency. Whether a result of a failed video adapter, a wrong driver, or a screen resolution that corrupts the display, the result is the same: an unreadable or blank monitor. If this happens along with the regular boot option, Window NT provides a workaround solution: the ability to boot into standard VGA mode. When VGA mode is selected, a standard video driver will be used, giving you access to the screen, even if it is only in 16-bit color. It might be ugly, but you will most definitely be glad to see it.

Files Required to Boot

Although an in-depth knowledge of the Windows NT and Windows 2000 boot process is not necessary, a general understanding of the boot process can help you troubleshoot errors. Windows NT and Windows 2000 uses only a handful of files in their boot process, so when things go wrong, it is not too hard to find the problem. The following is a quick summary of the Windows NT and Windows 2000 boot files for an Intel-based system:

■ **Ntldr**   The Ntldr program performs a range of tasks including the initialization of file system drivers and the inspection of the Boot.ini file (discussed next). If Windows NT or Windows 2000 is the chosen operating system, Ntldr also loads the OS kernel into memory.

■ **Boot.ini**   The Ntldr program reads the Boot.ini file to search for the location of available operating systems. If you have multiple operating systems installed, you can modify this text file to determine boot options for the system. For example, you can set which OS will boot by default.

■ **Bootsect.dos**   This file holds the boot sector information of any other operating systems that are loaded on the system.

- **Ntdetect.com**   The Ntdetect.com file detects hardware and builds a hardware list.

- **Ntbootdd.sys**   This file is used only when the server boots from a SCSI device that does not have a BIOS installed.

Test Smart   Only three of these files are actually needed to boot the system, Ntldr, Boot.ini, and Ntdetect.com. Be sure you can identify the function of each of these files before taking the test.

Creating an Emergency Repair Disk

Perhaps the last step in the Windows NT installation is to make a recovery disk. The recovery disk holds the default information that can be used to recover Windows NT if it becomes corrupt or damaged. Recovery disks can be made from the Windows NT command prompt with the Rdisk.exe command, and they should be made periodically to keep the information on the disk as current as possible. The data on the disk is a backup of key registry files, including system, security, account information, and software configurations. Because the Windows NT Emergency Repair Disk (ERD) holds registry and security information, it should be treated with the same security considerations as a tape backup. Rdisk will back up security information only if you are logged on with administrator permissions and if Rdisk is used with the /s option.

Test Smart   Rdisk is used to create Emergency Repair Disks in Windows NT.

Recovery disks for Windows 2000 are no less important than those for Windows NT 4, and they should be made after the installation as well as after any changes in the hard-disk partition information. In Windows 2000, the Emergency Repair Disk utility is found within the Backup utility—who knows why that is? Rdisk does not work in Windows 2000 as it did with Windows NT.

Windows XP and the ERD

As mentioned with Windows NT 4 and 2000, an Emergency Repair Disk (ERD) could be used to attempt to repair a damaged system. With Windows XP, the ERD is gone and has been replaced with Automated System Recovery (ASR). ASR is an advanced tool designed to repair a damaged system and is often the last resort when other methods such as Safe Mode, Last Known Good Configuration, and Recovery Console have been unable to restore our systems.

There are two components needed to create an ASR backup. The first component is the actual backup of the data and files and the second is the creation of a floppy disk required to restore the system to its original state. The ASR Wizard will guide you through the process of creating both of these components. Like the Windows 2000 ERD disk, the ASR Wizard can be started from the Windows XP backup utility.

System Recovery and Restore Using ASR   Once the Windows XP backup utility has been used to create the ASR, if the system were to fail in the future, the system can be recovered from the time when the ASR backup was created. To restore the system state using the ASR, follow these steps:

1   Boot from the Windows XP Professional CD-ROM.

2   When prompted, press F2 to begin the ASR recovery process.

3   Insert your most recent ASR floppy disk in the drive when prompted.

4   Insert the backup data when prompted.

5   Follow the onscreen instructions to complete the installation.

Note   ASR is not a utility designed to be used for backing up or restoring data.

Windows XP Restore Points

In the case of a corrupt system, there is a new feature in Windows XP that might be able to get you back on your feet in a hurry, the System Restore feature. The System Restore Wizard is used to return a corrupt system to a point where it was once working and does so without losing user data such as document files, e-mail settings, or Internet favorites. To return the system to a previous state, you must load *restore points,* which are essentially saved system configurations.

These restore points are made automatically by Windows XP either daily or when a significant change occurs to the system such as the installation of a new driver. You can also create restore points manually using the System Restore Wizard. This is often done before making major changes to your system to give you a point to return to if things do not go as planned. To access the System Restore Wizard, click Start, All Programs, Accessories, System Tools, and select System Restore from the list.

Note   You can turn the System Restore feature on and configure the disk space it uses from the System Restore tab in the System utility.

 Test Smart   When trying to recover a system, you should try to use the System Restore feature first before using the ASR.

Installing Device Drivers

When you add a new hardware device to a Windows 9x or Windows 2000/XP system, Plug and Play will (normally) automatically detect the device and install the appropriate drivers. If the system doesn't have suitable drivers for the device, it will prompt you to supply them. You should always bear in mind that even if Windows does have a driver for the device, it might not be the latest driver available. If you have not checked for new drivers, let Windows install the device and then check the manufacturer's Web site for the latest drivers. You can then update them as described in the next section, "Updating Drivers."

 Test Smart   When installing a new hardware device, you should always make sure that you have the latest drivers for the device.

Although Plug and Play is an increasingly reliable system, it is still relatively complex and requires that the operating system, the BIOS, the drivers, and the peripheral itself are all in agreement as to what the device being installed is, and how it should be installed. As you can imagine, there are times when all of the four *moons* are not in alignment, and that's when you need to install devices manually. Fortunately, that's not very difficult either.

Note   As we have discussed, Windows NT 4 does not support Plug and Play. Therefore, if you add devices to the system, you must install the drivers and configure the devices manually.

If you add new hardware and it is not automatically detected by the system, you can force the system to try to recognize it by using the Add New Hardware Wizard, accessible through the Control Panel. Alternatively, with the Add New Hardware Wizard you can also manually specify a device and load drivers. If you are adding new devices that are not plug and play, this is the method you will need to use.

Updating Drivers

You should check on a regular basis to determine whether there are new device drivers available for your system. If there are, you can download them and install them using the Update Drivers feature, which can be accessed from the device's properties dialog box in Device Manager.

Rollback Drivers

New to Windows XP is the driver rollback feature. This feature is a useful addition to Windows XP because even though new drivers are intended to improve the performance of a system or correct a problem, that's not always the case. Sometimes new drivers cause more problems than they fix. Fortunately, with the driver rollback feature, it's possible to easily revert to the previous driver and at least get back to where you were before the drivers were updated. To use the driver rollback feature, from Device Manager, right-click on the hardware device concerned to open its properties dialog box. Click the Driver tab, and then click the Roll Back Driver button.

Installing and Running Programs

Although Windows operating systems offer a basic range of programs like Word-Pad and Paint, the limited nature of these programs makes it extremely unusual to find a PC that does not have additional programs installed. In many cases, as a PC technician, it will be you who is called upon to install programs.

Installing Additional Windows Components

When you install Windows, it is unlikely that you will install all of the programs that come with the OS. Because of this, and the realization that you are likely to want to install additional Windows programs at a later date, Microsoft has made it simple to install additional Windows components. In Windows 9x and Windows NT 4, simply open Add/Remove Programs in Control Panel and select the Windows Setup tab. On a Windows 2000/XP system, open Add/Remove Programs in Control Panel, then select Add/Remove Windows Components from the menu bar on the left. This will start the Windows Components Wizard, through which you can add or remove Windows components and programs. You can see the Windows Components Wizard in Figure 8-5.

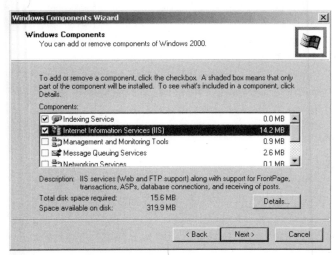

Figure 8-5 In Windows 2000, Windows components are added or removed through the Windows Components Wizard.

Test Smart   Windows components are added through the Add/Remove Programs utility in Control Panel in both Windows 9x and Windows NT 4 or Windows 2000/XP.

Installing Third-Party Programs

Third-party programs—that is, software not supplied by Microsoft (or yourself)—are generally as easy to install as inserting a CD into a drive, thanks to the AutoRun feature, which automatically starts the CD when inserted. Even if a program doesn't have AutoRun, you can still expect it to be no harder than double-clicking a setup program and following a wizard.

> **Note**   You can install a program through the Add/Remove Programs utility if you want to, but you will still need to specify the path to the setup file. It's probably easier just to run the setup file from its location.

In terms of what to consider when installing a program, there are really only two things:

■ **System requirements**   All programs will state what the minimum hardware requirements are for running the program. They will also tell you how much disk space will be required. Be sure that your system meets these specifications before starting your install.

■ **Program associations**   When you double-click on a file in Windows, the program that is started to show or work with the file is defined by program associations. For example, double-click a file with a .txt extension. Windows, by default, will start Notepad. It's the same thing with .bmp files and Paint. When you install a new program, it will often lay claim to files with a certain extension (in some cases without warning). If you are OK with this new association, fine. If not, you can normally reclaim file associations from within the program. Figure 8-6 shows the File Types tab of the Folder Options dialog box.

Test Smart   Before installing a program, it's a good idea to back up the system. That way, if the installation fails and you run into problems, you can restore the system to its previous state.

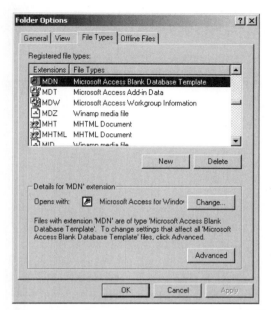

Figure 8-6 You can configure file associations through Windows Explorer.

Running DOS Programs   Even though Windows has been with us for many years, you might still find yourself working with DOS programs. This is normally because the program is one that has been used for many years, and the user has not upgraded to a Windows version or a Windows version is not available.

Working with DOS programs is relatively straightforward in that you can still create a shortcut to the program on the Windows desktop, but when you double-click the shortcut, it opens the program (or a batch file that starts the program) in a DOS window.

The only other thing you might need to consider is printing, which can be an issue because the DOS program will not understand the normal method of printing in Windows. In this case, it will be necessary to redirect or capture the printer port to the printer.

Uninstalling Programs

Most Windows programs now come with an uninstall feature, and simply running the utility will cause the program to be uninstalled. Alternatively, you can remove programs using Add/Remove Programs in Control Panel.

After you have run the uninstall program, you might find that icons and menu entries for the program still exist. This is because sometimes the system requires a reboot before it is able to completely remove the program. After a restart, you should find that all traces of the program have been removed.

Test Smart   Often, you will need to reboot the system in order to completely uninstall a program.

Installing and Configuring Printing

Chances are very high that each and every PC you work on will either have a printer attached to it, or it will connect to a printer over a network. For this reason, it is very important to understand how to set up, configure, and work with printing.

Installing a Printer

With each version of the Microsoft operating system, Microsoft has made it easier and easier to install a printer. In the latest versions of Windows, it is simply a case of running a wizard. During the printer installation, you might or might not need to supply printer drivers. Windows ships with a wide range of drivers, though you should not assume that these are up-to-date.

Windows 9x and Windows NT/2000 have an Add Printer Wizard that will take you through the process of adding a printer to the system. There are four basic steps to the process. First, you must specify whether the printer is a local (directly attached to the system) or a network printer. If the printer is local, you can ask Windows to automatically install the printer using Plug and Play. If the printer is local, and you choose to install it manually, you must specify the port to which the printer is attached. For a network printer, you need to supply the path to the printer (its UNC), or you can choose to browse the network to locate the printer. You can also connect to a printer on your intranet or the Internet by providing its URL. If the printer is local, and you choose not to let Windows install it automatically, you must then select a make and model of the printer. If you have new printer drivers on a CD or from the Internet, you can click Have Disk and use the latest drivers. If you are connecting to a network printer, the need for printer drivers will depend on what platform you are connecting to.

Do You Have the Right Drivers?   In printing, as with just about anything else, having the right driver makes all the difference. Using the wrong printer driver can result in a number of errors such as blank pages being printed, garbled text, or hieroglyphic codes being displayed on the pages. In other less dramatic cases, it might be that you can print correctly but that certain features of the printer are unavailable or do not work correctly. A good example of this is drivers for laser printers, many of which are cross compatible as far as basic printing of documents goes, but features like double-sided printing or tray selection might not be available. Bottom line—always make sure that you are using the correct printer driver for the printer and also ensure that you have the latest version of the driver by checking on the manufacturer's Web site.

Managing Printing

With printing installed and working correctly, hopefully management of printing tasks will be infrequent. Even so, expect to be managing printers on a regular basis.

Managing Jobs in the Queue   When print jobs are sent to the printer, they are placed in a print queue. In reality, they are actually stored as files in a special directory called a spooler—more about that in a minute.

Once in the queue, print jobs can be paused, resumed, and cancelled. All of these functions are performed through a screen that is accessed by double-clicking the printer in the Printers folder. Figure 8-7 shows print jobs in the print queue and a Cancel task being performed.

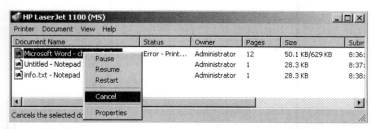

Figure 8-7 Print jobs can be can be paused, resumed, and cancelled while in the print queue.

In Windows 98 anyone can delete a print job from the print queue, but in Windows 2000/XP, only users with special privileges can control print jobs in the queue.

Managing the Spooler   The spooler is the name given to an area of disk space in which print jobs are stored before being sent to the printer. Spooling allows you to send multiple jobs to the printer at one time and have them print when the printer is free to do so. It's a great system, but it does have its considerations.

■ **The spooler uses space.**   Print jobs in the spooler are stored as files, and the files take up space on the hard disk. Today's highly graphical programs can create very large print files that can fill up a hard disk in a hurry if there is not enough room. For example, you might think that 100 MB of free space on a hard drive is plenty. Send three or four large print jobs and you will fill that space in short order. Running out of space due to the spooler will at best give you a printing error, and at

worst crash your system. Be sure that you have enough space available
to accommodate print requirements.

■ **Files in the spooler can become corrupt.**   Sometimes, a print job
in the spooler can become corrupted, causing pages to be printed in
garbled text and even blank pages to be spit out by the printer. If your
printer was working fine, but becomes flaky on a single job, the spool
file has probably become corrupted. Try printing the job again—if it
prints OK, the problems with the print spool might have been an isolated incident. If you find that you are continually experiencing problems, you might have to delve deeper into the problem.

If you would rather not, you don't have to use the spooler and
instead can print directly to the printer. Doing so circumvents the
spooling process and eliminates any problems caused by it, but it also
means that you will only be able to send a print job to the printer when
it is not busy. It will also mean that your program will be unavailable
until the print job has been completed. As you can imagine, this is
probably not ideal, so it is very uncommon not to use spooling.

If you do want to disable spooling, you can do it from the
Advanced tab of the properties dialog for a given printer. You can see
an example of a printer's Advanced tab in Figure 8-8.

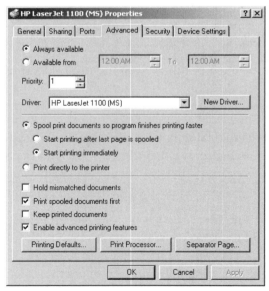

Figure 8-8 If necessary, you can choose to bypass the spooler by selecting Print Directly To The
Printer.

Note As we have already discussed, Windows NT 4 and Windows 2000 use a different architecture than Windows 9x. One of the major differences in the architecture is that Windows NT and Windows 2000 use services for system functions. One of these is the Spooler service, which can be stopped and restarted as necessary. If you are having printing problems in Windows NT or Windows 2000, stopping and restarting the spooler can often allow printing to restart automatically, or at the very least allow you to remove a print job that is stuck in the queue.

Setting the Default Printer Because Windows allows you to have more than one printer installed, it also provides a mechanism to assign a printer as the default. The default printer is used either when programs provide a quick link to printing, like a Print toolbar button, or when you are printing from a program that does not have a printer selection screen, like some versions of Notepad.

To configure the default printer, follow these steps:

1 Open the Printers folder either from the Start menu or Control Panel.

2 Select the printer you want to make the default. From the File menu, select Set As Default Printer or right-click and select Set As Default Printer. A small black circle with a check mark should appear next to the printer.

Figure 8-9 shows the Printers folder with a default printer assigned.

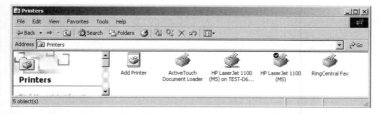

Figure 8-9 The default printer is denoted by a small circle with a check mark in it.

If you choose to delete the default printer, Windows will give you a message notifying you of the fact and then automatically set another printer as the default. If you only have one printer defined and you delete it, the system will notify you that there are no other printers installed, and thus there is no default printer.

 Test Smart Deleting the default printer will cause the system to select another printer as the default.

Network Printing

Printers are a commonly shared network resource on both home and business networks, sometimes to centralize print jobs and other times simply to save on the cost of owning multiple printers. The popularity of networking printers means that you as a PC technician will become well acquainted with configuring (and troubleshooting) network printers on a regular basis.

See Also   *For more information on sharing printers on the network, refer to Chapter 5.*

Connecting to a Printer in Windows 95/98   In a workgroup setting, it's very common for a printer to be shared from a Windows 9x system. Even in a server-based network, a departmental printer often will be shared from a Windows 9x system, allowing the printer to be close to the people who use it.

There are a number of ways to connect to a printer hosted on a Windows 9x system.

1   Use the Add Printer Wizard in the Printers folder of Control Panel.

2   Using Network Neighborhood, locate the printer, and then right-click the printer and select Capture.

3   From the command prompt, type the command **net use lptx:** **\\\server\printername** (where *x* is the number of the LPT port you wish to capture).

The last of these commands is particularly useful because it can be placed into batch files, which are used to start DOS programs. Also, creating batch files can give nontechnical users a simple way to connect to infrequently used printers. It should be noted, though, that connecting to a printer from a command prompt does not require that you specify printer drivers, and so on. You must rely on the program to specify the correct drivers for the device or you might experience problems.

Connecting to a Printer in Windows NT 4 or Windows 2000/XP

Windows NT/2000 has an advanced printing subsystem that makes it an ideal candidate for use as a network print server. Windows 2000 can act as the print server for printers attached directly to the system, or for network-attached printers. You can attach to a printer on a Windows NT 4 or Windows 2000 system in the same way as the three steps just described in the Windows 9x section.

One particularly useful advantage of connecting to a printer hosted on a Windows 2000 or Windows NT 4 system is that it's possible to load the printer drivers for the client operating systems on the server. When a client connects to the server and chooses to use a network printer, the printer drivers are automatically downloaded to the client. In an environment with many systems, this is a particularly timesaving feature because it allows printer drivers to be managed and updated centrally.

Key Points

- If you have a bootable CD in the CD-ROM drive and the system halts with a "no operating system found" error message, ensure that the BIOS is set to boot from the CD.

- New hard disks must be partitioned before they can be formatted and used by the operating system.

- If a hard disk is partitioned into two or more parts, it gives the appearance of having more than a single physical drive.

- To be able to boot from the hard disk, you must have at least one primary partition because this partition stores the operating system and is the one you actually boot from.

- Fdisk is a utility used in Windows 9x systems to partition the disk.

- Primary partitions are bootable, whereas logical partitions are not.

- The Fdisk utility can be used with the /mbr switch to repair a damaged master boot record.

- The Windows 2000 Disk Management utility is a graphical utility that allows you to fully configure the partitions on your system.

- After creating the partitions on the hard disk, the partitions must be formatted before they can be used by the operating system.

- The formatting of a drive can be done from the command line using the Format utility.

- To manually start the installation of a Windows 9x OS the Setup command is used.

- Winnt.exe and Winnt32.exe are used to install Windows NT and Windows 2000.

- Windows 3x cannot be directly upgraded to Windows 2000.

■ In a dual operating system configuration, the operating systems are separate and will each need their own configuration and programs installed.

■ Windows 95 does not include CD-ROM drivers on the startup disk.

■ The primary program used to enable CD-ROM support is the Mscdex driver.

■ If a floppy disk or a hard disk has already been formatted, we can make it bootable using the Sys command.

■ Windows systems include a safe mode that loads minimal drivers to attempt to get into a damaged system.

■ When making a boot disk with Windows NT, ensure that you copy the three files, Ntldr, Ntdetect.com, and Boot.ini.

■ The Windows 2000 Recovery Console is a feature that allows you to access the system's hard drive and perform commands to attempt to correct the problem.

■ In Windows NT, Emergency Repair Disks are made using the Rdisk.exe command.

■ In Windows 2000, the Emergency Repair Disks are made using the Backup utility.

■ You can add or remove Windows components using Add/Remove Programs in Control Panel.

■ The default printer is the one that print jobs will be sent to unless you specify otherwise in the program.

■ Spooling allows the system to print in the background, but it requires disk space and system resources.

Chapter Review Questions

1   You have a Windows 98 system that uses FAT32. You decide to install Windows NT 4 into a dual-boot environment on a partition that uses NTFS. What will the result be? (Choose two.)

a)   Windows 98 will be able to access the FAT32 partition but not the NTFS partition.

b)   Windows 98 will be able to access both partitions.

c)   Windows NT will be able to access both partitions.

d)   Windows NT will be able to access the NTFS partition but not the FAT32 partition.

Answers a and d are correct. Windows 98 can read FAT32 partitions, but not NTFS partitions. Windows NT can access NTFS partitions but not FAT32 partitions. Answers b and c are incorrect.

2   Which of the following operating systems is not directly upgradeable to Windows XP?

a)   Windows 95

b)   Windows 98 SE

c)   Windows 2000

d)   Windows Me

Answer a is correct. Windows 95 does not directly upgrade to Windows XP. Instead, it must first be upgraded to Windows 98. All of the other answers are operating systems that can be directly upgraded to Windows XP.

3   You are working for a marketing company that has over 100 PCs. Some of the PCs are running Windows 98, and the remainder are running Windows NT 4. You decide to upgrade all of the systems to Windows 2000. Which of the following statements is correct about the upgrade process?

a)   The Windows 98 systems can be upgraded directly to Windows 2000.

b)   The Windows NT 4 systems can be upgraded directly to Windows 2000.

c)   The Windows 98 systems must be upgraded to NT 4, then they can be upgraded to Windows 2000.

d)   The Windows 98 systems must be upgraded to Windows Me, then they can be upgraded to Windows 2000.

Answers a and b are correct. Both Windows 98 and Windows NT 4 are directly upgradeable to Windows 2000. Answer c is incorrect. Windows 98 systems cannot actually be upgraded to Windows NT 4. Answer d is incorrect. Windows 98 can be upgraded directly to Windows 2000.

4   You want to create a boot disk for Windows NT 4. After formatting the disk, which of the following files must you copy to the disk?

a)   Ntoskernel.exe

b)   Boot.ini

c)   Ntldr

d)   Ntdetect.com

e)   Bootsect.dos

Answers b, c, and d are correct. After formatting the disk, you need to copy the Boot.ini, Ntldr, and Ntdetect.com files to the disk. Answers a and e are incorrect.

5   You are troubleshooting a Windows NT 4 system that won't boot. What should your first troubleshooting step be?

a)   Use the Recovery Console.

b)   Use the Last Known Good Configuration.

c)   Use a boot disk.

d)   Reinstall the OS.

Answer b is correct. When troubleshooting a Windows NT 4 system that won't boot, your first troubleshooting step should be to use the Last Known Good Configuration. Answer a is incorrect. The Recovery Console is a feature of Windows 2000, not Windows NT 4. Answer c is incorrect. Although you could try a boot disk, the most obvious choice is to use the Last Known Good Configuration. Answer d is incorrect. Reinstalling the OS should be considered a last-resort troubleshooting step.

6   While troubleshooting an error in Windows 95, you decide to boot into safe mode. What will the video mode be?

a)   VGA, 600×800

b)   VGA, 640×480

c)   VGA, 1024×768

d)   XGA, 1024×768

Answer b is correct. When using safe mode, video is displayed in Standard VGA (640×480). All of the other answers are incorrect.

7   A user calls to report that she is having problems with printing. Each time she hits the print shortcut in her program, the print job comes out on the wrong printer. Where would you direct her to go to correct the problem?

a)   Control Panel, Printers, Properties, Spool Setting

b)   Control Panel, Printers

c)   Control Panel, Printers, File

d)   Control Panel, System, Printers

Answer b is correct. The problem being described sounds like an issue with the default printer. The default printer assignment is made from the Printers folder in Control Panel. All of the other answers are incorrect.

8   Which of the following commands would you use to format the D: drive?

a)   format /drive=c:

b)   fdisk d:

c)   format d:

d)   format d: /mbr

Answer c is correct. The drive letter is appended to the Format command to indicate which drive to format. Answer a is incorrect. The only required switch for the Format command is the drive letter. Answer b is incorrect. The Fdisk command is used for creating and deleting partitions, not formatting them. Answer d is incorrect. The /mbr switch is used with the Fdisk command, not the Format command.

9   While running Fdisk, you are asked if you would like to enable large disk support on the disk. What will the result be if you answer Yes to the question?

a)   The file table will be created using NTFS.

b)   The file table will be created using FAT.

c)   The file table will be created using FAT32.

d)   The file table will be created with FAT if it is under 8 GB, and with FAT32 if it is over 8 GB.

Answer c is correct. If you answer Yes to enabling large disk support, Fdisk will prepare the drive as a FAT32 system. All of the other answers are incorrect.

10 You have installed an incorrect device driver in your Windows XP system and now the hardware device fails to function. Which of the following would you do first?

a) Run the ASR recovery process.

b) Return the system to the most recent restore point.

c) Use the Windows XP driver rollback feature.

d) Download the most recent driver from the manufacturer's Web site.

Answer c is correct. The quickest way to recover when a bad or incorrect driver has been installed in Windows XP is to use the driver rollback feature. All of the other answers are valid steps to take but using the driver rollback feature would be the first way to try to recover the system from a corrupted device driver.

11 You have decided to upgrade your Windows 98 system to Windows 2000. Which of the following steps describes the best way to do this?

a) Insert the Windows 2000 CD-ROM and boot the system.

b) While in Windows 98, insert the Windows 2000 CD-ROM and then choose upgrade.

c) Using the Windows 2000 CD, run the Upgrade Wizard from the root directory.

d) While in Windows 98, disable AutoRun. Then insert the Windows 2000 CD and let the setup program run automatically.

Answer b is correct. Upgrading from Windows 98 to Windows 2000 is started by inserting the Windows 2000 CD in the drive while in Windows 98. The AutoRun feature will automatically start the Setup program. All of the other answers are incorrect.

12 A user calls to tell you that they are having sporadic problems with print jobs. Sometimes the print job is only half complete, other times they get pages of garbled text. There have been no configuration changes to the computer and it has been running well for some time. Which of the following troubleshooting steps are you likely to perform first?

a) Replace the printer drivers.

b) Replace the printer cable.

c) Check that the system has enough available disk space.

d) Check that the correct drivers are installed for the printer.

Answer c is correct. Although the problem described could be any one of the symptoms suggested, the easiest to check, and also a very possible cause, is that the system is running out of disk space for the spooling of print jobs. In this instance, you would check that the disk space was not an issue before investigating and trying one of the other possible solutions. All of the other answers are incorrect.

13 Which of the following utilities is used in Windows NT 4 to manage disk partitions and volumes?

a) Fdisk

b) Disk Manager

c) Disk Management

d) Disk Administrator

Answer d is correct. The tool used ion Windows NT 4 to manage disk partitions and volumes is called Disk Administrator. Answer a is incorrect. The Fdisk tool is associated with MS-DOS and Windows 9x systems. Answer b is incorrect. There is no Windows tool called Disk Manager. Answer c is incorrect. The Disk Management tool is used to manage volumes and partitions on a Windows 2000 system.

14 You want to create a Windows 95 boot disk that provides CD-ROM support. Which of the following files must be on the disk? (Choose two.)

a) Command.com

b) Bootsect.dos

c) Cddrv.exe

d) Bootcd.drv

e) Mscdex.exe

Answers a and e are correct. On a Windows 95 boot disk with CD-ROM support, the Command.com file along with the Mscdex.exe file are required. The disk will also need to contain Config.sys, Autoexec.bat, and a CD-ROM driver file. Answer b is incorrect. The Bootsect.dos file is used to denote the location of DOS boot files on a dual-boot system. Answers c and d are incorrect. There are no boot files with these names.

15 A user complains that each time she double-clicks on a document, the file opens in the wrong program. Where would you go to correct this problem?

a) Control Panel, File Associations, Folder Options

b) Control Panel, System, File Options

c) My Computer, Tools, Folder Options

d) Internet Explorer, Tools, Folder Options

Answer c is correct. You can configure file associations through My Computer, Tools, Folder Options. All of the other answers are incorrect.

16 Which of the following Winnt32.exe switches can be used to check for any potential issues with upgrading a Windows NT 4 system to Windows 2000?

a) /checkupgradeonly

b) /Nt42win2k

c) /Upgrdchk

d) /Windows Upgrader

Answer a is correct. The /checkupgradeonly switch is supplied so that you can determine a Windows NT 4 system's suitability for upgrading to Windows 2000. All of the other answers are incorrect.

17 You are troubleshooting a problem in Windows 98 and wish to boot into safe mode. Which of the following procedures will allow you to do this?

a) In Windows, select Start, Shutdown, Boot Into Safe Mode.

b) During boot-up, press the F8 key.

c) During boot-up, press the F10 key.

d) During boot-up, press Ctrl+Alt+Delete.

Answer b is correct. To enter safe mode, you must press the F8 key during boot-up. Answer a is incorrect. Boot Into Safe Mode is not an option on the restart menu. Answer c is incorrect. Pressing F10 will not have any effect on the system. Answer d is incorrect. Pressing Ctrl+Alt+Delete during boot-up will most likely cause the system to reboot again.

18 You are using Windows NT 4 and decide to upgrade to a SCSI host adapter that does not have a BIOS installed on it. Which of the following files must be added to the system to accommodate this?

a) Hba.sys

b) Nobios.sys

c) Bootsect.dos

d) Ntbootdd.sys

Answer d is correct. If you install a SCSI host adapter that does not have a BIOS installed on it, you must ensure that the Ntbootdd.sys file is installed in order for a Windows NT 4 system to boot. Answers a and b are incorrect. These are not recognized files used in the Windows NT boot process. Answer c is incorrect. The Bootsect.dos file is used to boot to DOS on a dual-boot system. It is not involved with the initialization of SCSI devices.

19 What are two ways of uninstalling a program in Windows 2000?

a)   From Control Panel, select Windows Components, Add/Remove Programs.

b)   From Control Panel, select Add/Remove Programs.

c)   Locate the directory in which the program is installed, delete all of the files, and then delete the shortcuts to the program.

d)   Run the program's own uninstall utility.

Answers b and d are correct. The two correct ways to remove a program in Windows 2000 are to run the uninstall utility or to go to Control Panel, Add/Remove Programs and remove it from there. Answer a is incorrect. The Add/Remove Programs utility is found directly in Control Panel. Answer c is incorrect. Although this procedure will remove all of the files and the shortcuts, it will not remove registry entries and so will not result in a clean uninstall.

20 In Windows 2000, in which file would you configure boot options such as OS selection, defaults, and timeouts?

a)   Boot.ini

b)   Autoexec.bat

c)   Win.ini

d)   W2kboot.ini

Answer a is correct. The Boot.ini file contains options such as OS selections, default choice of operating system, and timeouts. Answer b is incorrect. Autoexec.bat is a boot file used with MS-DOS. Answer c is incorrect. Win.ini is a Windows 9x startup file. Answer d is incorrect. There is no such file as W2kboot.ini.

Chapter 9

Diagnosing and Troubleshooting

Setting up a system is one thing, but quite often the real fun starts when the troubleshooting begins. Diagnosing and troubleshooting really is an art form, or at least we like to think so. In this chapter, we take a whirlwind tour through some of the errors you will find when working in the Windows world. Of course, in the limited space we have, we cannot discuss all of those errors you are going to encounter but we can at least get to the roots of a few of them. Perhaps the best place to start is with those annoying startup errors.

A Problem with Your Boots

It would be unfair to say that booting up is the only time that your system will have a problem, although sometimes it might seem that way. There are a variety of errors that you might encounter during the boot phase or during the system startup. Some of them are as simple to correct as removing a floppy disk from the drive; others can leave you scratching your head and scrambling for a solution. In this section, we look at some of the causes of these boot errors and what you can do to fix them.

Invalid Boot Disk and Inaccessible Boot Device

Things seem pretty bad when the system reports an error that it can't find a valid boot disk or boot device. At first, it might seem that someone has walked off with your hard disk but this is generally not the case. There are several factors that can cause the invalid boot disk error, including

- There is a non-bootable floppy or CD in the drive with the BIOS set to boot from the floppy or CD.

- The BIOS is not set to the correct boot sequence; for example, it is set to boot from a network.

- The hard disk does not have any bootable files on it or boot files are corrupt.

- The hard disk is not physically connected correctly.

- The hard drive is damaged.

Of course, some of these errors are easier to fix than others and when faced with this error, the best practice is to start with the most obvious solutions and work from there. If you suspect that the hard drive has lost or damaged boot files, the next move would be to see if you can get the system to boot from a boot disk. To do so, remember to change the BIOS to boot from the floppy drive. If you still cannot access the hard disk when using a boot disk, you might need to verify that the hard disk is correctly attached to the system. If you can see the hard disk in the BIOS, the boot files might be damaged or corrupt. You might need to manually replace the boot files or reinstall the OS.

Missing Ntldr Error Message

The Ntldr is a boot file used with Windows NT/2000 and Windows XP. Ntldr is the operating system boot loader, and without it there will be no system boot. As you might recall from Chapter 7, Ntldr is the file responsible for initializing the boot process. One error message sometimes seen on startup is the "Missing NTLDR" error message. As anyone who has ever seen this message will tell you, it can be a heart stopper. Still, as dramatic as this error is, it often has an easy remedy.

Troubleshooting a "NTLDR not found" error normally comes down to determining what drive you are booting from. A common issue is that a floppy disk that was formatted under Windows NT/2000 or Windows XP is in the floppy drive and the system is attempting to boot from it instead of the hard drive. This will cause the system to generate the "NTLDR not found" error. If there is not a disk in the floppy drive and you are receiving the error, your problem might be slightly more complex. The first step in the troubleshooting process is to verify the boot order set in the BIOS. This will at least confirm that the system is set to boot from the hard disk and not the floppy drive, CD, or even a network boot.

Once confirmed, you might try a Windows NT/2000/XP boot disk to start the system from the floppy drive.

Note For more information on the boot files for Windows 2000, refer to Chapter 7.

Bad or Missing Command.com Error Message

The command interpreter, Command.com, provides basic functionality to an MS-DOS or Windows 9x system, and without it, the system will be unusable. When this happens, you will receive the error message "Bad or Missing Command.com" or the equally irritating "Bad or Missing Command Interpreter."

In some cases, you might find that Command.com has become corrupt—it is, after all, a file like any other and just as susceptible to corruption. If you suspect that this is the case, you can copy a new version of Command.com from the Windows directory on a Windows 9x system, or from the first disk of a set of MS-DOS disks. You can also use the DOS Sys.com utility, which, as well as copying the files Io.sys and Msdos.sys, will transfer a new copy of the Command.com file to the target drive. When you copy Command.com, or use the Sys.com command, make sure you are using the correct version for your OS!

Note To get to the error "Bad or Missing Command.com," the system must have already accessed (at least) the Io.sys and Msdos.sys files. Therefore, the system is able to access the hard disk—it just can't find the Command.com file.

Error in Config.sys Line *XX*

The Config.sys file is one of the startup files used with MS-DOS and Windows 9x, and is used for loading device drivers and configuring certain memory parameters. When a command in the Config.sys file cannot be processed properly, you might receive an error that says "Error in Config.sys line *xx*," where *xx* indicates the actual line within the file that contains the error. In most cases, the error is caused by the incorrect syntax being used. For example, if the command `Buffers-40` were placed in the file, it would produce an error because the correct syntax is `Buffers=40`.

Correcting such errors is simple if you know the correct syntax. Since Config.sys is a text file, you can use the Edit utility, Notepad, or just any other plain text editor to make the necessary changes. In Windows 9x you can also use the Sysedit utility because Config.sys is one of the files that is automatically opened when you start the utility. If you would rather not delete the offending line, and instead want to simply bypass it on the next boot, add a semicolon (;) or put the word *Rem* at the beginning of the line. This will cause the system to ignore that line.

In some cases, the error is not one related to syntax but is instead related to a missing driver file. If a device driver is referenced in the Config.sys file and the system cannot locate that file or it is not in the directory specified, an error along the lines of "Missing Device Driver" will be displayed. Keep in mind that when the Config.sys file is processed, the Autoexec.bat file has not yet been run. Therefore, any Path statements that appear in the Autoexec.bat file will not yet have been executed. It is for this reason that the path to device drivers in the Config.sys file must be explicit. To really get a good idea of what is going on in a Config.sys file, take some time to look at one in action. If you have access to an old DOS or Windows 3.*x* machine, they often have interesting Config.sys files. Just by editing these files, you are certain to get a few of those "Missing Device Driver" errors and a better idea of how to correct them.

Himem.sys Not Loaded Error Message

Himem.sys is the extended memory driver used for both MS-DOS and Windows 9x. The bad news is that without Himem.sys, Windows 9x will not load properly and will leave you with nothing more than a DOS prompt. If you receive the "Himem.sys not loaded" error message, there can really only be one of two explanations. Either the Himem.sys file can't be found or it's corrupt.

Missing or Corrupt Himem.sys

On a Windows 9x system, the Himem.sys file should be found in the Windows directory. You can check its existence by using the Dir command. If the file is there and you are still receiving the "missing or corrupt" error message, you must assume that it has been corrupted. Simply copying a new copy of Himem.sys from the original installation CD on top of the old one should fix the problem.

In some cases, the Himem.sys file might not be the problem itself; instead, it identifies that there is a problem with the memory installed in the system. Himem.sys is able to detect problems because it performs a very fast (but surprisingly thorough) check of the memory when it loads. If Himem.sys senses a problem with the memory, you really don't have very many options available to you. You might try a reboot to determine if the problem was just a one-time occurrence, but the chances are that you will find yourself troubleshooting and possibly replacing RAM modules in order to correct the problem.

Errors in System.ini, Win.ini, or the Registry

Because device drivers (and background programs and services) can be loaded through the System.ini and Win.ini files and the registry, you might find that you receive a message that a device referenced in one of these places cannot be accessed. To determine what the problem is, you will need to examine either the files or the registry—which is often easier said than done.

The System.ini and Win.ini files can be opened in any text editor, although the easiest way to open them is with the Sysedit utility, which opens them both at the same time, along with the Autoexec.bat and Config.sys files. Sysedit has a search facility that makes it easier to find offending lines in the files.

Problems with an entry in the registry are a little more complex because the registry itself is more complex than the text files used for Win.ini and System.ini. When you are troubleshooting an entry in the registry, you will need to use the appropriate registry editing tool—Regedit.exe in Windows 9x and Windows XP and Regedt32.exe in Windows NT 4/Windows 2000 systems. Both utilities have an advanced search capability, which you will almost certainly need to take advantage of. Of the two, however, it is generally accepted that Regedit.exe is the better editor due to its better search capabilities. To prepare for the A+ exam, it would be a good idea to take a look at the registry using these editors, but be warned, do not make any changes to the registry without knowing what you are doing and without a backup of the registry.

Irrespective of whether the error occurs in one of the INI files or the registry, the type of error will invariably be predictable. If the error occurs on a system that has been working, and to which no changes have been made, you are most likely dealing with a corrupted driver file or program. In this case, replacing the driver or program with a new copy will probably do the trick.

If the error is occurring after a new program or driver has been installed or uninstalled, it is likely that the recent changes to the system are at the root of the problem. It is not always the case, but at the very least, it gives a good place to start looking for the problem. In either case, refer to the documentation that came with the program or device and consult both the Web site of the manufacturer of the device or program and Microsoft's OS support pages.

Generally speaking, only background programs and services are loaded through the registry and INI files. Such programs might include virus checkers, memory optimizers, and the like. Other programs that you just want to start automatically are more likely to be placed in the Startup group.

Note   Another useful troubleshooting tip is to bypass the processing of Autoexec.bat and Config.sys, which can be achieved on a Windows 9x system by using the Interactive Startup menu option. Once again, the Interactive Startup option is available by pressing the F8 key during boot.

Protection Is the Real Thing Bypassing the Autoexec.bat and Config.sys files is useful if the files are being used to load device drivers. In some cases it is necessary to load drivers through these two files if they are *real mode* drivers. Unlike *protected mode* drivers, real mode drivers can only be run in base memory (the area of memory between 0 and 640 KB), and do not support modern OS features such as multitasking and paging. In contrast, protected mode drivers support all of these features, which is why almost all device drivers made for Windows versions since Windows 95 are protected mode drivers.

The term *protected mode* actually comes from the fact that these drivers are able to prevent other programs or drivers from using their memory space. Real mode drivers, on the other hand, have the ability to use memory already allocated to another driver or program.

On today's systems, the need to load real mode drivers is diminishing quickly, but there are still legions of Windows 9x systems out there (and some Windows NT 4 systems) that use real mode drivers to support some legacy hardware device or another. When you experience an odd device driver problem, it is certainly worth keeping the real mode driver issue in mind.

Event Viewer—Event Log Is Full

As was discussed in Chapter 7, Windows NT 4 and Windows 2000/XP include a utility called Event Viewer. Within Event Viewer are a number of separate log files that are used by the system, via the Event Log service, to record, well, events that occur on the system.

By and large, Event Viewer is relatively maintenance free, although it is important to understand how it deals with log files when they get full. Unless you have a detailed auditing strategy in place, the log most likely to fill up is the System log. You can specify the criteria for management of each of the logs separately. Figure 9-1 shows the Event Viewer on a Windows XP system and the System log with errors.

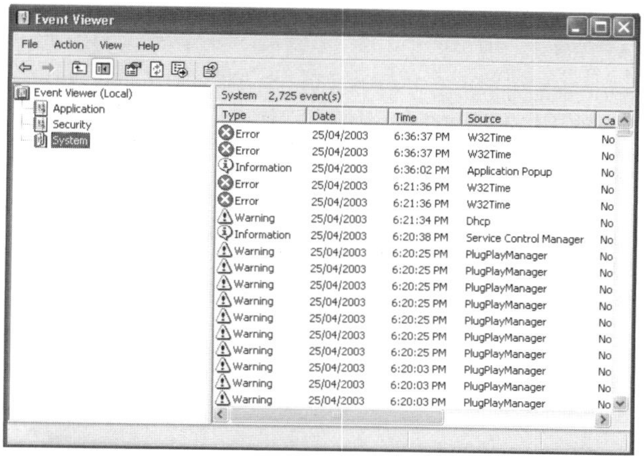

Figure 9-1 Errors in the System log are identified with a red *X*.

There are plenty of things of you can do with these log files. For instance, you can specify the location of a log file and the maximum size of a log file, as well as what you would like to happen once the maximum log size is reached. There is also a button that allows you to clear the log. One option, Do Not Overwrite Events (Clear Log Manually), can be a little risky; even if there is a maximum size set, the log file will discard all new events because there isn't room to store them, at least not until the log file is cleared manually. The best way to prevent this from occurring is to use one of the other options that automatically restrict the size of the log file. If you really must use the Do Not Overwrite Events option, you should implement a regular schedule of manually checking and clearing log files.

Note   One of the key features of Event Viewer is that it will record Stop errors, a.k.a. the Blue Screen of Death, to the System log. When the system experiences a Stop error, information about the state of the system and the cause of the error will be provided, albeit in a cryptic form, in a System Log event.

Aside from familiarizing yourself with the managing of log files, you would do well to familiarize yourself with Event Viewer and the ways in which you can read, search for, and filter log entries. Over the course of your career as a PC technician, you will find that a tool like Event Viewer becomes a regularly used resource.

Failure to Start GUI

In most cases, we will boot up our systems and before long we will be staring at our familiar desktops, but as we all know, this isn't always the case. Sometimes we are left staring at a graphical interface that won't start. One of the most common causes of graphical user interface (GUI) failure is corrupted, or incorrectly configured, display drivers. The easiest way to get around this is to boot into safe mode, which will boot the system with a minimal set of drivers, including a basic generic video driver at 640×480 resolution. Once the system has booted in safe mode, you can then troubleshoot the video driver problems. If you boot into safe mode and the GUI still doesn't start, the problem might be with a corrupt Windows system file such as one of those responsible for initializing and displaying the GUI. If you find that this is the case, you might be left with no option but to reinstall the operating system or restore it from a backup.

Note   If the system simply freezes during startup, you might find that a program that has been configured to run at startup is having a problem. In this case, you can bypass the loading of programs from the Startup folder by holding down the Ctrl key while Windows loads. You should not forget, however, that programs and services can also be loaded through the Windows startup files and the registry.

Windows Protection Errors

Of course, the sight of any error is undesirable, but Windows protection errors can be particularly troublesome. Windows protection errors are caused when the operating system is unable to load or unload a virtual device driver (VxD). Oftentimes, but not always, the VxD that failed to load will be listed in an error message when the Windows protection error halts the system. If it is, you have a better chance of searching for the offending device driver. Often the Windows protection error will be displayed on boot with no clues as to its cause.

What makes Windows protection errors harder to isolate are the numerous conditions in which they can occur. The following is a list of a few things that might cause the dreaded Windows protection error:

- Damaged registry

- Damaged or virus-infected Win.com or Command.com file

- Resource conflict between devices

- Plug and Play feature in the BIOS not working correctly

- Malfunctioning cache or memory in the system

- Faulty motherboard

These are just a few of the potential causes but are enough for you to see how difficult these errors can be to track down. Fortunately, when they do occur, they can often be traced to recent changes to the system, such as the addition of new hardware or new software packages. If you do get one of these error messages, the Internet will likely be your best resource for finding the answer to the problem. The best place to start is with the support pages on the Microsoft Web site.

The Untechnical Solution Without question, some of the problems we encounter while supporting PCs will require complex solutions, replacing expansion cards, reconfiguring software, and the like. However, in the real world, the majority of problems we face have an easy solution. Startup errors are no exception. Many of the startup files we access as technicians are just as accessible to us as they are to the system users—a frightening thought. This means that many of the startup errors we encounter can be a result of user-modified settings that prevent the system from booting. It is common for users to change simple settings such as the graphical settings, but equally, it is not uncommon to find users changing more sensitive settings and removing software packages that can and will cause startup errors. Because of this, when confronted with a system with startup errors, interview the user just to see if they have made any system modifications.

Searching for Answers

We all know that we are going to have problems with our systems; what we all don't know is what tools and utilities are available to help us when we encounter a problem. Like the problems themselves, however, there are a seemingly endless number of tools and utilities available, making it confusing to know which ones to use. In this section, we review a few of these utilities and resources, focusing on the ones that are likely to appear on the A+ exams.

Working with the Startup Disk

One of the first and most needed utilities is the trusty startup disk. When a system is refusing to boot, the startup disk might be the only friend you have. Each of the various Windows operating systems provides a method of creating boot disks; however, in some instances that method might require a little manual labor. Windows 95 included only those files necessary to boot the system, and Windows 3.*x* actually did not provide a way to create boot disks. For those of us who worked with those systems, one of the more irritating things about these boot disks is that they did not provide CD-ROM drivers. This meant we had to manually add support for CD-ROM devices to the boot disk files. Thankfully, Windows 98 boot disks changed all that, offering support for a wide range of CD-ROMs.

There are actually only a handful of files you need on a boot disk to get the system up and running. These files were introduced in Chapter 7 but include Io.sys, Msdos.sys, and Command.com for DOS-based boot disks. To format a floppy disk and copy these files to it, simply issue the command **format a: /s**.

Remember that the preceding command will only get the system booting up from the floppy drive. Additional files are often added to the boot disk to make it more usable.

Windows NT/2000/XP boot disks are quite different than those used with their Windows 9x cousins. Windows NT/2000/XP does not use the Io.sys, Msdos.sys, Command.com, Autoexec.bat, or Config.sys files used with DOS-based disks. Rather, the boot disks must contain the Ntldr, Boot.ini, and Ntdetect.com. A description of these files was provided in Chapter 7. To create a boot disk for one of these systems, you must first format a floppy disk with your OS, then manually copy the required files to the disk.

CD-ROMs and a Few More Helpful Files for the Boot Disk

Getting the system up and running is the basic function of the boot disk, but there are a few additional files and software you might want to include to make the boot disk that much more useful. If you are using a DOS-based system like Windows 9x, it's a good idea to include the Config.sys and Autoexec.bat files on the boot disk. These files can be transferred from the hard disk using the Copy command.

Without question, disk formatting and disk partitioning files would be handy on the boot disk. The files you would want for this include the Fdisk.exe, Format.com, and Sys.com commands. These files will also have to be manually transferred. Make sure you use the versions corresponding to the operating system you put on the disk, or the programs will give an "Incorrect DOS version" error and will not run.

In addition to formatting and partitioning utilities, it is also helpful to include diagnostic software just to see if something is wrong with the hard disk. The utility most often included is Scandisk.exe, which can detect and report errors on the disk. If working on an older DOS system, the Msd command might also be useful.

If a boot disk is created in Windows 98, the disk will be created with CD-ROM support. Sometimes, however, you might need to manually make a boot disk with CD-ROM support. There are two pieces to the puzzle when enabling CD-ROM support: an entry needs to be placed in the Config.sys file to load the device driver, and the Microsoft CD Extensions (Mscdex.exe) need to be placed in the Autoexec.bat file.

To give you some idea, the line in Config.sys would look something like this:

DEVICE=driver.SYS /D:Homer

The line in Autoexec.bat would look like this:

MSCDEX.EXE /D:Homer

The device line in the Config.sys file loads the CD-ROM driver, in this case, Driver.sys. Of course, you would put the actual name of your CD-ROM driver here. The /D switch names the CD-ROM device, in this case, Homer. The name can be anything you like but must be eight characters or less.

The function of Mscdex.exe in Autoexec.bat is to assign a drive letter to the device; hence, /D:Homer has to be the same in both files. Remember to put the Mscdex.exe file onto your boot disk. If all goes as planned, you will have access to the CD-ROM from the boot disk.

Note   A discussion about diagnostic tools and utilities would most certainly include the different boot methods used for troubleshooting startup problems. These boot methods, including safe mode and similar strategies, are discussed in Chapter 8.

Asd.exe (Automatic Skip Driver)

Every now and then, you will load a bad driver onto a system or a working driver will become corrupt. When this happens, the malfunctioning driver can, and often will, prevent the system from loading. To help prevent a bad device driver from causing problems on the system, Windows 98 includes the Asd utility, which is designed to automatically detect potentially faulty device drivers and skip over them during startup. With the faulty device driver not loaded, you should be able to get into the system and troubleshoot the driver.

The Asd utility runs in the background, and if you want to see if it has detected a potentially bad driver, you can type **asd.exe** in the Run dialog box. A dialog box will appear, letting you know if any faulty device drivers were detected.

Installation/User Manuals

While some consider those manuals and installation guides as optional reading and, in some cases, simply recycling material, things really do go more smoothly when we take the time to read those manuals. Often, the troubles we are experiencing can be resolved and even prevented by simply flipping through the manual that came with the device. Equally, if we need to get updated drivers for a device or troubleshoot a specific device, the manual gives clues on where to go and the exact name and model of the device.

It is always recommended to keep all of that recycling material that ships with PC products; you never know when you are going to need it!

Internet/Web Resources

The Internet has become the technician's right arm. It gives us quick access to not only drivers but a vast collection of tips, hints, and solutions to the most complex of PC problems. On the Internet, we can find solutions from formal sites such as Microsoft's or Novell's support pages, or from informal sources such as newsgroups. The bottom line is, because of the Internet, we never need to face a troubleshooting problem alone; we have thousands of others waiting to lend a hand. As far as Windows is concerned, one of the first places we can turn to in times of trouble is the Microsoft support page at *www.microsoft.com /support*. The solution to virtually every problem we face can be tracked down in this massive database. As a future PC technician, it certainly would be a good idea to check out this support page and acquaint yourself with how it works.

Windows Task Manager

Windows Task Manager is one of those utilities that can be used both in the gathering of information and to fix certain problems. Because of this, it is often used by both technicians and users. To access Task Manager, you can press the Ctrl+Alt+Delete keystroke combination. In Windows NT/2000/XP, this will open the Windows Security dialog box, which provides a button to open Task Manager. The same keystroke sequence will open the Close Program dialog box in Windows 9x.

Task Manager provides a quick look at what is going on in your system, what processes are running, and what resources are being used. The Windows NT and Windows 2000 Task Manager has three tabs: the Applications tab, which shows the applications that are running, the Processes tab, which displays the processes running, and finally the Performance tab, which shows overall resource usage. The Task Manager utility in Windows XP also includes a Networking tab, which displays network-related statistics, and might include a Users tab, which shows information about the currently logged-on users.

In the troubleshooting process, Task Manager is often used to manually end a process or an application that is either hung or unresponsive. The Processes tab and the Applications tab both provide a button to do just that. This makes it possible to end a specific program or process without having to reboot the computer system. Figure 9-2 shows Task Manager and the Performance tab from a Windows XP system.

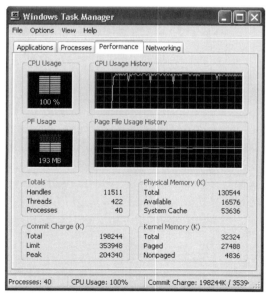

Figure 9-2 Windows Task Manager is used to both view system resource usage and troubleshoot applications or processes.

Dr. Watson

Windows versions since Windows 95 include a utility called Dr. Watson. Dr. Watson is a troubleshooting utility that can be used to determine why a program or process is causing problems. Figure 9-3 shows the Dr. Watson dialog box on a Windows 2000 system.

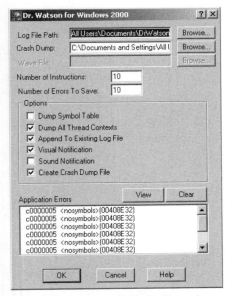

Figure 9-3 In Windows 2000, Dr. Watson has only one view.

In basic terms, the function of Dr. Watson is to collect information about the system at the time of the problem. Information collected includes a listing of the services that were running, details of what was in memory, and so on. As well as displaying the information on screen, a log file is also created. On a Windows 2000 system, the default location for the log file is C:\Documents and Settings\All Users\Documents\DrWatson. On a Windows 9x system, the file is placed in C:\Windows\Drwatson by default. The name of the log file is User.dmp in Windows 2000/XP, Drwtsn32.log in Windows NT, and in Windows 9x the name will vary but will have the .wlg extension.

Test Smart   At this point, don't worry about interpreting the information presented by Dr. Watson. On the A+ exam, the questions related to Dr. Watson will tend to be fairly basic, such as where the log files are and their names.

One thing worthy of note is that Dr. Watson does not start automatically, although some programs can be configured (or do it by default) to start Dr. Watson in the event of an error. You can have Dr. Watson start through the Startup folder if you want, in which case it will sit dormant, waiting for an error, or you can start it up when you receive an error message.

Note   In Windows 2000/XP and Windows 98, you can start Dr. Watson from the Run dialog box with the command **drwatson**.

Dr. Watson might look slightly different on each platform; however, the basic functionality is the same. On a Windows 98 system, you can elect to view Dr. Watson in Standard mode, which just displays the Diagnostics tab, or Advanced view, which shows a range of tabs including Startup, Tasks, and MS-DOS Drivers. Windows 2000 does not offer multiple views.

Note   Just why the program was called Dr. Watson is not clear. We would have felt more comforted if the super sleuth himself, Sherlock Holmes, had been on the case rather than his assistant, but there you go.

Dr. Watson can be of great help when it comes to troubleshooting errors because it provides a snapshot of the system at the time of the problem. Combining the information provided with additional information from tools like System Information, Task Manager, and Event Viewer can make the troubleshooting process considerably easier.

Device Manager

The Device Manager utility is used to provide a graphical representation of what and how devices are configured in the system. Device Manager is a one-stop utility used to view and manage hardware and drivers on the system. This includes viewing installed ports, viewing and updating device drivers, changing I/O settings, disabling a device, and in Windows XP, even rolling back a driver if the wrong or a corrupted one has been installed.

Device Manager is used in the troubleshooting process to disable hardware that might be causing system problems, to update drivers, to change the resources used by devices, to uninstall devices, and to see if the system has detected any conflict with devices. Because Device Manager is a key utility used by PC technicians, we would certainly advise that you spend some time familiarizing yourself with it before taking the A+ exam. Figure 9-4 shows Device Manager from a Windows XP system.

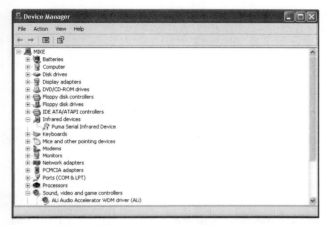

Figure 9-4 Windows Device Manager is used to manage hardware and settings from within Windows.

 Test Smart   Device Manager can be started using the System utility in Control Panel.

MSD and WinMSD

Way back in the days of DOS, we had the Microsoft Diagnostics (MSD) utility to report on the internal configuration of the PC. The MSD utility would provide information on hard disks, basic drivers, and resource information such as IRQs and I/O addresses.

We no longer use that original MSD utility; rather, we use the Windows NT Diagnostic (WinMSD) utility. The WinMSD utility is a graphical utility that provides detailed configuration information about the system. The current WinMSD utility does more than report on hardware; it also provides information on hardware resources used, drivers, print jobs, network connections, Internet, and installed applications. Given the flexibility of the utility and the amount of information that can be easily accessed, it should be widely used by technicians supporting PCs. Figure 9-5 shows the WinMSD utility on a Windows XP system.

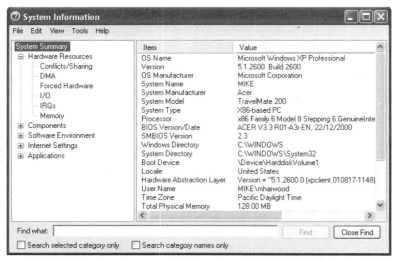

Figure 9-5 The WinMSD utility is used to gather information on a variety of system software and hardware.

Eliciting Problem Symptoms from Customers

Troubleshooting computer systems with which you are familiar is one thing, but as a PC technician you will be working on systems with which you have no history. You are not sure what programs are used, how the system has been functioning in normal operation, or even what the problem is. In such cases, you will often rely upon the information you can gather from customers to pinpoint what the error is. There are many questions you need to ask, including: Are programs locking up? Is a single program locking up? Is the system slow? Are there any particular error messages being displayed? Has this problem happened before? Has anything been tried to correct the problem? What changes have been made?

Only by asking such questions can you begin to isolate the problem. Over time, you will find that many of these problems are common and a few helpful pointers from the customer will easily pinpoint a familiar error.

One common strategy used by technicians is to have the customer re-create the error. This gives the technician first-hand experience with the issue, which is always better than an explanation of it.

Test Smart   When gathering information from a customer, ensure that you ascertain whether there have been any recent changes to the computer system including the adding or removing of files or programs. These changes can often be isolated as the cause of the issue.

Perhaps the most important thing to consider when dealing with customers is that attitude is everything. In many cases the customer will probably be frustrated by the fact that their PC is not working properly, and the temptation for them to take out their frustration on the technician is more common than you might think. So, you should work hard at developing an understanding with the user that you are there to correct the problem.

Personalities aside, there are certainly many conditions that you will be called upon to correct. The following sections detail some of the more common situations you might find yourself working on.

See Also   *More information and general troubleshooting procedures were covered in Chapter 2.*

Common Windows Operational Errors

Spend enough time working with and troubleshooting Windows operating systems and you are sure to notice that many of the errors you encounter are repetitive. This is particularly true of those Windows errors we see in daily operation. This doesn't mean that you are always going to see the same thing over and over again, but that during the course of your career, you will most likely get to build a large mental database of situations, symptoms, conditions, and, of course, solutions. It can take years to develop a large database of symptoms and solutions; here are some pointers to start you along that path.

Troubleshooting Windows-Specific Printing Problems

When it comes to common computer errors, printing and the print process seem to have more than their fair share of issues. Printing has become a very integral part of home and business environments and is relied upon to be there when needed. You will be called upon to make sure that printing is always available. For the most part, the printer errors that occur tend to be recurring ones and are therefore easy to identify.

The Print Spooler Is Stalled

When a printer is configured to use print spooling, print jobs are first sent to the spooler, which saves the print job to the hard disk. This method allows Windows to hold print jobs in a queue until the printer is free. When all works as it should, it is a seamless operation, and the print spooling process is invisible to the user. From time to time, however, the print spooler stalls and the print jobs held in the queue are frozen there. Your mission is to get the print spooler functioning—preferably while retaining the print jobs in the queue.

Typically, there are no error messages displayed when a print spooler stalls; rather, you are likely to find out when someone complains that their document won't print. The first thing you are likely to do when troubleshooting a print

spooler stall is open the printer's print queue. This can be done by double-clicking the printer icon in the bottom right corner of the taskbar or by double-clicking the printer in the Printer Settings dialog box. The Printer Settings dialog box
can be accessed through Windows Control Panel. Figure 9-6 shows a print
queue with various documents in it.

Document Name	Status	Owner	Pages	Size	Submitted
Microsoft Word - chapter9.doc	Printing	Administrator	56	46.1 KB/2.50 MB	7:26:11 AM 1/6/2003
		Administrator	1	29.8 KB	7:26:27 AM 1/6/2003
http://dhmail01.dollarhost.com/X0...		Administrator	5	1.34 MB	7:26:51 AM 1/6/2003
http://dhmail01.dollarhost.com/X0...	Spooling	Administrator	5	1.32 MB	7:26:51 AM 1/6/2003

HP LaserJet 1100 (MS)
Printer   Document   View   Help
4 document(s) in queue

Figure 9-6 The printer's print queue window shows the print jobs in the queue.

Each pending print job is listed in the print queue. The print job at the top
is the one currently printing, and, if the print spooler is stalled, it's the potential
problem. To get the print spooler going again, you can try to delete this print job
and the following print jobs will hopefully carry on through to the printer.

If removing the print job does not get the print spooler going, on a Windows NT or Windows 2000/XP system you can stop and restart the print spooler
service. To access the print spooler service, go into Control Panel, select the
Administrative Tools icon, and then the Services shortcut. The Services dialog
box will open. Scroll down the list until you find the Print Spooler service. In
Windows 2000 and Windows XP you can restart the service by right-clicking on
the Print Spooler and selecting Restart from the shortcut menu.

Test Smart   To re-initiate the print spooler on a Windows 2000 or Windows XP system, try
restarting the Print Spooler service.

Note   Windows 9x does not use a print spooler service, so this troubleshooting step is not valid
on these platforms.

If the print spooler problem persists, you do have the option of restarting
the computer system and in most instances this will clear the problem. The print
jobs in the queue, however, will be lost and will need to be resent. If the problem continues after a reboot, you might have to verify that there is enough hard
disk space for the print spooler to operate. If there is not enough hard disk
space for the print spooler to function, it will certainly freeze every time.

Test Smart   Sometimes it might appear that a print spooler has stalled when a large document or one with a large number of graphics is printed. Such a document can tie up resources and just slow the process down, but it will work its way through the print spooler.

Incorrect or Incompatible Driver for the Printer

A very common step when troubleshooting printers is to verify that the correct drivers are being used for the printer. All manner of seemingly unrelated problems can be corrected by installing the correct or updated printer driver. It is always best to get the latest printer driver from the manufacturer's Web site. If a printer is using the wrong or a corrupted driver, a technician must know how to update and replace the printer driver.

When replacing or updating a printer driver, you need to access the Printers dialog box. Right-click on your printer and choose Properties from the shortcut menu to display the properties dialog box for that printer. On the Advanced tab, click the New Driver button to add or change the driver. Figure 9-7 shows the Advanced tab of a printer's properties dialog box.

 Test Smart   One sure sign that a printer is using the wrong driver is garbled print jobs coming out of the printer. If this happens, updating the driver should correct the problem.

Figure 9-7 Modify print drivers on a Windows 2000 system in the printer's properties dialog box.

Out of Memory Errors While Printing

There are two memory-related issues that you can encounter while printing. The first has to do with the system being out of memory, which is relatively uncommon. The second is running out of memory on the printer, which occurred quite frequently with older laser printers. Today it is less of an issue—many high-performance printers now have hard disks of their own, and even those that don't generally have more than enough RAM to cope with even the most graphically demanding documents.

Even so, you might come across errors on laser printers along the lines of a memory overflow or page buffer overflow that indicates the printer does not have enough installed memory to cope with the amount of information it has been supplied to print the current page. If you experience such an error, there are really only two things you can do. Either install more memory in the printer to accommodate the large quantities of data, or reduce the size of the print file. You will find that many graphics programs (the ones most likely to create this kind of problem) have multiple settings that will allow you to reduce the size of the print file.

As for dealing with system memory errors while printing, there is little that you can do apart from increasing the amount of installed memory or reconfiguring the swap file to create more virtual memory.

> **Note**   Don't forget, the spooling process uses disk space to store print files. If there is not enough free space on your hard disk, you might find yourself unable to print large files irrespective of how much memory is installed in the system or in the printer.

General Protection Faults

If you work with Windows long enough, you are at some point going to have the opportunity to experience a General Protection Fault (GPF). A General Protection Fault occurs when a program attempts to start but the system detects a procedure in that program that could compromise another program or even the OS itself. A common cause of a GPF is when a program or device attempts to access a corrupted or unsupported device driver.

The Blue Screen of Death

When a GPF error does occur, your system might give you the infamous "blue screen of death." Text on the blue screen outlines the cause of the problem, but the information provided is often very cryptic and might require some research to determine exactly what the cause of the problem is. Before going down that route, however, try simply restarting the computer. Many GPF errors occur once and then you might never see the same error again. GPF errors are really only a problem when they are recurring and keep halting the system. When this happens, you will need to identify the cause of the problem. If a single program causes a GPF every time it is started, that program might need to be reinstalled or you should refer to the manufacturer's Web site to isolate the cause of the GPF.

The text on the blue screen error messages seems very cryptic, filled with hexadecimal characters and numbers that seem more like the scribblings of an ancient civilization than anything modern. Still, hidden in these cryptic codes is often the answer to the blue screen riddle. Armed with this information, a trip to the Microsoft support database might give you the answer you are seeking.

Blue screen error messages seem very dramatic because they bring a system to a halt. The exact cause of a blue screen error varies, but we have found that most blue screen errors can be traced back to recent changes made to the system, whether hardware or software. Naturally, as part of the troubleshooting process, determining if any recent changes have been made to the system would be a priority.

While there isn't a universal method for solving blue screen errors, there are a few things you can try to get the system back up to a functional state. The first thing to do would be to isolate those system changes. As we have mentioned throughout this book, recent changes to a system are often the cause of the problem. Undoing these changes will often get you back in the system. To undo these changes, we often have to rely upon the Last Known Good and Safe Mode options to get us back into our systems.

While working with blue screen errors, we have found that many of them can be traced to corrupt or incorrect drivers being used, which is where the Last Known Good and Safe Mode options really shine. However, we have seen some blue screens that were simply unrecoverable and the system had to be restored from backup. Even after that, some blue screens persisted, which led to the discovery of some faulty hardware components.

When all is said and done, blue screen errors can be simple to fix or they can permanently bring down a system. The only really good way to deal with them is to use the Microsoft support pages and keep those backups up to date.

Illegal Operation

Illegal operation errors are unfortunately not uncommon in the Windows world, and can certainly add an element of frustration to a computer user's life. In very basic terms, an illegal operation is reported when a program tries to perform a function that the operating system is unable to carry out. This is sometimes caused by a particular bug in the program itself, which creates the illegal operation. Most programs today are tested thoroughly under differing conditions and different hardware configurations. This testing process has served to reduce the number of illegal operation errors, but they still occur.

Illegal operation errors can be particularly difficult to troubleshoot and some are triggered only sporadically, which makes them even more difficult to nail down. You can sometimes isolate the cause if you can re-create the error; other times, a simple reboot will correct the problem. If the cause can be pinned to a specific program, then that program might need to be reinstalled.

The Microsoft support Web site at *http://support.microsoft.com* contains detailed information on illegal operation errors and program troubleshooting. This is often the best place to go when trying to pinpoint an illegal operation error.

Invalid Working Directory

A working directory is typically the directory where a program's primary files are kept, and it is used by a program to store the temporary files it needs. If you receive an error message stating an invalid working directory, then the program cannot find the directory. This can happen if the directory is moved, renamed, or deleted. To correct the error, you will need to put the directory back in its original location, or you might be able to correct the problem by editing the shortcut to the program, which has a field for the working directory. In some cases, if the working directory has been completely deleted, the entire program will need to be reinstalled.

System Lockups

System lockups, or freezing, are probably the most frustrating of all computer errors and perhaps the most common. Troubleshooting system lockups is particularly difficult because there are many different things that can cause the system to hang. To make it more difficult, system lockups are often sporadic, and re-creating them or pinpointing them to one particular program or process can be very difficult. Lockups can be caused by a hardware malfunction; for instance, if the system is hanging after new memory is added, the memory might not be correctly installed or configured. In addition to hardware, system lockups can also be caused by conflicting device drivers or failing programs.

To recover from a system lockup, you can press Ctrl+Alt+Del to open the Close Program dialog box in Windows 9x. The same command will bring up a link to Task Manager in Windows NT and Windows 2000/XP. Both of these utilities will identify a program that is locked and not responding. If you can close the program from within these utilities, you might be able to recover the system. Be warned, however, that if you close down a program in this manner, everything you have been working on will be lost. In some cases, the system will not function even after the program is terminated, leaving a system reboot as the only option. Figure 9-8 shows Task Manager and the Applications tab.

Figure 9-8 Use Task Manager to close down a locked program.

Identifying Device Errors with Device Manager

When it comes to verifying that hardware is configured and working with the operating system, Windows Device Manager provides all you need. Device Manager is used to view the hardware devices detected by the system, and it's the main utility used to verify devices and device drivers in a Windows operating system.

Devices in Device Manager are organized by type; for instance, all network cards are organized under the Network Adapters category. This structure makes navigating Device Manager very easy. To see the devices listed within a particular category, simply click on the category heading to display all installed devices and the current status of that device. If the device is listed with a red *X*, it is not functioning or has been disabled. Alternatively, if there is a yellow circle with a black exclamation point, the device is not functioning correctly, which might mean a resource conflict or that incorrect drivers are being used.

Test Smart If a device is listed with a red *X* or yellow circle with black exclamation point, the associated device is not functioning correctly and will need some troubleshooting.

Device Manager is commonly used to change the drivers used by a device, manually set system resources used by a device, and even disable a device. To see the properties of any device, right-click on the device and select Properties from the menu to display the configurable properties for the device. Several of the configurable options change depending on the device you are monitoring, but there are some common ones used. Every device's properties dialog box has a General tab that shows the current status of the device, provides a trouble-shooting button used to help troubleshoot devices, and has a Device Usage section that allows you to manually disable the device. Figure 9-9 shows the General tab of an Ethernet adapter's properties dialog box in Device Manager.

Figure 9-9 The General tab of a device's properties dialog box in Device Manager helps you troubleshoot or even disable the device.

In addition to a device's General tab, a device's properties dialog box might also have a Resources tab. As you might imagine, the Resources tab is used to view the resources used by a hardware device and displays whether or not there is a resource conflict. If there is a resource conflict, you can manually change the resources used from the Resources tab. Figure 9-10 shows the Resources tab of a network card's properties dialog box in Device Manager on a Windows 2000 system.

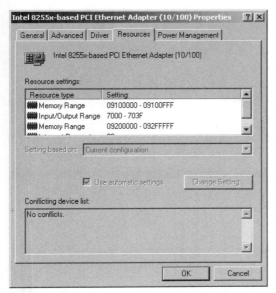

Figure 9-10 The Resources tab is used to view resources and manually set resources used by the system.

The final tab to consider when configuring a hardware device is the Driver tab. The Driver tab is used to view the driver currently used by a hardware device, update that driver, or uninstall that device driver. Figure 9-11 shows the Driver tab for a device.

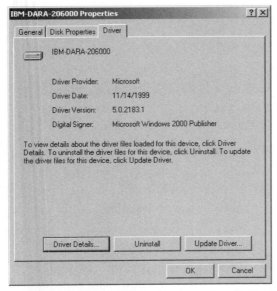

Figure 9-11 The Driver tab is used to view and modify the driver used by a particular device.

Signed or Unsigned Drivers One of the problems that technicians struggle with is corrupt or poorly written device drivers. Of course, we have to have device drivers, but some of them seem to be more trouble than they are worth. Introduced with Windows 2000 is a safeguard measure aimed at ensuring that the device drivers used on systems will not cause the system to fail. This strategy is known as driver signing. Signed drivers are those that have been tested and verified to work with Windows; for a driver to become classified as a signed driver, it must meet the standards set out by the Windows Hardware Quality Labs (WHQL). Once the driver has passed the testing process, a digital signature is embedded into the device driver, hence the term *signing*. Many manufacturers offer both unsigned and signed device drivers, but only those that are signed have been confirmed to work with the Windows version in question. Wherever possible, you should try to use signed drivers.

Test Smart   If after adding a new hardware device, it doesn't work or another device stops working, there might be a resource conflict. To verify this, use the Resources tab from the device's properties dialog box.

Troubleshooting Programs

PC technicians truly are jacks-of-all-trades. In addition to managing and troubleshooting hardware, they also have to have sufficient knowledge to troubleshoot program errors. Troubleshooting program errors offers a range of different challenges for a technician and in many cases is much more difficult than hardware troubleshooting.

Programs Won't Install

You can install a program a hundred times, and then the 101st time it will refuse to install under what appear to be the same conditions. Sometimes when a program fails to install, an error message will appear to help identify the nature of the problem; other times, the install will just stop without warning. When a program refuses to install, consider the following:

- **System resources**   If you are trying to install a newer program onto an older system, it might not meet the minimum requirements for that program. Refer to the program's documentation to identify its minimum requirements.

- **Program conflict**   Sometimes a program will fail to install if another program is running. For instance, a screen saver that starts during the install might cause the installation to fail. Similarly, a virus checker running in the background might do the same. When installing a program, it is suggested that you shut down all other programs.

- **Installation media**   Sometimes the installation medium itself is corrupt; it might be a scratch on the installation CD or a damaged installation file on the floppy disk. If possible, try reinstalling the program with different media.

- **Incorrect installation procedures**   Most modern programs will start their setup program automatically when you insert the CD and almost install themselves, but there are those that require a bit more work. Refer to the manufacturer's installation procedures to verify that the installation procedures are correct.

A Program Will Not Start or Load

After you install a program, you expect that you'll be able to click on the program's shortcut and the program will begin. While this is most often the case, sometimes the newly installed program simply won't run, and in some cases a program that used to run no longer does. There are many reasons why a program will not load; ordinarily, an error message displayed on the screen can help isolate the cause. When a program fails to load, consider the following:

- **System resources**   If the program has just been installed, verify that the system has enough resources—memory, hard disk space, and processor power—to run the program.

- **Corrupted installation**   It might be that the program did not install successfully. Sometimes when a program fails to load, you will need to reinstall it to see if the problem is corrected.

- **Virus**   If a program has been running and now fails to start, it might be that a virus has damaged the program's files. Run a virus checker to see if there is a virus on the system.

- **Incorrect shortcut path**   If a program won't start from its shortcut on the desktop, try starting it directly from the program's main executable file. This file is located in the program's directory. It might be that the path for the shortcut is just wrong.

- **Deleted or moved files**   If a program used to work but now does not, it might mean that the program files have been deleted or moved. Use Windows Explorer to verify that the files are still where they need to be.

- **Expired software**   If you were using trial software that has an expiration date, it might just be that the time has expired. Refer to the manufacturer's Web site for more information.

> **Note**   When a program fails to run, the first step is often a simple reboot of the computer system. Many programs require a reboot of the program to function after installation, and other programs sometimes just get buggy and a reboot gets things up and running again.

A Program Loads but Performs Poorly

You might find that some programs can be installed and will load, but their performance is so slow that they cannot be realistically used. This is almost always due to a lack of system resources, most likely hard disk space or memory. You might need to refer to the manufacturer's specifications to ensure that you have what you need to run the program.

To verify whether or not a program is using too many system resources, you will need to monitor resource usage using a performance monitoring utility. In Windows NT and Windows 2000/XP, you can open Task Manager and select the Performance tab to see if the memory and processor usage is too high. In Windows 9x, you can use the System Monitor utility to do the same.

You Cannot Log on to a Network

Many of the systems you will be supporting will be connected to a network rather than be stand-alone systems. Because of this, you will need to have a basic understanding of network troubleshooting, at least from the client end of things. While the A+ exam does not require an advanced level of knowledge on network troubleshooting, you will be expected to know how to identify logon errors.

When troubleshooting a system that cannot log onto the network, consider the following:

- **Network card resources**   With the network card installed, verify that there are no resource conflicts and that it is recognized by the system. You can do this from within Device Manager.

- **Verify link light**   Most modern network cards have an LED on them, referred to as the *link light*, that lights up when the card is making a connection to the network. If the LED is not lit, then no connection is present. This could be caused either by a problem with the network card or some kind of connectivity issue elsewhere on the network.

- **User name and password combination**   Network connectivity problems are sometimes as simple as the wrong password or user name being entered. Ensure that Caps Lock is off and that the password and user name, especially if they are case-sensitive, are being entered correctly. Be sure these are correct before taking the troubleshooting procedure any farther.

■ **Network card drivers**   If you cannot connect to the network, you might need to verify that the correct network card drivers are being used. If in doubt, update the driver using Windows Device Manager. Be sure to use the latest driver from the manufacturer's Web site.

TSR (Terminate-and-Stay-Resident) Programs   In days gone by (which in computing terms can mean just a few years ago), a popular approach to drivers was to use *terminate-and-stay-resident (TSR)* programs. TSRs are called such because they load into memory via a program that then terminates. Although the program has finished (terminated), the driver is still in memory, that is to say, resident.

In a sense, you could say that all drivers are TSRs to some degree—after all, they all load and then stay loaded so that the device for which they are responsible can be accessed.

Viruses and Virus Types

It really is unfortunate that something as useless and destructive as a virus has to be a consideration for PC technicians, but it definitely must be a consideration, and at some point you can expect to be trying to solve a virus-related problem.

In a very general sense, a virus is a program that is often intended to damage the data files, programs, and operating system of a computer. Some viruses are more successful in this respect and some of the more harmful can certainly wipe out the contents of your hard disk. While many viruses do such damage, others are harmless and do not adversely affect the computer system. Still, you really don't want to take the chance.

There are four main types, or categories, of viruses that you need to deal with, each targeted at a different area of the computer system. These virus categories include boot sector viruses, Trojan horse programs, executable viruses, and macro viruses.

Boot Sector Virus

As you might have guessed, boot sector viruses are targeted at the system's boot sector. Specifically, the boot sector virus changes the code of the Master Boot Record (MBR). If a virus is successful in writing itself to the MBR, it can be a huge problem as it then sits there in memory trying to do the same to other devices such as floppy disk drives, other hard disks, and even those drives connected by the network. Once the virus has written itself to the MBR, it can do a variety of damage to the system depending on what its designer had in mind. To remove a virus from the MBR you can use the Fdisk command, using the following syntax: *fdisk /mbr*.

> **Note**   Many BIOSs now include a setting that can be used to protect the boot sector of the hard disk from virus infection. Given the destructive nature of boot sector viruses, if your BIOS has such a feature, you should certainly enable it.

Trojan Horse Program

A Trojan horse program is so named because it disguises itself as something it isn't. A Trojan horse program is often used to locate local passwords on the computer system, make the system vulnerable for a remote attack, or simply damage files on the local system. Typically Trojan horses do not replicate themselves to other computers; rather, they are commonly downloaded from the Internet in the form of free games, screen savers, or other system utilities, and then run their destructive program code when the user starts the "masquerading" program. The best prevention for Trojan horse programs is to only download proven and trusted programs.

Executable Virus

One of the most dangerous types of virus is embedded in an executable file. It can basically do anything, including mailing itself to everyone in your address book, and wiping out your system and any system yours is connected to.

If there were any good news about executable viruses, it would be that they are an increasingly unpopular method of transmitting viruses, and the majority of people are now aware of the risks that running unknown EXE files can present. The bad news is that the virus writers have simply developed other ways of distributing their malicious code.

> **Note**   Executable viruses can be embedded in any executable file, not just EXE files. These include BAT, COM, and CMD files.

Macro Virus

A macro virus is a bit of a different monkey. The macro virus is written in a macro language and placed within a macro, which can then be embedded in a document or spreadsheet. The problem with macro viruses is that they come as part of the document or spreadsheet and are practically undetectable unless you are using antivirus software. To their credit, programs that have macro languages, and thus are susceptible to macro viruses, often have the ability to switch macros off, or warn you when you open a document with embedded macros and offer to disable them.

Is It a Virus?

As if it weren't hard enough trying to determine if a problem is hardware- or software-related, now you also have to add viruses to that equation. So, just how do you know if there is a virus on a computer system? Unfortunately, it is not always easy to tell.

The first step in being able to identify the presence of a virus is developing an awareness of viruses and what they are designed to do. Companies that make antivirus software provide detailed information about the latest viruses, how they spread, and what they are designed to do. When it comes to fighting the virus threat, education is definitely the key and PC technicians will need to check these sites out to stay ahead of the game.

General Signs and Symptoms

Early detection of a virus is important, and while it might be difficult to detect the presence of a virus, there are some general signs to keep an eye on. Again, these are not sure signs of a virus but they are potential indicators.

- **Unusual messages on the screen**   Keep an eye out for unusual messages or display windows that appear. If these are not part of any program that you have installed, they might be the work of a virus.

- **Sound files or music played at random times**   Though most viruses are not overt, some will play sound files or music that will alert you to their presence. One common virus would cause the computer to say the *Space Odyssey* line "I can't let you do that, Dave" every time you tried to access certain areas of the hard disk—funny, but very annoying.

- Missing or corrupt files or programs

- If you are looking for a program or a file and can't find it, it could be a virus. Some viruses rename or delete files and program executables. When this happens, you will not be able to find them. If you suspect that this is happening, the best thing to do is run your virus checker right away.

- **System performance**   Some viruses will drain your system's resources and the entire system will noticeably slow down. If you use system resource utilities to check the memory usage, you will find that it is extremely high considering the programs that are running on it. You might notice that the hard disk keeps running out of space and that overall performance, including loading programs, is noticeably slower, often confirmed by unusually high CPU usage.

■ **New files or programs**   If you are looking through a computer system and notice new files or programs that shouldn't be there, they
could be virus programs or the by-product of a virus infection. To verify this, refer to the Web site of your antivirus software manufacturer.

Where Do Viruses Come From?

There are many different ways to get a virus on the system. Most of these virus
sources can be shut down with a little common sense but many users are not
always aware of the virus threat. Common methods by which you can get
viruses include the following:

■ **Floppy disks**   The problem with floppy disks is that they are often
transferred between users and computer systems. If one of these
floppy disks has a virus on it, the virus can easily find its way into other
systems. One way to safeguard against this is to use a virus checker
with an autodetect feature that will check the disk when it is inserted.
This can also be done manually, which can be a bit of a nuisance but
is better than getting a virus.

■ **E-mail**   E-mail has become one of the most common methods of distributing, and therefore contracting, viruses. Many of us don't bother to
look closely at e-mail messages we receive and open them without
hesitation. Then, before you know it, you have a virus in your system.
Nowadays, there are several methods commonly used to prevent the
spread of viruses through e-mail. One strategy is to purchase a virus
checker that has the ability to scan incoming e-mail and attachments.
In addition to virus checkers, a good virus strategy will also include
educating users about what to look for in terms of a virus.

Test Smart   Keep an eye on those e-mail attachments—they are a breeding
ground for viruses.

■ **Network**   When a computer system is connected to a network, especially the Internet, it opens up the potential for viruses to spread themselves around the other computers on the network. Of course, the only
real way to prevent this is to make all computers stand-alone systems
as they once were, which of course is a very impractical solution.

■ **Downloading software**   Many of us spend time on the Internet and
at some point will download files onto our local computer. These files,
many of which are executables, can contain viruses. Before installing
any software or opening any files that you have downloaded, be sure
to check the files for viruses.

Removing Viruses

As a PC technician, you will be called upon to remove viruses from computer systems. There are many different types of viruses and each one requires a different approach to removal. In the modern fight against viruses, you have access to virus-removal software from companies that specialize in it. When you are attempting to rid a system of a virus, running one of these virus removal tools is the first step. To work effectively, these virus checkers need to be up to date. If they do not detect a virus, you might need to upgrade the virus checker to search for the latest viruses.

Even after the antivirus program has removed the virus, there might still be file damage to the system. Much of this will have to be repaired manually. In a worst-case scenario, if too many files are damaged, the entire operating system might need to be reinstalled or you will need to restore it from a backup.

It is also worth noting that antivirus software is often configured to always be on, running in the background, as well as periodically scanning the hard disk for viruses. While this is a good thing, sometimes this feature must be turned off to prevent it from conflicting with other system functions. For instance, the virus checker should be disabled before running a defrag or installing some software. If it is not, such functions might be disrupted and fail to complete.

Key Points

- When a command in the Config.sys file cannot be processed properly, you might receive an error that says "Error in CONFIG.SYS line xx," where *xx* indicates the actual line within the file that contains the error.

- If you would rather not delete the offending line in the Config.sys file, and instead want to simply bypass it on the next boot, add a semicolon (;) or put the word *Rem* at the beginning of the line.

- Without Command.com, the system will be unusable. To install a new copy of Command.com, copy it from the original media or boot from a bootable floppy disk and use the Sys.com utility.

- Without Himem.sys, Windows 9x will not load properly, leaving you with nothing more than a DOS prompt.

- Troubleshooting a "Ntldr not found" issue normally comes down to determining what drive you are booting from. A common issue is that a floppy drive that was formatted under Windows NT or Windows 2000 is in the floppy drive.

- Windows 9x, Windows NT 4, and Windows 2000/XP include a utility called Dr. Watson. Dr. Watson is a troubleshooting utility that can be used to determine why a program or process is causing problems.

■ You can have Dr. Watson start through the Startup folder if you want, in which case it will sit dormant, waiting for an error, or you can start it up when you receive an error.

■ Windows protection errors are caused during startup by a problem with a virtual device driver (VxD). The offending driver will most likely be named in the error message.

■ Generally speaking, only background programs and services are loaded through the registry and .ini files.

■ One common strategy used by technicians is to have the customer re-create the error. This gives the technician first-hand experience with the issue, which is always better than an explanation of it.

■ When a printer is configured to use print spooling, print jobs are first sent to the spooler, which saves the print job to the hard disk.

■ To get the print spooler going again, you can try to delete the offending print job, and the following print jobs will hopefully carry on through to the printer.

■ In Windows 2000/XP, the spooler service can be stopped and restarted.

■ If there is not enough hard disk space for the print spooler to function, it will certainly freeze every time.

■ A very common step when troubleshooting printers is to verify that the correct drivers are being used for the printer. All manner of seemingly unrelated problems can be corrected by installing the correct or updated printer driver.

■ One sure sign that a printer is using the wrong driver is garbled print jobs. Updating the driver should correct the problem.

■ A General Protection Fault occurs when a program attempts to start but the system detects a procedure in that program that could compromise another program or even the OS itself.

■ An illegal operation is reported when a program tries to perform a function that the operating system is unable to carry out.

■ A working directory is typically the directory where a program's primary files are kept, and it is used by a program to store the temporary files it needs.

■ To recover from a system lockup, you can press Ctrl+Alt+Del to open the Close Program dialog box in Windows 9x; the same command will bring up a link to Task Manager in Windows 2000.

■ Device Manager is used to view the hardware devices detected by the system and is the main utility used to troubleshoot devices and device drivers in a Windows operating system.

■ Signed drivers have been tested and verified to work with Windows; for a driver to become classified as a signed driver, it must meet the standards set out by the Windows Hardware Quality Labs (WHQL).

■ If after adding a new hardware device, it doesn't work or another device stops working, it might be due to a resource conflict. To verify, check the Resources tab in the device's properties dialog box in Device Manager.

■ Sometimes a program is added to the system and even though it loads, its performance is so slow it cannot be used. This is almost always due to a lack of system resources, most likely hard disk space and memory.

■ Network connectivity problems are sometimes as simple as the wrong password or user name being entered.

■ Most modern network cards have an LED on them, referred to as the link light, that lights up when the card is making a connection to the network.

■ In a very general sense, a virus is a program that is often intended to damage the data files, programs, and the operating system of a computer.

■ The four main types or categories of viruses, each of which is targeted at a different area of the computer system, are boot sector viruses, Trojan horse programs, executable viruses, and macro viruses.

■ Boot sector viruses change the code of the Master Boot Record (MBR). To remove a virus from the MBR, you can use the Fdisk command using the following syntax: *fdisk /mbr*.

■ A Trojan horse program is so named because it disguises itself as something it isn't. The best prevention for Trojan horse programs is to only download proven and trusted programs.

■ Executable viruses can be embedded in any executable file, not just EXE files. These include BAT, COM, and CMD files, and executable scripts such as VBS files.

■ Macro viruses are written in a macro language and placed within a macro, which can then be embedded in a document or spreadsheet.

■ The first step in being able to identify the presence of a virus is developing an awareness of viruses and what they are designed to do.

■ Even after a virus checker has removed a virus, there might already have been file damage to the system.

Chapter Review Questions

1   What are the two ways in which you can start the Dr. Watson utility? (Choose two.)

   a)   Control Panel, Diagnostics, Dr. Watson

   b)   Start, Run, Drwatson

   c)   Start, Run, drw

   d)   Start, Programs, Accessories, System Tools, System Information, Tools, Dr. Watson.

   Answers b and d are correct. The Dr. Watson utility can be started in either of these ways. Answers a and c are incorrect.

2   You get the message "Error in Config.sys Line xx" when you boot your system. Which of the following are valid troubleshooting steps?

   a)   Run Regedit to find the offending line. Determine why the driver is failing to load.

   b)   Run Sysedit to find the offending entry in Config.sys. Determine why the driver is failing to load.

   c)   Run Regedt32 to find the offending line. Determine why the driver is failing to load.

   d)   Run Confed to determine the offending line. Determine why the driver is failing to load.

   Answer b is correct. The Config.sys file is a text file and as such can be edited through a utility such as Sysedit. Answers a and c are incorrect, because the Regedit and Regedt32 utilities cannot be used to edit the Config.sys file. Answer d is incorrect. There is no Windows utility called Confed.

3   Which of the following keys would you press on a Windows 98 system to start the system in safe mode?

   a)   F6

   b)   F7

   c)   Tab

   d)   F8

   Answer d is correct. On a Windows 98 system, when the F8 key is pressed during boot-up the system will select the interactive startup option. From there you can elect to enter safe mode. The other answers are incorrect.

4 In which area of memory do real mode drivers load?

a) Extended

b) Conventional

c) Real

d) Stable

Answer b is correct. Real mode drivers can only be loaded into conventional memory. All of the other answers are incorrect.

5 Which of the following are you likely to try first after receiving a blue screen error message?

a) Safe mode

b) Last Known Good boot option

c) Checking the System log in Event Viewer

d) Using a boot disk

Answer b is correct. One of the first steps in recovering from a blue screen error is to reboot the system and see if you can restart the system using the Last Known Good boot option. If this fails to start the system, it would be necessary to take troubleshooting a little further. Answer a is incorrect. Safe mode might be used, but typically not after you try to recover the system using the Last Known Good boot option. Accessing safe mode will allow you to remove or replace device drivers that might be causing the error. Answer c is incorrect because you cannot access the Event Viewer until you can get into the system. If you do get back into your system, it would be a good idea to see if any errors are recorded in the Event Viewer. Finally, answer d is incorrect because the boot disk might need to be used but not until you try to recover with other methods.

6 Which of the following characters would you place at the beginning of a line in the Config.sys file if you wanted the system to ignore the line during boot?

a) ;

b) *

c) :

d) %

Answer a is correct. Placing a semicolon at the beginning of a line in a file such as Config.sys will cause the operating system to ignore the line. All of the other answers are incorrect.

7   You are troubleshooting a problem with a device driver that is loaded through Config.sys. The system has been working fine up to this point and no configuration changes have been made. When you check to see that the file still exists in the location specified in the Config.sys file, it is indeed there. What troubleshooting step are you most likely to perform next?

a)   Delete the line out of the Config.sys file.

b)   Copy the file to the root directory of the drive and amend the path in the Config.sys file accordingly.

c)   Rename the device driver to .VXD.

d)   Copy a new version of the file over the old.

Answer d is correct. If the device driver has been working correctly up to this point, and the file is still in its original location, chances are that the file has become corrupted. In this case, the first troubleshooting step should be to copy a new version of the file over the old. Answer a is incorrect. Removing the line from the file would cause the device driver to not load. Answer b is incorrect. Copying the file to a different location and amending the Config.sys entry would most likely not help. Answer c is not a valid troubleshooting step.

8   While working on a Windows 95 system, you receive the message "Bad or Missing Command.com." What troubleshooting step are you likely to perform first?

a)   Boot from a floppy disk and run Comrest.exe to restore the boot files.

b)   Boot from a floppy disk and run *fdisk /mbr*.

c)   Boot from a floppy disk and run Sys.com to restore the boot files.

d)   Boot from a floppy disk and reformat the drive.

Answer c is correct. The bad or missing Command.com message is produced when the boot process is unable to locate the Command.com file in its normal location. By booting from a floppy disk and using the Sys.com utility, you can replace the Command.com file. Answer a is incorrect. There is no utility called Comrest.exe. Answer b is incorrect. Replacing the Master Boot Record will not replace a missing or corrupted Command.com file. Answer d is incorrect. Formatting the drive will delete any and all of the data on it. This should not be done.

9   Through which file is the Himem.sys file loaded?

a)   Win.ini

b)   Config.sys

c)   Autoexec.bat

d)   System.ini

Answer b is correct. The Himem.sys driver is loaded through the Config.sys file. All of the other answers are incorrect.

10 On a Windows 2000 system, what is the name of the Dr.Watson log file?

a) Drwtsn32.log

b) User.dmp

c) Watson.log

d) Repair.log

Answer b is correct. The User.dmp file is the Dr.Watson log file on a Windows 2000 system. Answer a is incorrect. Drwtsn32.log is the Dr.Watson log file on a Windows NT system. The other answers are incorrect because they are not valid log file names for Dr.Watson.

11 You receive the message "Could Not Find Ntldr" when you start up your computer. What is the first thing you would check?

a) That the BIOS settings for the hard disk are correct

b) That the data connections for the hard disk are in place

c) That there is not a floppy disk in the floppy drive

d) That the power connections for the hard disk are in place

Answer c is correct. Most commonly, the "Could Not Find Ntldr" error appears when a floppy disk that was formatted under Windows NT 4 or Windows 2000 is left in the floppy drive and the system is restarted. Because this is one of the easiest things to check, this would also be one of the first things to check. Answer a is incorrect. If the BIOS settings for the hard drive were incorrect, the system would most likely not boot at all. Answers b and d are incorrect. If the power or data connectors for the hard drive were not connected properly, chances are that the system would give an error before you reach the Ntldr error.

12 You are working on a Windows 2000 system that is experiencing problems printing. Where would you go to restart the print spooler?

a) Control Panel, Administrative Tools, Services

b) Control Panel, Printers

c) Control Panel, Performance

d) Control Panel, Administrative Tools, Printers

Answer a is correct. The Print Spooler service is stopped and started through the Services utility, which is accessed through Control Panel. Answer b is incorrect. Although spooling is directly related to printing, the Print Spooler service is not stopped or started through the Printers utility. Answer c is incorrect. There is no Performance utility in Control Panel. Answer d is incorrect. There is no Printers utility under Administrative Tools in Control Panel.

13 When starting up a program, you get a message about an invalid working directory. What are you most likely to do to correct this problem? (Choose two.)

a) Edit the properties of the shortcut to the program.

b) Edit the setting within the program.

c) Reinstall the program.

d) Create a new directory with the same name as the program under C:\Temp.

Answers a and b are correct. The properties for a shortcut to a program can be edited to correct the path to the working directory, or some programs allow you to edit the path to the working directory within the program. Answer c is incorrect. Generally speaking, a problem with the working directory does not require that you reinstall the program. Answer d is incorrect. Creation of a directory under Temp will have no bearing on the situation.

14 What symbol is used in Device Manager to indicate that a device is not functioning correctly?

a) A yellow triangle with a black exclamation mark.

b) A red circle with a white *X* in it.

c) A red triangle with a white exclamation mark in it.

d) A yellow circle with a black exclamation mark in it.

Answer d is correct. A yellow circle with a black exclamation mark indicates that a device is not operating correctly. Answer a is invalid. Answer b describes a symbol that is used to identify a device that is missing or disabled. Answer c is invalid.

15 While installing a new device driver on a Windows 2000 system, you receive a message that the driver is unsigned. What does this mean?

a) The driver does not have any information in it about who wrote it.

b) It has not been approved by Microsoft to work with Windows 2000.

c) The driver has not yet registered itself with the system.

d) The driver has not yet been assigned system resources.

Answer b is correct. Signed drivers have been approved by Microsoft for operation with Windows 2000. You should try to avoid using unsigned drivers whenever possible. Answers a, c, and d are all incorrect.

16 A user calls you regarding a problem with logging on to the network. When you visit their workstation, you notice that the link light on the network card is not lit. Which of the following troubleshooting steps are you least likely to attempt?

a) Logging on with a different user name and password

b) Reinstalling the device drivers for the network card

c) Replacing the network card

d) Checking the network cabling between the user and the server

Answer a is correct. If the link light on the network card is not lit then there is no connection with the network. Therefore, attempting to log on with a different user ID and password will not yield any results. Answers b, c, and d are all valid troubleshooting steps.

17 You have determined that your system has a boot sector virus. Which of the following commands would you use to create a new Master Boot Record?

a) format c: /mbr

b) sys c: /mbr

c) fdisk /mbr

d) fdisk +mbr

Answer c is correct. To write a new Master Boot Record the command fdisk /mbr is used. All of the other answers are incorrect.

18 Which of the following is *not* a symptom of a virus infection?

a) Periodic system freezing

b) Unusual behavior in programs

c) Files being renamed or deleted

d) Power supply failure

Answer d is correct. Viruses can affect many aspects of the operation of the system, but they are not able (yet) to create symptoms like a power supply failure. Answers a, b, and c are incorrect. All of these are valid symptoms of a virus infection.

19 During the day, your antivirus software alerts you to the fact that your system has a virus on it. What is a correct procedure for removing the virus?

a)   Boot the system from a known clean floppy disk and run the anti-virus software.

b)   Disable the BIOS, boot the system from a known clean floppy disk, and run the antivirus software.

c)   Reboot the system and run the antivirus software.

d)   Reboot the system and run the *format /mbr* command.

Answer a is correct. If you suspect a virus on your system, you should restart the system from a known virus-free floppy disk and then run the antivirus software to remove the virus. Answer b is incorrect. If you disabled the BIOS the system would not boot at all. Answer c is incorrect. It is best to restart the system from a known clean working floppy disk before running the antivirus software. Answer d is incorrect. Even if you did suspect a boot record virus, you would use the Fdisk utility to correct it, not the Format command.

20 On a Windows 2000 system, how would you go about closing a program that has frozen?

a)   Press Ctrl+Alt+Delete and select Task Manager.

b)   Press Ctrl+Alt+Delete and select Programs.

c)   Press Ctrl+Alt+Delete and select Processes.

d)   Press Ctrl+Alt+Delete and select Close Current Program.

Answer a is correct. You can close a program that is not responding from within Task Manager. You can start Task Manager by pressing Ctrl+Alt+Delete and then selecting Task Manager. All of the other answers are incorrect.

Chapter 10

Networking the Operating System

In our modern computing world, networking has become the name of the game. Many homes and most offices now have at least a few computers networked and rely on these networks to conduct their day-to-day business. For us as PC technicians, the popularity of networks means that we will need to have a working knowledge of how they function and how they are configured and accessed from within the operating system.

Introducing the Network

So common are networks today that many of the new computer systems we buy ship with a network card and a modem as part of the package. In fact, many systems have such devices built right onto the motherboard. The world of networks can certainly be a confusing one, providing us with an endless variety of terms, acronyms, and jargon that are often as confusing to seasoned network administrators as they are to newcomers. Fortunately, as far as the A+ exams are concerned, we skirt the edge of these technologies, just dabbling our fingers in the murky abyss that is networking. As far as the exam goes, you will be expected to know basic networking terms and concepts.

> **Note**   The topic of networks is very broad and much of it falls well beyond the scope of the A+ exams. This chapter stays online with the CompTIA objectives in terms of content. If you want to explore the world of networking further, we recommend you investigate CompTIA's Network+ certification.

Configuring Protocols

Network protocols are the languages that make networking possible. They govern how devices on the network interact and provide systems that allow data to travel reliably on the network. We need protocols because unless two devices on the network know *how* to talk, they won't be able to. It's a bit like talking to someone who's speaking a language you do not understand; unless you agree with that person to speak your language, you won't be able to understand them. Entiendes?

There are three primary networking protocols used on today's networks— they are the Transmission Control Protocol/Internet Protocol (TCP/IP), Internetwork Packet Exchange/Sequenced Packet Exchange (IPX/SPX), AppleTalk and the NetBIOS Extended User Interface (NetBEUI).

TCP/IP

TCP/IP is now by far the networking protocol of choice. As well as being the preferred protocol for wide area networks, TCP/IP is also the protocol used on the Internet. Because almost every business (and many homes) has Internet access, it stands to reason that TCP/IP has become the standard network protocol. Although the term TCP/IP is used as if it is describing a single protocol, the TCP/IP suite of protocols actually comprises a large number of protocols. The term TCP/IP comes from the fact that these two protocols are the most commonly used of the suite.

When configuring TCP/IP, there are a number of different concepts and terms that you need to be familiar with.

TCP/IP Addressing   TCP/IP uses software-configured addresses to identify the system on the network. At the minimum there are two pieces of information that are required for addressing. These are the *IP address* and the *subnet mask*. The IP address uniquely identifies the system, and also defines what network segment the system is attached to. Because the IP address defines two things (the IP address of the system and the network to which it is attached), another number called a subnet mask is used by the system to determine what parts of the IP address denote the system, and what parts refer to the network ID.

In most cases it is also necessary to define the *default gateway*, a parameter that tells the system how to find a path from the network to which it is attached to remote networks. TCP/IP addresses can be assigned automatically via DHCP, which is discussed later in this chapter, or manually.

Domain Name System   The Domain Name System (DNS) is a network service that allows easy-to-remember host names such as www.microsoft.com to be translated into an IP address. The service is useful because it means that we can access a site by remembering the domain name instead of the much-harder-to-remember IP address.

For a system to be able to use DNS it must be configured with the IP address of at least one DNS server. These servers are the systems that actually perform the domain name to IP address translation. As with the IP addressing information, the DNS server information can be supplied automatically via DHCP, or configured manually.

Note   Because DNS is such an important service, it is common to provide the addresses of two DNS servers so that if the first DNS server is unavailable there is another server that can answer requests. The DNS servers are referred to as the primary and secondary DNS servers in this instance.

Try This   There is a more detailed discussion about the DNS service later in this chapter.

Windows Internet Naming Service   One final network service we should mention is the Windows Internet Naming Service (WINS). Like DNS, WINS is designed for those of us who cannot remember those IP address numbers. Unlike DNS, however, WINS is designed to map computer (NetBIOS) names to IP addresses. For example, if you have a computer with the address 192.168.23.45, it can resolve this address to the computer's name, which might be something like secretary1, server1, or bobs-computer.

 Test Smart   WINS is used to resolve NetBIOS names to IP addresses.

Automatic IP Address Assignment   An important element of understanding TCP/IP is that of addressing. Each and every computer wanting to use the Internet needs to have a TCP/IP address assigned to it. TCP/IP addresses are assigned to the system's network card and can be viewed by looking at the properties of the network card. Figure 10-1 shows the TCP/IP settings on a Windows 2000 or Windows XP system.

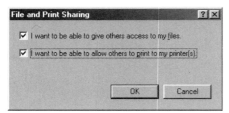

Figure 10-1 The network connection's properties dialog box shows the TCP/IP settings on a Windows 2000 or Windows XP system.

Dynamic Host Configuration Protocol   There are two ways in which a computer can get valid TCP/IP addressing information. One way is manually (statically), which requires that the information is typed in on each system individually; and the other is automatically (dynamically) via a system called the Dynamic Host Configuration Protocol (DHCP). Each time a computer attempts to connect to a network that uses DHCP for address assignment, it receives the IP address information from a DHCP server. The IP addresses are leased to the computer for a specified period of time from a predefined range of IP addresses. At various times during the lease, the IP address is renewed. If for some reason it is not possible to renew the same address, the DHCP server will supply a different but still valid address. For this reason, systems such as servers that need to have the same IP address all the time are unsuited to having dynamically assigned addresses.

Test Smart   The function of DHCP is to dynamically assign TCP/IP information to systems on a TCP/IP network.

To configure your TCP/IP information manually, you will need to ask your ISP or network administrator to provide you with the TCP/IP information. You will be required to input this information in the network connection settings on your system.

If a system configured for DHCP cannot find a DHCP server, it will assign itself an IP address automatically. These IP addresses are in the reserved private range of 169.254.*x.x*. This process is called *Automatic Private IP Addressing (APIPA)*. This feature was not available on Windows NT 4 and Windows 95.

Internetwork Packet Exchange/Sequenced Packet Exchange

TCP/IP is not the only protocol on the block, just the one most used. Once upon a time, the Internet Packet Exchange/Sequenced Packet Exchange (IPX/SPX) protocol was as popular as TCP/IP. IPX/SPX is a protocol suite like TCP/IP, comprising numerous individual protocols. IPX/SPX was used primarily with Novell NetWare networks.

Like TCP/IP networks, all computers in an IPX/SPX network must have a unique address assigned to them, and the IPX/SPX addresses are assigned to a system by modifying the network connection settings. Although IPX/SPX is a widely deployed protocol, TCP/IP, with the encouragement of software vendors, is quickly becoming the de facto standard for both local and wide area networks. Even Novell now uses TCP/IP as the default protocol on NetWare networks, with IPX/SPX supplied only for use if needed.

Test Smart   Do not expect to see any questions on the exam regarding IPX/SPX. Just know that it is another protocol used on networks.

AppleTalk

It will probably come as no surprise to learn that AppleTalk is a protocol introduced to network Apple computers. Today, even Apple networks are more likely to use TCP/IP, although parts of the AppleTalk protocol are still used.

Unless you are working on an Apple or Macintosh network, the chances are slim that you will find the need (or desire) to install AppleTalk on a system, though many of the commonly used operating systems can support it if needed.

Addressing on an AppleTalk network is basically automatic, though the network administrator does assign a unique number to each segment of the network. Then, when a system running AppleTalk is powered on, it generates a random address for itself and then checks with the other systems on the network to make sure that the address is not already in use. If, as is very likely, it is not, the system then uses that address.

NetBEUI

No discussion of network protocols would be complete without mentioning NetBEUI, or the NetBIOS Extended User Interface. Microsoft and IBM created NetBEUI in the mid-1980s as a protocol for small- to medium-sized networks. NetBEUI is very fast because it has a low overhead, but this low overhead also gives it limited functionality. NetBEUI is a non-routable protocol, and as such found its popularity on small localized networks. Perhaps the strongest appeal of NetBEUI is that it is arguably the easiest protocol to configure because it does not require addressing configuration.

NetBEUI is also basically self-configuring. For addressing, NetBEUI uses the NetBIOS computer name, which is the name by which the system is recognized on the network. Examples of a NetBIOS name include things like *bobspc* and *server1*.

Note   One thing to be aware of is that operating systems can use more than one protocol at a time. For example, it might be that you use TCP/IP for Internet access and AppleTalk to communicate with Apple Macintosh machines on the network.

Configuring Client Options

With your network card installed and your protocol configured, the next step in connecting to the network is the client software. Client software is what makes it possible to use the services of other systems on the network. Ever since the early versions of Windows, Microsoft has included Client For Microsoft Networks with its operating systems. In early versions of Windows, the software had to be installed separately; in today's versions, it is integrated into the OS and installed by default if you have a network card. All that remains after you have installed (or verified) the client software is to configure it for connection to the network.

Note   To connect to other server systems it might be necessary to install additional client software. A good example of this is Novell NetWare, which, to use all of the functionality available, requires that you install additional client software on your system.

Domain or Workgroup?   Windows OS–based networks can operate on one of two principles—domain or workgroup. Domain networks are associated with a client/server network model, while workgroups are used with the peer-to-peer model. In a domain environment, a server is used to perform centralized authentication and other tasks. In a workgroup environment, administration is decentralized with each system being responsible for authentication. To create a domain, you will need a network operating system on the server such as Windows NT Server or Windows 2000 Server. All Microsoft operating systems since Windows For Workgroups 3.1 support workgroup-based networks.

Configuring client software is as simple as supplying a couple of pieces of information. If you are using a PC and you want to become a member of a workgroup, you must specify the name of the workgroup in the network configuration. On a Windows 9x system this is done through the Network folder in the Control Panel. In Windows 2000, it's done on the Network Identification tab of the System Properties dialog box, accessed from the System icon in the Control Panel. Figure 10-2 shows this dialog box.

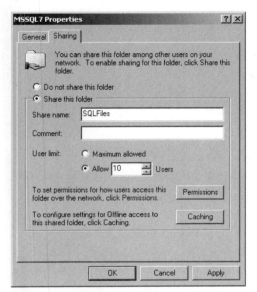

Figure 10-2 In Windows 2000 it is possible to join a domain using the Network Identification tab of the System Properties dialog box.

Becoming a member of a domain is a little more complicated and requires that you specify the name of the domain as well as supply credentials for a user account on the domain server that has the special privileges required to add your computer to the domain. The network administrator can provide these details to you.

Note Workgroups are an odd concept in that all they really are is a method of logically grouping computers together on the network. This makes it easier to find resources when using something like Network Neighborhood but does little else. For centralized administration you will need to operate in a client/server domain environment.

Configuring Novell NetWare Clients

If you are connecting a system to a Novell NetWare network, you will use client software. Novell provides client software, as does Microsoft. Which one you use will depend on the services and software installed on your network. The Novell-supplied client has more features than the Microsoft client, but both require the same information in order to connect to and use network resources. This information includes

- **User name** This would be the user name that you are supplied to log on to the network.

■ **Password**　You should be provided with a password along with the user name.

■ **Tree**　NetWare uses a concept known as trees to organize resources on the network. Because there can be more than one tree accessible to you, it is necessary to specify which tree you want to connect to.

■ **Context**　The context is the location within the tree where the user ID you want to log in as resides.

■ **Server**　Although it is not strictly necessary to do so, you can if you want specify the name of a server that you want to connect to. If a server name is not supplied, NetWare automatically selects the most appropriate server for you.

Generally speaking, you would ask the network administrator for information such as the tree name, the context, and the server. Once the information has been entered the first time, it is remembered by the client software (with the exception of the password, obviously) so that it need not be reentered each time the user needs to log on.

The Last Piece of the Puzzle

Finally, once all of the ingredients (network card, protocol, client software) are in place, the last thing you will need to be able to connect to the network is a user name and password. If you are using a client/server network, these will be managed and issued centrally. If you are in a workgroup environment, you will need to coordinate user IDs and passwords with other users who are granting you access to their systems or accessing yours.

Tools for Verifying the Configuration

A number of tools are used on a network to verify connectivity or get information about the network setting for a system. Because most networks now use TCP/IP, our focus (and that of the A+ objectives) is on those tools you can use to troubleshoot TCP/IP-related connectivity.

■ **Ipconfig**　The Ipconfig command displays the TCP/IP configuration on Windows systems. The most common command syntax used with the utility is *ipconfig /all*, which displays information on all network cards in the system. Information supplied includes the default gateway and the subnet mask, the MAC address of the network card, DNS server information, and DHCP lease information. Ipconfig can also be used to release and renew addresses obtained via DHCP.

- **Winipcfg** The Winipcfg utility is a graphical version of the Ipconfig utility found only in Windows 9*x* and Windows Me. Like Ipconfig, Winipcfg can report TCP/IP configuration information and can also be used to release and renew TCP/IP addresses obtained via DHCP.

Test Smart Ipconfig and Winipcfg are utilities used to verify TCP/IP information as well as to refresh and renew that information.

- **Ping** Perhaps the mostly widely used TCP/IP utility of all, the Ping utility tests connectivity between networked devices. Ping works by sending a certain number of data packets to another system and waits for it to send them back. Ping reports how many of the packets it received back, and how long the round trip between the two devices took to complete.

- **Tracert** You can think of the Tracert utility as a kind of advanced Ping. Whereas Ping verifies connectivity to a remote system, Tracert verifies the route to a remote system by reporting the status of every step on the journey. If a Ping fails, you can use Tracert to determine where along the path the problem exists.

- **Nslookup** The Nslookup utility can be used to troubleshoot the DNS configuration on a system. It is often used in advanced DNS troubleshooting and should not factor very much in the A+ exams.

Sharing

One of the fundamental and cornerstone functions of a network is the ability to easily share data with other users. When you wish to allow other network users access to your files and folders (whether located on a hard disk or a CD-ROM drive), you can choose to share a specific directory (including all subdirectories), or you can choose to share your entire hard drive. All operating systems offer some degree of security for shared drives, but some are more capable than others in this respect. For example, on a Windows 9*x* system you can specify a password that must be supplied when accessing the share, and another to provide limited access to the file. Windows NT and Windows 2000 take security one step further by including a set of permissions that can be applied to the share, and are then able to further secure data by making use of the secure file system (NTFS) that was discussed in Chapter 8.

Note When sharing your hard drive, be sure you understand the security implications.

Sharing Print and File Services

Sharing a drive or directory is a simple process, though depending on what operating system you are using there might be additional steps. By default Windows NT and Windows 2000 are configured to share resources. In Windows 9x and Windows Me, File And Printer Sharing must first be installed and then you must specify that you wish to make files and/or printers available to other users. Figure 10-3 shows the File And Printer Sharing dialog box from a Windows 98 system.

Figure 10-3 You enable file and printer sharing in Windows 98 through the File And Printer Sharing dialog box.

Test Smart   If you try to share a drive on a Windows 98 system and the Sharing option appears dimmed, you probably need to enable File And Printer Sharing.

The easiest way to share a drive or folder is to navigate through My Computer until you locate the directory or drive you want to share, right click, and then choose Sharing from the menu. You should see a screen similar to that shown in Figure 10-4.

Figure 10-4 There are a number of properties you can configure when sharing a folder in Windows 2000.

Once you have completed the fields and clicked OK, the resource will be available to other systems on the network. You can tell when a folder, printer, or drive is successfully shared because a hand appears under the folder, as shown in Figure 10-5.

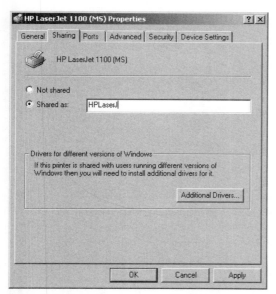

Figure 10-5 Shared files and folders appear with a hand underneath.

Accessing Shared Drives

Sharing resources on a computer is the first step in the process; the second is accessing those shares from another computer. Modern operating systems make it as easy as they can to access shared resources; it is really not that difficult. There are numerous ways to access a shared drive on another system. The following describes some of the most common.

■ **Using My Computer** When you right-click the My Computer icon, you have an option to map a network drive. You can either browse the network to find the resource you are looking for or connect directly by specifying the resource you want to access. When choosing to map a drive, you can specify whether or not to have the drive reconnected each time the system starts. Figure 10-6 shows an example of the Map Network Drive dialog box on a Windows 2000 system.

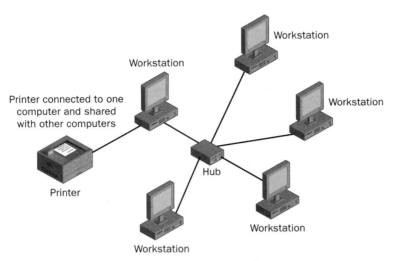

Figure 10-6 Mapping a drive can be done through My Computer.

Test Smart   If you don't select the Reconnect At Logon check box, the drive mapping will be lost when you restart the computer.

■ **Through Network Neighborhood**   On Windows 9*x* platforms, you can browse the network through Network Neighborhood to locate a share or resource that you want to access. Then you can choose to map a network drive to that point. You can also map a drive by right-clicking Network Neighborhood and selecting Map Network Drive from the menu.

■ **Right-click My Network Places**   In Windows 2000, you can map a drive by right-clicking My Network Places and selecting Map Network Drive from the menu. As with Windows 9*x*, you can also browse the network and then select a network resource to map to.

■ **From the command line**   Though it might seem a little old school to connect to a network share using the command line, it can, and often is, still done. If you want, you can map a network drive from the command prompt by using the *Net Use* command. This is useful if you want to map network drives through a batch file or logon script.

UNCs—What's In a Name?   When mapping to resources, a format known as the *Universal Naming Convention (UNC)* is used. The UNC was created to make a uniform method of referring to resources on the network. The basic format of a UNC is \\servername\sharename\subdirectory\subdirectory. The only required elements are the *servername* and the *sharename*. The *subdirectory* elements are optional. So, if you were trying to access a shared folder called info on a server called server1, the UNC would be \\server1\info.

In Windows networking, the NetBIOS name (discussed later) is used as the server element of the UNC and the resource you are accessing is the sharename. This method of UNC naming works both for file shares and for printers. For example, you could connect to a folder share called \\bobspc\data as well as a printer share called \\bobspc\laser.

Sharing Printers

As well as sharing folders and drives, you can also share resources, such as printers, that are connected to your system. As with file sharing, you must first ensure that the system is set up to make printers available on the network. This function is enabled automatically in Windows NT 4 and Windows 2000, but it will need to be enabled manually on other Windows platforms.

Once your system is set up to share the printer, the actual sharing is as easy as clicking a button. From the Printers folder in Control Panel, right-click the printer you want to share and select the Sharing option from the shortcut menu. As with files, once the printer has been successfully shared, a hand will appear under its icon. Figure 10-7 shows the process of sharing a printer.

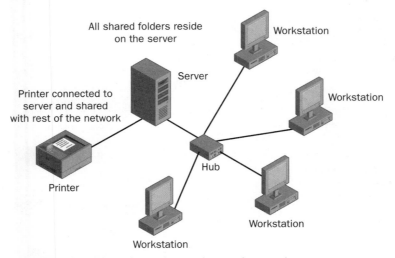

Figure 10-7 Select the option to share a printer on the network.

Setting Permissions to Shared Resources

An important consideration when sharing resources is that of protecting them with permissions. Without permissions, unauthorized users could potentially gain access to files on your computer.

When you create a share, there are four levels of security that you can apply to it. These permissions are

- **No Access**   The No Access permission is a restrictive permission because it can take away all other permissions.

- **Read**   The Read permission enables a user to view and list all the files within the share, but not to make any changes to the files.

- **Change**   The Change permission allows a user to view, list, make changes to, and rename files within the share. The only thing it doesn't do is allow a user to modify the permissions to a share. For that you need the Full Control permission.

- **Full Control**   With the Full Control permission, a user can do anything to a share including renaming files, changing permissions on the share, and even renaming the share. This is a powerful permission and should only be assigned to users that absolutely need this level of permission.

An important consideration when assigning rights is understanding that user and group rights can be combined, with one exception. If you assign a user or a group No Access to a share, that will override all other permissions to that user or group. For example, if a user was assigned Full Control to a share but the user was a member of a group that was assigned No Access to the share, the user's rights to the share would be none. The No Access permission overrides all others. All of the other rights are cumulative. So, if you assigned a user the Read permission, but assigned a group of which that user was a member the Change permission, the user's rights would be Change.

> **Note**   A further consideration when assigning permissions is that NTFS permissions can combine with share permissions. This can create problems; it might seem like a user should have access to something but they don't because the permissions are combined. Likewise, a user might be able to access something they shouldn't!

When assigning permissions to shared resources, be sure that you understand what you are granting access to and to whom.

Configuring the Network Card

The *network card* is an important piece of hardware in terms of networking and provides the physical connection to the network. Computers within a network communicate from network card to network card over some type of network media, such as UTP cable. In the past, the type of media connection was a major consideration when buying a network card. Nowadays, almost every network card comes with a UTP connection. If you need some other type of connection like coaxial or fiber-optic, you will likely have to order it specially.

Once the network card is installed in the system, you need to make sure that it is recognized by the operating system. Thanks to Plug and Play, this is now a simple task and often there is very little or no configuration required. As was discussed in Chapter 6, it is important to have the latest drivers for your network card. Even if your system does plug and play the network card straight away, you should still make sure you have the latest version of the drivers installed. To make sure that your network card has been correctly installed, you can check it in Device Manager. If you are using Windows 9*x*, you should then be able to further configure the card through the Network folder in Control Panel. On a Windows 2000 system, configuration is performed through the Network And Dial-Up Connections folder in Control Panel.

Accessing the Internet

The Internet is itself the world's largest network. When you log on to the Internet, your system actually becomes part of that giant network and can access resources like any other network. In this section, we look at some of the concepts and terminology that you will need to understand when supporting users who access the Internet.

Internet Service Providers

By now, many of us are familiar with Internet service providers (ISPs) simply because we have Internet access available in our homes. ISPs are companies that specialize in providing Internet access to home and business users. ISPs can provide different types of Internet access including dial-up phone access, cable access, and digital subscriber line (DSL).

Some ISP connections, such as cable, allow you to log on to the Internet and do not require you to input a user name and password to do so. Other connection methods, such as dial-up using a modem, will require that you input a valid user name and password every time you make the connection to the ISP's server. If your ISP connection requires that you enter a user name and password and you are having problems, make sure that you are entering this information correctly.

TCP/IP

You won't get far in a discussion about networking without bumping into TCP/IP. This is especially true with respect to the Internet, because it is TCP/IP that makes the Internet possible.

TCP/IP is suited to both wide area networks, such as the Internet, and local area networks. TCP/IP is actually more than a single protocol; it is a *protocol suite*, meaning that there are several individual protocols that operate under the TCP/IP banner. In the following sections we look at some of these protocols and the services that they perform.

E-Mail

One function many of us have come to rely on is e-mail. E-mail allows us to send and receive messages via the Internet. To use e-mail, your system must have a connection to the Internet and you must have a means, and an account, to connect to an e-mail server.

Most of the e-mail services we use today require the use of the Simple Mail Transfer Protocol (SMTP) to send mail and Post Office Protocol (POP) to receive mail. The current version of POP being used is version 3 (POP3).

 Test Smart   The SMTP protocol is used to send e-mail and the POP3 protocol is used to receive it.

An additional e-mail retrieval protocol is the Internet Message Access Protocol or IMAP. IMAP is similar to POP in that it is used for retrieving e-mail and not sending it, which is still the responsibility of SMTP. One of the most significant differences between POP and IMAP is that the latter has a more robust authentication system. POP actually transmits passwords in clear text, whereas IMAP does not. In order to use IMAP, both the server and the client must be configured to use it.

HTML

The Hypertext Markup Language (HTML) and the Internet are like Batman and Robin. One without the other is only half the fun. HTML is a special language that makes it possible to use tags to define how a certain string of text should be treated within a file. For example, the HTML tag Hello will cause the word *Hello* to be displayed in bold when viewed through a program that can translate the tag language. In the case of HTML, the program doing the translation is a browser such as Internet Explorer. HTML is not the only tag file format used on the Internet, but it is by far the most common.

> **Note** Talking about HTML brings up an interesting point. Many people think that the World Wide Web is the Internet, which in fact is incorrect. The Internet is actually a computer network. The WWW is a collection of servers all providing information to people who access the information using the Hypertext Transfer Protocol (HTTP). So, the WWW and the Internet are actually different things, though one could not exist without the other.

HTTP

Hypertext Transfer Protocol (HTTP) is used to establish a connection with a Web server and transmit HTML pages to the client browser. HTTP is a relatively simple protocol with a limited number of actions that it can perform. One of the drawbacks of HTTP is that requests and responses are sent in an unsecure manner. For that reason, a variation of HTTP called HTTPS is available, which provides more security.

> **Note** Although the correct designation of a URL for an Internet Web site is http: //www.microsoft.com, modern browsers assume that you are going to be using HTTP and so don't require that you explicitly define it. That's why you can just type www.microsoft.com into your browser and it will still work.

HTTPS

The Hypertext Transport Transfer Protocol Secure (HTTPS) protocol is used for accessing a secure Web server such as in online banking or other secure Internet transactions. Using HTTPS in the URL instead of HTTP directs the browser to establish a secure connection. The URL for an HTTPS connection will always start with HTTPS instead of HTTP; for example, https://www.phoneybank.com.

Secure Sockets Layer

The Secure Sockets Layer (SSL) is the security system used by HTTPS. SSL works by encrypting information sent to and received from a remote host, making it unreadable by a third party. For SSL to be used, both the Web server and the client software (the browser) must support it. Fortunately, SSL is a very widely supported protocol and you should not experience any problems accessing a secure site with any modern Web browser.

Telnet

Telnet is a protocol that allows a session to be opened on a remote host. You can use the remote host as if you are actually sitting at that system. Telnet is popular for accessing UNIX and Linux systems as well as for configuring network devices such as routers and switches.

FTP

File Transfer Protocol (FTP) is used to send and receive files from a remote computer—for example, it can be used when downloading a program from the Internet. FTP has a simple set of commands that can be used with it, such as GET, which retrieves a file, and PUT, which sends a file. Although command line FTP can still be used with all FTP servers, many people prefer to use a graphical FTP client such as CuteFTP. It makes the FTP process almost invisible and makes it unnecessary to remember usage and syntax for the FTP commands.

Domain Name System

In a TCP/IP network, computers identify themselves using IP addresses. An IP address is composed of four sets of numbers, each separated by periods. A valid IP address would be 192.168.34.23. This number strategy is fine for computers. But for most of us, remembering one number is hard enough; a set of four is out of the question. As we discussed earlier, to make things a bit easier on us, we have the Domain Name System (DNS). DNS is used to correlate those difficult-to-remember IP addresses with more friendly names. For example, instead of typing in our browsers the IP address **http://207.46.134.155**, DNS allows us to go with the friendlier **www.microsoft.com**.

 Test Smart   For the exam, remember that the function of DNS is to resolve host names to IP addresses.

.com or .org?   On the Internet, organizations are defined by their domain name and also by a domain name extension. Although the policing of these extensions is somewhat lax, there are some basic guidelines that determine what the domain name extension is supposed to be, based on the function of the organization. Table 10-1 lists the major domain name extensions.

Table 10-1   Internet Domains

Extension	Purpose	Example
.com	Commercial business	www.microsoft.com
.org	Not for profit organizations	www.comptia.org
.edu	Educational organizations	www.harvard.edu
.gov	Government organizations	www.whitehouse.gov
.mil	Military organizations	www.nic.mil
.net	Internet organizations	www.att.net

In addition, domain names can include country extensions; for example, Canada has the .ca extension, Australia has .au, and England has .uk. There are also a growing number of alternative domain names such as .info and .fm.

Internet Connectivity Technologies

Nowadays, it almost seems like it's hard to find a computer or network that doesn't have Internet access. For that reason, understanding the various methods by which Internet access is provided is a key consideration for anyone working with PCs on a technical level.

In the following sections, we will look at some of the methods used to gain Internet access, including modem, cable, DSL, and satellite, to name a few. Of these methods, dial-up networking via a modem is the one you are likely to encounter the most, and the one that has the most considerations.

Dial-up Networking

Many of us have at least seen a dial-up Internet connection and perhaps at some point configured one. A dial-up connection to the Internet requires a modem and a special protocol called the Point-to-Point Protocol (PPP). The many wizards used in modern operating systems make configuring a dial-up connection to the Internet fairly straightforward. To initiate the connection to the Internet using a dial-up connection, we need a few things, including

- An installed dial-up adapter
- The correct telephone number to dial the Internet connection
- The TCP/IP protocol installed
- The TCP/IP settings from the ISP
- A valid user name and password

Configuring your dial-up connection depends on the operating system you are using; however, both the earlier Windows 9*x* systems right up through Windows XP provide wizards to guide you through the configuration of the dial-up Internet connection. Regardless of the OS used, you will need the same configuration information from the ISP to make the connection to the Internet.

Note   If you are installing dial-up networking on a Windows NT 4 system, you have one additional step. You will need to install the Remote Access Service. The procedures for this are clearly identified by Microsoft.

Anyone who has used a dial-up connection has no doubt at some point needed to troubleshoot it. Whether the connection fails completely or is simply too slow, there are some common errors that seem to creep up all the time. Table 10-2 identifies some dial-up networking connection problems and potential solutions.

Table 10-2   Troubleshooting Dial-up Connections

Connection Problem	Solution
You cannot log on using your user name or password.	This is often caused by either the user name or password being incorrectly typed. You might need to contact your ISP to ensure that you have the correct data.
When the modem dials, you hear someone answer the phone.	If you have incorrectly entered the phone number to connect to the ISP, you might dial a regular number. In such a case, you might hear someone attempt to answer your modem. Verify that you have the correct number entered.
You receive an error message indicating that the ISP server cannot negotiate the protocol.	This error is often a result of TCP/IP not being installed on your system. Verify that TCP/IP is installed.
Your modem connects but operates too slowly.	Verify that you are using the correct and most recent drivers for your modem.
Your modem connects but periodically hangs up.	This often happens because the incorrect modem driver is being used or sometimes because the settings for the modem are not correct. Ensure that the settings you entered are the same as those provided by the ISP.

Test Smart   For the A+ exam, you will be expected to be able to identify common problems with dial-up connections. Be sure you are familiar with the material presented in Table 10-2.

DSL Networking

Digital subscriber line, or DSL, is an always-on Internet access method that uses a phone line to deliver high-speed Internet access. It is a popular means of accessing the Internet but is only available in certain areas. The main factor limiting the availability of DSL is that you must be within a certain distance of the telephone company's exchange in order to use it. This makes DSL popular in urban areas but less so in less populated areas.

When you sign up for DSL access, the provider will either rent or sell you a DSL modem. This modem translates the signals from your computer into a format that can be sent over the phone line. In most cases the rental of the modem is just part of the overall monthly fee.

When the company supplies the DSL modem they might also supply a network card to be installed in your PC. Often they will even come and install the network card. The card will most likely be a UTP network card and the DSL provider will give you a UTP cable to connect the card to the modem. The DSL modem is then plugged into the wall socket and, from a hardware point of view, the connection is ready to go.

The DSL provider will give you information on how to configure the network connection for the DSL service, along with information relating to e-mail servers, news servers, and so on. Nowadays it is almost certain that IP addressing information will be automatically supplied via a DHCP server. For this reason you should not manually configure addressing information for the connection unless the DSL provider explicitly tells you to do so.

With the addressing information set to be obtained automatically, you should now just be able to start the Web browser and use the Internet. It might be necessary to configure the browser so that it knows to use the DSL connection, which would actually be regarded as a LAN connection in many browser configurations. Again, the DSL provider will most likely supply all of the information you need to configure browsers and e-mail software.

Because the DSL modem is not a user-configurable piece of equipment, troubleshooting a DSL connection is really limited to checking all of the physical connections and ensuring that all of the software settings are configured correctly. If you have checked and double-checked these things, you should contact the DSL provider for help.

ISDN Networking

Although ISDN is not as popular today as it once was, this high-speed Internet access method is still a common sight in corporate environments and in some homes where other methods of high-speed Internet access are not available.

ISDN uses a special phone line and specialized equipment called terminal adapters to provide a connection. A terminal adapter can be either a card that is installed in a system, a dedicated external device, or a port on another piece of networking equipment such as a router. The function of the terminal adapter or TA is to convert the signals so that they can be transmitted over the line.

Although ISDN is a high-speed service, it is still considered a dial-up method because the connection is only established when there is traffic to be sent or received. Another consideration is that unlike services such as DSL or cable, with an ISDN service you are normally charged for each second that you are using the connection. This raises additional concerns such as ensuring that the connection is not left on unnecessarily. Software configurations such as the address settings will be supplied by the ISP.

Troubleshooting ISDN connections often requires a call to the telephone company that provides the service, because apart from checking the software configuration and hardware connections, there is little else to do. In the early stages of deployment of an ISDN connection, tweaking of the configuration to minimize line time or optimization of the connection might produce unexpected results. For this reason, make changes one at a time and ensure that you wait to see if the changes cause any problems before making any more.

Cable

In areas that have cable television service, many cable television providers have now started to provide Internet access. Cable Internet is an always-on service that provides high-speed Internet access.

To get cable Internet access, apart from a cable company that provides the service, you will also need a cable modem and a network card installed in your computer system. The cable modem is a special device that translates the signal from the network card into a format that can be sent over the cable connection. In many cases the network card will be supplied and fitted into the system by the cable provider. In other cases you might be required to fit the card, or have it fitted, yourself.

In terms of software configuration, the cable ISP will provide you with the necessary information for configuring e-mail clients and Web browsers. They will also provide you with information for configuring the addressing of the system. As with the other connectivity methods discussed in this section, the likelihood is that addressing will be performed automatically via DHCP, although it is also possible to obtain static addresses where necessary.

When it comes to troubleshooting, the first thing to check with a cable Internet connection is that the hardware connections are correct and that any software configurations are as they should be. Often, cable modems have LEDs on them, which can indicate a problem with the actual connection. Many cable ISPs prefer that you do not cycle the power on a cable modem or disconnect the cable that is used to transmit the signal without first checking with them.

As with many of the other Internet connectivity methods discussed here, the cable ISP is normally able to perform remote diagnostics on your connection and modem, so if you are experiencing a problem, don't wait too long to phone them. If the problem is with the connection or the modem, a call to the tech support department can get you up and running faster. If it is not, at least you can exclude that from the troubleshooting process.

Satellite

Satellite Internet access is becoming popular in areas where other high-speed Internet access methods such as cable and DSL are not available. In terms of configuration, satellite Internet access can be reasonably complex because there are a number of components, including dishes, special interface cards, cabling, and software. For this reason, it is very common for satellite Internet access providers to provide a complete service that includes installation. Of course, in really remote areas this might be impractical, in which case detailed instructions and phone support will normally be available to make the installation process as easy as possible.

As we discussed in Chapter 6, there are two ways in which satellite Internet access can be implemented. In a one-way configuration, requests are sent over a modem to the provider and the replies are received over the much faster satellite link. In a two-way configuration, both the request and replies are sent over the satellite link. The advantage of the two-way system is that it is faster and does not require a modem and phone line. The downside is that the hardware and configuration for the link is even more complex.

From a software perspective, aside from any special driver software needed for the satellite hardware, the same e-mail and Web browser programs will be used with a satellite link as with any other. The satellite ISP will provide the necessary information for the configurations.

When it comes to troubleshooting problems with a satellite Internet access link, apart from checking software configurations and physical connections there is probably not much more you should do before contacting the satellite ISP.

Wireless

Wireless Internet access is becoming increasingly popular in populated areas where a single wireless access point can provide service to a large number of people.

To get access to a wireless Internet connection, you will need a wireless network card and an account with the ISP that is providing the service. In some environments, an account with an ISP is not necessary because the service is provided free of charge by the establishment you are in.

In environments where wireless Internet access is provided as a courtesy, there is unlikely to be any significant amount of technical support. Therefore, if you are experiencing a problem you might well have to troubleshoot it yourself. Apart from making sure that the wireless network card is functioning correctly, you should also ensure that your software configuration is correct for the environment you are in. In almost all cases this means that addressing information is obtained automatically.

> **Note**   Sometimes, if you find that you are moving between different areas that provide wireless Internet access, you might need to reboot the system or refresh the network addressing information in order to get a connection.

LAN

In a corporate environment, providing Internet access over a LAN is becoming the norm. One or more systems or even dedicated hardware devices are connected to the Internet, and that connection is then shared between systems on the network. In a home environment, the availability of high-speed Internet access methods such as cable and DSL, and the availability of affordable network devices that can be used to share an Internet connection, has led many a home network to now have shared Internet access as well.

> **Note**   Discussing the mechanisms by which Internet access is provided over a LAN is beyond the scope of A+ and, to be honest, there are so many possible configurations that it would be impossible to cover them all.

The key element in configuring and troubleshooting an Internet connection over a LAN is to remember that there is nearly always another system or device between you and the Internet. That means that during the troubleshooting process you must keep this in mind. It also means that the configuration of software such as browsers and e-mail clients will depend on the configuration of the network.

Internet Connection Sharing   For those who remember, Windows 98 Second Edition included a new and well-promoted feature, Internet Connection Sharing (ICS). ICS is a simple concept and is designed to allow one system to share its Internet connection with the other computers on the network. This provides an easy way to allow several systems to access the Internet without each one needing to have its own connection. ICS functionality has been included with subsequent Windows operating systems including Windows Me, Windows 2000, and Windows XP.

 Test Smart   ICS allows a computer on a network to share the Internet connection to other users on the network.

Installing and Configuring Browsers

Browsers are programs that are used to view pages formatted in certain languages such as the Hypertext Markup Language (HTML) or the Extensible

Markup Language (XML). Browser programs are often referred to as Web browsers because that's what they are mostly used for—browsing the Web. Nowadays, however, many other programs take advantage of the browser's functionality, including help systems and reference material.

Perhaps the most common browser program is Microsoft Internet Explorer, though there are other browser programs, such as Netscape Navigator and Mozilla. Generally speaking, functionality between browsers is very similar and all of the major browser software is free to download and install. On PC systems that get their configuration information via DHCP, there is typically no configuration required to get a browser working and accessing pages from the Internet. If you are using a system that is manually configured for TCP/IP, you might need to provide additional information, such as the addresses of DNS servers and perhaps even a default gateway, before the browser will be able to access the Internet. Figure 10-8 shows the Internet Explorer Web browser.

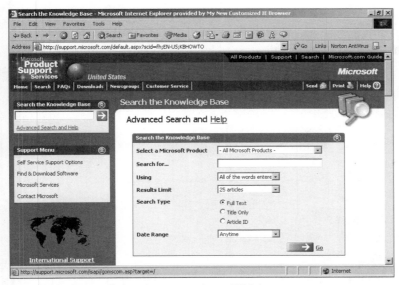

Figure 10-8   Internet Explorer is a commonly used Web browser.

As a PC technician, you will often be asked to configure browsers for Internet connectivity. In the A+ objectives, CompTIA specifies three areas of browser configuration that you need to be aware of.

Enabling/Disabling Script Support

Scripts are small programs embedded within Web pages that can add functionality to or enhance the appearance of a Web page. The problem is that these same scripts can also contain malicious code that can perform actions on or from your

PC without you knowing. As you can imagine, this can cause some concern, so browser programs commonly provide facilities that allow you to disable the running of scripts and thus negate the risks presented by running scripts.

In Internet Explorer, you can configure support for scripts by selecting Tools, Internet Options, Security and then clicking the Custom Level button. You can then enable or disable script support as appropriate.

Configuring Proxy Settings

As many people, particularly those on a business or home network, access the Internet through a LAN, understanding how to configure access through a proxy server is important. A proxy server is a system that processes Internet requests and responses on behalf of another system. Proxy servers can either be software running on a PC or dedicated hardware devices. In either case the configuration of the browser is the same.

When you access the Internet through a proxy server, you must tell the browser to send requests to the proxy server rather than directly to the Internet. In Internet Explorer this configuration is accessed through the Tools menu, by choosing Internet Options, Connections, and LAN Settings. You should then see the dialog box shown in Figure 10-9.

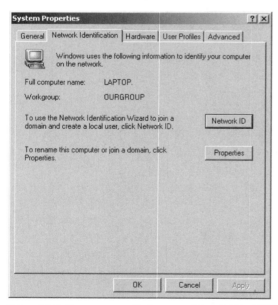

Figure 10-9 Proxy server settings are configured in the LAN Settings dialog box.

To use a proxy server, first click the Use A Proxy Server check box and then specify the address of the proxy server you wish to use. You can also configure a specific TCP/IP port. The default TCP/IP port for HTTP is 80, but it might be that your proxy server is configured to listen to requests on another port number. You should check with your network administrator to see if this is the case.

Configuring Security Settings

The Internet can be a dangerous place. OK, so that sounds a little dramatic but in terms of your computer, it's basically true. Numerous threats exist that can at worst affect the configuration of your computer system and at least cause personal information to be "extracted" from your PC. For this reason, browsers have features designed to protect your PC and the information on it from unscrupulous eyes. In Internet Explorer these features are configured by choosing Tools, Internet Options, and then selecting the Security tab. You can see an example of this screen in Figure 10-10.

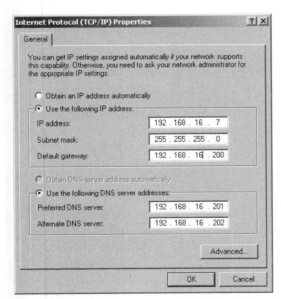

Figure 10-10 Security settings are configured on the Security tab.

There are four preset levels of security settings: Low, Medium, Medium High, and High. As the slider is moved between the levels, basic information is provided on-screen about that security level and what it does and does not allow. In addition, each of the security levels can be further configured by clicking the Custom Level button. Settings are applied to zones, making it possible to have different levels for each of the zones. In Internet Explorer 5.5 there are four zones: Internet, Local Intranet, Trusted Sites, and Restricted Sites. For the Local Intranet, Trusted Sites, and Restricted Sites zones, you can add sites that you wish to be included in that zone.

By configuring the security settings you can limit your exposure to Internet-borne threats.

Firewalling Under Windows XP

A new feature that Microsoft included in Windows XP is the Internet Connection Firewall, or ICF. The ICF is a firewall designed to protect a system that is connected to the Internet. In doing so, if that Internet connection is shared, it also indirectly protects the other systems on the network that use that connection.

The ICF works by monitoring all of the network traffic that passes over the Internet connection. The ICF monitors all of your outbound requests so that the inbound responses from those sites are allowed to pass through the firewall. All other traffic is discarded. Using ICF is a very important tool in protecting yourself from the various threats of the Internet.

The ICF feature is enabled in Windows XP through the Network And Internet Connections icon in Control Panel. Right-click the connection you want to enable ICF on, select Properties, and then Advanced. At the top of the dialog box there is a check box labeled "Protect my computer and network by limiting or preventing access to this computer from the Internet". Once you have selected this option, click OK. The ICF feature is now enabled.

Key Points

■ Protocols govern how devices on the network interact and provide systems that allow data to travel reliably on the network.

■ There are three primary networking protocols used on today's networks: TCP/IP, IPX/SPX, and NetBEUI.

■ TCP/IP is also the protocol suite used on the Internet.

■ To connect a system to a network using TCP/IP, you will at least need an IP address and a subnet mask.

■ DHCP can assign TCP/IP addresses dynamically. In the absence of a DHCP server, a system configured to receive an IP address automatically can use APIPA to get an address.

■ Client software has specific configuration information that is required to connect to servers on the network.

■ The Ping utility tests connectivity between networked devices.

■ The Ipconfig command displays the TCP/IP configuration on Windows systems. Ipconfig can also be used to release and renew addresses obtained via DHCP.

■ Tracert verifies the route to a remote system by reporting the status of every step on the journey.

■ The Winipcfg utility is a graphical version of the Ipconfig utility found only on Windows 9*x* and Me.

■ One of the fundamental and cornerstone functions of a network is the ability to easily share data and resources with other users.

■ In Windows 9*x* and Me, File and Printer Sharing must first be installed and then you must specify that you wish to make files and/or printers available to other users.

■ Accessing network resources can be done from Network Neighborhood, from My Computer, and from the command line.

■ The UNC was created to provide a uniform method of referring to resources on the network.

■ When sharing resources, be sure that you understand the permissions that can be assigned to resources to protect them from unauthorized access.

■ The network card is an important piece of hardware in terms of networking and provides the physical connection to the network.

■ To make sure that your network card has been correctly installed, you can check it in Device Manager.

■ ISPs are companies that specialize in providing Internet access to home and business users.

■ WINS is designed to map computer (NetBIOS) names to IP addresses.

■ The function of DNS is to resolve host names to IP addresses.

■ The SMTP protocol is used to send mail and the POP3 protocol to receive mail.

■ A dial-up connection to the Internet requires a modem and the PPP protocol.

■ Many methods of connecting to the Internet are available, including cable, DSL, wireless, and satellite.

■ ICS is a simple concept that enables one system to share its Internet connection with the other computers on the network. Windows versions from Windows 98 SE on allow Internet Connection Sharing.

■ Windows XP includes a feature called the Internet Connection Firewall (ICF) that can be used to protect the system from Internet-borne attacks.

Chapter Review Questions

1 You want to find out what kind of network card is installed in your Windows 98 system. Where would you go to do this?

   a)   My Network Places/Network

   b)   Control Panel/Network

   c)   Control Panel/Adapters

   d)   Control Panel/Network Cards

Answer b is correct. The network cards installed in a Windows 98 system can be found in the Network folder in Control Panel. Answers a, c, and d are invalid.

2 You have just finished installing a new Windows 2000 system but you have not yet joined the domain. Where would you go to do this?

   a)   Control Panel/System/Network Identification

   b)   Control Panel/Network/Network Identification

   c)   My Network Place/Identification

   d)   Control Panel/Identification

Answer a is correct. The Network Identification tab is found in the System dialog box, accessed from the System icon in Control Panel. Answers b, c, and d are all incorrect.

3 You are using Windows 98 and wish to enable ICS. How would you do this?

   a)   Control Panel/ICS

   b)   Control Panel/Network/ICS

   c)   Control Panel/Network/Internet/Internet Connection Sharing

   d)   None of the above

Answer d is correct. ICS is not supported in Windows 98. Answers a, b, and c are all incorrect.

4 Which of the following protocols is required to gain Internet access?

   a)   TCP/IP

   b)   IPX/SPX

   c)   NetBEUI

   d)   AppleTalk

Answer a is correct. TCP/IP is the protocol used on the Internet and so a system that wants to gain access to the Internet must accommodate TCP/IP. Answers b, c, and d are all incorrect. None of these protocols will allow you to access the Internet.

5 You are troubleshooting a TCP/IP configuration problem on a Windows 98 system. Which of the following commands could you use to view the DNS information for the system? (Choose two.)

a) Winipcfg

b) Ping

c) showDNSconf

d) D. ipconfig /all

Answers a and d are correct. The *ipconfig /all* command and the Winipcfg utility can be used on a Windows 98 system to see detailed TCP/IP configuration information, including DNS server information. Answer b is incorrect. The Ping utility is used to test connectivity, not to view TCP/IP configurations. Answer c is incorrect. There is no such utility as showDNSconf.

6 What is the tag language commonly used to create Web pages on the Internet?

a) HTML

b) VPML

c) HTTP

d) FTP

Answer a is correct. HTML is a tag language that is used to create a large percentage of the pages on the Internet. Answer b is not a valid answer. Answer c is incorrect. HTTP is a protocol used to retrieve pages from a Web server. Answer d is incorrect; FTP is a protocol used for transferring files to and from a remote system.

7 Which of the following domain extensions would you expect to see associated with a company that makes educational materials?

a) .edu

b) .com

c) .gov

d) .mat

Answer b is correct. Companies are assigned the .com suffix under the standard DNS naming system. Answer a is incorrect. The .edu domain suffix is reserved for educational establishments. Answer c is incorrect. The .gov domain suffix is reserved for governmental institutions. Answer d is incorrect. The .mat suffix is not a recognized domain designation.

8 A user calls to report that she is able to receive e-mail but is unable to send it. When you visit her computer, which of the following will you check first?

a) The POP3 configuration

b) The HTTP configuration

c) The NNTP configuration

d) The SMTP configuration

Answer d is correct. The SMTP protocol is used for sending e-mail. Answer a is incorrect. POP3 is a protocol used for retrieving mail from a server, not for sending it. Answer b is incorrect. HTTP is a protocol used to retrieve pages from the Internet. Answer c is incorrect. NNTP is a protocol used to access Internet newsgroup servers.

9 You want to configure your system so that it can receive IP addressing information automatically from a central server. Which protocol achieves this?

a) WINS

b) DNS

c) DHCP

d) HTTP

Answer c is correct. The Dynamic Host Configuration Protocol (DHCP) issues IP addressing information to clients automatically. Answer a is incorrect. The WINS service is used on Windows networks to resolve NetBIOS computer names to IP addresses. Answer b is incorrect. The Domain Name Service is responsible for resolving host names to IP addresses. Answer d is incorrect. HTTP is a protocol used to retrieve pages from the Internet.

10 The new banking program you have installed requires that you obtain a serial number from their secure Internet site. Which of the following addresses are you most likely to use?

a) http://secure.myfinancialsoftware.com

b) https://www.myfinancialsoftware.com

c) http:secure://www.myfinancialsoftware.com

d) ssl://www.myfinancialsoftware.com

Answer b is correct. When accessing a secure Web site, the HTTP Secure protocol is used. This means that the URL must be prefixed with https. Answer a is incorrect, although it is a valid address for non-secure Web sites. Answer c is not a valid URL address. Answer d is incorrect. Although the Secure Sockets Layer (SSL) is a component in Web page security, this prefix is not valid.

11 You want to verify that a remote system is connected to the network. Which of the following utilities could you use to do this? (Choose two.)

a)   Ping

b)   Ipconfig

c)   Tracert

d)   Winipcfg

Answers a and c are correct. Either the Ping utility or the Tracert utility can be used to verify connectivity to a remote system. Answers b and d are incorrect. Both of these utilities are used to view the TCP/IP configuration on a system.

12 Which of the following UNC paths is correct for accessing the data share on server7?

a)   \\data\server7

b)   \\s=server7\share=data

c)   \\server7\data

d)   \\server7\\data

Answer c is correct. When connecting to resources using UNC, the correct syntax is *computer-name**sharename*. In this case it would be \\server7\data. None of the other answers would work in this case.

13 Which network service performs IP address to computer name (Net-BIOS name) translations?

a)   WINS

b)   DHCP

c)   DNS

d)   Nslookup

Answer a is correct. WINS in a Windows network is responsible for mapping computer names to IP addresses. Answer b is incorrect because DHCP is used to dynamically assign TCP/IP information to systems on the network. Answer c is incorrect. DNS is used to resolve host names to IP addresses. Answer d is incorrect; Nslookup is used to troubleshoot the DNS configuration on a system.

14 While troubleshooting a TCP/IP connectivity problem on a Windows 98 system, you need to renew the dynamically assigned address. Which two utilities could you use to do this?

a)   Winipcfg

b)   DHCPrenew

c)   Ipconfig

d)   Ping

Answers a and c are correct. Both the Winipcfg and the Ipconfig utilities can be used to renew the TCP/IP information assigned to a computer system. None of the other utilities listed are designed to do this.

15 Users are complaining that they are unable to access the printer on your computer system but that they can see your computer. What is the most likely cause of this problem?

a)   They are using a different protocol than you.

b)   They are trying to access the printer using UNCs instead of dynamic printer mappings.

c)   The printer is not shared.

d)   You have set the permissions so that only you can access it.

Answer c is correct. If other network users can see your computer but not the resource you want to share, ensure that it is shared. It will appear with a hand underneath the device when shared. Answers a and b are not valid. Answer d is incorrect. Users would still be able to see the printer if the problem were related to permissions; they would, however, be denied access to the device.

16 While troubleshooting a TCP/IP connectivity problem, you discover that the system has an IP address from the 169.254.x.x range. What can you deduce from this?

a)   That the DNS server on the network is not running

b)   That the operating system has disabled the network card

c)   That the DHCP server on the network is not running

d)   That the static IP address is incorrect

Answer c is correct. If a system is configured to use DHCP to gather TCP/IP information and no DHCP server is available, it will assign itself an IP address in the 169.254.x.x range of IP addresses. None of the other answers are valid.

17 You want to make a printer attached to your computer available to other users on the network. Where in Windows 9*x* or Windows 2000 would you go to do this?

   a)   Control Panel/Printers

   b)   Control Panel/Sharing

   c)   Control Panel/Network

   d)   Control Panel/Network and Dial-Up Connections

   Answer a is correct. The Printers folder in Control Panel allows you to configure settings for printers connected to your system, including sharing the printer to other users on the network. None of the other answers are valid.

18 Which protocol is used by the modem when establishing a dial-up connection?

   a)   PPP

   b)   TCP/IP

   c)   IPX/SPX

   d)   NetBEUI

   Answer a is correct. The PPP protocol is designed to be used to establish a remote connection using dial-up networking. Answers b, c, and d are LAN protocols used to connect computers in a network.

19 You want to connect to a printer called laserj on the sales server. Which of the following UNCs would you achieve to do this?

   a)   \\sales\p=laserj

   b)   \\s=sales\p=laserj

   c)   \sales\laserj

   d)   \\sales\laserj

   Answer d is correct. To connect to a printer on a server called sales you would specify the server and then the printer share. In this case it would be \\sales\laserj.

20 What is the purpose of the FTP protocol?

   a)   It is used for establishing dial-up connections over a modem.

   b)   It used for transferring files to and from a remote server.

   c)   It is used for downloading Web pages from a remote system.

   d)   It is used for accessing newsgroups on a server.

Answer b is correct. The FTP protocol is part of the TCP/IP protocol suite and is widely used to transfer files to and from a remote computer system. Answer a is incorrect because this describes the function of PPP. Answer c is incorrect because this describes the function of HTTP. Answer d describes the NNTP protocol.

Check Yourself

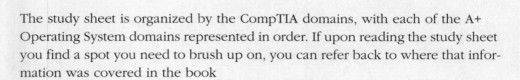

(before you test yourself)

The study sheet is organized by the CompTIA domains, with each of the A+ Operating System domains represented in order. If upon reading the study sheet you find a spot you need to brush up on, you can refer back to where that information was covered in the book

A+ Operating System Technologies

Domain 1.0 OS Fundamentals

Operating System Structure and System Files

Major Operating System Functions

- Operating systems provide an interface through which you can interact with the computer system.

- Operating systems provide the means by which you can store and organize data—one of the most fundamental computing requirements.

- Operating systems provide printer subsystems and drivers so that you can print to a multitude of different printing devices.

- Operating systems provide the ability to create, manage, organize, and secure data and programs.

- Windows 9x and Windows Me are operating systems designed for use in non-business settings where an affordable OS that offers compatibility with a wide range of applications and hardware is required, but other features like advanced networking support and high levels of security are not required. Windows 9x and Windows Me are no longer supplied by Microsoft, having been replaced with Windows XP.

- Windows NT was a robust operating system that built on the strengths of its predecessor, Windows NT 3.51 while implementing the new Windows 95–style interface. Windows NT 4 came in two primary versions—Windows NT Workstation, which was designed as a robust business-quality workstation operating system, and a server version designed as a corporate-level server operating system. Implementation of Windows NT was widespread and was largely responsible for establishing Microsoft in the server operating system market.

■ Windows 2000 is a business-level operating system that was released in a Professional edition designed for workstation use, and multiple server versions designed for corporate networking. Although Windows 2000 was built on Windows NT technologies, it came with many new features including support for Microsoft's directory services system—Active Directory.

■ Windows XP is the most recent workstation operating system release from Microsoft. It comes in two versions—Windows XP Home Edition is designed to replace Windows 9x/Me and Windows XP Professional is designed to replace Windows 2000 Professional. Windows XP has a slightly different user interface but in general terms it shares many of the same features as its predecessors.

■ To see which version of Windows you are running, right-click My Computer and select Properties, or access the System Properties dialog box by double-clicking the System icon in Control Panel.

Major Operating System Components

■ Registry

- The registry is a single hierarchical database that holds the system's hardware and software settings.

- The registry is the central location where all of the system configurations are kept.

- In a Windows 9x system, the registry is made up of two files, System.dat and User.dat.

- Changes are sometimes made manually to the registry using registry editors such as Regedit.exe and Regedt32.exe.

- A common method of making changes to the registry is by using the utilities in Control Panel.

■ Virtual Memory

- This is the name given to an area of space on the hard disk that is used by the operating system as if it were normal physical memory.

■ File Systems

- File systems are the means by which data (in the form of files) is organized on storage devices such as hard disks and CDs.

- The characteristics of a file system define such things as the maximum partition size, security measures, the permissible characters, and the organization of the files within folders.

- Windows 9*x* supports the FAT16 file system and starting with Windows 95 OSR2 the FAT32 file system is supported as well.

- Windows 2000 supports the FAT16, FAT32, and NTFS file systems.

Major Operating System Interfaces

- Windows Explorer

  - Windows Explorer shows all of the drives connected to the system. Clicking on any of these drives allows you to see the files and folders held within the drive.

  - Files and folders in Windows Explorer are organized in a tree-like structure with parent folders containing other folders and files.

  - Windows Explorer gives you a method of easily copying and moving files and folders around the system.

  - To view hidden files in Windows, you can select Folder Options from the Tools menu in Windows Explorer.

- My Computer

  - The My Computer window displays all of the installed system drives and shortcuts to some of the commonly accessed Windows utilities including Control Panel.

  - Selecting any of the drives in the My Computer window will open that drive and display the contents of that drive.

- Control Panel provides access to the areas used to perform system tasks such as installing, managing, and configuring hardware and software on Windows-based systems. Inside Control Panel, several utilities can be accessed to start management programs including:

  - **Add/Remove Programs:** Used to add or remove programs from the system. The Add/Remove Programs utility is also used in Windows 9*x* to create a startup disk.

  - **Add New Hardware:** When new hardware is added to the system that is not detected by Plug and Play, use the Add New Hardware utility to add devices to the system. You can also use the Add New Hardware utility to troubleshoot an existing device.

- **Display:** The Display utility is used to customize the display settings for the system. From within the applet, the hardware acceleration settings are modified when troubleshooting video display problems such as system freezing.

- **Printers:** The Printers utility in Control Panel is used to add, remove, and configure the printers connected to the computer system. From the Printers utility you can also stop and restart print jobs you have sent to the printer.

- **System:** Some of the key areas accessed through the System Properties dialog box include: Device Manager, which shows the installed hardware in the system and its status; Hardware Profiles, which enable you to establish different hardware profiles on your computer (a setting typically used with laptop systems); and Performance Options, which allow you to optimize program response and change the system's virtual memory.

- **Network or Network Connections:** The Network or Network Connections utility in Control Panel is where you go to configure the network. Options include adding and removing protocols, configuring network cards, and enabling file and print sharing.

- Computer Management Console

  - The Computer Management utility is available in Windows 2000 and Windows XP. It allows you to perform system configuration and management tasks such as working with hard disks, user accounts, and other system settings.

- Accessories/System Tools

  - The Accessories/System Tools program group contains many tools that are used in the maintenance and upkeep of the system. Which tools are included in this group will depend on the OS in use and the options installed.

- Command Line

  - There are many command line utilities that can be used in the management of the system. The command line can be accessed through the Accessories program group or by launching Command.com (and/or Cmd.exe in Windows NT 4/2000/XP) from the Run dialog box.

■ Network Neighborhood/My Network Places

● On a Windows 9*x*/NT 4 system, the Network Neighborhood utility allows you to view, or browse, the network and access resources. On Windows 2000 and Windows XP systems the utility is renamed My Network Places.

■ Taskbar/Systray

● The taskbar provides a home for the Start button and the system tray (systray). In a default configuration the taskbar can be found at the bottom of the screen, but it can be repositioned at any edge of the screen. It can also be resized as necessary.

■ Start Menu

● The Start menu is a pop-up menu present in all versions of Windows since Windows 95. The Start menu is intended as a way of easily accessing programs and utilities. The Start menu is activated by clicking the Start button on the taskbar.

■ Device Manager

● Device Manager is used to identify what hardware has been detected by the system, the resources used by the device, and whether the device is currently functioning.

● If a resource conflict is shown in Device Manager, you can manually change resources to correct the conflict.

● Devices that are not recognized by the system or that are incorrectly configured will be displayed with a yellow circle that contains either a question mark or an exclamation point. A red *X* indicates that the device has been disabled.

Identifying Major System Files

■ Windows 9*x* core system files include the following:

● Io.sys is located in the root directory (C:) and is responsible for loading system files and verifying their settings.

● Msdos.sys contains the multiboot configuration for Windows 9*x* systems. Msdos.sys must be at least 1024 bytes (1 KB) in size.

● Autoexec.bat is used during the boot process and contains the program and environment settings. Programs can be added and removed from the Autoexec.bat file using the Edit command or Sysedit from within Windows.

- Command.com provides the command interface for the user. Basic commands such as Dir, Copy, and Cd are built into Command.com.

- Config.sys is often used in conjunction with the Autoexec.bat file, but instead of handling the loading of programs, the Config.sys file is responsible for the loading of the device drivers and the configuration of the system's memory. Though not needed with Windows 9x versions, it is still used for backward compatibility for those programs that need to access a Config.sys file to operate. Device drivers loaded into Config.sys are added with the line Device= or Devicehigh= followed by the device driver name. The Devicehigh option loads the devices into upper memory.

- Himem.sys is an extended memory driver, which makes the memory area above 1 MB available for use by the operating system.

- Emm386 is an expanded memory manager that works by deceiving the process into thinking that it is storing data in a special type of memory called expanded memory when in fact it is using extended memory.

- Win.com is the startup file for Windows 9x. It is located in the root of the directory in which Windows is installed. There are a number of switches that can be used, but one of the most useful is /d, which causes Windows to start in safe mode.

- System.ini is held in the Windows root directory and is included with Windows 9x for backward compatibility. The System.ini file stores data about the system's hardware for use with DOS and Windows 3.x operating systems.

- Win.ini holds program settings and personalized settings such as fonts, screen savers, and display settings. The Win.ini file is included for backward compatibility only.

- System.dat is a registry file and maintains the settings for the system's hardware including resource allocation, device drivers, and hardware configurations. The backup file of System.dat, System.da0, is held in the Windows folder and will be used by the system in the event that the System.dat file fails.

- User.dat is the other file comprising the registry. User.dat holds only user-specific information such as passwords, personalized color settings, and installed programs. A backup file of User.dat, User.da0, is used should the original User.dat file become corrupt.

■ When you want to exclude a line from executing in the Config.sys or Autoexec.bat file, add a semicolon or the word *Rem* before the line and the entry will be ignored.

■ Editing text-based Windows files can be done using the Edit command-line program, and using Notepad or the Sysedit utility in Windows.

■ Windows NT/2000 core files include the following:

● Boot.ini defines the location of the Windows NT and Windows 2000 system files.

● Ntldr is responsible for loading the operating system.

● Bootsect.dos holds the boot sector information of any other operating systems that are loaded on the system.

● Ntdetect.com is responsible for detecting hardware and builds a hardware list.

● Ntbootdd.sys is used only when the system boots from a SCSI device that does not have a BIOS installed.

● Ntuser.dat is a file that stores a user's settings. When the user logs on, the information in the Ntuser.dat file is placed in the registry.

● A number of files comprise the registry. In a default installation they can be found in the C:\Winnt\System32\Config directory.

Using Command Line Functions

■ DOS commands are referred to as both internal and external commands. Internal commands are primary DOS commands and are built into the Command.com file. Internal commands include Dir, Cls, Copy, and Delete. External commands are not included in the Command.com file. Such commands include Xcopy, Attrib, and Edit.

■ Help for practically all DOS commands can be obtained by typing the command followed by the /? switch.

■ There are two wildcard characters you can use. The question mark (?) is used to denote a single character. The other permissible wildcard character is an asterisk (*), which is used to denote a group of characters.

Dir

■   The Dir command is used to list the contents of various directories. An example would be issuing *dir windows* from the root folder, which would give a listing of the files in the Windows directory.

Attrib

■   The Attrib command is used to view and modify the attributes of a file. File attributes include hidden (h), system (s), read-only (r), and archive (a). The + and – signs are used to add an attribute to or remove an attribute from a file or folder. An example of the Attrib command is *attrib +h +r comptia.bat*, which would change the attributes of the file Comptia.bat to hidden and read-only.

Ver

■   The Ver command is an internal DOS command used to identify which operating system version is being used on the system. The syntax is simply *ver*.

Mem

■   The Mem command is used to view the available memory including conventional, extended, and expanded memory. The simplest form of the command is *mem*.

ScanDisk

■   ScanDisk is a widely used utility and is used to detect and correct file problems and errors on hard disks and floppy disks.

■   During the ScanDisk operation, the hard disk is examined by looking for physical errors on it that will be marked as bad so no new data can be stored in that location.

Defrag.exe

■   The function of this utility is to rearrange the files on the disk in a contiguous fashion.

■   When using Defrag, you should really try to leave the system alone so that it can do its thing. Also, programs like virus checkers and screen savers can cause delays in the Defrag process because they use valuable system resources.

- Defrag can improve the performance of a hard disk by better organizing its contents.

- Defrag is not used to identify errors on a hard disk.

Edit

- The Edit command is widely used as a text editor to modify the key system files and even create batch files. The command *edit* will open the editor.

Copy

- The Copy command is used to copy a file from one location to another from the command line. For example, this command will copy a file from the floppy disk to the hard disk: *copy a:\text.doc c:*.

Xcopy

- The Xcopy command enables multiple directories to be copied at once. To copy subdirectories with the Xcopy command, the /s switch is used. Xcopy uses the same general command line syntax as the Copy command, but it includes many additional switches with added functionality.

Format

- The Format command is used after a hard disk has been partitioned. The formatting process prepares the disk for use. The Format command can also be used to prepare a floppy disk for use.

Fdisk

- The Fdisk command is used to partition a hard disk.

Setver

- The Setver command is used to manually set the DOS version reported to a program. This is typically done for backward compatibility.

Scanreg

- The Scanreg utility is used to make a backup copy of the system's registry, restore a copy of the backed-up registry, or attempt to fix the registry. Scanreg is issued with one of three primary switches: `Scanreg /fix`, `Scanreg /restore`, or `Scanreg /backup`.

Md/Cd/Rd

■   The Make Directory command (Md) is used to create directories from the command prompt. The Change Directory command (Cd) is used to move around the file structure. The Remove Directory command (Rd) is used to remove a directory from the structure. Note that the directory must be empty before it can be removed with the Rd command.

Delete/Rename

■   The Delete command is used to delete a file or files. The Rename command is used to rename a file. The commands can be shortened to Del and Ren, respectively.

Deltree

■   The Deltree command can be used to remove multiple directories, populated or unpopulated, at the same time.

Type

■   The Type command is used to display text files on the screen. Its only feature is the display of files—you cannot edit files with the Type utility.

Echo

■   The Echo command is used to cause a string of characters to be displayed on the screen. Echo is commonly used in batch files to turn on and off the showing of messages on the screen.

Set

■   The Set command is used to set environment variables.

Ping

■   The Ping utility is used to test connectivity between two devices on a network running the TCP/IP protocol.

Managing Disks, Directories, and Files

Disk Management

■   Windows 2000 and Windows XP use the Disk Management utility found in the Computer Management console to manage hard disks.

■ Within the Disk Management utility in Windows 2000 and Windows XP, hard disks can be formatted with either the FAT16, FAT32, or NTFS file systems.

■ Windows 2000 and Windows XP can use both basic disks and dynamic disks.

■ Windows 9x uses the Fdisk utility to manage hard disks.

■ Disks can be formatted from within My Computer and Windows Explorer.

Partitioning, Formatting, and File Systems

■ Partitions are logical divisions of the hard disk. Each partition can be formatted with a file system. There are two types of partitions, primary and extended. Primary partitions can be made bootable, in which case they are referred to as active partitions. There can be only one active partition on a disk at a time.

■ Extended partitions can be further divided up into logical partitions.

■ A hard disk can have a maximum of four partitions on it, either four primary partitions, or three primary partitions and one extended partition.

File Systems

■ FAT16

  ● The FAT16 file system will only recognize partitions up to 2 GB in size.

  ● The FAT16 file system offers no local security on files and folders.

  ● FAT16 partitions can be read and accessed by MS-DOS, Windows 3.x, Windows 9x, Windows NT, and Windows 2000/XP.

■ FAT32

  ● FAT32 was introduced with Windows 95 OSR2.

  ● FAT32 supports hard disk volumes up to 2 terabytes.

  ● FAT32 does not offer local security for files and folders.

  ● FAT32 does not support disk compression.

  ● FAT32 uses more efficient cluster sizes than FAT16, often enabling it to store more files in a given amount of space.

  ● Windows 9x since Windows 95 OSR2 supports FAT32; Windows 2000 and Windows XP support FAT32, but Windows NT 4 does not.

- NTFS

  - NTFS partitions cannot be accessed on Windows 9*x* systems.

  - **Security:** The NTFS file system allows for permissions to be applied to local files and folders.

  - **Volume size:** NTFS allows for large volume sizes, and a maximum volume size of 2 TB.

  - **Disk performance:** NTFS offers a higher level of performance than FAT, particularly with larger files.

- NTFS5

  - NTFS5 was introduced with Windows 2000 and offers enhancements to earlier versions of NTFS.

  - **Encryption:** Windows 2000 allows you to encrypt individual files and folders. Once a file or folder is encrypted, only those who have the decryption key can access it. Windows 2000 does this through a feature called the Encrypting File System (EFS).

  - **Disk quotas:** Disk quotas are a means to restrict the amount of space that a user can use to save files on the system. Any Windows 2000 NTFS partition can support disk quotas.

- HPFS

  - HPFS was not widely used in the Windows world and while Windows NT could read HPFS volumes, no other Windows OS offers support for HPFS. HPFS originated on the OS/2 platform.

- CDFS

  - This is the standard format used by data CDs.

- Converting File Systems

  - You can convert a FAT32 or FAT16 file system to NTFS on a Windows 2000/XP system using the following command: *convert x: / fs:ntfs* (where *x* is the drive letter you want to convert).

  - You can convert from a FAT16 file system in Windows NT 4 using the same command as in Windows 2000/XP.

  - NTFS cannot be converted back to FAT16 or FAT32.

  - FAT16 can be converted to FAT32 using the Cvt1.exe command.

Directory Structures

■ A directory structure provides a framework that allows you to organize files on a disk. At the very top of the directory structure is the root. This is reflected in commands such as the backslash (\). Under the root directory other folders are created. These are referred to as subfolders.

■ **Creating folders** You can create folders as you need them. There are a number of ways to create folders. The most common is now to create folders from within Windows Explorer, but you can also use the Make Directory command (Md) at the command prompt.

■ **Navigating the directory structure** You can navigate the directory structure from within Windows Explorer or by using the Change Directory (Cd) command at the command prompt.

Files

■ Files are typically created when you save a file through a program or when you copy files to or from your computer. You can also create new files by right-clicking in a folder in Windows Explorer and clicking New.

■ The most common file name extensions and their functions are listed in Table B-1.

Table B-1 Common File Name Extensions

File Name Extension	Associated Program or Function
.exe	Identifies an executable program. Examples of such files include Setup.exe and Install.exe.
.bat	Identifies an executable batch file. Batch files are used to run specific programs or sets of commands.
.com	Used to identify a command file. An example of a command file is Command.com.
.bmp	Identifies a graphics (bitmap) file.
.jpg	Identifies a graphics (JPEG) file.
.ini	Identifies an initialization file for a program. Good examples of .ini files include Win.ini and System.ini. These are text files and typically edited with the Sysedit utility.
.sys	Used with system files.
.doc	The file extension associated with Microsoft Word documents.
.txt	Documents saved in a text format.

■ Files with certain file names suggest that they are executable, that is, they can be run from the command line. Executable file name extensions include .bat, .exe, and .com. File names cannot include the following characters: \ / ? * : " < > |

■ File Attributes

● There are four attributes that can be assigned to individual files and folders: read-only (r), archive (a), system (s), and hidden (h). Table B-2 lists file and folder attributes.

Table B-2   File and Folder Attributes

Attribute	Description
Archive	When the archive attribute is applied, the file or folder will be marked for backup. Windows backup utilities can be set to back up files with the archive attribute set. By default, all files are assigned the archive attribute but folders will have to be done manually.
System	The system attribute is automatically assigned to key Windows and DOS files. System files are often also assigned the hidden attribute as an extra level of precaution.
Hidden	Files and folders assigned the hidden attribute will not be visible by default from within Windows or DOS.

● Attributes are modified from the command line using the Attrib command. When removing attributes the minus (<;$MI>) sign is used, and when adding attributes the plus (+) sign is used.

■ In Windows, you can view and modify the attributes for a file simply by right-clicking on the file you wish to view and choosing Properties from the menu.

■ File Compression

● File compression saves space on the hard disk by reducing a file to less than its original size. The compression algorithm is able to do this because the way that programs save files is not always the most efficient way of doing it. File systems like NTFS support file compression on a file-by-file basis.

■ File Encryption

● File encryption is a process that scrambles the file so that only someone with the appropriate access rights can access it. File encryption is available through third-party products and with some Windows operating systems through the Encrypting File System (EFS) feature.

■　File Permissions

● File permissions are attributes applied to files that denote who can perform what action to the file. NTFS supports the file permissions detailed in Table B-3.

Table B-3　　NTFS File Permissions

Permission	Description
Full Control	Allows full access and control over the file including changing the permissions and ownership.
Modify	Allows the user to see, change, and delete existing files. If applied to a folder, also allows the creation of new files.
Read & Execute	Allows the user to see the file and its contents. If the file is an executable, the user can also execute that file.
List Folder Contents	Allows the user to see the files in a folder and their attributes but not to actually open the file.
Read	Allows the user to see the files in a folder and to open them, but not make any changes to the file.
Write	Allows a user to create new files and make changes to the contents of existing files. It does not allow the user to delete a file.

● File permissions can be combined between users and groups but if a permission is denied through one or the other, it is not allowed.

■　File Types

● There are two types of files used on a computer. Text files, which can contain a standard set of numbers and characters, and can be read in a text editor, and binary files, which store information in code. The latter should not be opened in a text editor because even a small change will affect its ability to be used.

Major Operating System Utilities

Backup and Restore

■　There are three primary backup types used:

● A full backup saves all directories and files from the hard disk and does not use the archive bit to determine whether a file should be backed up. It does however clear the archive bit once the file or directory has been backed up.

- An incremental backup includes only the files that have changed or been created since the last full or incremental backup. To determine whether a file has changed since the last full backup, the backup software looks at the archive bit setting on the file. Only files and folders with the archive bit set to on will be backed up. Once the file has been backed up, the archive bit is cleared so that the file is not backed up again unnecessarily.

- Differential backups back up the files that have changed since the last full backup.

■ Chkdsk

- Chkdsk is a utility that is used to check, and if necessary repair, the file system on a hard disk. It is a DOS-based utility.

■ Disk Cleanup

- The Disk Cleanup feature in Windows 2000 and Windows XP scans your computer hard disk looking for files such as temporary files and temporary Internet files that can be deleted to free up space on the disk.

■ Format

- The Format command is the tool used in the final step to prepare a disk for use. The Format command can be used on both hard and floppy disks.

■ Device Manager

- Device Manager is used to identify what hardware has been detected by the system, the resources used by the device, and whether the device is currently functioning.

- If a resource conflict is shown in Device Manager, you can manually change resources to correct the conflict.

- Devices that are not recognized by the system or that are incorrectly configured will be displayed with a yellow circle that contains either a question mark or an exclamation point. A red *X* indicates that the device has been disabled.

■ Msconfig.exe

- The Msconfig utility enables you to safely modify legacy Windows files without making permanent changes. It allows you to customize these files, determining which of the legacy files Windows is to use.

- Regedit.exe

  - The Regedit utility enables you to navigate through the registry, modify and search through the values in the registry, and manually export the entire registry to create a backup.

  - Regedit is used by all versions of Windows since Windows 95.

  - Regedit can be used to export the registry for backup purposes and import that file when needed.

- Regedt32.exe

  - This is a registry editing tool used on 32-bit operating systems like Windows NT 4 and Windows 2000.

  - When editing the registry, you normally use Regedit in Windows 9*x* and Regedt32 in Windows NT 4 and Windows 2000. Where possible, you should always try to configure the system through Control Panel rather than with a registry editor because it is safer.

- Sysedit.exe

  - The Sysedit utility lets you edit the legacy system files simultaneously, including the Autoexec.bat, Win.ini, System.ini, Config.sys, and Protocol.ini files.

- Event Viewer

  - The Event Viewer utility in Windows NT/2000/XP provides access to the various system logs. These provide useful information on how the system is running and any issues that have occurred.

- Task Manager

  - The Task Manager can be activated by pressing Ctrl+Alt+Delete on a Windows NT/2000/XP Professional system and selecting Task Manager. Information provided by the Task Manager can help you determine the current state of the system and is useful in tracking down problems.

- Attrib.exe

  - This command line utility is used to change or view the attributes of a file or folder.

- Extract.exe

  - The Extract utility is used to manually extract Windows installation files.

- The Extract utility must be run from the command line. To extract a compressed file, use the syntax *extract* followed by the file you wish to decompress.

- Extract lets you retrieve a single file from a .cab file, which can be useful if a user deletes an important file by accident.

■ Edit.com

- The Edit command is used as a text editor to modify the key system files and even create batch files. Issuing *edit* at a command prompt will open this simple text editor and allow you to save, print, and edit text files.

■ Windows Explorer

- Windows Explorer is an all-in-one file management tool that allows you to create, delete, modify, and move files and folders through one interface.

Domain 2.0 Installation, Configuration, and Upgrading

Installing Windows

Startup (Starting the Installation)

■ Older operating systems, including Windows 3.*x* and early Windows 95, were installed from floppy disks.

■ There are two ways you can access the CD-ROM on a non-bootable system. The first method is to use a bootable floppy disk with CD-ROM drivers on it; the second is to configure the BIOS to boot directly from the CD-ROM drive.

■ Windows 98 included a method of creating a bootable floppy disk that will take you to the command prompt with CD-ROM access.

■ If you have a bootable CD in the CD-ROM drive and the system halts with a "No Operating System Found" error message, ensure that the BIOS is set to boot from the CD-ROM drive.

Partition the Hard Drive

■ New hard disks must be partitioned before they can be formatted and used by the operating system.

- When a hard disk is partitioned, it can be divided into several partitions or use the entire hard disk as a single partition.

- To be able to boot from the hard disk, you must have at least one primary partition. This partition stores the operating system and is the one you actually boot from.

- In addition to primary partitions, you can use an extended partition, which can then be divided into logical partitions. Logical partitions receive a drive letter and are referred to as logical drives.

- Primary partitions are bootable whereas logical drives within an extended partition are not.

- Fdisk is a command line utility used in DOS and Windows 9x to create partitions, delete partitions, display partition information, or mark a partition as being active.

- The active partition is one that can be booted from. A system must have an active partition and there can be only one.

- Though not widely used, the Fdisk utility can be used with the /mbr switch to repair a damaged master boot record.

Format the Hard Drive

- After creating the partitions on the hard disk, the partitions must be formatted before they can be used by the operating system.

- Formatting the hard disk has two key functions—it creates a file system on the drive and a root directory.

- Formatting a drive can be done from the command line using the Format.exe command. The exact syntax for this command is *format drive letter:*, where *drive letter* is replaced by the letter of the drive being formatted.

Run the Appropriate Setup Utility

- To manually start a Windows 9x installation, the Setup.exe command is used.

- When installing Windows NT or Windows 2000, the Winnt.exe command is used if you are installing from a Windows 9x system or from DOS. The Winnt32.exe command is used to start an installation from a Windows NT or a Windows 2000 system.

■   Table B-4 shows some of the switches for Winnt.exe and Table B-5
     shows the same for the Winnt32.exe command.

Table B-4   Commonly Used Winnt.exe Options

Option	Description
/s:path	Specifies the location of the Windows 2000 installation files.
/u:file	Allows you to specify the location of the answer file, which is used in unattended installations.
/a	Enables accessibility options.

Table B-5   Commonly Used Winnt32.exe Options

Option	Description
/s:path	Specifies the location of the Windows 2000 installation files.
/checkupgrade-only	Performs a test to see if the system will support Windows 2000.

■   The Windows NT 4 version of the Winnt command had a switch, /ox,
     that allowed you to create a set of boot disks from which you could
     start the installation. Microsoft removed the /ox switch in Windows
     2000 and replaced it with a utility called Makeboot, which allows you
     to create the 4 boot disks used to install Windows 2000.

Performing an Operating System Upgrade

Upgrade Considerations

■   Hardware requirements

  ●   Before performing the upgrade make sure that the current hard-
       ware meets the minimum hardware requirements for the new OS.
       Pay special attention to hard disk space and memory.

■   Hardware compatibility

  ●   Operating systems have a hardware compatibility list (HCL). The
       HCL is a list of the hardware tested and proven to work with the
       OS. If you want the upgrade to go as smoothly as possible, you
       will want to verify that the hardware works with the new OS. To
       verify hardware compatibility when upgrading to Windows 2000,
       you can use the *winnt32 /checkupgradeonly* command to verify
       hardware.

■   Backups

  ●   Before upgrading a system, a complete backup should be made.
       Ensure that both the data and key system files, such as the .ini and
       registry files, are saved somewhere safe.

■ Check the disk

● You will want to know that your hard disk is error free and finely tuned before the upgrade process. To ensure this, it is a good idea to run the disk defragmenter utility and perform a ScanDisk on the hard disk.

■ Virus scan

● It is always a good idea to perform a quick virus scan on the system before the upgrade. Afterwards, it is important to disable the virus checker for the upgrade because it can cause an error and halt the system during the upgrade process.

■ Verify upgradeability

● It might sound obvious, but you might want to ensure that the OS you have can be upgraded to the one you want. Windows 3.x won't make the leap to Windows 2000 but Windows 9x and Windows NT 4 will.

Upgrading Windows 95 to Windows 98

■ To upgrade the Windows 95 system, simply put the Windows 98 upgrade CD in the CD-ROM drive from within Windows 95, and, if AutoRun is enabled, you will be asked if you would like to upgrade your system to the newer Windows 98 operating system.

■ The upgrade from Windows 95 to Windows 98 will typically keep all of the settings and programs intact; in addition, most of the drivers used with Windows 95 work with Windows 98.

Upgrading from Windows NT Workstation 4 to Windows 2000

■ When upgrading from Windows NT to Windows 2000, there are some hardware devices that will not function properly until new Windows 2000 drivers are installed.

■ Most programs will transfer over when upgrading from Windows NT to Windows 2000.

Replacing Windows 9x with Windows 2000

■ Windows 2000 and Windows 9x are architecturally very different from each other, making upgrading to Windows 2000 more troublesome than other upgrades.

■ Many programs, such as games and utilities, will not work after the upgrade, and you will need to find new device drivers for much of your hardware.

■ From within Windows 9*x* you can run the Windows 2000 Setup program, and you will be asked if you would like to upgrade the Windows 9*x* system to Windows 2000.

■ The upgrade process is one-way; Windows 2000 does not have an uninstall feature to return to Windows 9*x*.

■ To upgrade to Windows 2000 from a Windows 3.*x* system, you will first need to upgrade to Windows 98 or Windows 95.

Dual-Booting Windows 9*x* with Windows NT 4 or Windows 2000

■ In a dual-boot configuration, the computer system has two working operating systems and during the boot process you will be able to decide which of the operating systems you will boot into.

■ In a dual operating system configuration, the operating systems are effectively separate and will each need their own configuration and programs installed.

■ If you are dual-booting and cannot see the other OS, it is likely that the file system is not recognized.

Booting Windows

Startup Disk

■ When making a boot disk using Windows NT, ensure that you copy the three files, Ntldr, Ntdetect.com, and Boot.ini.

■ In Windows 9*x*, the startup disk is made using the Add/Remove Programs utility in Control Panel.

■ An important point to remember is that Windows 95 does not include CD-ROM drivers on the startup disk.

■ Bootable floppy disks can be made from the command line using the Format command. The correct syntax is *format a: /s*.

■ If a floppy drive or a hard disk has already been formatted, you can make it bootable using the Sys command.

Windows 9x Boot Options

- Safe Mode

  - Safe mode is used to troubleshoot a system that will not boot.

  - When booting into safe mode, only necessary device drivers are loaded. Only the device drivers for the keyboard, mouse, and VGA display are loaded. If the cause of the system failure is not hardware-related, the system should boot by bypassing most of the files at startup.

- MS-DOS Mode

  - In MS-DOS mode, only those drivers needed to get DOS going are loaded, including the Config.sys and the Autoexec.bat files.

  - Table B-6 shows some of the more commonly used Windows 9x boot options.

Table B-6   Commonly Used Boot Options for Windows 9x

Boot Option	Function
Logged Mode	Windows will try to load normally and then create a log file of the boot activities. The log file is named Bootlog.txt.
Safe Mode with Networking	This works in much the same way as the safe mode boot option; however, the network drivers are loaded, providing you with access to the network.
Step-by-Step Confirmation	The step-by-step feature allows you to say yes or no to the loading of each device specified in the Autoexec.bat and Config.sys files.
Command Prompt Only	This option is sometimes used when the system will not even get into safe mode. This option gets you to a command prompt.

Windows 2000 Boot Options

- To access the different boot options for Windows 2000, you need to press the F8 key when prompted during the boot process.

- Safe Mode

  - Similar to safe mode in Windows 95/98, this safe mode starts the system with minimal files and drivers, including those for mice, keyboard, base video, and mass storage.

- Safe Mode with Networking

  - This option starts the system with minimal drivers, as with safe mode, but includes network connections.

- Safe Mode Command Prompt
  - This option starts the system with minimal drivers and goes directly to a command prompt, instead of to the Windows desktop.

- Enable Boot Logging
  - When you're booting into Windows, this option logs the services and drivers that were loaded on startup.

- Enable VGA Mode
  - This option starts Windows with a basic VGA driver.

- Last Known Good Configuration
  - When this option is used, the system attempts to start by using the information saved when Windows was last shut down.

- Directory Services Restore Mode
  - Used only on Windows 2000 domain controllers, this option attempts to restore the Active Directory service on a domain controller.

- Recovery Console
  - The Recovery Console is used primarily to recover from a failed system. If the system refuses to boot, you can start the Recovery Console from the Windows 2000 setup disks, from the Windows 2000 CD, or from the system itself if the utility is installed.
  - The basic procedure used to install the Recovery Console is to access the Windows 2000 CD, go to the i386 file folder, and run the *winnt32.exe /cmdcons* command.

- Ntldr, Boot.ini
  - The Ntldr (NT Loader), Boot.ini, and Ntdetect.com files are required to boot the Windows NT or Windows 2000/XP system.

- Creating an Emergency Repair Disk (ERD)
  - An Emergency Repair Disk (ERD) is a floppy disk that contains key system information that can be used in the recovery process of a failed system.
  - In Windows NT, recovery disks can be made from the Windows NT command prompt with the Rdisk.exe command.
  - In Windows 2000, the Emergency Repair Disk utility is found within the Backup utility.

- Windows XP Professional has done away with the ERD in lieu of the ASR (Automatic System Recovery) disk. As in Windows 2000, this disk is created from within the Backup utility.

■ Navigating Without a Mouse

- The basic keys used in keyboard navigation are the Tab key, which can be used to move around between elements on the page or buttons in a dialog box, and the arrow keys, which can be used to move between icons on the desktop.

- The Alt+Tab combination allows you to switch between running applications.

- You can bring up the Start menu by pressing Ctrl+Esc.

- The Alt+F4 combination can be used to close applications.

Installing and Running Programs

Windows 9x and Windows 2000/XP Plug and Play

■ When you add a new hardware device to a Windows 9x or Windows 2000/XP system, Plug and Play will (normally) automatically detect the device and install the appropriate drivers.

■ Even if Windows does have a driver for the device, it might not be the latest driver available. If you have not checked for new drivers, let Windows install the device and then check the manufacturer's Web site for the latest drivers.

■ Plug and Play requires that the operating system, the BIOS, the drivers, and the peripheral itself are all in agreement as to what device is being installed, and how it should be installed.

■ Windows NT 4 does not support Plug and Play. Therefore, if you add a device to the system, you must install the drivers and configure the device manually.

Identify the procedures for installing and launching typical Windows and non-Windows applications.

■ To add a Windows component on a Windows 9x or Windows NT 4 system, simply click the Add/Remove Programs utility in Control Panel and select the Windows Setup tab.

- On a Windows 2000/XP system, click the Add/Remove Programs utility in Control Panel and select Add/Remove Windows Components from the menu bar on the left.

- Third-party software, that is, software not supplied by Microsoft, is generally as easy to install as inserting a CD into a drive—the AutoRun feature has seen to that.

- All programs will state what the minimum hardware requirements are for running the program. They will also tell you how much disk space will be required. Be sure that your system meets these specifications before starting your install.

Procedures for Setting Up and Configuring a Windows Printing Subsystem

- Windows versions since Windows 95 have the Add Printer Wizard that will take you through the process of adding a printer to the system.

- When installing a local printer, Windows might automatically install the printer using Plug and Play. If the printer is local, and you choose to install it manually, you must specify the port to which the printer is attached and supply the driver.

- To install a network printer, you need to supply the path to the printer (in UNC), or you can choose to browse the network to locate the printer.

- Setting the Default Printer

  - The default printer is used either when applications provide a quick link to printing, like a Print button on a toolbar, or when you are printing from an application that does not have a printer selection screen, like some versions of Notepad.

  - To set a printer as the default printer, right-click on the printer and select the default printer option from the menu.

  - Deleting the default printer will cause the system to select another printer as the default.

- Spooler Settings

  - The spooler is the name given to an area of disk space in which print jobs are stored before being sent to the printer.

  - Spooling allows the system to print in the background while you perform other tasks, but it requires disk space and system resources.

- Once in the queue, print jobs can be paused, resumed, and cancelled. All of these functions are performed through a window that is accessed by double-clicking the printer in the Printers folder.

- In Windows 98, anyone can delete a print job from the print queue, but in Windows NT and Windows 2000/XP only users with the required permissions can control print jobs in the queue.

Domain 3.0 Diagnosing and Troubleshooting

Common Errors in the Boot Sequence

Safe Mode

- Safe mode allows Windows 2000 and Windows 9*x* to load with only a minimal set of drivers.

- Safe mode provides just enough of an environment so that you can proceed to troubleshoot the OS using the built-in tools.

- On both a Windows 9x and a Windows 2000 system, you enter safe mode by pressing the F8 key during boot. You will be taken to a menu that allows you to access safe mode.

- In Windows 98, to enter Interactive Startup, and subsequently safe mode, press the Ctrl key while booting.

Common Windows Errors

- **No operating system found** This means that the BIOS could not find the boot loader, which is Io.sys in Windows 9*x* and Ntldr in Windows 2000. Possible causes include:

  - The boot loader is missing or corrupt.

  - The hard disk was not detected by the BIOS.

  - A floppy disk could be in the floppy drive, preventing a normal boot process.

  - Physical installation of the hard disk was performed improperly.

  - You have a boot sector virus.

- **Error in Config.sys line *xx*** When a command in the Config.sys file cannot be processed properly, you might receive this error message, where *xx* indicates the actual line within the file that contains the error.

- Config.sys is a text file. To correct errors or modify the settings, use the Edit command, Notepad, or the Sysedit utility.

- To bypass a line in the Config.sys file, add a semicolon (;) or put the word *Rem* at the beginning of the line. This will cause the system to ignore the line.

■ **Bad or missing Command.com**   The Command.com file cannot be located during the boot process. The Command.com file might have become corrupt or has moved.

- To correct the error, copy a new version of Command.com to the root directory from the Windows directory on a Windows 9*x* system, or from the first disk of a set of MS-DOS disks.

- Sys.com can be used to transfer a new copy of the Command.com (as well as Io.sys and Msdos.sys) file to the target drive.

■ **Himem.sys not loaded**   If you receive this error message, the Himem.sys file is missing or corrupt. The Himem.sys file should be found in the Windows directory; if it's not there, it might have been moved. If it is there, and the error message continues, it might be corrupt.

■ **Swap file**   The swap file is the space on the hard disk used to store temporary data that will not fit into regular memory.

- A system that frequently hangs or freezes might indicate a problem with the swap file.

- To correct a damaged swap file in Windows 9*x*, delete the Win386.swp file and restart the system.

- To correct a damaged swap file in Windows 2000, simply restart the computer.

■ **Windows NT boot issues**   Perhaps the most common Windows NT and Windows 2000/XP boot error message is "Could not find Ntldr." To correct the error, consider the following:

- Ensure that there isn't a disk in the floppy drive when the system boots.

- Check the physical installation of the hard disk.

- Verify that the BIOS detects the hard disk.

- The Ntldr file might be missing or corrupt.

■ **Dr. Watson**   This is a troubleshooting utility that can be used to determine why a program or process is causing problems. In both Windows

2000 and Windows 9*x,* you can start Dr. Watson from a command prompt with the command `drwatson`.

■ **Failure to start graphical user interface (GUI)**   One of the most common causes of no GUI is corrupted, or incorrectly configured display drivers. Another cause might be corrupt Windows files. To correct GUI errors:

- Try booting into Windows safe mode and replace the video drivers.

- Use the Windows NT or Windows 2000 Last Known Good Configuration option during bootup.

- Use the Windows 2000 Recovery Console.

■ **Windows protection error**   This error is caused during startup by a problem with a device driver. The device driver with the problem may have been loaded through the system.ini file or by the registry. To correct the Windows protection error:

- Try booting Windows in safe mode.

- If in safe mode, update the device driver.

- Use the Windows NT or Windows 2000 Last Known Good Configuration option.

- Use the Windows 2000 Recovery Console.

- Edit the System.ini file to not load potentially problematic device drivers.

■ **A device referenced in System.ini, Win.ini, or the registry is not found**   This error is caused by a driver being specified when its device is not present on the system. To correct the problem, remove the entry for the device.

- The System.ini and Win.ini files can be opened in any text editor like Notepad, or with the Sysedit utility.

- When you are troubleshooting an entry in the registry, you will need to use the appropriate registry editing tool: Regedit in Windows as well as Regedt32 in Windows NT or Windows 2000.

- Editing the registry is more safely accomplished by using the Control Panel utilities.

Recognizing and Solving Common Problems

Eliciting Problem Symptoms from Customers

- Gather information from users including any error messages, how frequently the error occurs, and what the exact error is.

- Wherever possible have the customer re-create the error.

- When gathering information from a customer, ensure that you ascertain whether there have been any recent changes to the computer system, including the adding or removing of files or programs. These changes can often be isolated as the cause of the problem.

Troubleshooting Windows-Specific Printing Problems

- Print Spool Is Stalled

  - When a printer is configured to use print spooling, print jobs are first sent to the spooler, which saves the print job to the hard disk.

  - Each pending print job is listed in the printer's properties dialog box. The print job at the top is the one next in line for printing; cancel this print job if the spooler is stalled.

  - If removing the print job does not get the print spooler going, on a Windows NT or Windows 2000/XP system you can stop and restart the print spooler service.

  - To access the print spooler service, go to Control Panel, select the Administrative Tools icon, and then open the Services shortcut.

  - Windows 9x does not use a print spooler service, so the system might need to be restarted to clear the print spooler.

  - Sometimes it might appear that a print spooler has stalled when a large document or one with a large number of graphics is printed. Such a document can tie up resources and just slow the process down, but will work its way through the print spooler.

  - The spooling process uses disk space to store print files. If there is not enough free space on your hard disk, you might find yourself unable to print large files irrespective of how much memory is installed in the system or in the printer.

- Incorrect or Incompatible Driver for the Printer

  - If a printer fails or text is garbled in print jobs, update the printer driver.

- The latest printer drivers can be downloaded from the manufacturer's Web site.

Other Common Problems

■ General Protection Faults

- A General Protection Fault (GPF) occurs when a program attempts to start but the system detects a procedure in the program that could compromise another program or even the OS itself.

- A common cause of a GPF is when a program or device attempts to access a corrupted or unsupported device driver.

- When a GPF error does occur, your system might "blue screen." This refers to the system halting with the display of a blue screen displaying white text outlining the cause of the problem. The text is often cryptic but can be used in conjunction with Microsoft's support Web site.

■ Illegal Operation

- An illegal operation is reported when a program tries to perform a function that the operating system is unable to carry out.

- Illegal operations are sometimes caused by a bug in the program itself.

- Sometimes an illegal operation error will be corrected after a reboot and sometimes a program might need to be reinstalled.

- The Microsoft support Web site (*http://support.microsoft.com*) contains detailed information on illegal operation errors and program troubleshooting.

■ Invalid Working Directory

- An invalid working directory error can occur when a program's directory has been moved, renamed, or deleted.

- To correct the error, you will need to put the directory back in its original location, or you might be able to correct the problem by editing the shortcut to the program, which has a field for the working directory.

- In some cases the program might need to be reinstalled.

■ System Lockup

- Troubleshooting system lockups is particularly difficult because there are many different things that can cause the system to hang.

- Lockups can be caused by a hardware malfunction; for instance, if the system is hanging after new memory is added, the memory might not be correctly installed or configured.

- System lockups can also be caused by conflicting device drivers or failing programs.

- To recover from a system lockup, you can press Ctrl+Alt+Del to open the Close Program dialog box in Windows 9*x*.

- In Windows NT and Windows 2000/XP, the Task Manager can be used to shut down a frozen program. Press Ctrl+Alt+Del to invoke the Windows Security dialog box. From here you can access the Task Manager.

■ Optional Device (Sound Card, Modem, Input) Will Not Function

- Device Manager is used to view the hardware devices detected by the system, and is the main utility used to view devices and device drivers in a Windows operating system.

- If the device is listed with a red *X*, it is not functioning or has been disabled. Alternatively, if there is a yellow circle with a black exclamation point, the device is not functioning correctly, which might mean there is a resource conflict or incorrect drivers being used.

- If a hardware device is not working, use Device Manager to locate any resource conflicts.

- Device Manager can be used to manually configure resources used by a hardware device and to update device drivers.

■ Programs Don't Install

- If you are trying to install a newer program onto an older system, the system's resources might not meet the minimum requirements for that program. Refer to the program's documentation to identify the minimum requirements.

- **Program conflict**   Sometimes a program will fail to install if another program is running. For instance, a screen saver that starts during the install might cause the installation to fail. Similarly, a virus checker running in the background might do the same. When installing a program, it is suggested that you shut down all other programs.

- **Installation media**   It is possible that the installation medium itself is corrupt; it might be a scratch on the installation CD or a damaged installation file on the floppy drive. If possible, try rein-stalling the program with different media.

- **Incorrect installation procedures**   Most modern programs install using the AutoRun feature and almost install themselves, but there are some that require a bit more work. Refer to the man-ufacturer's installation procedures to verify that you have installed the program correctly.

■ Program Will not Start or Load

- **System resources**   If the program has just been installed, verify that the system has enough resources—memory, hard disk space, and processor speed—to run the program.

- **Corrupted installation**   It might be that the program did not install successfully. Sometimes when a program fails to load, you will need to reinstall it to see if the problem is corrected.

- **Virus**   If a program has been running and now fails to start, it might be that a virus has damaged the program's files. Run a virus checker to see if there is a virus on the system.

- **Incorrect shortcut path**   If you are unsuccessfully trying to start a program from the shortcut on the desktop, try starting it directly from the program's main executable file. This file is located in the program's directory. It might be that the path for the shortcut is just wrong.

- **Deleted or moved files**   If a program used to work but now does not, it might mean that the program files have been deleted or moved. Use Windows Explorer to verify that the files are still where they need to be.

- **Expired software**   If you were using trial software that has an expiration date, it might just be that the time has expired. Refer to the manufacturer's Web site to confirm.

■ Cannot Log on to Network (Option—NIC Not Functioning)

- **Network card resources**   With the network card installed, ver-ify that there are no resource conflicts and that it is recognized by the system. You can do this from within Device Manager.

- **Verify LED**   Most modern network cards have an LED on them, referred to as the *link light*, that lights up when the card is making a connection to the network. If the LED is not lit, no connection is present. This could be caused either by a problem with the network card or some kind of connectivity issue elsewhere on the network.

- **User name and password combination**   Network connectivity problems are sometimes as simple as the wrong password or user name being entered. Be sure they are correct before taking the troubleshooting procedure any farther.

- **Network card drivers**   If you cannot connect to the network, you might need to verify that the correct network card drivers are being used. If in doubt, update the driver using Device Manager. Be sure to use the latest driver from the manufacturer's Web site.

■ Viruses and Virus Types

- **Boot sector virus**   Boot sector viruses are targeted at the system's boot sector; specifically, the boot sector virus changes the code of the master boot record (MBR). To remove a virus from the MBR, you can use the Fdisk command, using the following syntax: `Fdisk /mbr`. Many BIOSs now include a setting that can be used to protect the boot sector of the hard disk from virus infection. Given the destructive nature of a boot sector virus, if your BIOS has such a feature you should certainly enable it.

- **Trojan horse program**   A Trojan horse program is so named because it disguises itself as something it isn't. A Trojan horse program is often used to locate local passwords on the computer system, make the system vulnerable for a remote attack, or simply damage files on the local system.

- **Executable**   One of the most dangerous types of virus is one embedded in an executable file because it can basically do anything, including mailing itself to everyone in your address book, or wiping out your system and any system yours is connected to. Executable viruses can be embedded in or launched from any executable file, not just those with .exe extensions. These include .bat, .com, and .cmd files. Viruses can also be embedded in or launched from script files which will be run by the operating system.

- **Macro virus**   A macro virus is written in a macro language and placed within a macro, which can then be embedded in a document or spreadsheet.

■ Virus Sources

● **Floppy disks**   If a floppy disk has a virus on it, the virus can easily find its way to other systems. One way to prevent this is to use a virus checker with an autodetect feature that will check the disk when it is inserted.

● **E-mail**   This has become one of the most common methods of distributing, and therefore contracting, viruses. Use a virus checker to ensure that no viruses are contained in e-mail attachments.

● **Network**   When a computer system is connected to a network, especially the Internet, it opens up the potential for viruses to spread themselves around to the other computers on the network.

● **Downloading software**   Many of us spend time on the Internet and at some point will download files onto our local computer. These files, many of which are executables, can be filled with viruses. Before installing any software that you have downloaded, be sure to check the files for viruses.

● **How to Determine the Presence of a Virus**   Keep an eye out for unusual messages or window display boxes that appear on your screen. If these are not part of any program that you have installed they might be the work of a virus. Though most viruses are not overt, some will play sound files or music that will alert you to their presence. If you are looking for a program or a file and can't find it, that could indicate a virus. Some viruses rename or delete files and program executables. When this happens, you will not be able to find them. If you suspect that this is happening, the best thing to do is run your virus checker right away. Some viruses will drain your system's resources and the entire system will noticeably slow down. If you use a system resource utility to check the memory usage, you will find that it is extremely high considering the programs that are running on it. You might notice that the hard disk keeps filling and that overall performance, including loading programs, is noticeably slower. If you are looking through a computer system and notice new files or programs that shouldn't be there, they could be virus programs or the by-product of a virus infection. To verify this, refer to the Web site of your virus software manufacturer.

Domain 4.0 Networks

Networking Protocols and Connectivity

Protocols

- Protocols govern how devices on the network interact and provide systems that allow data to travel reliably on the network.

- There are a number of commonly used protocols including TCP/IP, IPX/SPX, AppleTalk, and NetBEUI. Of these, TCP/IP is by far the most popular.

- In a TCP/IP network, the system requires at the very least an IP address and the subnet mask, and, in most cases, a default gateway, to get onto the network.

- DNS is a system that resolves host names to IP addresses. In order for a system to be able to send resolution requests to a DNS server, it must be supplied with the address of the DNS server. It is a common practice to supply the IP addresses of more than one DNS server.

- WINS is a service that resolves NetBIOS system names to IP addresses. WINS is commonly used on Microsoft networks but is now being replaced by DNS.

- TCP/IP information can be assigned manually, or dynamically using a DHCP server.

- Some operating systems (Windows 2000, Windows XP) support APIPA. If a system that is configured to use DHCP is unable to get an IP address from the DHCP server, APIPA will cause the system to assign itself an IP address, providing limited network functionality.

- IPX/SPX was created by the computer networking software company Novell. IPX/SPX is a suite of protocols designed primarily for use on local area networks (LANs).

- IPX/SPX has all but been replaced by TCP/IP and even Novell now uses TCP/IP as the default protocol in their networking products.

- AppleTalk is a networking protocol designed to be used on networks with Apple Macintosh computers.

- NetBEUI is a LAN protocol designed for relatively small networks. NetBEUI is simple to configure and easy to use.

- Configuring Client Options

- Certain options must be configured on client systems in order for them to connect to the network correctly.

- When connecting to a Microsoft network, clients need to know information such as the domain that the system is a member of and the correct user name and password.

- When connecting to a Novell network, information such as the user name, the name of the NDS tree to which you want to connect, and the location of the user ID in tree (referred to as the context) is required.

■ Ipconfig.exe

- The Ipconfig command displays the TCP/IP configuration on Windows systems.

- The most common command syntax used with the utility is *ipconfig /all*, which displays information on all network cards in the system including the default gateway, the subnet mask, the MAC address of the network card, DNS server information, and DHCP lease information.

- Ipconfig can also be used to release and renew addresses obtained via DHCP.

■ Winipcfg.exe

- The Winipcfg utility is a graphical version of the Ipconfig utility found only in Windows 9*x* and Windows Me.

- Winipcfg can report TCP/IP configuration information and can also be used to release and renew TCP/IP addresses obtained via DHCP.

■ Ping

- The Ping utility tests connectivity between networked devices that use the TCP/IP protocol.

■ Tracert

- Tracert verifies the route to a remote system by reporting the status of every step on the journey.

■ Nslookup

- The Nslookup utility can be used to troubleshoot the DNS configuration on a system.

Network Sharing

■ Sharing Disk Drives

- To share a hard disk drive, File and Printer Sharing must be enabled on the system.

- To share a drive, right-click on the drive you wish to share and select Sharing from the menu.

- Once a drive is shared, a hand will appear underneath the drive icon to let you know it is shared.

- Access to shared drives over the network is controlled by permissions. Windows NT and Windows 2000/XP offer more share security that Windows 9x.

- Shared drives can be accessed through My Computer, Network Neighborhood, and from the command line.

■ Sharing Print and File Services

- By default, Windows NT and Windows 2000 are configured to share resources.

- In Windows 9x and Windows Me, File and Printer Sharing must first be installed and then you must specify that you wish to make files and/or printers available to other users.

- You can map to a share on a network using the NetBIOS name or the IP address and the sharename in a UNC format.

■ Setting Permissions to Shared Resources

- Shared resources can be assigned permissions so that only intended users can gain access to them.

- Windows NT and Windows 2000/XP provide four levels of share permissions—No Access, Read, Change, and Full Control.

- Permissions assigned to a user and group can be combined to gain a greater set of rights, but the No Access permission cannot be overridden.

- When you create a share, by default the Full Control permission is assigned to the group Everyone.

- Permissions can be viewed and changed through Windows Explorer.

■ Network Type and Network Card

- Two types of networks are used, peer-to-peer and client/server networks.

- In a peer-to-peer network, PCs can act as both a client and a server. As well as sharing their own resources, systems can be used to access other machines that make their own resources available.

- Peer-to-peer networks are small, typically restricted to 10 computer systems.

- Peer-to-peer networks do not use a dedicated network server.

- Client/server networks use a dedicated server to manage network authentication, security, and access to network resources.

- Client/server networks can accommodate thousands of interconnected systems.

- The OS must have a network card installed and configured in order to connect to network resources. The network card provides the physical connection to the network.

- The OS has to have a network protocol installed to communicate over the network.

Internet Concepts and Connectivity

■ An ISP (Internet service provider) is a company that specializes in providing Internet access to home and business users. ISPs can provide different types of Internet access including dial-up phone access, cable access, and DSL.

■ **TCP/IP** A protocol suite used by default by most operating systems and the protocol used on the Internet. TCP/IP information can be assigned manually (statically), or automatically using a DHCP server. Some of the protocols found within the TCP/IP protocol suite are included in Table B-7.

Table B-7   **TCP/IP Protocols and Their Functions**

Protocol	Function
File Transfer Protocol (FTP)	FTP is used to send and receive files from a remote computer—for example, it can be used when downloading a program from the Internet.
Hypertext Transfer Protocol (HTTP)	HTTP is used to establish a connection with a Web server and transmit HTML pages to the client browser.
Hypertext Transfer Protocol Secure (HTTPS)	This protocol is used for accessing a secure Web server such as for online banking or other secure Internet transactions. Using HTTPS in the URL instead of HTTP directs the browser to establish a secure connection.
Secure Sockets Layer (SSL)	SSL is the security system used by HTTPS. SSL works by encrypting information sent to and received from a remote host making it unreadable by a third party.
Network News Transfer Protocol (NNTP)	This protocol is used to connect to, browse, and retrieve messages from newsgroups on the Internet. To connect to a news server, at the very least you will need the IP address of your ISP's NNTP server.
Post Office Protocol 3 (POP3)	POP3 is a single-user e-mail retrieval protocol, which allows a user to download e-mail from a remote mail host.
Point-to-Point Protocol (PPP)	This is a dial-up networking protocol used to establish network connections over a modem link.
Simple Mail Transfer Protocol (SMTP)	SMTP is used to send e-mail across a network such as the Internet.
Internet Messaging Application Protocol (IMAP)	A protocol, like POP3, that is used for retrieving e-mail from a remote host. IMAP has more features than POP and is more secure.

■ **Telnet**   Telnet is a protocol that allows you to open a session on a remote host and perform actions through that session that are executed at the remote host as if you were actually at that host. Telnet is popular in the Linux/UNIX environment and for the configuration of network devices such as routers.

■ **HTML**   Tag language used to develop Web pages for the Internet. Web browsers interpret pages that are written in HTML and display the results in the browser window.

■ **DNS**   As discussed, the Domain Name Service is responsible for resolving host names to IP addresses. On the Internet, organizations are defined by their domain name and also by a domain name extension. Common domain name extensions are listed in Table B-8.

Table B-8   Common Domain Name Extensions

Extension	Purpose	Example
.com	Commercial business	www.microsoft.com
.org	Not-for-profit organizations	*www.comptia.org*
.edu	Educational organizations	*www.harvard.edu*
.gov	Government organizations	*www.whitehouse.gov*
.mil	Military organizations	*www.nic.mil*
.net	Internet organizations	*www.att.net*

Installing and Configuring Browsers

■ Browsers are programs that are used to view pages formatted in certain languages such as the Hypertext Markup Language (HTML) or the Extensible Markup Language (XML).

■ Internet Explorer is configured in the Internet Properties dialog box. Configurable options include connection method, LAN settings, security, home page, and privacy settings.

Internet Connectivity Technologies

■ Dial-up Internet access, that is, access via a modem, is still the most popular method of connecting to the Internet. Dial-up networking is currently limited to 56 Kbps, making it slow in comparison to other Internet access methods such as DSL and cable.

■ A dial-up connection to the Internet requires a modem and a special protocol called the Point-to-Point Protocol (PPP).

■ Many methods of connecting to the Internet are available including cable, DSL, wireless, and satellite. Availability of these services depends on your location and the local ISP's offerings. Most urban areas have DSL and cable Internet access, while satellite Internet access is gaining ground in rural areas where DSL and cable are not available.

■ ISDN is a high-speed Internet access service that uses phone lines to provide speeds of up to 1.544 Mbps. There are two versions of ISDN—Basic Rate Interface (BRI), which is limited to 128 Kbps, and Primary Rate Interface (PRI), which is capable of the aforementioned 1.544 Mbps. By sacrificing some of the bandwidth on an ISDN line, you can also use voice traffic over the same link.

■   Internet access across a LAN is becoming almost standard in networks of all sizes. When accessing the Internet across a LAN, specialized proxy server software is often used to manage and control Internet access.

Installing and Configuring Browsers

■   Enabling and Disabling Script Support

- Scripts are small programs embedded within Web pages that can perform simple functions that add functionality or enhance the appearance of a Web page. The problem is that these same scripts can also contain malicious code that can perform actions on or from your PC without you knowing about it.

- In Internet Explorer, you can configure support for scripts by selecting Tools, Internet Options, Security, and then clicking the Custom Level button. You can then enable or disable script support as appropriate.

■   Configuring Proxy Settings

- If you are using a Web browser on a network that uses a proxy server to provide Internet access, you will most likely need to tell the Web browser the IP address of the proxy server. In Internet Explorer this is done by selecting Tools, Internet Options, Connections, LAN Settings.

- The normal port number for HTTP traffic is 80. You should check with the network administrator to determine if the default TCP/IP port is being used for Web browsing.

- Internet Connection Sharing (ICS) is a simple concept that enables one system to share its Internet connection with the other computers on the network. Windows versions from Windows 98 SE on allow Internet Connection Sharing.

■   Configuring Security Settings

- Internet Explorer has security settings that allow you to define what Internet-borne scripts and associated files can be downloaded and run from your computer. You can access the security settings in Internet Explorer by clicking Tools, Internet Options, Security.

■   Firewall Protection Under Windows XP

- Windows XP includes a feature called the Internet Connection Firewall (ICF) that can be used to protect the system from Internet-borne attacks.

Index

Inside *security information* you can trust

Microsoft® Windows® Security Resource Kit
ISBN 0-7356-1868-2   Suggested Retail Price: $59.99 U.S., $86.99 Canada

Comprehensive security information and tools, straight from the Microsoft product groups. This official RESOURCE KIT delivers comprehensive operations and deployment information that information security professionals can put to work right away. The authors—members of Microsoft's security teams—describe how to plan and implement a comprehensive security strategy, assess security threats and vulnerabilities, configure system security, and more. The kit also provides must-have security tools, checklists, templates, and other on-the-job resources on CD-ROM and on the Web.

Microsoft Encyclopedia of Security
ISBN 0-7356-1877-1   Suggested Retail Price: $49.99 U.S., $72.99 Canada

The essential, one-of-a-kind security reference for computer professionals at all levels. This encyclopedia delivers 2000+ entries detailing the latest security-related issues, technologies, standards, products, and services. It covers the Microsoft Windows platform as well as open-source technologies and the platforms and products of other major vendors. You get clear, concise explanations and case scenarios that deftly take you from concept to real-world application—ideal for everyone from computer science students up to systems engineers, developers, and managers.

Microsoft Windows Server 2003 Security Administrator's Companion
ISBN 0-7356-1574-8   Suggested Retail Price: $49.99 U.S., $72.99 Canada

The in-depth, practical guide to deploying and maintaining Windows Server 2003 in a secure environment. Learn how to use all the powerful security features in the latest network operating system with this in-depth, authoritative technical reference—written by a security expert on the Microsoft Windows Server 2003 security team. Explore physical security issues, internal security policies, and public and shared key cryptography, and then drill down into the specifics of the key security features of Windows Server 2003.

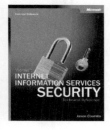

Microsoft Internet Information Services Security Technical Reference
ISBN 0-7356-1572-1   Suggested Retail Price: $49.99 U.S., $72.99 Canada

The definitive guide for developers and administrators who need to understand how to securely manage networked systems based on IIS. This book presents obvious, avoidable mistakes and known security vulnerabilities in Internet Information Services (IIS)—priceless, intimate facts about the underlying causes of past security issues—while showing the best ways to fix them. The expert author, who has used IIS since the first version, also discusses real-world best practices for developing software and managing systems and networks with IIS.

To learn more about Microsoft Press® products for IT professionals, please visit:

microsoft.com/mspress/IT

Drew Bird

Drew Bird (A+, Network+, Linux+, Server+, MCNE, MCP) is the author of numerous computer books, including study guides for CompTIA's A+, Network+, Server+, and Linux+ certifications. He has written more than 150 articles that have been published on technology-related Web sites and in magazines. Over the course of thirteen years in the IT industry, Drew has been a systems manager, a systems analyst, an instructor, and all-round tech. Drew lives in Kelowna, B.C., Canada, with his wife, Zoë, and their dog Merlin.

Mike Harwood

As well as being a husband and a father of two, Mike Harwood (A+, Network+, Server+, Linux+, MCSE), has authored books on numerous CompTIA certifications, including A+, Server+, Network+, and Linux+. A system manager for a multi-site network, Mike has also donned the hat of trainer for a community college and of consultant for an Internet service provider.

The manuscript for this book was prepared and submitted to Microsoft Press in electronic form. Pages were composed by Microsoft Press using Adobe FrameMaker+SGML for Windows, with text in Garamond and display type in ITC Franklin Gothic Condensed. Composed pages were delivered to the printer as electronic prepress files.

Cover designer:	Methodologie, Inc.
Interior Graphic Designer:	James D. Kramer
Principal Compositor:	Kerri DeVault
Electronic Artist:	Joel Panchot
Principal Proofreader:	nSight
Indexer:	Pamona Corporation

Get a **Free**
e-mail newsletter, updates,
special offers, links to related books,
and more when you

register online!

Register your Microsoft Press® title on our Web site and you'll get a FREE subscription to our e-mail newsletter, *Microsoft Press Book Connections.* You'll find out about newly released and upcoming books and learning tools, online events, software downloads, special offers and coupons for Microsoft Press customers, and information about major Microsoft® product releases. You can also read useful additional information about all the titles we publish, such as detailed book descriptions, tables of contents and indexes, sample chapters, links to related books and book series, author biographies, and reviews by other customers.

Registration is easy. Just visit this Web page and fill in your information:

http://www.microsoft.com/mspress/register

Microsoft®

Proof of Purchase

Use this page as proof of purchase if participating in a promotion or rebate offer on this title. Proof of purchase must be used in conjunction with other proof(s) of payment such as your dated sales receipt—see offer details.

Faster Smarter A+ Certification
0-7356-1915-8

CUSTOMER NAME

Microsoft Press, PO Box 97017, Redmond, WA 98073-9830